Dr. Hazzan and colleagues exemplify the global mindset and practical problem-solving approach that is fundamental to Hult's philosophy of busin[illegible] not only a thoughtful, experience-based view of the realities [illegible] sion, but also actionable tools and frameworks to foster th[illegible] desirable behaviors essential for success in dynamic market[illegible]

Dr. Matt Lilley, *President, Hult* [illegible]

This much-needed book fills an important gap in postgraduate teaching resources. It stands out for its practical classroom utility and focus on entrepreneurial growth. It is rich with contemporary case studies, and provides numerous frameworks which connect academic theory to real-world action. As educators of the next generation of global business leaders, we have an imperative to provide a global perspective and underline the importance of solving the challenges the world faces and advancing humanity for all. Dr Hazzan and his colleagues have provided an important contribution to this effort.

Dr. Darren Dahl, *Dean, UBC Sauder School of Business*

This book incorporates a thoughtful and scholarly exploration of how culture, tradition, and belief shape business practices across emerging markets. Leading with recognition of indigenous language and traditions, it gives strong attention to property rights and the cultural and ethical dimensions of development. Hazzan, Amlani, and Davis include many references to Nigeria as a case study to interrogate both the promise and complexity of global finance and sustainability. By addressing traditional land tenure systems, adverse possession, and the powerful role of religion in shaping organizational behavior, it invites scholars to reconsider the ethics of international business and the cost of growth. The text is brilliantly written and meticulously researched, making it a particularly noteworthy and timely contribution to the scholarship and evolving discourse on international development.

Dr. Jacob K. Olupona, *Hugh K. Foster Professor of African and African American Studies, and Professor of African Religious Traditions, Harvard University*

International Business Growth Strategies for Emerging Markets provides a pragmatic view on both the realities and opportunities of emerging markets. This insightful book explains the impact these dynamic markets have on global growth. Excellent for future leaders.

Dr. Monique Jordan, *Boston Undergraduate Campus Dean, Hult International Business School, Boston, Massachusetts*

International Business Growth Strategies for Emerging Markets

International Business Growth Strategies for Emerging Markets: Creating Sustainable Entrepreneurial Expansion is a comprehensive introductory guide to taking sustainable business into, and doing business within, the world's fastest growing economies.

The authors, multicultural seasoned experts in accounting, finance, law, and strategy, stress the fundamental importance of sustainability. They underline the critical role of research and analysis before action. The potential positive impact of AI and digital transformation is a consistent theme. Drawing on their own experiences and a rich panoply of relevant literature, the authors highlight opportunities, risks, and proven techniques for market entry.

Primarily written to inform undergraduate and postgraduate business students, the book also appeals to executives and managers tasked with crafting successful plans for businesses contemplating foundation or expansion in a world of unlimited potential.

Seni Hazzan has taught at Berkeley, Harvard, Yale, Menlo, and Pepperdine Universities; he is now a member of faculty at Hult International Business School based in Boston, Massachusetts. A graduate of the Universities of Maiduguri, Yale, Berkeley, and Pepperdine, he holds both Chartered Professional Accountant (CPA) and Fellow Chartered Accountant (FCA) professional designations.

Alym Amlani, CPA, is a recognized thought leader and highly respected educator at the University of British Columbia's Sauder School of Business, the Langara School of Management, and Kwantlen Polytechnic University's Melville School of Business.

Paul Davis, LL.D., has returned to academia after a lifetime in international business. Trained as a lawyer in the United Kingdom, he emigrated to Canada and earned his doctorate in law from the University of Ottawa.

Small Business & Entrepreneurship

The field of Small Business & Entrepreneurship is dynamic, constantly evolving and worth billions worldwide: it's no wonder that Entrepreneurship has come to occupy a central position within the Business School globally. This series meets the need for rigorous yet practical and accessible textbooks that cover the full spectrum of the Small Business and Entrepreneurial world views.

Collectively, the Small Business & Entrepreneurship Series is a valuable resource for advanced undergraduate and postgraduate students at Business Schools globally, helping them gain an in-depth understanding of contemporary concepts and the realities of entrepreneurial practice across the entire subject area – from development and product sourcing to relationship management, communications, sustainability, and sales and marketing. Individually, each text provides essential reading for a core topic. A range of consistent pedagogical features is used throughout the texts, including international case studies which highlight the practical importance of theoretical concepts.

Advanced Undergraduate and Graduate level students studying for degrees in Entrepreneurship, Leadership, and Business Management will find each text invaluable reading, providing the knowledge and tools to approach a future in Entrepreneurial ventures with confidence.

More information about this series can be found at www.Routledge.com/small-business-and-ENT

International Business Growth Strategies for Emerging Markets
Creating Sustainable Entrepreneurial Expansion
Seni Hazzan, Alym Amlani, and Paul Davis

International Business Growth Strategies for Emerging Markets

Creating Sustainable Entrepreneurial Expansion

Seni Hazzan, Alym Amlani, and Paul Davis

Routledge
Taylor & Francis Group
NEW YORK AND LONDON

Designed cover image: Renato Michel Moura, Artur Nogueira, Brazil

First published 2026
by Routledge
605 Third Avenue, New York, NY 10158

and by Routledge
4 Park Square, Milton Park, Abingdon, Oxon, OX14 4RN

Routledge is an imprint of the Taylor & Francis Group, an informa business

ISBN: 978-1-041-07028-3 (hbk)
ISBN: 978-1-041-06543-2 (pbk)
ISBN: 978-1-003-63849-0 (ebk)

DOI: 10.4324/9781003638490

Typeset in Sabon
by SPi Technologies India Pvt Ltd (Straive)

Access the Support Material: www.routledge.com/9781041065432

We humbly dedicate this book to future generations – our children and their children – who will inherit the world we shape today. May they live in a sustainable, equitable, and prosperous world, built upon the lessons we learn and the actions we take today.

Contents

Territorial acknowledgment

The authors researched and wrote this book on the ancestral territories of the First Nations in the countries today known as Canada and the United States.

Author Seni teaches at Hult International Business School, on the traditional home of the *Massachusêuck* (Massachusett) people, members of the Algonquin family who have stewarded the land for generations. We recognize their enduring commitment to the earth, pay respect to their elders, past and present, and honor their resilience and contributions as they continue to live and work in the region.

Authors Alym and Paul teach, and Paul lives, at the University of British Columbia on the unceded territory of the *xʷməθkʷəy̓əm* (Musqueam) people. For thousands of years, they have sought to walk gently on this land. We honor their deep connection to the land, water, and resources of the Gray Peninsula.

Alym lives, and also teaches, on the unceded territories of the Coast Salish First Nations: *Semyone* (Semiahmoo), *q̓ic̓əy̓* (Katzie), and q̓ʷaƛ̓ən (Kwantlen), who have cared for and stewarded the land for thousands of years.

We honor their histories, their cultures, and their ongoing contributions to these regions. It is important that we reflect on the legacy of colonization and affirm our commitment to respectful relationships with Indigenous communities. We express gratitude for the opportunity to meet, learn, study, teach, and write on their lands.

Acknowledgments

Each of us has enjoyed the support of our precious families as we made time to move this project to completion. They have our gratitude and endless love.

We are fortunate to have had the support and insights of valued colleagues, for which we are profoundly grateful. Rodrigo Andai, in Chile, provided input and explanations regarding resource exploration and mining around the world. Gabriel Roberts of Oxford Brookes University significantly aided our research by developing custom software to streamline data collection. These contributions were instrumental in forming our analytical view of growth and emerging markets.

We extend our gratitude also to the institutions where we found invaluable assistance. Kimberly Lace Fama of the David Lam Management Research Library at the University of British Columbia worked tirelessly to track down obscure works.

Harvard Business School's Baker Library is home to a truly remarkable archive of interviews with business leaders, titled *Creating Emerging Markets Oral History Collection*. Comprising 185 interviews at the time of writing, this collection is a deeply valuable resource which has provided us with a treasury of illustrative examples and insights. Standing tall among the capable interviewers, Professor Tarun Khanna's work demonstrates his deep knowledge of the field and extraordinary ability to draw out meaningful discussions from his subjects. While writing, we were deeply honored to receive supportive communications from Professors Geoffrey Jones and Tarun Khanna, who are strongly engaged with the Collection and significant contributors to it.

We benefitted from access to the *Financial Times* newsletter *fDi Intelligence*, which provides regular updates on projects and initiatives all around the world. We refer frequently to useful articles.

While acknowledging assistance from all these sources, we take full responsibility for the content of this book and for any errors that remain.

Acronyms, abbreviations, definitions, and conventions

Occasionally, we use the term *organization* where it is worthwhile to emphasize that a concept or insight is broadly applicable to businesses, not-for-profits, non-governmental organizations (NGOs), and other institutions generally. However, this book is about *business*, which is usually conducted by *companies*, and we will use those two terms as appropriate to refer to commercial enterprises. By *entrepreneurs*, we mean individuals who make innovative commercial steps forward in business environments. *Company* denotes an operating legal entity, without distinguishing partnerships, unincorporated entities, or sole traders; this level of granularity is never required by the context.

We use first-, second-, and third-party terms. "We," and occasionally "I," denote actions or thoughts of the authors or collaboration with the reader. "I" is used when just one of us is speaking. "You" means we are directly addressing the reader.

For whom did we write this book?

The idea for this book was conceived in a postgraduate university course. The primary intended reader is the student, whether undergraduate, postgraduate, or in professional training. Consequently, the narrative is framed in the context of *teaching* students *about* doing business in emerging markets. However, as we also attempted to deliver actionable descriptions of policy and strategy, it might also be relevant to entrepreneurs and executives who, for business reasons, want to know more about the opportunities, challenges, and risks that characterize these alluring places. We will primarily address the student but from time to time cast the reader in the role of a business decision-maker to invoke their imagination and drive home key points.

For educational focus, each chapter starts with a set of learning objectives. All objectives are aligned with the higher learning functions (4-6) of Bloom's Revised Taxonomy (Anderson and Krathwohl, 2001).

Reference

Anderson, L. W., & Krathwohl, D. R. (Eds.). (2001). *A taxonomy for learning, teaching, and assessing: A revision of Bloom's taxonomy of educational objectives*. Longman.

Authors

Seni Hazzan epitomizes the value of real-world experience applied to academic excellence. A graduate of the Universities of Maiduguri, Yale, Berkeley, and Pepperdine, he holds both CPA and FCA professional designations. After early successes at Goldman Sachs, Arthur Andersen, and PricewaterhouseCoopers (PWC), he was headhunted to become CEO of FCMB Capital Markets in Nigeria and then applied his entrepreneurial skills with the Central Bank of Nigeria to found and oversee Entrepreneurship Development Centers to support startup and employment initiatives.

Professor Hazzan has taught at Berkeley, Harvard, Yale, Menlo, and Pepperdine Universities; he is now a member of faculty at Hult International Business School based in Boston, Massachusetts.

Alym Amlani is a recognized thought leader and highly respected educator at the University of British Columbia's Sauder School of Business, the Langara School of Management, and Kwantlen Polytechnic University's Melville School of Business. His multidisciplinary background in psychology, business education, and cognitive systems, combined with his experience as a professional magician, fuels his passion for edutainment (merging education and entertainment) to make classes both engaging and memorable. His broad skillset also includes advanced expertise in online teaching technologies.

Paul Davis has returned to academia after a lifetime in international business. Trained as a lawyer in the United Kingdom, he emigrated to Canada and earned his doctorate in law from the University of Ottawa. Since then, he has enjoyed work periods as a law professor, currency trader, commercial pilot, in-house counsel for two multinational businesses, and most recently as a forensic accounting consultant. He has lived and worked in Mexico, Brazil, Indonesia, and several developed countries.

Table of abbreviations and acronyms

3G	Global Growth Generators: Bangladesh, China, Egypt, India, Indonesia, Iraq, Mongolia, the Philippines, Sri Lanka, Vietnam
4IR	Fourth Industrial Revolution
a.k.a.	also known as
ABGF	Agência Brasileira Gestora de Fundos Garantidores e Garantias S.A.
ADB	Asian Development Bank
AEO	Authorized Economic Operator
AfCFTA	African Continental Free Trade Area
AFD	Agence Française de Développement
AfDB	African Development Bank
AI	Artificial Intelligence
AIIB	Asian Infrastructure Investment Bank
AKAM	Aga Khan Agency for Microfinance
AKFED	Aga Khan Fund for Economic Development
AKRSP	Aga Khan Rural Support Programme
ANC	African National Congress
ASM	Artisanal and Small-Scale Mining
BAE Systems	British Aerospace Electronics Systems
BBC	British Broadcasting Corporation
BCBA	Buenos Aires Stock Exchange
BESS	Battery Energy Storage System
BIA	B Impact Assessment
BII	British International Investment
BoP	Bottom of the Pyramid
BPO	Business Process Outsourcing

BRICS	Brazil, Russia, India, China, and South Africa
CAPM	Capital Asset Pricing Model
CDC	CDC Group plc, recently renamed BII
CDS	Credit Default Swap
CEO	Chief Executive Officer
cepo	Cepo cambiario (currency clamp)
CIA	Central Intelligence Agency
COD	Cash on Delivery
CPA	Chartered Professional Accountant
CPM	Cost Price Method
CPTPP	Comprehensive and Progressive Agreement for Trans-Pacific Partnership
CRP	Country Risk Premium
CSIR	Council of Scientific and Industrial Research (India)
CSO	Chief Sustainability Officer
CUP	Comparable Uncontrolled Pricing
DBA	Doctor of Business Administration
DEI	Diversity, Equity, and Inclusion
DHL	Dalsey, Hillblom, and Lynn
DRC	Democratic Republic of Congo
DTAA	Double Taxation Avoidance Agreement
DXB	Dubai International Airport
EDC	Export Development Canada
EIB	European Investment Bank
EITI	Extractive Industries Transparency Initiative
EM	Emerging Market
EME	Emerging Market Economy
EMNC	Emerging Market Multi-National Corporation
EMO	Emerging Market Organization
ERP	Enterprise Resource Planning
ESG	Environmental, Social and Governance
EU	European Union
EUR	Euro (currency)
EV	Electric Vehicle
FATF	Financial Action Task Force
FCPA	Foreign Corrupt Practices Act
FDI	Foreign Direct Investment
FMCG	Fast-Moving Consumer Goods
FPIC	Free, Prior, and Informed Consent
G7	Canada, France, Germany, Italy, Japan, the United Kingdom, and the United States
GDP	Gross Domestic Product
GDPR	General Data Processing Regulation 2018 (Europe)
GEM	Global Entrepreneurship Monitor
GLOBE	Global Leadership and Organizational Effectiveness
GPS	Global Positioning System

GST	Goods and Services Tax
HBS	Harvard Business School
HNA	Hainan Airlines Group Co., Ltd.
HSBC	Hongkong and Shanghai Banking Corporation
IBRD	International Bank for Reconstruction and Development
ICMA	International Capital Markets Association
ICT	Information and Communication Technology
IDB	Inter-American Development Bank
IFC	International Finance Corporation
IIRC	International Integrated Reporting Council
IKEA	Ingvar Kamprad Elmtaryd Agunnaryd
ILO	International Labour Organization
IMF	International Monetary Fund
INSEAD	Institut Européen d'Administration des Affaires (European Institute of Business Administration)
IP	Intellectual Property
IPEF	Indo-Pacific Economic Framework
IPS	Industrial Promotion Services
IR	Integrated Reporting
IRIS+	Impact Reporting and Investment Standards Plus
IRP	Industry Risk Premium
IT	Information Technology
ITA	International Trade Administration
KPI	Key Performance Indicator
LAC	Lakeside and American Corporation
LDC	Least Developed Country
LGBTQ(2S)+	Lesbian, Gay, Bisexual, Transgender and Queer (or Questioning) (2-spirit) plus
LGPD	Lei Geral de Proteção de Dados
LL.D.	Doctor of Laws
MENA	Middle East and North Africa
MFN	Most-favored-nation
MIGA	Multilateral Investment Guarantee Agency
MINT	Mexico, Indonesia, Nigeria and Türkiye
MNC	Multi-National Corporation
MRP	Market Risk Premium
MSCI	Morgan Stanley Capital International
N-11	Next Eleven. Bangladesh, Egypt, Indonesia, Iran, Korea, Mexico, Nigeria, Pakistan, the Philippines, Turkey, and Vietnam
NAFTA	North American Free Trade Agreement
NGO	Non-Governmental Organization
NIC	Newly Industrialized Country
NTBF	New Technology-Based Firm
NYSE	New York Stock Exchange
OECD	Organisation for Economic Co-operation and Development

P2	Pollution Prevention
PE Diamond	Private Equity Diamond
PEP	PepsiCo
PESTEL	Political, Economic, Social, Technological, Environmental, and Legal
PIN	Personal Identification Number
PLC	Public Limited Company
PLI	Production-Linked Incentive
PM	Prime Minister
POCD	People, Opportunity, Context, Deal
PPP	Public-Private Partnership
PR	Public Relations
PSM	Profit Split Method
PWC	PricewaterhouseCoopers
QR Code	Quick Response Code
R&D	Research and Development
RBV	Resource-Based View
RPM	Resale Price Method
SAIC	Shanghai Automotive Industry Corporation
SCM	Supply Chain Management
SDG	Sustainable Development Goal(s) (United Nations)
SEBI LODR	Securities and Exchange Commission (Listing Obligations and Disclosure Requirements) Regulations
SEZ	Special Economic Zone
SIM	Subscriber Identity Module
SLB	Sustainability Linked Bond
SMART	Specific, Measurable, Achievable, Relevant, Time-Bound
SME	Small and Medium-Sized Enterprise(s)
SP	Size Premium
SROI	Social Return on Investment
STA-IDEAAS	Sistemas de Tecnologia Agroelectro – Instituto para o Desenvolvimento de Energías Alternativas e da Auto Sustentabilidade
SWOT	Strengths, Weaknesses, Opportunities, Threats
TAV	Tepe-Akfen-Ventures
TBL	Triple Bottom Line
TPS	Toyota Production System
TQM	Total Quality Management
TRIPS	Trade-Related Aspects of Intellectual Property Rights
TWh	Terawatt-hour(s)
UAE	United Arab Emirates
UNSDG	United Nations Sustainable Development Goal or Group
UPI	Unified Payments Interface
USD	United States Dollar
USLP	Universal Sustainable Living Plan
USMCA	United States-Mexico-Canada Agreement
VAT	Value Added Tax

VC	Venture Capital
VPC	Value Proposition Canvas
VRIN	Valuable, Rare, Inimitable, Non-substitutable
VUCA	Volatility, Uncertainty, Complexity and Ambiguity
WACC	Weighted Average Cost of Capital
WTO	World Trade Organization

Preface

For courses like Professor Hazzan's *Developing Business Strategies for Emerging Markets*, a highly popular elective course at Hult International Business School, there is no current comprehensive text. We wrote this book to fill that critical gap in the available literature.

Harvard Business Press published the most recent edition of Khanna and Palepu's seminal work *Winning in Emerging Markets* in 2010. Pacek and Thorniley published their excellent volume *Emerging Markets* in 2007. Since these fine texts last appeared, new global realities have transformed the world politically, economically, and technologically. The term "growth markets" has become popular as an optimistic category which encompasses almost all emerging markets and adds a handful of developed economies.

Seismic changes have taken place in the world of emerging markets over the last two decades. In 2007, Bulgaria and Romania joined the European Union. Russia was a relatively peaceful destination for investment. The western world was just beginning to sanction Iran. Ukraine was a mixed economy with a strongly emerging middle class. Today, we see prominent wars and armed conflicts, accelerating urbanization, the growth of digital economies and new, inventive trade policies reshaping the challenges and opportunities facing business leaders.

We don't just update the earlier literature but also place the study of emerging markets in the context of contemporary business realities and opportunities.

As we scoured libraries and online resources for published data and narratives, collaborated across continents, and dug deep into firsthand experiences for insights and illustrations, we were greatly impressed beyond all else by the evident and growing importance of sustainability in approaching new business development. Hence the title, and we trust that we have delivered on our promise in our treatments of the interwoven elements which require consideration.

You will find stories here which we are sharing for the first time; others are tried-and-true histories that remain cogent and relevant. There are many short, integral paragraphs which illustrate concepts; longer case studies are separated by shading and boxing so that they can be read in context, or independently so that they do not interrupt the flow of the narrative.

A new administration took charge in the United States early in 2025. A period of trade hostility, marked by massive tariff changes, rhetoric, and retaliation, ensued. The new order threatens to reshape global supply chains and deeply impacts the era of open trade upon which so much emerging market success was predicated. Many businesses will require fundamental rethinking of cross-border investment and marketing policies. Vietnam's manufacturing rise and Mexico's integration into American supply chains are among the many success stories which may reverse course. Depending on individual businesses' sourcing and marketing models, the rapid changes that are occurring may reinforce the need for adaptable sourcing strategies and scenario planning for uncertainties.

We are humbly confident that this book will be a vital resource for students, present and future business leaders, and decision-makers, who share an interest in these fascinating markets.

Boston, MA
Vancouver, BC
3rd March 2025

References

Khanna, T., & Palepu, K. (2010). *Winning in Emerging Markets. A road map for strategy and execution*. Harvard Business Press.

Pacek, N. & Thorniley, D. (2007). *Emerging markets. Lessons for business success and the outlook for different markets*. The Economist and Profile Books Ltd.

CHAPTER 1

Market categories

Learning outcomes

After studying this chapter, you will be able to do the following:

1. Critically compare growth and emerging markets, distinguishing them from developed growth markets and least developed countries.
2. Assess the key factors that distinguish developed markets from emerging markets.
3. Assess the geopolitical risks of doing business in emerging markets.
4. Analyze different classifications of emerging markets and evaluate their validity or usefulness in making investment decisions.
5. Examine active companies in emerging markets and analyze how they strategize for success.

Why study emerging markets?

Emerging markets are the drivers of global growth. They offer vast, unparalleled business opportunities but challenge familiar economic models. Current and future business leaders must understand their potential, be aware of their risks, and take full note of the urgency of managing their growth in a sustainable, inclusive manner.

Imagine a country in which most of the population is poor and underprivileged. However, it has resources, human or physical, which can fuel rapid economic growth. Over a protracted but relatively recent period, economic development has accelerated, driven by structural reforms, institutional development, and global economic and investment cycles. A middle class emerges and grows rapidly; there is increased demand for goods, services, education, and a better quality of life. Local companies grow rapidly;

DOI: 10.4324/9781003638490-1

international players want to enter the market. But there is a disconnect: demand is there, but some or all of the institutions, infrastructure, and mechanisms to meet that demand are struggling to keep up. This is an *emerging market.*

We identify 26 countries as being currently in this position. They are home to over 68% of the world's population; in them, *billions* of people are joining the global economy. Industry is accelerating, and fortunes are being made. Their middle classes are swelling at an unprecedented rate.

More than half of those countries are among the fastest-growing economies in the world. They are sustaining real Gross Domestic Product (GDP) growth at or above the global average of 3.2%. They are reinventing established views of business and challenging our understanding of supply chains and consumer demand. Already seismic, the rate of change is still increasing. What is happening? Why? What are the opportunities? How do businesses strategize to join the party? These are the questions we will help you to address.

No doubt you are anxious to know which countries we have chosen as our focus. They are listed in Table 1.1.

Trying to draw precise boundaries between emerging markets and other groups is rather an unproductive exercise, as there will always be countries that are on the margin and subject to debate. That said, to understand our selection and the elevation of some countries into the *emerging growth* category, we must start with a view of the whole world.

Setting aside a few disputed areas, there are about 195 countries in the world. Figure 1.1 illustrates a division into three main groups.

The International Monetary Fund (IMF) classifies 40 countries as having *advanced economies*, based on income per capita. Most other writers use the term *developed countries*. Here you will find Canada, the United States, almost all of Europe, and the wealthier Asian-Pacific nations.

In the lowest circle are the *Least Developed Countries* (LDCs).[1] The United Nations (UN) places 46 nations, 33 of them in Africa and most of the rest in Asia-Pacific, in the category. Their progress is "insufficient," and they have not met benchmarks for income levels, human assets, economic progress, or environmental vulnerability.

Table 1.1 Growth and emerging markets

Type	*Countries*
Emerging growth markets *Sustained real GDP growth ≥ 3.2%*	**Africa:** Egypt, Ethiopia, Ghana, Kenya, Morocco, Nigeria. **Asia:** Bangladesh, India, Indonesia, Kazakhstan, Malaysia, the Philippines, Sri Lanka, Vietnam. **Europe:** Türkiye. **Latin America:** Brazil.
Emerging markets *Sustained real GDP growth*	**Africa:** South Africa. **Asia:** China, Pakistan, Thailand. **Europe:** Romania. **Latin America:** Chile, Colombia, Mexico, Peru. **Middle East:** Saudi Arabia

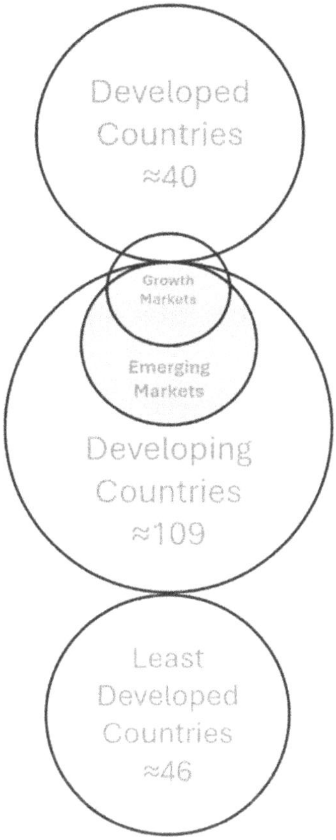

Figure 1.1 Prosperity ranking of countries

They typically have severe economic problems and structural deficiencies (UN Trade and Development, 2024).[2]

In the middle group, we find *developing countries*. They are not yet fully developed, they still have high dependence on agriculture or resource extraction, and they have weaker financial and legal institutions. Their populations have limited access to healthcare, education, and technology, and their economies are volatile. However, because some progress is being made overall, they are distinct from LDCs.

Emerging markets are a subset of developing countries, effectively the upper half, that have sustained and relatively consistent economic growth, institutional development, and improving financial markets.

Growth markets are not a separate group. Growth market status overlays the top half of the emerging markets and a sliver of the developed markets. It is determined by economic trajectory. Growth markets are business environments which exhibit strong rates of economic expansion or increased consumer demand (Indeed Editorial Team, 2023).

Emerging growth markets have fast-growing economies, with sustained real GDP growth rates matching or above the global average. They are clearly making economic and social progress. They have rising consumer demand, especially from a growing middle class, industrial growth, and urbanization. While they may have some challenges (e.g., in infrastructure or regulation), the growth potential is highly attractive to investors.

Emerging markets outside the growth overlay manifest greater risk due to economic volatility, political instability, or underdeveloped regulatory bodies and institutions; typically, they have lower real GDP growth rates, lower average incomes, and less access to global financial markets. Despite all this, their growth is sustained and positive. They still attract interest from investors, for example, in natural resource industries, infrastructural development, and consumer goods.

In summary, in developing countries, there is some economic and social progress, though it may be halting and erratic. In emerging markets, there is sustained progress. And in emerging growth markets, there is sustained progress above the global average.

Extraordinary growth comes with extraordinary risks to the environment, to society, and to the laws and institutions which govern society. *Sustainability*, to which we are deeply committed, refers to the immediate necessity of preserving the future value of the world's resources for our children and their descendants. Emerging markets offer extraordinary promise for businesses, but the opportunities must be grasped in a way that preserves our planet. Environmental threats are the most visible: U.S. President Barack Obama noted at the 2015 Paris Climate Conference that "We're the first generation to feel the effect of climate change and the last generation who can do something about it" (Obama, 2015).

Vietnam's Success Story

In 2024, as the world struggled with political turmoil, economic instability, and unfolding environmental threats, Vietnam stepped onto the world stage as a prime example of transformation. Rising from the ashes of war, Vietnam has averaged a real GDP growth rate of over 5% annually, compared to a global average of 2.72%. It has become one of the fastest-growing economies in the world (Macrotrends, n.d.-c). The government has put money into infrastructure, entered public–private partnerships, and spawned an expanding middle class which innovates and consumes like never before. Retail spending in the country grew over the last ten years at an average rate of over 8.5%.

The story of modern Vietnam exhibits the promise of a better future and the challenges along the way: power shifts, transportation bottlenecks, and an urgent need to ensure that growth aligns with environmental protection, social responsibility, and economic stability. It seems reasonable to say that everyone wants the growth to continue, as it brings improved living standards and a reduction of poverty, but the growth must be sustainable.

Other definitions

There are 26 countries in our list of emerging markets. Authors and authorities never quite agree: a comparative table prepared in 2010 listed 37 potential members and then looked at half a dozen different agencies' lists. The International Monetary Fund. (IMF) recognized 23 of them, the Financial Times 22, Morgan Stanley 24, Standard and Poor's 21, and Dow Jones 22. Despite the similar totals, the constituent nations were markedly different, with only the first five BRICS countries (Brazil, Russia, India, China, and South Africa) plus Mexico, Indonesia, the Philippines, and Türkiye making it onto every list (Panibratov, 2017: 36–37).

In 1981, International Finance Corporation's Antoine van Agtmael had suggested that an emerging market was "A market growing in size and sophistication in contrast to a market that is relatively small, inactive, and gives little appearance of change" (Mobius, 2012). The Economist said, "An economy that is not too rich, not too poor and not too closed to foreign capital" (The Economist, 2017).

To say that emerging markets are the middle countries – those that are neither fully developed, nor suffering at the low end of the *Legatum Prosperity Index* (2023) – does not separate them from the much larger "developing countries" group. Over the last two decades, many great minds have been applied to finding a working definition, and they have produced a surprising variety of opinions.

In 2010, Professors Khanna and Palepu (2010) concluded, sensibly, that defining emerging markets are those which have not yet developed was an "unhelpful tautology" and pointed out that other writers and authorities have taken distinct approaches to formulating a definition. A deeper discussion, they said, "might elicit a list of the persistent headaches of doing business in Emerging Markets," leading to their own definition: "Emerging markets reflect those transactional arenas where buyers and sellers are not easily or efficiently able to come together." Existence of institutional voids was the defining characteristic. It is not intuitively straightforward, however, to look at a country, ask "does it have institutional voids?" then base a classification on that question alone.

In 2021, Professor Tamer Cavusgil and colleagues published the most thorough modern analysis of country groups to date (Cavusgil, Ghauri & Liu, 2021). Their categories embrace four groups: advanced, emerging, frontier, and developing economies. Frontier markets sit between the LDCs and emerging markets and carry the alternative descriptor "pre-emerging markets." They, say the authors, have "advanced further economically, than developing countries, but [are] still in a transitional phase." For the Cavusgil team, Egypt, Morocco, and Nigeria are frontier economies. Saudi Arabia, on the other hand, has the characteristics of an emerging market but is "different" because of its political structure. We feel these distinctions to be slightly over-thought and are confident to include the frontier markets in the emerging category below the growth circle overlap.

The IMF is widely recognized as having great authority in matters of countries' wealth and rankings, due to its access to data, expertise, and global reach. It works closely with the World Bank and UN (International Monetary Fund, n.d.). Despite this analytical powerhouse, one universal system of classification simply does not exist. However, at least everyone seems to agree that a developed country cannot be an emerging market, nor can one which is stagnant or in a state of decline. Growth is about economic trajectory; emerging market status is about positive change.

Other country classifications: N-11, 3G, NICs, income levels, BRICS, and MINT

There are many groups of countries, identified by mnemonics or acronyms, which belong logically together for one reason or another. For example, Goldman Sachs has separated the Next-11 (N-11) countries which it considered had the potential to join the world's largest economies. That list included Iran (Goldman Sachs, 2005).

Citigroup published its own concept, the Global Growth Generators (3G), which recognized Iraq and Mongolia as worthy of attention (Buiter & Rahbari, 2011).

The term "NICs" refers to newly industrialized countries; the list of members is very similar to that of emerging markets. Another popular classification scheme categorizes countries by income levels. Of the three divisions – low, middle, and high income – emerging markets live in the middle group.

There are yet more subgroupings. The best known is BRICS, comprising Brazil, Russia, India, China, and South Africa. The acronym started life in 2001 as BRICs, as Goldman Sachs' Global Investment Research Division published a report titled "Build Better Global Economic BRICs" (O'Neill, 2001). At that time, the "s" functioned as a pluralizer, but it became capitalized and represented South Africa from 2010 when the original four invited a new member to join. Jim O'Neill, author of the Goldman Sachs paper, pointed out that the growth rate of emerging economies was outpacing that of developed economies and argued that the G7 should include BRIC representatives.

The acronym became an organization, with annual summits from 2009, establishment of its own development bank in 2014, and other collaboration initiatives. In 2024, four new countries – Iran, Egypt, Ethiopia, and the United Arab Emirates – attended their first summit as new members. Saudi Arabia received an invitation to join BRICS but as of December 2024 had not responded. And BRICS' flirtation with Argentina in 2023 ended with a change of government and its withdrawal from the membership process. BRICS is a formidable bloc (the word refers to a group of countries which cooperate on specific issues, with or without a formal governance structure) – the current membership, although dominated by China with 70% of the group's total GDP, accounts for 26.67% of the world's land surface and close to half of its population.

Russia's invasion of Ukraine has engendered some serious geopolitical issues, but the BRICS countries continue to collaborate on their initiatives; while some members have expressed condemnation of Russia's actions, only a shadow has been cast, and the group appears to be taking steps to adapt to the new conditions.

Jim O'Neill added to his list of creations in 2013, introducing MINT as a new acronym for Mexico, Indonesia, Nigeria, and Türkiye. These countries, he felt, were emerging markets with strong potential for growth (O'Neill, 2013).

Characteristics of emerging markets

In all emerging markets, we find volatility, uncertainty, complexity, and ambiguity. These are the ingredients of the VUCA conceptual lens, which is not a test for emerging market status but offers a framework to organize shared difficulties. We will devote the whole of Chapter 2 to VUCA.

A productive and consistent method to identify emerging markets depends on examination of their characteristics, as we outlined above. We will now go on to describe the typical characteristics shared by most emerging markets, most of the time.

Above-average real GDP growth rate

International Monetary Fund projections for 2024 and 2025 suggest that the global average real GDP growth rate will be approximately 3.2% (International Monetary

Table 1.2 2024 projected real GDP percentage increases in growth and emerging markets

India	6.6	Brazil	3.2
Ethiopia	6.1	Peru	3.1
Vietnam	6.1	Morocco	2.9
Bangladesh	5.8	Nigeria	2.9
Philippines	5.8	Thailand	2.6
Malaysia	5.1	Pakistan	2.4
Indonesia	5	Chile	2.3
China	4.9	Sri Lanka	2.2
Kenya	4.7	Mexico	2.1
Ghana	4	Colombia	1.5
Kazakhstan	3.6	Saudi Arabia	1.5
Egypt	3.6	Romania	1.4
Türkiye	3.2	South Africa	1.1

Fund, 2024); for an emerging market to be classified in the "growth" category, it should meet or exceed this level. The World Bank, International Monetary Fund, Organization for International Co-operation and Development (OECD), various commercial enterprises, and national statistics offices all publish annual tables of actual and predicted growth rates (World Bank, n.d.-a), from which we have extracted a ranking using the most conservative estimates from reliable sources (Table 1.2). These figures represent the most recently reported actual growth rates, while growth market and emerging market status are based on potential, rather than recent results. Fourteen countries meet the 3.2% benchmark, while 12 do not. The latter group do not have sustained above-average growth, but their underlying fundamentals remain strong enough that they are viewed as making economic progress and thus "emerging."

Real GDP is an important metric, as it includes the impact of factors like infrastructure development, technology adoption, education, and industrial output, which also underpin market status. A country with a broad, diversified economy can continue to be an emerging market despite short-term setbacks to real GDP growth. Türkiye and South Africa, for example, have suffered from political and economic issues, but they have strong industrial bases, advanced financial markets, and exhibit potential for strong recoveries.

Figure 1.2 plots GDP per capita (X axis) against 2023–2024 real GDP growth rate, using the most conservative estimates from the International Monetary Fund (IMF) and World Bank. The shaded area below 3.2% real GDP growth rate contains emerging markets; above the line are growth markets which have not yet achieved developed status. Movements between classifications will occur if we change the predicted period. In 2025, China will likely drop back into the shaded area. Brazil, currently on the dividing line, will sink deeper into it.

The inclusion of *per capita* GDP adds perspective on the distinction between growth and wealth. In the upper-left quadrant are countries which have high-growth economies but low average incomes, indicating the most significant investment opportunities.

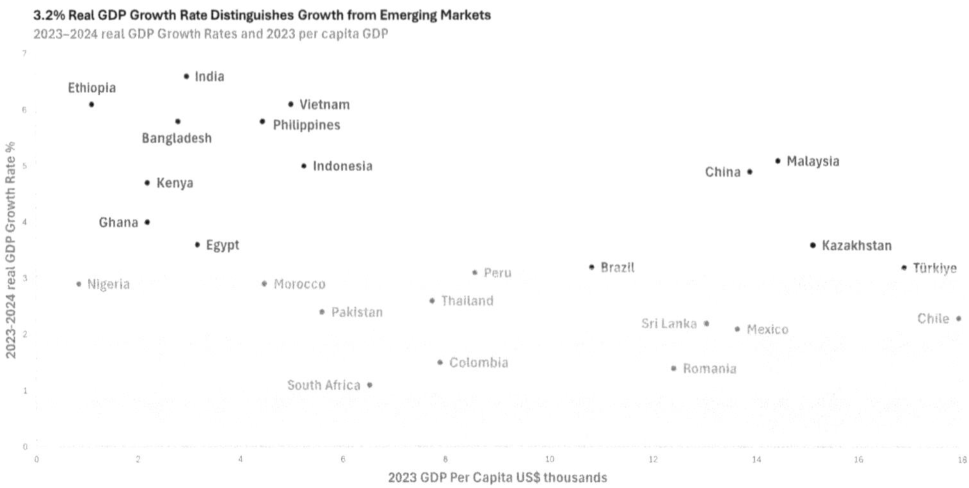

Figure 1.2 Distinguishing growth and emerging markets

In the upper-right quadrant, we find countries that are on their way to becoming fully developed and leaving the emerging markets category altogether.

Contrasting the left and right *halves* of the chart captures the trade-off between risk and opportunity. Low incomes, indicated by low GDP per capita on the left half, are a strong indicator of political instability and weak infrastructure. Although the countries in the upper-left quadrant thus exhibit the most opportunity, they also pose higher risks.

INCREASING STANDARD OF LIVING

While still less than *per capita* income in developed countries, the population should be seeing a real increase in standard of living. Vietnam, for example, has seen improvements in education, healthcare, and infrastructure as its manufacturing hub status has grown exponentially.

In the early 2000s, Vietnam consistently invested 9–10% of GDP in infrastructure (World Bank, 2006). Over time, this has declined, dwindling to 2.5% in 2020 (World Bank, n.d.-b). The significant use of public–private partnerships, especially in transport and logistics, coupled with government tax incentives, has resulted in over 5% annual growth in real GDP, strongly supported by exports (Vu & Nguyen, 2025). Strategic investment in infrastructure has directly contributed to an improvement in living standards, including health, education, and connectivity.

MIDDLE-CLASS GROWTH

The most visible and important attraction for a seller of consumer goods and services is an expanding middle class. A large, expanding pool of consumers has increasing purchasing power. A notable example of the emergence of a large middle class is India, where over the last 25 years millions of people have experienced a hefty increase in disposable income (Varma, 2007). Despite the difficulties of estimation and different definitions, the East Asia Forum concluded that from 2000 to 2012, the middle-class population doubled in size from 300 to 600 million (Krishnan, 2024).

Transition from rural poverty to urban affluence has profound political and economic implications. In the Mexican presidential election of 2006, Felipe Calderon won "largely because he understood what his contender, Andres Manuel Lopez-Obrador, did not: that Mexico was rapidly becoming a majority middle-class nation" (De la Calle & Rubio, 2012).

De la Calle and Rubio expand while seeking to define middle class:

> A middle-class household ... is generally a family living in an urban context ... The transformation from a mostly rural and mostly poor country to a less poor, mostly middle-class country occurred, in large part, thanks to the communications revolution, improved transportation, and the benefits of emigration, including remittances.
>
> The definition of the middle class also includes a positive worldview, an interest in enjoying life beyond the day-to-day, an expectation of systematic economic advancement, and a belief that education is essential to the development of one's children.
>
> *(De la Calle & Rubio, 2012, p. 15)*

ECONOMIC POLARIZATION

Economic polarization refers to an increase in wealth disparity between a small rich segment of the population and a large segment enduring poverty. It can occur purely through an increasing concentration of wealth, between regions (often due to urbanization), or between sectors (e.g., when IT employees advance while agriculture declines). It is a two-edged sword.

Wealth disparity often causes or fuels protests and social instability, sometimes leading to political insecurity. It can limit the ability of consumers to purchase products and services and increase the difficulty of implementing sustainable development. Inequality can fuel populist movements in emerging markets, thus multinational companies must be especially vigilant not to appear to be exploiting marginalized populations.

At the same time, the increasingly wealthy sector, be it upper or middle class, increases the potential for product and service sales. Companies operating in emerging markets may find opportunities to gain recognition with this group by investing in training and educational programs.

Economic polarization is an important indicator of emerging market status as it is exacerbated by the rapid advancement of urban centers, while the traditional sector (agriculture, low-skilled labor) is left behind. India and Mexico are prime examples, where some cities participate strongly in global markets, while rural areas see little advancement and still lack decent infrastructure. Although growth is rapid, it is unevenly distributed. Brazil is another stark example, where highly successful, wealthy businesspeople live in Rio and Sao Paulo alongside vast slums (favelas).

Economic polarization is thus a source of risk, an opportunity for social impact, and an indicator that several market strategies may be required to run in parallel, due to the gap between population segments.

GROWTH OF MANUFACTURING AND SERVICES

Continued growth is usually driven by a movement away from agricultural and mineral dependence toward increased reliance on production of goods and services.

Figure 1.3 shows the dramatic change in Vietnam over 20 years. Not only has real GDP grown by a factor of eight over the period, but also the proportion of real GDP which is non-agricultural has grown exponentially. Despite real growth in both sectors, agricultural production has shrunk from 21.8% in 2003 to 13.7% in 2023. This has accompanied explosive urbanization (General Statistics Office of Vietnam, n.d.).

GROWTH OF MARKET ACCESS

None of the above features will be attractive if an incompetent government hangs onto archaic restrictions, prohibitive regulatory systems, or financial roadblocks. Without inward investment, a country will struggle to continue impressive growth. Vietnam's economic growth and success as a manufacturing center for multinational businesses have resulted from deliberate government policies aimed at attracting foreign investment, reducing tariffs, privatization of public enterprises and infrastructure investments (Le, Singh & Nguyen, 2016).

A large-scale success in developing market access was Mexico's entry into trade agreements like the United States-Mexico-Canada Agreement (USMCA), formerly known as the North American Free Trade Agreement (NAFTA), which significantly enhanced two-way traffic with the developed markets of the United States and Canada. However, these trade relations have an uncertain future in 2025 as America transitions to the newly elected Republican administration. President Trump's policy indications point toward renegotiation or cancellation of agreements which he perceives as damaging to American

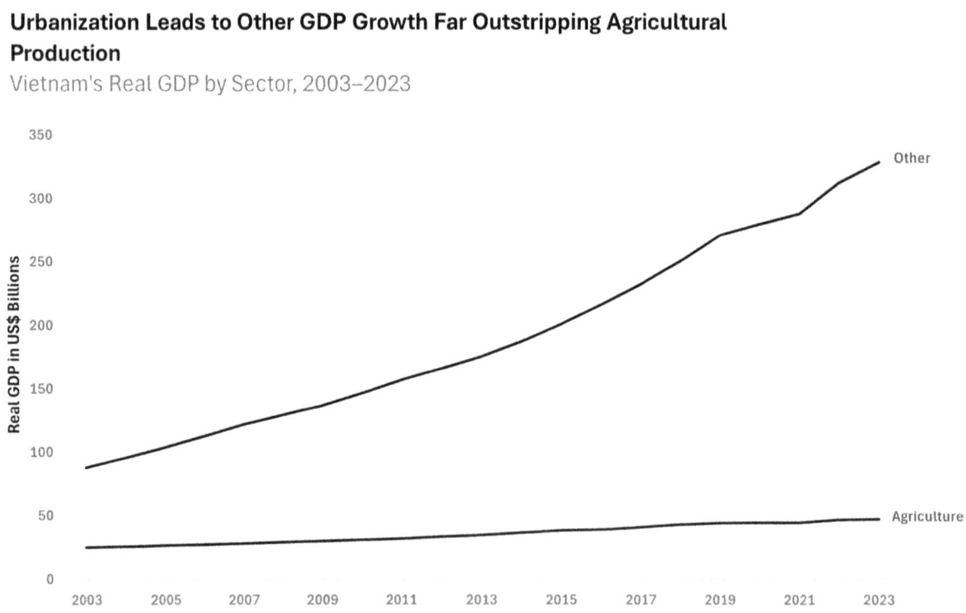

Figure 1.3 Vietnamese agriculture versus other

economic interests; new tariffs raise questions about future cross-border flows. Businesses in Mexico and around the world are anxiously bracing themselves for fundamental shifts in trade policy (The White House, 2025).

"Tariff wars" have far-reaching effects beyond simply reducing international trade volumes. They disrupt global supply chains. They raise input costs, as the American auto manufacturing sector has already seen. They destabilize cross-border investment planning. Businesses reviewing their existing strategies, like those making new plans, must incorporate greater flexibility into their sourcing strategies and reevaluate choices of market entry type. Emerging markets which have predicated their success on exports to advanced economies, particularly the United States, have the difficult task of revising their growth projections even as the eventual levels of tariffs are unknown and changeable daily. Any assumption that trade networks are resilient or even predictable is no longer valid.

INFRASTRUCTURE DEVELOPMENT

The movement toward industrialization drives improvements in roads, utilities, and communications. China's internal development sets the standard for the developing world as it has shown over a period of 40 years the results of massive investment in roads, airports, railways, power generation, sustainable energy, and digital technology (Qiu, 2019).

India has similarly made impressive, targeted investments in infrastructure. It has created programs like "Make in India" (2014) and "Digital India" (Ministry of Electronics & IT, 2022). A relentless quest for development has led to the Delhi-Mumbai Industrial Corridor (DMIC, 2025), new electric railways, and connectivity for millions of rural inhabitants through the BharatNet Initiative (Digital Bharat Nidhi, 2025).

GEOPOLITICAL RISK

Geopolitics, the influence of geography, politics, economics, and culture on international relations and power dynamics, is particularly strong in emerging markets. Access to water or waterways near borders, control over trading routes, and possession of resources have deep influence on government policies. Trade relations, competition, and sanctions have powerful effects on supply chains. Even soft power, such as the export of ideologies and political frameworks, affects global business. Emerging markets are especially vulnerable to geopolitical influence if they are in strategic locations, subject to resource exploitation, or implicated in climate agreements.

Indonesia, for example, has become the epicenter for strategic competition between China and the West. While China is courting Indonesia with huge investments in infrastructure projects, the United States is making Herculean efforts to build its own influence through the Indo-Pacific Economic Framework (U.S. Department of Commerce, n.d.).

Geopolitical forces can be strong enough to relegate a country to or below the list of emerging markets. Very recently, political protests and a devastating conflict have severely impacted Israel's progress. In the first quarter of 2023, graphically demonstrating the impact of volatility in growth markets, the country saw a 60% decline in inward investment (Wrobel, 2023). It remains to be seen what the medium- and long-term effects of these disruptions will be.

There are countries which were great prospects in 2007 when Pacek and Thorniley published the second edition of their seminal work *Emerging Markets* but have suffered such economic decline that they are no longer strong contenders for the attention of ethical, risk-averse global corporations. If we look at countries which have fallen out of the list of emerging markets, the cause is often a war, economic sanctions, or both. Economic mismanagement, hyperinflation, and political instability account for the rest.

Ukraine, once a budding EU member and a rapidly advancing technology hub, is now a war-ravaged country that one day will need to rebuild from the ground up. Real GDP growth rate in Ukraine for 2022 was sadly negative 29.1% (Worldometers, n.d.-a; Macrotrends, n.d.-a). Russia, the aggressor which has brought this about, still has some characteristics of an emerging market, but the military concentration, the main growth area, has little interest for entrepreneurs outside supporting regimes (Macrotrends, n.d.-b). Figure 1.4 shows the close correlation between Ukrainian and Russian GDP growth.

Iran, with a population exceeding 90 million, has a ruined economy due to international sanctions intended to control its anti-western policies and support for terrorist regimes and organizations. Its currency is almost worthless, and its oil is unwelcome in most markets; no ethical global business can consider Iran a viable target for expansion. Iran has rapid economic growth, a large young population and increasing urbanization, but it also exhibits deep political instability, poor infrastructure, and an appalling level of corruption. It has been relegated below the category of emerging markets (Worldometers, n.d.-b).

Authorities differ as to whether Argentina should be considered an Emerging Market; it is still included in some indices. However, with a projected real GDP contraction of 3.5%, and indications that contraction will continue for the foreseeable future, we do not feel its inclusion is presently warranted.

Geopolitical risk often manifests itself most visibly in currency devaluation. We will return to this in Chapter 2 as we address currency volatility.

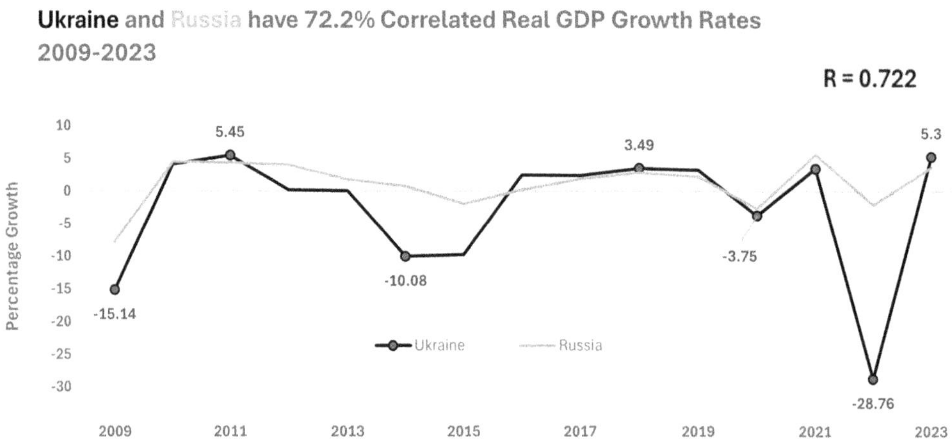

Figure 1.4 Ukrainian and Russian real GDP growth

STABLE GOVERNMENT

Emerging market status is difficult to maintain if government is unstable, constantly changing, or unable to progress its own economic objectives. It is the factor which leads some analysts to separate countries such as Nigeria into a subcategory and deny them full emerging status.

In March 2023, Bola Tinubu, former governor of Lagos and a noted kingmaker, won the presidency of Nigeria. His new government was determined to increase the country's investment appeal and attract more foreign direct investment (BBC Africa Visual Journalism Team, 2023). It immediately instituted two economic reforms – the removal of fuel subsidies, and a change to a market-reflective exchange rate. The instant effect on cost of living and doing business was dramatic – gasoline prices at the pump rose by over 150%, and the naira depreciated over 40% against the U.S. dollar (around 30% in the unofficial market) (Abdulrahman, 2024).

Unstable government can drive a country back into least developed status after a period of prosperity. Fifty years ago, after independence Zimbabwe had a serious chance to become a regional leader in Africa. It had so much fertile land it was called the "breadbasket of Africa" (the term is used for any area which supplies large quantities of food, not necessarily grains) and had a large skilled workforce. Controversial land redistribution decisions, expropriations, and economic mismanagement caused one of the worst financial crises in history. Violence, political oppression, and a brain drain followed. The country remains trapped in a cycle of poverty and underdevelopment and is thus not considered an emerging market (Godwin, 2011).

Government turbulence can cause businesses to move completely out of a country, causing deep harm to its economy. Bomagra, which half a century ago was a massive Argentinian business with global reach, did exactly that, demonstrating the critical importance of legal stability. In response to political upheaval, it moved its headquarters to Brazil despite enormous cultural differences and executive resistance. Eventually, it left Latin America and relocated to the United States (Born, 2008).

When the population is unhappy, violence can flare; strikes and protests can disrupt business operations, and people and property are at risk. Conflagrations can occur suddenly and without warning, as happened in Bangladesh in the summer of 2024 (Corea & Erum, 2024). Sudden changes in the political environment can cause unexpected currency devaluations and supply chain disruption.

Even the mere threat of political upheaval can spook markets and investors. In Venezuela, a radical change of regime caused massive devaluation of the local currency, the bolivar, resulting in hyperinflation. At the turn of the century in Argentina, loss of confidence in the government caused unsupportable outward movement of foreign capital, which contributed to an unbreakable spiral of hyperinflation and unemployment (Kiguel, 2016).

Thailand is a current case in point. On August 14, 2024, Prime Minister Srettha Thavisin lost his job for violating his office's rules on ethics. He had been in power for less than a year and was the third Prime Minister in 16 years removed by the same court. As the BBC reports, "Politics in Thailand is not known for its ethics; bribery is commonplace and ministers with more serious convictions have been allowed to serve in the past" (Head & Tan, 2024).

There are rare cases where political upheaval has occurred, yet emerging market status has been maintained. The 2011 revolution in Egypt, for example, gave rise to a new wave of entrepreneurship, particularly among younger people. The experience of driving change led to empowerment of the youthful population, a shift in societal attitudes, and a sharp rise in startups and creativity (El Tahri, 2023).

The events of late 2024 and early 2025 in the United States showed that trade protectionism can become a geopolitical force. Before even taking the official reins of government, the incoming administration began talking of 60–100% tariffs on imports from BRICS countries, suggesting that they would address currency manipulation and restore economic sovereignty. As the levels and scope of tariffs escalated in spring 2025, profound implications became apparent for emerging markets dependent on exports to, or integrated with, the United States. In an atmosphere of economic nationalism, tariff-based disruptions have become foreseeable crises where they were once mere exceptions.

INSTITUTIONAL VOIDS AND FINANCIAL CONSTRAINTS

The concept of *institutional frameworks* broadly covers formal systems, such as laws, regulations, and regulatory agencies, and informal expectations and ways of doing business that are societally policed. Together these two groups form the structures which lead to effective governance, balancing economic interests with societal and environmental responsibility.

Weakness in institutions is pervasive among emerging markets. Patchy enforcement, corruption, or the mere absence of policies and standards can be a significant hindrance to good business. Governments and businesses alike have a responsibility to fill these gaps wherever they find them.

INFORMATION ASYMMETRY

Partially due to such institutional voids, market data are often incomplete, inaccurate, or inaccessible. Cultural differences, especially informal procedures, make it difficult to make decisions from a distance. Geographical diversity and weak reporting standards may leave investors in the dark about important factors. Information asymmetry can be a barrier to investment, increase transaction costs, reinforce inequality, and lead to mispricing.

These deficiencies create opportunities for innovation, especially through digital platforms and consumer education. Organizations which acknowledge and address asymmetry earn trust, while supporting growth and equity.

BANKRUPTCY LAWS

Abrupt financial changes and persistent risks make the risk of failure in emerging markets greater than in developed markets. The enhanced risk of failure is acknowledged when a country moves toward a settled framework for assisting business survival in troubled times. Insolvency frameworks are important to investors because they reduce financial risk and definite personal liability, both important considerations for business expansion.

In 2009, Stephen Lubben, a noted bankruptcy lawyer in his practicing days, but latterly a professor at Seton Hall, published a paper which reviewed progress on implementing bankruptcy laws in emerging markets (Lubben, 2009). He did not intend to enter the definitional debate, but to provide an empirical view of progress in the emerging world toward legislation which prioritizes corporate rescue over liquidation. America's adoption of Chapter 11 in 1978 drove such reforms all over the world (11 U.S.C. §§ 1101–1174 (2024)). When Professor Lubben was writing, not all emerging markets had fully developed such laws.

However, over the past 40 years, all emerging markets have adopted legislation which views corporate distress in this manner. The changes came more or less in regional waves; while South Africa and Nigeria had older insolvency legislation, Egypt, Kenya, and Morocco signed up from 2008 to 2015. Bangladesh led the Asian countries in 1997, with Sri Lanka completing reforms in 2017. The European members accomplished their reforms between 2008 and 2015, while the Latin American wave was in the mid-late 1990s. The Middle Eastern nations recognized the need for reform between 2013 and 2018.

The presence or absence of a mature corporate bankruptcy regime is not a defining element for emerging market status. However, if corporate regulation has not yet restructured in this manner, like in least developed nations such as Chad, the Central African Republic, and Haiti, this is a clear sign that the economy is not yet positioned to move toward emerging market status.

We have concluded our rather lengthy description of the characteristics and defining features of emerging and growth markets. The remainder of this book will develop themes relating to doing business in emerging markets; before we dig deeper, however, we must explain that the successful businesses which will illustrate these themes are expanding in three very distinct ways. We will be drawing examples and telling the stories of all these types.

The three growth trajectories

Scholars of business growth in emerging markets describe successes on three pathways.

(1) Entrepreneurs from developed countries expanding successfully into emerging markets.
(2) Emerging Market Multi-National Corporations (EMNCs) successfully expanding into developed countries.
(3) Visionary people in emerging markets accomplishing extraordinary growth at home or in multiple emerging markets.

Each of these trajectories requires further comment and examples.

Expanding *into* emerging markets

"Emerging markets are the next frontier for global business expansion" (Villamarin, 2024).

They are not just a frontier. They are the star player in prospects for global growth. However, writers in the field often espouse a developed world view, focusing on western expansion into new territories. Companies from developed countries have indeed built new empires in emerging markets and are the focus of many excellent academic works. They are the exclusive focus of Pacek and Thorniley (2007), and the subject of a highly readable and compelling work by Guillen and Garcia-Canal (2013). However, that is only one-third of the picture.

For companies presently seated in developed countries, even if we espouse the dated view that the primary purpose of every business is to increase profits, there are compelling reasons to consider emerging markets for expansion. Rapidly expanding middle classes create significant business opportunities; competitors might not yet be part of the landscape; the growth rates of emerging markets encourage governments to create favorable operating conditions for inward investors. An inward investor is a natural or legal person from one country that injects capital into another country (Chen, 2021). These conditions can include not only lower charges for materials and services but also tax incentives, subsidies, and guarantees. Being first-to-market with a product can have significant benefits for a brand not only in the target country but also back home.

Whatever the reason, commercial or altruistic, a business is likely to find government support for expansion into or within an emerging market. Encouragement of business growth is a sound policy; the World Bank's 2024 *Business Ready* report stresses the vital contribution of the private sector to job creation, accounting for 90% of jobs and 80% of government revenue (World Bank, 2024).

When things are stagnating or entering a downturn at home, a successful venture in a new market will spread risk and may be a source of new expertise and innovation. In the midst of a stagnating domestic market in 2009, Sony expanded its PlayStation® business into Latin America (IGN Staff, 2009). Its success in the region has proved durable, with the latest phase being the 2024 announcement that it has set up a production line for PlayStation 5 game discs in the Manaus Free Trade Zone in northern Brazil (Scullion, 2024).

Populations with growing wealth in a domestic middle class will need goods and services which may be sparsely available; providing them improves lives. German company Jumia, a massive presence in African e-commerce, today has a physical presence in 11 countries and 2.3 million customers. Started in 2012, Jumia saw that online shopping had poor availability across the continent and moved quickly to fill the gap. Despite German registration, Jumia is a quintessentially African business with deep roots in Nigeria. It has earned the nickname "the Amazon of Africa."

It has not all been smooth sailing for Jumia. After a euphoric listing on the New York Stock Exchange, its shares fell quickly, and its operations and valuation were severely affected by the COVID-19 pandemic and management challenges (BBC News, 2020). In 2022 it was forced to restructure after ousting its co-founders (Adeoye, 2022).

The African continent is also fertile ground for innovative companies filling gaps in the financial ecosystem. Flutterwave, Inc., though based in San Francisco, set a record for African startups by securing $170 million in new funding. It achieved *unicorn* status by doing so. The name unicorn refers to a privately held company, valued at over US$1 billion, with high growth prospects and a disruptive business model. An early major success was its 2022 switching and processing license from the Central Bank of Nigeria, enabling it to participate in fund transfers and other payment services; by 2024, it had entered 34

African markets with the latest license granted by Ghana. Not surprisingly Flutterwave has encountered significant governance challenges, which it has met by strengthening compliance practices and a partnership with the Nigerian Economic and Financial Crimes Commission. Flutterwave is a thought leader in prevention of cybercrime.

An element of national pride is often found in such successful organizations. Infosys, today a global IT giant, was founded in India in 1981 with US$250 capital; thanks to adept management and a marriage of quality services to low costs, it grew rapidly from a small, local software business to a multinational behemoth with over 300,000 employees in 50 countries (Infosys, 2024).

Red Tiger

There is more to entering an emerging market than simply selling products or services to its residents, exploiting its resources, or adopting its technology. The NetEnt acquisition of Red Tiger Gaming provides a striking example of another potential avenue: building a successful business overseas using an inexpensive yet highly educated labor pool. Red Tiger, founded in the Isle of Man, set up in Sofia, Bulgaria, as a development center for gaming software. Instead of attempting to lure Bulgarian programmers away from home to work for higher salaries, Red Tiger took the enterprise to their country, employing at peak over 400 young developers *in Bulgaria*. After only five years, the business, with its proprietary software, changed hands in an all-cash deal worth £220 million (NetEnt, 2019). The shareholders deployed the profits from the sale in philanthropic causes. This beautiful story illustrates all three aspects of success in an emerging market – economic growth, demographic advantage, and global integration.

Expanding *from* emerging markets

EMNCs have become powerful players on the world stage, taking their unique skills, passion, and hunger to other countries in their own quest for success. The common theme is the recognition of extraordinary potential: to grow, to innovate, and to make positive contributions to society.

These companies are now evolving as global market leaders, representing a challenge and a threat to established businesses in developed countries. By 2006, research published by top academics in the field, including Harvard's Professor Tarun Khanna, was bringing attention to the shifting landscape (Khanna & Palepu, 2006). *Business Week* used apocalyptic language to warn its readers of the phenomenon: "be afraid, be very afraid," while Bloomberg Business headlined "American companies should be very afraid" (Braunstein, 2006).

Ten years later, Robert Grosse eloquently expressed the continuing threat:

> They will enter local markets outside their home countries and take business away from local competitors there as well. Even this threat is not the complete picture. As the emerging markets themselves become the most attractive places to build

> sales in the future these emerging market companies are already established there, and are likely to prove to be formidable competitors.
>
> *(Grosse, 2016)*

What were the reasons for the extraordinary growth of the emerging market Multi-National Corporations (MNCs)? In 2012, INSEAD Professor Chattopadhyay and colleagues published the results of their interviews with top executives of 39 such companies, commenting that the key challenges were to build global businesses and global brands.

The team identified four successful strategies:

- Cost leadership, leveraging cost advantages and high volumes to attack developed markets.
- Knowledge leverage, tapping into knowledge of home markets to expand into other emerging markets.
- Niche customization, combining cost advantages and low-cost research and development to develop unique brands for other markets.
- Global brand building, taking focused innovation into developed markets and acquiring the skills and resources to do so through strategic acquisitions (Chattopadhyay, Batra & Ozsomer, 2012).

Cost leadership is also a highly visible strategy for inward investors from developed markets, which might be eyeing the labor costs in emerging markets and thinking about deploying them to reduce their own costs. Extreme competency in maintaining low costs, lean engineering, frugal innovation, cheaper natural resources, and economies of scale all help give such companies a price advantage that plays well in markets seeking lower priced products.

India's Mahindra Tractors, the authors say, became the world's largest tractor manufacturer (units sold) by creating large-volume operations in their home market then applying their models in others. Companies like Mahindra leverage knowledge to take lessons learned in one market and apply it in others where similar conditions apply.

The first two strategies are well-established and natural extensions of corporate growth within markets. Niche customizers, however, are a newer development, focusing on "small, neglected, and special-needs segments primarily, but not exclusively, in developing markets" (Chattopadhyay, Batra & Ozsomer, 2012, p. 11). Mahindra Tractors is in this group too, with a focus on small, rugged tractors for the hobby farmer and golf course markets. Niche customizers use their knowledge of poor customers and inexpensive products, aiming not to compete with the massive multinationals but to find the customers that they ignore or underserve.

Chattopadhyay's last category, global brand builders, is a larger extension of the third group. Stressing the importance of focused innovation and aggressively deploying the fruits of their low-cost research and development, companies like Arçelik and Lenovo consistently develop world-class, highly desirable products and features that compete strongly in world markets with the very largest MNCs.

In the early 2020s, the full circle extent of emerging market entities' ability to grow from within, then dominate a world market, came fully into focus. Then in November 2024, Northvolt, the most prominent European electric vehicle (EV) battery maker, filed for bankruptcy with debts of billions of dollars. It failed, says analyst Michael Dunne, "because it could not match Chinese competitors on quality, cost or speed to market" (Dunne, 2024).

Leaders in developed countries appear to be very aware of the threat from expanding emerging market multinationals. Late in 2024, under President-elect Donald Trump, the United States adopted an adversarial position toward the BRICS countries' discussions about creation of a new currency.

> The idea that the BRICS Countries are trying to move away from the Dollar while we stand by, and watch is OVER. We require a commitment from these Countries *(sic)* that they will neither create a new BRICS Currency, nor back any other Currency to replace the mighty U.S. Dollar or, they will face 100% Tariffs and should expect to say goodbye to selling into the wonderful U.S. Economy.
>
> *(Trump, 2024)*

While the prospect of a new common currency seems unlikely given the cultural and economic distances between members, it is noteworthy that then President-elect Trump saw this as such a threat. It is a demonstration of the size and raw power of emerging markets as a group.

Expanding *within* emerging markets

There are compelling histories of visionary people in emerging markets who have made extraordinary accomplishments at, or close to, home. The seminal work concentrating on home-grown social entrepreneurs is *The power of unreasonable people* (Elkington & Hartigan, 2008). Large, successful companies which originated inside emerging markets have used local advantages to dominate their industries. Typically, they have leveraged family solidarity, cultural awareness, and profound local understanding to build remarkable businesses.

The family business structure is far more important in emerging than in developed markets. Because large-scale industrialization and development are more recent, even large, leading commercial companies often remain in the first generations of family ownership. The Turkish Corporate Governance Association, for example, estimates that 95% of businesses in the country are family owned (Dogan, 2024).

Collaborating with family members and appointing them to key roles are viable responses to the still-nascent legal frameworks in emerging markets. Cultural aspects, particularly a high value placed on family loyalty and a long-term vision of providing for future generations, may lessen the urgency of making immediate profits for shareholders, and underdeveloped capital markets can make family money an important source of finance. Of course, family businesses still exist in developed markets but often have more dispersed ownership structures with capital market investors and professional managers.

Exemplary large businesses which epitomize the family ethic are the Angelini Group (COPEC) in Chile (uncle, father, and son) (Rossi, 2018); Zamil Group in Saudi Arabia (CEO Adib AlZamil is one of 15 brothers and sisters who carry on the business started by their father) (AlZamil, 2023), and Akbar Brothers in Sri Lanka (chairman Abbas Akbarally represents the third generation at the reins) (Akbarally, 2015).

Laura Catena, managing director of Bodega Catena Zapata and founder of the Catena Institute of Wine, continued at the head of a wine business founded in Argentina by her great-grandfather. She debates the upsides and downsides of family domination, particularly considering the long-term perspective required in businesses where rewards are not immediate (Catena, 2022). Her conclusions underline the importance of leadership transition, which may be within families or, with globalization, to a wider pool of executive talent.

Beyond profit: Making a difference

Many mature businesses have grown above the notion that pure profit is the only viable motivation for a new venture. Sustainability is central to the business philosophy of many notable leaders.

Alberto Baillères, CEO of Grupo Bal, gave an impactful interview in 2013 in which he continually underlined his love for his country, Mexico; through the media of education and business he stressed the role of emerging market companies in the building of nations (Baillères, 2013). "Purpose goes beyond making a profit; it is about creating a positive impact on society and leaving a lasting legacy," says inspirational speaker Chinedum Azuh (2023).

Patagonia, Inc., the American outdoor clothing retailer, was effectively given away in 2022 by founder Yvon Chouinard – its entire profits are used to combat climate change and protect land (Gelles, 2022). While Patagonia is not itself based in an emerging market, its practices, ethics, and influence have profound importance in its supply chain, for example in its ethical sourcing of products from Southeast Asia. Its pursuits of sustainable, regenerative agriculture in India and Argentina are exemplary.

Entrepreneurs who achieve success from within emerging markets frequently combine a desire for profit with other noble goals; if unemployment is rife, a desire to see compatriots in gainful work can be a powerful driver. Grameen Bank in Bangladesh, while pursuing profitability, set course with the main ambition of creating employment and improving lives. It did this by being a first mover in the emerging area of microcredit, empowering poor residents, 97% of them women, to start their own businesses. Founder Muhammad Yunus, awarded a Nobel Prize for his pioneering work (Grameen Bank, 2024), recently became the interim leader of his country after a period of unrest (The Economist, 2024).

Conclusion

This chapter explored definitional debates and selected a list of emerging markets. We explained that "growth markets" is a term which overlays the most rapidly advancing emerging markets and a handful of developed markets. We contrasted emerging markets with other groupings and identified their characteristics. We explained why emerging markets are so attractive as a base or destination for a business hoping for extraordinary success. We explored the characteristics of these markets and hinted at the importance of understanding their unique characteristics and strategizing to cope with them.

As we continue, we will develop the theme that the most successful companies in emerging markets are those that not only expand but also do so responsibly.

They must moderate the desire for profit with purposeful ideals, ensure that their growth does not degrade their sustainability, and temper boundless ambition with planning for resilience.

The companies with global impact tomorrow may not come from Silicon Valley or London, Frankfurt, or Tokyo. They could just as easily have roots in Jakarta, Lagos, Mumbai, or Beijing. The question for future business leaders inside emerging markets is, "Are you ready to take on the world?" For outsiders, it is, "Are you ready to compete with these forces?"

A business expanding within, or into, a growth or emerging market may be attracted by the opportunity yet daunted by the extent of complexity and diversity. Market dynamics are increasingly shaped by global forces, which bring VUCA together. In the next chapter, we will discuss how these four elements engage the VUCA framework, which helps business leaders to organize and strategize for these challenges.

Notes

1 The delineation of **markets**, amidst a classification of **countries**, does not mean that market and country are synonymous. A market can be a country, but it can also be an industry or a segment of a population. As our concentration is on geographies, we can regard markets, countries, and economies as interchangeable.

2 The UN regularly reviews its classifications of LDCs. Countries, including Cambodia, Laos, Nepal, Rwanda, and Uzbekistan (Jivraj, 2024), have made significant reforms and achieved economic advancement, making them candidates for promotion to the emerging markets list. Uzbekistan has been a major recipient of sustainable development investment, including $2.6 billion U.S. dollars from the Asian Infrastructure Investment Bank, which held its ninth annual meeting in Samarkand in 2024 (Cross, 2024). Reasons for delaying reclassification vary but focus on the need for further improvements in political stability, infrastructure, or the filling of institutional voids.

References

Abdulrahman, A. (2024, May 30). Nigeria: One year later, Tinubu struggles with the economic question. https://africanarguments.org/2024/05/nigeria-one-year-later-tinubu-struggles-with-the-economic-question

Adeoye, A. (2022, November 23). 'Amazon of Africa' Jumia restructures after ousting co-founders. *The Financial Times*. https://www.ft.com/content/cb1fcc33-473a-420f-8065-4e3533e54f63

Akbarally, A. (2015, December 23). Interview by V.G. Narayanan. *Creating Emerging Markets Oral History Collection*. Baker Library Special Collections, Harvard Business School.

AlZamil, A. (2023, May 16). Interview by T. Khanna. *Creating Emerging Markets Oral History Collection*. Baker Library Special Collections, Harvard Business School.

Azuh, C. (2023, April 17). The importance of defining the purpose of your business. *LinkedIn*. https://www.linkedin.com/pulse/importance-defining-purpose-your-business-chinedum-azuh/

Baillères, A. (2013, April 15). Interview by R.G. Cuéllar. *Creating Emerging Markets Oral History Collection*. Baker Library Special Collections, Harvard Business School. Bankruptcy Code, 11 U.S.C. § 1101–1174.

BBC Africa Visual Journalism Team. (2023, May 28). Bola Tinubu: Timeline of how Nigeria's kingmaker became king. https://www.bbc.co.uk/news/resources/idt-966cd330-15e7-40de-9b22-3008247d1911

BBC News. (2020, April 28). Jumia: The e-commerce start-up that fell from grace. https://www.bbc.com/news/world-africa-52439546

Born, J. (2008, August 21). Interview by A. Lluch. *Creating Emerging Markets Oral History Collection*. Baker Library Special Collections, Harvard Business School.

Braunstein, D. (2006, July 31). *American companies should be very afraid*. Bloomberg. https://www.bloomberg.com/news/articles/2006-08-21/american-companies-should-be-very-afraid

Buiter, W., & Rahbari, E. (2011). *Global growth generators: Moving beyond 'Emerging Markets' and 'BRIC'*. Citigroup Global Markets.

Catena, L. (2022, April 11). Interview by A. Lluch. *Creating Emerging Markets Oral History Collection*. Baker Library Special Collections, Harvard Business School.

Cavusgil, S.T., Ghauri, N., & Liu, L.A. (2021). *Doing business in Emerging Markets*, 3rd ed. Sage.

Chattopadhyay, A., Batra, R., & Ozsomer, A. (2012). *The new emerging market multinationals. Four strategies for disrupting markets and building brands*. McGraw Hill.

Chen, J. (2021, November 17). Inward investment: Meaning, overview, disadvantages. https://www.investopedia.com/terms/i/inward-investment.asp

Corea, H., & Erum, N. (2024, July 29). *What is happening at the quote-reform protests in Bangladesh?* Amnesty International. https://www.amnesty.org/en/latest/news/2024/07/what-is-happening-at-the-quota-reform-protests-in-bangladesh/

Cross, A. (2024, November 8). Harnessing Central Asia's infrastructure opportunity. *fDi Intelligence*. https://www.fdiintelligence.com/content/opinion/opinion-harnessing-central-asias-infrastructure-opportunity-84288

De la Calle, L., & Rubio, L. (2012). *Mexico: A middle class society*. Woodrow Wilson International Center for Scholars.

Digital Bharat Nidhi. (2025). BharatNet Project. https://usof.gov.in/en/bharatnet-project

DMIC. (2025). Delhi-Mumbai Industrial Corridor (DMIC). https://www.nicdc.in/index.php/delhi-mumbai-industrial-corridor-dmic.htm

Dogan, O. (2024, November 19). Family businesses boost Turkey's FDI possibilities. *fDi Intelligence*. https://www.fdiintelligence.com/content/opinion/opinion-family-businesses-boost-turkeys-fdi-possibilities-84296

Dunne, M. (2024, November 26). Northvolt collapse lays bare Chinese EV supremacy. *fDi Intelligence*. https://www.fdiintelligence.com/content/opinion/opinion-northvolt-collapse-lays-bare-chinese-ev-supremacy-84346

El Tahri, N. (2023, August 9). Interview by G. Jones. *Creating Emerging Markets Oral History Collection*. Baker Library Special Collections. Harvard Business School.

Elkington, J., & Hartigan, P. (2008). *The power of unreasonable people*. Harvard Business Press.

Gelles, D. (September 14, 2022). Billionaire no more: Patagonia founder gives away the company. The New York Times.

General Statistics Office of Vietnam. (n.d.). https://www.gso.gov.vn

Godwin, P. (2011). *The fear: Robert Mugabe and the martyrdom of Zimbabwe*. Little, Brown and Company.

Goldman Sachs. (2005). *How solid are the BRICs?* (Global Economics Paper No. 153). Goldman Sachs.

Grameen Bank. (2024). About Grameen Bank. https://grameenbank.org.bd/about/introduction

Grosse, R. (2016). *Emerging markets: Strategies for competing in the global value chain*. Kogan Page.

Guillen, M., & Garcia-Canal, E. (2013). *Emerging markets rule: Growth strategies of the new global giants*. McGraw-Hill.

Head, J., & Tan, Y. (2024, August 14) Thai court dismisses PM for violating constitution. *BBC News*. https://www.bbc.com/news/articles/c98415kzxy9o

IGN Staff. (2009, February 20, updated 2012, June 15). Sony Computer Entertainment America expands in Latin America. https://www.ign.com/articles/2009/02/20/sony-computer-entertainment-america-expands-in-latin-america

Indeed Editorial Team. (2023, August 21). Growth markets: Key attributes, opportunities and risks. https://uk.indeed.com/career-advice/career-development/growth-market

Infosys. (2024). The Infosys Story. https://www.infosys.com/about/overview.html#

International Monetary Fund. (2024, October). Policy Pivot, Rising Threats. https://mediacenter.imf.org/news/imf---world-economic-outlook-july-2024-update/s/6ae9bf9c-586c-4078-8e5c-90ace9de89b1
International Monetary Fund. (n.d.). *IMF essentials: A guide to the International Monetary Fund*. International Monetary Fund. https://www.imf.org
Jivraj, H. (2024, September 2). Uzbekistan opening up, but yet to fulfil its FDI potential. *fDi Intelligence*. https://www.fdiintelligence.com/content/News/uzbekistan-opening-up-but-yet-to-fulfil-its-fdi-potential-83947
Khanna, T., & Palepu, K.G. (2006, October). Emerging giants: Building world-class companies in developing countries. *Harvard Business Review*. https://hbr.org/archive-toc/BR0610
Khanna, T., & Palepu, K.G. (2010). *Winning in emerging markets: A road map for strategy and execution*. Harvard Business Press.
Kiguel, M. (2016, June 11). Argentina's 2001 economic and financial crisis: Lessons for Europe. https://www.brookings.edu/wp-content/uploads/2016/06/11_argentina_kiguel.pdf.
Krishnan, S. (2024, May 21). Understanding India's evolving middle classes. https://eastasia forum.org/2024/05/21/understanding-indias-evolving-middle-classes/
Le, M.S., Singh, T., & Nguyen, D-T. (2016). *Trade liberalisation and poverty: Vietnam now and beyond*. Routledge.
Legatum Institute. *The Legatum Prosperity Index™* 2023. https://prosperity.com/rankings
Lubben, S.J. (2009). Financial distress and Emerging Markets. In Gregoriou, G.N. (Ed.). *Emerging markets: Performance, analysis, and innovation* (pp. 635–647). Chapman & Hall.
Macrotrends. (n.d.-a) https://www.macrotrends.net/global-metrics/countries/RUS/russia/gdp-growth-rate
Macrotrends. (n.d.-b) https://www.macrotrends.net/global-metrics/countries/UKR/ukraine/gdp-growth-rate
Macrotrends. (n.d.-c). Vietnam GDP growth rate (1985-2025). https://www.macrotrends.net/global-metrics/countries/VNM/vietnam/gdp-growth-rate
Make in India. (2014). About us. https://www.makeinindia.com/about
Ministry of Electronics & IT. (2022, December 23). Achievements Made under Digital India Programme. https://www.pib.gov.in/PressReleaseIframePage.aspx?PRID=1885962
Mobius, M. (2012). *The little book of Emerging Markets: How to make money in the world's fastest growing markets*. John Wiley & Sons.
NetEnt. (2019, September 5). NetEnt acquires casino software provider Red Tiger. https://www.netent.com/en/netent-acquires-casino-software-provider-red-tiger/#
O'Neill, J. (2001, November 30). *Build better global economic BRICs* (Global Economics Paper No. 66). https://www.goldmansachs.com/pdfs/insights/archive/archive-pdfs/build-better-brics.pdf
Obama, B. H. (2015, November 30). *Remarks at the First Session of COP21*. White House Archives. https://obamawhitehouse.archives.gov
Oneill, J. (2013, May 2). *The growth map: Economic opportunity in the BRICs and beyond*. Penguin Books.
Pacek, N., & Thorniley, D. (2007). *Emerging markets. Lessons for business success and the outlook for different markets*. The Economist and Profile Books Ltd.
Panibratov, A. (2017, pp.36–37). *International strategy of emerging market firms*. Routledge.
Qiu, X. (2019). *China 40 years infrastructure construction*. Springer Publishing.
Rossi, R. A. (2018, January 16). Interview by A. Lluch. *Creating Emerging Markets Oral History Collection*. Baker Library Special Collections, Harvard Business School.
Scullion, C. (2024, March 21). Sony has set up a production line in Brazil to make physical PS5 discs for Latin America. *Video Game News*. https://www.videogameschronicle.com/news/sony-has-set-up-a-production-line-in-brazil-to-make-physical-ps5-discs-for-latin-america/
The Economist. (2017, October 5). Defining Emerging Markets: A self-fulfilling prophecy. https://www.economist.com/special-report/2017/10/05/defining-emerging-markets

The Economist. (2024, August 10). Muhammad Yunus, a microcredit pioneer, is Bangladesh's interim leader. https://www.economist.com/asia/2024/08/10/muhammad-yunus-a-microcredit-pioneer-is-bangladeshs-interim-leader

The White House. (2025, February 1). *Fact sheet: President Donald J. Trump imposes tariffs on imports from Canada, Mexico and China*. The White House. https://www.whitehouse.gov/fact-sheets/2025/02/fact-sheet-president-donald-j-trump-imposes-tariffs-on-imports-from-canada-mexico-and-china/

Trump, D. [@realDonaldTrump]. (2024, November 30). *The idea that the BRICS Countries are trying to move away from the U.S. Dollar ... [Truth Social post]*. Truth Social. https://www.truthsocial.com/

U.S. Department of Commerce. (n.d.). Indo-Pacific Economic Framework for prosperity. https://www.commerce.gov/ipef

UN trade & development. (2024, December). UN list of least developed countries. https://unctad.org/topic/least-developed-countries/list

Varma, P.K. (2007, July 1). *The great Indian middle class*. Penguin Books.

Villamarin, P. (2024, July 24). Why Emerging Markets are the next frontier for global business expansion. *Merchant Risk Council*. https://merchantriskcouncil.org/learning/resource-center/member-news/blog/2024/why-emerging-markets-are-the-next-frontier-for-global-business-expansion

Vu, K., & Nguyen, P. (2025, January 5). Vietnam's 2024 GDP growth accelerates to 7.09%, driven by strong exports. https://www.reuters.com/markets/asia/vietnam-2024-gdp-growth-quickens-709-2025-01-06/

World Bank. (2006). *Vietnam: Infrastructure challenge in a market economy* (Report No. 37184-VN). World Bank. https://documents1.worldbank.org/curated/en/918311468308974645/pdf/371840VN0Cross17184to3718901PUBLIC1.pdf

World Bank. (2024). Business Ready. https://openknowledge.worldbank.org/server/api/core/bitstreams/131b6383-30a1-44b3-8e66-f425d715503d/content

World Bank. (n.d.-a). GDP growth (annual %). Retrieved March 3, 2025, from https://data.worldbank.org/indicator/NY.GDP.MKTP.KD.ZG

World Bank. (n.d.-b). Infrastructure investment as a percentage of GDP [Data set]. *Prosperity Data* 360. https://prosperitydata360.worldbank.org/en/indicator/GIH%2BGIO%2B2

Worldometers. (n.d.-a). https://www.worldometers.info/gdp/ukraine-gdp/

Worldometers. (n.d.-b). https://www.worldometers.info/demographics/iran-demographics/

Wrobel, S. (2023, September 6). Foreign investment in Israel plunged 60% in first quarter of 2023 – Finance Ministry data. https://www.timesofisrael.com/liveblog_entry/foreign-investment-in-israel-plunged-60-in-first-quarter-of-2023-finance-ministry-data

CHAPTER 2

The VVUCA framework

Learning outcomes

After studying this chapter, you will be able to do the following:

1. Critically evaluate the VUCA (volatility, uncertainty, complexity, and ambiguity) framework as a lens for viewing emerging markets.
2. Compare and assess the influence of VUCA factors on emerging markets.
3. Synthesize insights from real-world case studies to develop frameworks for identifying and mitigating VUCA factors in individual markets.
4. Deconstruct and critically analyze complex risk scenarios which implicate more than one VUCA factor, demonstrating their compounding effects.
5. Recommend strategic and risk management plans to address VUCA risks.
6. Develop innovative strategies to turn VUCA challenges to advantage in an emerging market.

Introduction to VUCA

VUCA is a framework for analyzing risk. In this chapter, we will apply it to emerging markets. The acronym stands for:

(1) Volatility (rapid, unpredictable change in the present)
(2) Uncertainty (lack of predictability about the future)
(3) Complexity (multiple, interconnected forces)
(4) Ambiguity (unclear cause-and-effect relationships, leading to multiple interpretations).

DOI: 10.4324/9781003638490-2

The presence of VUCA factors does not enable classification of countries or markets. VUCA is rather a lens for examination of business challenges. VUCA factors permeate emerging market business environments; mastery of VUCA concepts can turn challenges into competitive advantage.

Volatility

Volatility is the current state of being vulnerable to fast, large, unpredictable changes of situation. Sudden departures from the norm can be environmental, political, or economic. Respective examples are earthquakes, military coups, and currency devaluations or tariffs. Volatility requires a constant state of readiness to respond at short notice and remain adaptable.

Environmental volatility is commonplace because many emerging markets are situated in regions where extreme weather events are becoming more frequent: many parts of India are prone to flooding, drought, monsoons, and heatwaves; the Philippines suffers most of these with the added danger from earthquakes.

Economic growth volatility is characteristic of emerging markets; sudden declines may follow periods of swift growth, to the point of recession. Thailand (shown in Figure 2.1) and Türkiye, for example, have experienced exactly this pattern.

Currency volatility is one of the most visible risks of doing business across borders. It implicates the tightrope-walking act of accepting and making payments in a foreign currency which often, in emerging markets, is unstable.

Very few of the domestic currencies of emerging markets are stable; only one, the Saudi Riyal, is viewed as a secure monetary asset. Several emerging markets have domestic currencies which have experienced continuous decline against stable currencies such as USD, Euro, and Swiss Francs for years or decades.

The performance of the South African rand against the U.S. dollar over the last decade, shown in Figure 2.2, is illustrative; it continues a downward trend since the millennium. Some currencies, like the Turkish lira, have also suffered sudden and dramatic falls.

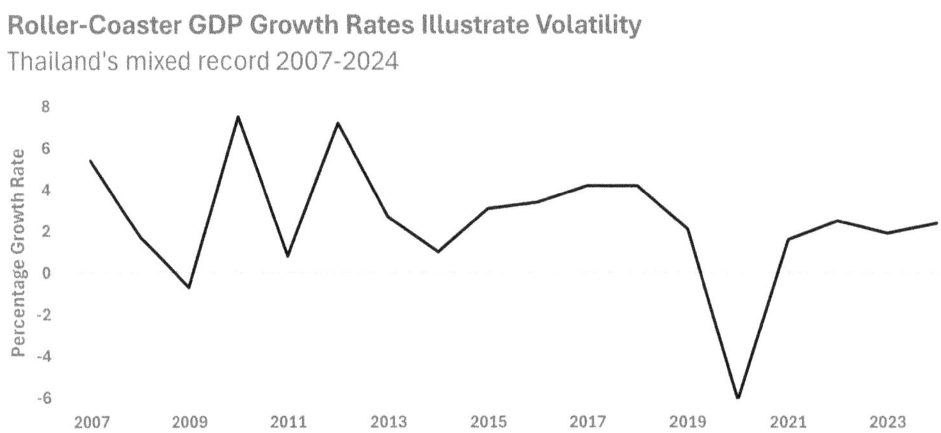

Figure 2.1 Thailand's real GDP growth rate

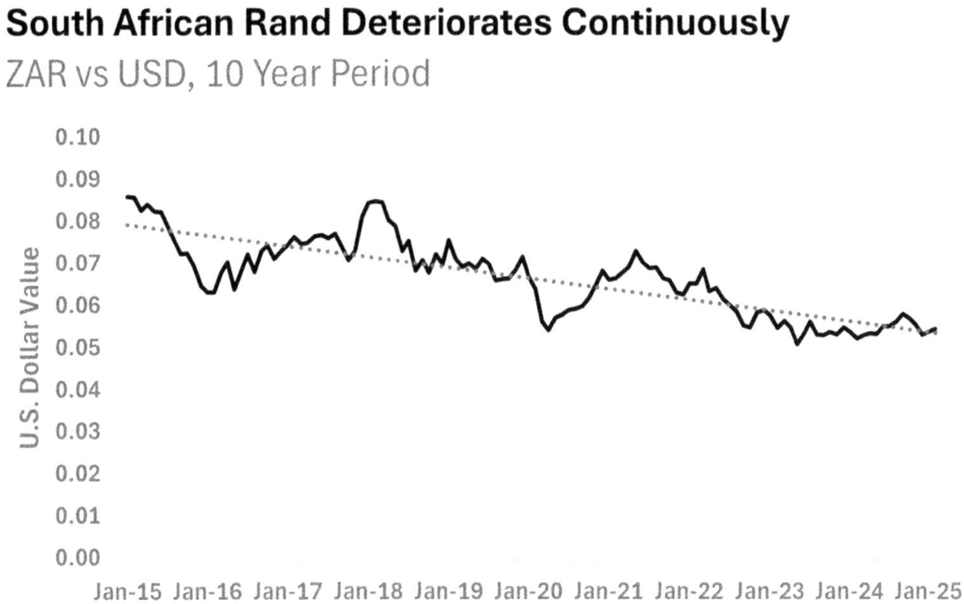

Figure 2.2 South African rand versus U.S. dollar

(Board of Governors of the Federal Reserve System, 2025, H. 10 Foreign Exchange Rates)

An external investor into a country with an unstable currency must manage the currency risk carefully, using hedging and other sophisticated mechanisms. It is rarely an option to complete all contracts or make sales in a stable currency; consumers in Morocco, for example, will not want to purchase household products using U.S. dollars or Euro. Where local contracts with suppliers or even government departments use foreign currency pricing, at a time of devaluation, there is a serious risk of default because the local currency cost of buying foreign currency for repayment becomes unmanageable.

Exotic currencies (the label often used for the currencies of developing nations) may be traded at dual exchange rates: one controlled by the government and used for official transactions, while another is used for businesses. Often, a third *parallel market* then operates at the real value of the currency.

Parallel markets typically arise where there is high inflation. Of the 20 countries identified by the World Bank as having significant inflation, only four do not also have parallel exchange markets (World Bank, 2022). They gain strength when governments attempt ineptly to curb inflation. If prices are controlled, goods become scarce and are sold illegally at higher prices. If exchange rates are fixed or currency restrictions are imposed, people circumvent them, paying a premium on the street. As local currency loses trust, foreign currencies become attractive, carry a premium, and may be used in all-cash transactions to avoid inflation. A vicious circle can ensue.

Currency instability can threaten the profitability and even existence of an otherwise powerful business. In August 2024, African telecom giant MTN reported its first annual loss since 2016. It lost its entire profits for the previous year in the devaluation of the Nigerian currency, the naira (Biznews Editor, 2024).

Government and political volatility demand continuous vigilance. Governments can become unstable very quickly. Policy changes, regulatory interventions, and capital flight can severely disrupt business plans.

Recent examples include the "Arab Spring" in 2010–2011, when popular uprisings attempted to reform authoritarian regimes in Bahrain, Egypt, Morocco, and Tunisia, among others. While the eventual result in some areas was a more favorable investment and growth environment, the immediate political instability and threat of violence were a significant disincentive to entry and led to significant economic downturns (Bowen, 2021).

Businesses operating in emerging markets must engage in scenario planning and develop strong local partnerships to mitigate these risks.

Infrastructure volatility plays havoc with supply chains and distribution networks. In emerging markets, geographical and political threats to infrastructure are more pronounced than in developed economies, as recent events in Nigeria demonstrate.

In March 2024, internet service suddenly stopped, throwing the economy into severe disarray. Banks were unable to function; telecommunications, already a problem sector, degraded even more. It became apparent that the stoppage was caused by the cutting of a submarine cable in the offshore region near Côte D'Ivoire (Mom, 2024). To date it has not been determined whether the cut was caused accidentally by an anchor or other equipment, deliberately, or by a seismic event.

Uncertainty

Uncertainty has a strong relationship with volatility. It is the state of not knowing what to expect in the future. Businesspeople seek to predict the future, understand what might happen, and plan for it. In emerging markets, however, predictions of future exchange rates, inflation, GDP growth, or government policy are highly uncertain.

Uncertainty can have compounding effects; uncertainty in one area can interact with uncertainties in another, amplifying the effects of both. Egypt, with its rapid population growth and strong regional influence, is a great case study in compound uncertainties.

In the last decade, the Egyptian government has evinced a deep desire to attract foreign businesses, creating free trade zones and enacting business-friendly legislation. However, the very businesses the government most wanted to attract were the same ones least able to function effectively in the uncertain climate (Sayigh, 2023). In 2016, the government suddenly floated the national currency, the Egyptian pound. It was immediately devalued by 50% on world markets. The intention was to stabilize the currency; in fact, it destabilized a large part of the economy. In 2022–2023, there were further sharp falls in value. Meanwhile, inflation was fluctuating wildly, exceeding 30% in 2023 (Trading Economics, 2025). Setting wages, pricing supplies and markets, importing, and exporting all became exceedingly complex operations. The government was at the same time lifting and reimposing capital controls without notice (U.S. Department of State, 2023). Foreign investors were sometimes denied access to their money and profits, making it impossible to synchronize multinational company operations. Inward investors simply did not know what would happen next.

Complexity

Complexity occurs where there are several interconnected components in a business environment, especially if they act in unpredictable ways. It is often intensified in emerging markets.

Governmental complexity comes in a variety of forms. Governments, their departments, and institutions can be weak, ineffective, or corrupt. Figuring out how the system works or how to work despite the system can call for significant investments of time, money, or both.

An example is the corporate taxation system in Brazil. Analyst Lara Rizerio, writing for InfoMoney, states that the average time spent by businesses in the world to calculate taxes is 268 hours. In contrast, for a foreign business operating in Brazil, the number is 2,600 hours (Rizério, 2015)!

Countries with federal and state tax systems frequently have conflicts or inconsistencies between the two. Although developed countries, like Canada, are not immune, examples are more common and less easily understood in emerging markets. An example is India's GST (goods and services tax) law, where the national government strives to implement a unified structure for the whole country. Meanwhile, states such as Kerala are not in agreement with the national plan, imposing additional sales taxes on goods or services previously taxed by the federal government at an allegedly uniform rate (which is not uniform at all) (Drishti IAS, 2024).

Financial complexity lies in the complicated interconnected web of financial systems, operations, and instruments. The interrelationships of markets, regulators, and investors make systems difficult to analyze or control.

Exchange and currency controls contribute to financial complexity. Underdeveloped and informal institutional structures don't help, and abrupt changes in financial policies and tax rates compound the issue. Financial complexity is a major contributor to the popularity of informal economies, such as undocumented lending and unreported cash-based hiring and sales. It can be exceedingly difficult for a business which wishes to operate transparently to compete, because workers in the informal sector prefer to be paid in untaxed cash than receive reported, taxable income.

Nigeria's underdeveloped credit system underlies the fact that 70.7% of all business credit comes from family and friends. The primary motivation for starting an informal business is unemployment. Despite that social safety net, Agwaibor (2024) calculates that 90% of the informal businesses which he surveyed, although they had significant turnover, showed profits under half a million naira – around US$300 – per month.

Labor complexity invokes the issue of informal economies – the areas of commerce which are hidden from governments. Informal economic activity – working for cash, evading income taxes, failing to remit sales taxes – occurs everywhere. As a primary driver is poverty and perceived unfairness of government, emerging markets suffer especially from this persistent and difficult feature.

How big is the problem? Take Nigeria as an example. Even a casual visitor will quickly observe the vast numbers of people operating street businesses. In the countryside, 80% of agricultural production relies on workers who have no business registration with government. Analyst Stephen Agwaibor, writing for TechCabal, estimates that the informal economy is significantly larger than the formal economy, at 58% of GDP (Agwaibor, 2024).

Lest you think that 58% is an extreme number, recent estimates for Sub-Saharan Africa suggest that in that region, 85% of all commerce occurs in informal systems. It can be challenging indeed for a foreign investor, accustomed to working and effective sales and payment channels, to gain an understanding of how to operate in such an environment.

Market complexity refers to the intricate challenges involved in understanding how institutions, cultures, and regulations interact in an unpredictable manner. The consumer side of market complexity is the most pronounced, often compounded by a lack of reliable market research and data. Consumer segmentation can be difficult or fractionated.

Brazil and India exhibit complex, highly fragmented consumer landscapes, with similar features. In Brazil, there are vast differences between income levels of urban and rural populations; even within those segments, there are great disparities between individual cities. Consider that in the north of Brazil, communities like Salvador, Bahia, have strong African culture, while in the south, Holambra has predominantly Dutch culture, and Blumenau has primarily German architecture, festivals, food, and language. Market complexity reflects social complexity.

Similar divides exist in India. The wealthy upper classes in the cities have money on a scale unimaginable to the rural poor; consumer preferences vary across the diverse geographies, languages, and cultures; and a large and growing population has vast differences in educational levels.

In both Brazil and India, income inequality, urban-rural contrasts, and deep cultural differences complicate market entry, customer segmentation, and targeting. The complexity of consumer behavior is multidimensional, making the design of products, marketing strategies, or distribution networks abnormally difficult. One-size-fits-all approaches to business are unlikely to succeed.

Logistical complexity describes the challenge of managing supply chains and distribution channels involving multiple parties and components, from manufacturers to transporters and distributors. This form of complexity severely impacts the costs of moving supplies, goods, and services between stakeholders.

Nigeria presents a perfect storm of challenges in this respect; the country has poor roads outside major cities (Punch Editorial Board, 2023), insufficient railway connectivity (Ayoola, 2023), and frequent congestion in its ports (GoComet, 2024). Compounding distribution delays are inefficiencies in customs clearance, while nationwide the electricity supply is unreliable and causes even small businesses to need their own generators to guarantee operating through business hours (Pelz et al., 2023).

Social complexity captures diversities of culture and language and reminds us of the need to know, understand, and respect unfamiliar customs and beliefs. Businesspeople must also understand that expectations regarding meetings, behavior, and social interaction outside the business context will vary widely.

Indonesia is a prime example of a linguistic mosaic. Although Bahasa Indonesia became the official language in 1945 after independence from the Netherlands, the country has over 700 languages and dialects – hardly surprising in a nation comprised of over 17,000 islands. Island populations originate from separate places, have different religions (Bali, for example, is Hindu while Java is 96% Muslim), and have evolved differently and sometimes independently over thousands of years.

Complex gift-giving practices and expectations characterize Chinese business interactions. The giver must take great care in choosing a gift that aligns with the relationship, the reason, and the context and must carefully choose the wrapping paper, especially its color. When giving the gift, the choice of words and body language, even the way of holding it, are important, and reciprocity is the norm. There are also taboos around certain gifts, such as clocks. You might ask if this is real. Yes, it is. Embarrassment awaits the over-anxious young executive who fails to heed these social norms when attempting to complete a deal in China or even with Chinese counterparts abroad.

There are two keys to successfully addressing social complexity. The first is research, reading, and questioning. In preparation for a visit to, or any negotiations in, a target market, it is essential to research the local cultures fully. The second is to engage help with local knowledge and ask an assistant to attend meetings and steer around potential difficulties.

Complexity also highlights the folly of seeing a country as a single unit, assuming the same market forces play throughout. In markets like Brazil, China, or India, focusing on a smaller geographical or other segment for early launch is often an excellent choice.

Unilever Hindustan

Unilever's success in Hindustan is a compelling example of leveraging logistical, social, and market complexity into competitive advantage. Recognizing that there are profound differences in preference between India's regions, it developed and produced personal care product lines which vary in packaging and size for different settings. The company built a huge distribution network for small stores (*kiranas*) and promoted its *Shakti* program to employ rural women as micro-entrepreneurs. All this was achieved in the face of vast numbers of different regulations in each local area; a significant element was localized production and distribution. The company's ability to develop resonance and relevance with multiple small markets translates into a competitive advantage which makes its products the market leaders across India.

Ambiguity

Ambiguity refers to an inability to understand the present, current situation. The causes of ambiguity can be external (generated by the situation) or internal (generated by deficiencies of research, understanding, or even patience). Legal, policy, and cultural ambiguities are the prevalent forms.

Legal ambiguity is commonplace especially in fast-moving areas of governance and regulation.

An example is India's data protection law, where hastily drafted legislation is deficient in defining key terms, relying on interpretation, assisted policies, and promised future guidelines to amplify meanings. It is not clear how a business with significant data privacy or transfer needs can be sure to operate effectively under such a regime (Ajaykumar, 2022).

A business entering a market with unclear data protection legislation must plan its hardware, software, internal compliance, and training investments in a way that can accommodate varied outcomes from light regulation to a heavy hand. Responses could range from improving compliance to rapid expansion with positive developments or delaying or stopping investment with negative indications.

Policy ambiguity results when a government's actions conflict with its own legislation or declared intentions.

South Africa is an early mover in the renewable energy sector. To encourage investment in projects, in 2009, the government opened a competitive bidding process. Once the money was in and the projects were under way, the government failed to honor its commitment to fixed feed-in tariffs (money paid to producers for supplying energy to the grid) and often delayed payments. This introduced a state of ambiguity to the entire program, as investors and producers were unable to determine the government's true intentions (Mukherjee, 2023).

External ambiguities are difficult to manage, as they result from factors beyond the control of market participants. By contrast, *cultural ambiguity*, failure to understand local practices, beliefs, and expectations, lies squarely within the reach of the inward investor to manage. The answers again are quality research and building strong relationships with local advisors and experts.

Starbucks' 2012 entry to the Indian market was fraught with cultural ambiguities. Starbucks knew the facts – drinking tea, not coffee, is the staple of most Indian regions. In a market where tea is inexpensive, there was ambiguity regarding perceptions of coffee, Starbucks' standard food items, and the positioning of coffee shops as a place to socialize.

The company addressed these challenges by producing locally relevant drinks and snacks, adjusting pricing to local conditions, and partnering with a trusted Indian partner, Tata Group (Fischer & Roy, 2019). Starbucks is now the largest organized café operator in India (Economic Times, 2024).

VUCA factors rarely operate in isolation. For example, political volatility fuels uncertainty about future legislation, while complexity of regulation impairs risk assessment. In such a situation, ambiguity may force a business to make decisions without complete information. In the next section, we'll demonstrate some real-world situations which implicate multiple VUCA factors, further complicating the challenges of operating effectively in emerging markets.

Combined VUCA factors

As examples we will discuss expropriation/nationalization, sanctions, and various types of legal issues, especially crime.

Expropriation refers to governmental seizure of private property, such as land or buildings; nationalization involves the government taking over an entire industry or sector, such as railways, oil production, or banking. Both may occur with or without payment of compensation.

Expropriation and nationalization encompass all four VUCA elements. They can be volatile events, happening abruptly and without warning. They can be a manifestation of uncertain policies and engage multiple layers of complexity. Multiple drivers may also introduce complexity, while investors encounter ambiguity in struggling to understand the implications of a specific case, wondering whether it is the outcome of a single dispute or a worrying trend.

In February 2024, the government of Nigeria seized coastal property worth about US$25 million from the Landmark Group. As of this writing, the government has paid no compensation (Jackson-Obot, 2024). Also in Nigeria, the Ogun state government's seizure of a complete Free Trade Zone has led to the opinion that the country "risks becoming a stark example of how not to attract FDI" (Skjelford, 2024).

Nationalization is often a result of a sudden deep change in political policy. Venezuela, once considered an emerging market, is no longer on our list thanks to fundamental economic interference by Hugo Chavez and Nicolas Maduro. In succession, these two leaders nationalized key industries such as oil, telecoms, utilities, and cement (Manasseh, 2011); foreign companies lost billions of dollars without compensation, and the population suffered a reversal of fortune so severe that it became a humanitarian crisis (Johnson, 2018). Despite all this, Venezuela still needs FDI to bolster its oil and gas production and is seeking some of it in emerging markets – for example, from Atlas Oranto of Nigeria (McIlhagga, 2024).

Expropriation and nationalization do not always involve governments taking 100% of assets away from private owners. A significant impact was felt on Malaysian businesses in 1971 when the government introduced its New Economic Policy, in direct response to the race riots of 1969. The policy resulted in redistribution of corporate wealth to the majority Bumiputra (Indigenous) population from other ethnic groups, and disproportionately affected members of the Chinese community. Owners of Indian origin also suffered. The goal was to have 30% of all major industries in Malay/Bumiputra hands.

The original intention was to run the policy for 20 years, but enforcement of versions of it has continued throughout the country. There are still significant Bumiputra quota requirements in education, government contracting and employment, and businesses (Chandran, 2018).

Sanctions also implicate all four VUCA elements.

Political disagreements do not only underly problems on foreign soil. When the home government has serious disagreements with a foreign country, economic sanctions are powerful weapons of persuasion or coercion. In recent years, it has become somewhere between difficult and impossible (inclusive) for American organizations to do business in countries at loggerheads with the U.S. government; while Cuba and North Korea are the obvious examples, Iran, Syria, Russia, and even some parts of Ukraine are today no-go areas for American business. Canada, the United Kingdom, and the European Union also impose economic sanctions on foreign governments, businesses and persons, and criminal penalties on citizens who flaunt the sanctions.

Civil and criminal legal situations invoke VUCA elements in tortuous combinations. We will describe some examples which demonstrate the difficulties.

Contractual Issues. It is a serious mistake to believe that honoring of contracts, or keeping of promises, occurs according to European or Canadian standards in all parts of the world. Equally, enforcement of contracts is not uniform but a patchwork of unequal legal procedures.

We previously mentioned Zimbabwe under the mismanagement of Prime Minister, then President, Robert Mugabe. One of the notable features of his autocratic rule was the government's willingness to tear up contracts and renege on its obligations, especially to foreign organizations (Slinn, 1983).

In India, a litigant might wait ten or even 15 years for a court date, only to find that the appointed judiciary accepts bribes, responds to coercion, or is simply predisposed to favor the local litigant. An inefficient court system or corrupt judiciary seriously impairs the confidence of the business community.

Violence and Crime. A damaging level of local criminal activity exists in many emerging markets, and perpetrators may see inward investors as natural targets. Criminals may even rationalize theft on the basis that the victims can afford the losses, as they are so much richer than local people. Author Paul writes:

> About a decade ago I visited a friend who transferred to Lagos, Nigeria, to supervise the building of a hotel for an international chain. He told me frankly that of every seven truckloads of building materials that arrived at the site, five went into the building and two just disappeared. He shrugged and said that the company accepted this level of loss as "normal" in that economy, at that time.

South Africa, a country with fabulous natural resources and a well-educated population, perennially suffers from its high violent crime rate. The resultant risk for businesses and their people, locals, and visitors is a significant disincentive to investment (Associated Press, 2024).

Paul has also experienced firsthand the disincentives to working or investing in an area where law and order have broken down.

> In the 1980s one of my clients had a group of financial relationships in Brazil. As they broke down due to poor communications, I went to Rio to work things out with the national bank. During one ten-day stay in Rio, I was robbed, on the street, three times. One of those robberies took place within five meters of a uniformed police officer, who saw the whole thing but took no action.
>
> Ironically, having sorted out the institutional problems and retrieved the company's funds, they were then all stolen by the local agent, against whom we had little recourse.

Organized crime, at local, national, and transnational levels, poses a substantial threat to companies seeking to do business in emerging markets. While it is omnipresent, few countries have suffered so deeply as Mexico from the omnipresent threat of drug cartels. Despite being so close to the United States, or perhaps because of proximity, criminal enterprises control vast areas within major cities and large swathes of territory outside them. Their ruthless domination of major illicit enterprises, including drug production and trafficking, kidnapping, and extortion, is legendary and the stuff of movies and documentaries. Despite all this, Mexico remains a significant market and has a strong tourism industry; however, infiltration of criminals into government and law enforcement remains a serious obstacle to inward investment and market confidence (Holmes, 2014).

Terrorism, whether historical or an ongoing threat, is a significant damper on economic opportunity.

This shadow looms over several emerging economies like that of Pakistan (Murphy, 2013); within the country, militant groups such as Tehrik-i-Taliban and Lashkar-e-Taiba have committed atrocious, highly visible attacks which shatter investor confidence. Just one example was the Peshawar school massacre in 2014, involving the murder of over 150 (mostly young) people (Rashid, 2015). Not only are individuals and businesses vulnerable, but also key infrastructural components such as power plants and transportation are at risk (Yusuf, 2012).

Corruption is a fundamental problem throughout emerging markets, yet not in developed growth markets. It is one of the most significant governance risks, and we will discuss its impact, regulatory position, and strategies for response in Chapter 3.

Analysis of VUCA risks creates opportunities for businesses that can strategize for quick adaptations. While VUCA elements may appear at first sight to be obstacles, successful businesses view them as signposts to innovation and competitive market positioning. In the next section, we'll outline the key steps to be taken.

Addressing VUCA risks

In adversity lies opportunity; rewards await companies that can "'Embrace Chaos': learn and profit from adverse institutional environments." These words are from one of the most beautifully written and entertaining volumes about emerging markets – while it was produced over a decade ago, its mastery of storytelling and capture of history makes it timeless (Guillén & García-Canal, 2013).

Companies entering emerging markets have several tools available, at the planning and operational stages, to reduce the risks engendered by VUCA factors.

To organize information, risk assessment, scenario modeling, and current market intelligence gathering are the three typical steps.

PESTEL analysis of risks, demonstrated in Appendix 1 (Political, Economic, Social, Technological, Environmental, and Legal), helps categorize challenges. This can be followed by the analysis of what-if scenarios sculpted to match local conditions.

Specialists within the business, or consultants, may be asked to model theoretical outcomes of risks such as currency devaluations, infrastructural breakdowns, or regulatory changes, alongside recommendations to mitigate potential disruptions or losses. Financial arrangements include purchasing insurance, hedging foreign currency, and building up contingency funds (usually in a stable currency)

A team consisting of experts from the local community and the incoming business may also model and assess unexpected events, then develop contingency plans and train staff to deal with them. This team should include exit plans in its modeled responses.

Scenario planning exercises can be highly productive; these involve identifying the drivers of ambiguity, working out plausible scenarios from worst-case to best-case, evaluating their impacts, developing strategies that address each of them, and then putting them into practice by continually monitoring developments as more information becomes available.

A common risk area in a new business is over-dependence on single suppliers. Diversification in the supply chain must be a priority from the very beginning, so that a single point of failure does not doom entire operations. Suppliers in this context include banks and other sources of financing. Banks can fail completely in emerging markets;

dependence on a line of credit from a bank which disappears overnight can severely impact operations and planned investments.

Sberbank.CZ

In April 2022, Sberbank CZ, the Czech subsidiary of Russia's Sberbank, found itself the object of a "run," and its banking license was abruptly withdrawn by the Czech National Bank. It took depositors years to recover approximately 95% of their funds, forcing businesses to move their lending arrangements instantly to other providers. Sberbank was a significant provider of credit to small- and medium-sized businesses in the country; its liquidation had a powerful negative effect on the economy.

Gathering quality market data will help with decisions about how to enter a market. For example, in a situation of high uncertainty, an investing business may choose to partner with a local entity to improve its knowledge pipeline. High currency volatility may indicate that exporting to a market is preferable to investing in plant and equipment inside it.

The ability to navigate through VUCA factors is a hallmark of businesses that grow within emerging markets. Nando's, today a South African multinational fast-food business, enjoyed its early growth during the period when its home country was transitioning to democracy. The political scene was highly uncertain; labor laws, taxes, and the market all changed unpredictably and regularly undermined operations and strategy. Robert Brozin, the co-founder, drove the business ahead despite these challenges with a concentration on brand-building, humor and creativity, and corporate culture (Brozin, 2019).

Successful operations in emerging markets require resilience against VUCA risks. The "Five A's" framework (Alignment, Agility, Alliance, Adjustment, and Alertness) provides a structured approach to simultaneously managing uncertainty, crises, and market opportunities.

Alignment. Product and service alignment, as opposed to reliance on a specific product or service, reduces overall business risk. Similarly, a policy which aligns investment into more than one market but uses the same infrastructure reduces risk in a single market.

Agility. Installing or hiring an empowered local team, with the knowledge, experience, and ability to make rapid decisions permits the timely grasping of opportunities and mitigation of risks. A faithful partner of agility is *lean operation*; if the local operation reduces waste and prioritizes efficiency, it can respond faster to changed conditions.

Alliance. In volatile markets, collaboration is a valuable two-way street. Partnership with local vendors, distributors, and advisors provides a better flow of relevant information; for smaller businesses, alliances with larger multinationals can leverage multiple resources. Local partners and experts can be invaluable assets in keeping current with knowledge about developments.

Adjustment. When the market is constantly changing, so must the business. Constant alertness and consideration of challenges and opportunities will drive constant adaptation. VUCA factors heavily underline the importance of flexible strategies and the ability to make fast, effective decisions. Success will come to businesses which can adapt quickly, remain flexible, and leverage local relevance and connections to remain resilient in the face of sudden change.

Alertness. Successful businesses with a first foothold secure market advantage by modeling future scenarios, continuing research into consumer behavior and choices, and experimenting with new products.

Case study – Kashagan

Kashagan is the fifth largest oil field in the world, and the largest outside the Middle East (KazMunayGas, 2024). Its development is an object lesson in how badly an emerging market initiative can go wrong.

Drawn by the lure of potentially massive profits, Shell, ExxonMobil, Total, and Eni all joined state-owned KazMunayGas in the venture. At the turn of the millennium, it was heralded as a game-changer for Kazakhstan's energy sector.

By 2013, cost overruns and delays were the primary features of the project. The original forecast investment was $10 billion; the joint venturers had spent more than five times that. Production was originally scheduled for 2005, but technological problems resulting from high sulfur levels delayed it to 2013 (Eni, 2013). One month after it started, the project stopped again while millions more were spent on repairs to a critical pipeline.

The government did not help. Despite the mounting costs of the project and delays caused in part by regulatory complexity, there were constant renegotiations of terms and conditions. The government wanted to increase its share of the revenues (Reuters, 2024). Environmental interest groups also intervened, criticizing the project for its handling of the sulfur issue and risk management for impacted residents (Eurasian Research Institute, 2021).

The project was surrounded by rumors of bribery and corruption. The Milan prosecutor's office was reported to be investigating "at least $20 million in bribes paid to 'a certain Kazakhstan politician'" (Radio Free Europe/Radio Liberty, 2013).

Production resumed in 2016, but Shell executed a broader strategy to reduce its risks in difficult projects and removed itself from the partnership. On exit, Shell recognized a monetary loss of approximately $2 billion (Shell International, 2022).

The Kashagan failure dramatically illustrates how, despite massive resources, realized risks can doom a promising expansion project. It is still in trouble (Parkhomchik, 2020).

Strategy summary

There are strategies and methodologies to reduce risks and enhance the possibilities of success under VUCA conditions.

(a) Invest affirmatively and sensibly in market research and local expertise. Invaluable insights will come from partnerships, local experts, government officials, and industry associations. Building effective partnerships may benefit from identification of local champions – people within the community who can help foreign businesses to integrate. Long before operating resources are committed, gain a thorough understanding of culture, regulation, and consumer behavior.
(b) Use financial instruments, including insurance and hedging, to protect against inflation, fluctuation, expropriation, and instability.
(c) Consider diversification of markets to spread risk.
(d) Establish local supply chains to insulate from currency fluctuations and international supply chain disruptions.
(e) Set firm compliance guidelines, including an anti-bribery policy, zero tolerance for corruption, and anti-money-laundering controls. Where financial crime risk is high, establish internal whistleblowing mechanisms and appropriate staff training. Conduct due diligence on all political relationships and explore which international organizations or legal frameworks (like investment treaties) might provide protection.
(f) Build strong relationships with governments, from local authorities to national.

Conclusion

This chapter explored the VUCA concept as a lens for viewing the risks, challenges, and opportunities that exist within emerging markets. We described and illustrated each VUCA factor and considered strategies for addressing each.

In the next chapter, we will embrace the integration of sustainability principles as a core policy when expanding into an emerging market. Alignment with sustainability goals reduces risk, builds resilience, and supports continuity. We will introduce frameworks for systematic incorporation of sustainability into decision-making. As interconnected national and international crises make headlines every day, this is not a nice-to-have but a necessity. We will explore how to turn a genuine desire for sustainability into a competitive advantage which satisfies expansionary ambitions, addresses risks to the maximum possible extent, and supports global ambitions.

References

Agwaibor, S. (2024, July 10). Nigeria's informal economy in five charts. *TechCabal Insights*. https://insights.techcabal.com/nigerias-informal-economy-in-five-charts/

Ajaykumar, S. (2022, December 17). The ambiguities in India's attempt at data protection. *Observer Research Foundation*. https://www.orfonline.org/expert-speak/the-ambiguities-in-indias-attempt-at-data-protection.

Associated Press. (2024, January 7). As police lose the war on crime in South Africa, private security companies step in. *NPR*. https://www.npr.org/2024/01/07/1223358578/as-police-lose-the-war-on-crime-in-south-africa-private-security-companies-step-

Ayoola, T.A. (2023, October 15). Nigeria wants to revamp its railway network. Four things it needs to do to succeed. *The Conversation*. https://theconversation.com/nigeria-wants-to-revamp-its-railway-network-four-things-it-needs-to-do-to-succeed-213385

Biznews Editor. (2024, August 19). MTN posts first loss since 2016 due to Naira devaluation. *BizNews*. https://www.biznews.com/sa-investing/2024/08/19/mtn-loss-naira-devaluation

Board of Governors of the Federal Reserve System. (2025), H.10 Foreign Exchange Rates. https://www.federalreserve.gov/releases/h10/hist/

Bowen, J. (2021, February 11). Arab Spring: How the uprisings still echo, 10 years on. *BBC News*. https://www.bbc.com/news/world-middle-east-56000950

Brozin, R. (2019, September 23). Interview by N. Hsieh. *Creating Emerging Markets Oral History Collection*. Baker Library Special Collections, Harvard Business School.

Chandran, M.R. (2018, June 25). Interview by V. Giacomin. *Creating Emerging Markets Oral History Collection*. Baker Library Special Collections, Harvard Business School.

Drishti IAS. (2024, January 12). Navigating GST challenges. https://www.drishtiias.com/daily-updates/daily-news-analysis/navigating-gst-challenges

Economic Times. (2024, October 18). Starbucks brews up success; now India's largest café chain. https://economictimes.indiatimes.com/industry/cons-products/fmcg/starbucks-brews-up-success-now-indias-largest-caf-chain/articleshow/114351613.cms

Eni. (2013, September 11) Eni: first oil from the Kashagan field has been produced. https://www.eni.com/en-IT/media/press-release/2013/09/eni-first-oil-from-the-kashagan-field-has-been-produced.html

Eurasian Research Institute. (2021). *Environmental issues and regulations at the Kashagan oilfield*. Eurasian Research Institute. https://www.eurasian-research.org/publication/environmental-issues-and-regulations-at-the-kashagan-oilfield/

Fischer, D., & Roy, K. (2019). Market entry in India: The curious case of Starbucks. *Rutgers Business Review* 4:2, 124–139. https://rbr.business.rutgers.edu/article/market-entry-india-curious-case-starbucks

GoComet. (2024, August 13). Nigeria port congestion. https://www.gocomet.com/real-time-port-congestion/nigeria

Guillén, M., & García-Canal, E. (2013). *Emerging markets rule: Growth strategies of the new global giants*. McGraw-Hill.

Holmes, C. H. (2014). *Organized crime in Mexico: Assessing the threat to North American economies*. Potomac Books.

Jackson-Obot, I. (2024, August 19). Demolition eats into Nigeria's FDI confidence. *FDI Insights*. https://www.fdiintelligence.com/content/feature/demolition-eats-into-nigerias-fdi-confidence-83952

Johnson, K. (2018, July 16). How Venezuela struck it poor. *Foreign Policy*. https://foreignpolicy.com/2018/07/16/how-venezuela-struck-it-poor-oil-energy-chavez

KazMunayGas. (2024). Kashagan growth projects. https://www.kmg.kz/en/company/projects/all/proekty-uvelicheniya-dobychi-na-m-r-kashagan/

Manasseh, S. (2011). Breaking the Cemnet: Venezuela's move to nationalize Cemex leads to dispute over arbitral jurisdiction, 3 *Arb. L. Rev*. 416.

McIlhagga, S. (2024, October 31). Venezuela still trying to lure FDI into offshore gas. *fDi Intelligence*. https://www.fdiintelligence.com/content/feature/venezuela-still-trying-to-lure-fdi-into-offshore-gas-84152

Mom, C. (2024, March 18). Explainer: Who cut the undersea cables and disrupted internet? *The Cable*. https://www.thecable.ng/explainer-who-cut-the-underwater-cables-and-disrupted-internet/

Mukherjee, P. (2023, July 18). South Africa's green power push falters as projects fail. *Reuters*. https://www.reuters.com/business/energy/south-africas-green-power-push-falters-projects-fail-2023-07-18/

Murphy, E. (2013). *The making of terrorism in Pakistan: Historical and social roots of extremism*. Routledge.

Parkhomchik, L. (2020). *Current challenges for the Kashagan offshore oil field project*. Eurasian Research Institute. https://www.eurasian-research.org/publication/current-challenges-for-the-kashagan-offshore-oil-field-project/

Pelz, S. et al. (2023, May 12). Electricity supply quality and use among rural and per-urban households and small firms in Nigeria. *Sci Data* 10, 273.

Punch Editorial Board. (2023, November 21). Nigeria's road infrastructure remains decrepit. https://punchng.com/nigerias-road-infrastructure-remains-decrepit

Radio Free Europe/Radio Liberty. (2013, October 11). *Kazakhstan's Kashagan oil field faces setbacks*. Radio Free Europe/Radio Liberty. https://www.rferl.org/a/kazakhstan-kashagan-oil-field-setbacks/25390847.html

Rashid, A. (2015, 13 December). Viewpoint: How Peshawar massacre changed Pakistan. *BBC News*. https://www.bbc.com/news/world-asia-35051628.

Reuters. (2024, April 17). Kazakhstan claims against Kashagan oil firms top $150 bln, Bloomberg reports. https://www.reuters.com/markets/commodities/kazakhstan-claims-against-kashagan-oil-firms-top-150-bln-bloomberg-reports-2024-04-17

Rizério, L. (2015, November 9). 10 problemas que inda travam a aposta de estrangeiros no Brasil, segundo gestor. *Open Logic*. https://www.infomoney.com.br/mercados/10-problemas-que-ainda-travam-a-aposta-de-estrangeiros-no-brasil-segundo-gestor/

Sayigh, Y. (2023, May 8). Assessing Egypt's State Ownership Policy: Challenges and Requirements. *Carnegie Endowment for International Peace*. https://carnegieendowment.org/research/2023/05/assessing-egypts-state-ownership-policy-challenges-and-requirements?lang=en

Shell International. (2022). Reserves. *Shell*. https://reports.shell.com/annual-report/2022/strategic-report/segments/oil-and-gas-information/reserves.html

Skjelford, I. (2024, July 9). Nigeria must seize FDI, not assets. https://www.fdiintelligence.com/content/locations/global/asia-pacific/opinion-nigeria-must-seize-fdi-not-assets-83902

Slinn, P. (1983). Foreign investment contracts – Host country's concerns. *Third World Legal Studies*: Vol. 2, Article 2.

Trading Economics. (2025). Egypt Inflation Rate. https://tradingeconomics.com/egypt/inflation-cpi

U.S. Department of State. (2023). 2023 Investment Climate Statements: Egypt. https://www.state.gov/reports/2023-investment-climate-statements/egypt/

World Bank. (2022, December 7). *Accounting for parallel exchange rates*. World Bank Group.

Yusuf, H. (2012). Conflict Dynamics in Karachi. *United States Institute of Peace, Peaceworks* No. 82.

CHAPTER 3

Sustainability and the pillars of ESG in emerging markets

Learning Outcomes

After studying this chapter, you will be able to do the following:

1. Critically evaluate the role of sustainability in emerging markets and explain its strategic importance in building longevity and market competitiveness.
2. Analyze the environmental, social, and governance (ESG) pillars in relation to sustainability, and explain why they are crucial to long-term success.
3. Discuss the trade-offs between economic growth, environmental protection, and social equity.
4. Critique and compare the major global frameworks for sustainability planning and reporting.
5. Assess the effect of government policy and administrative regulation on adopting sustainability goals while operating in emerging markets.
6. Conduct comparative case studies of how existing organizations have integrated ESG principles into their endeavors, successfully or unsuccessfully.
7. Advocate for consideration of ESG in major business decisions, using financial, ethical, and strategic methodologies.

DOI: 10.4324/9781003638490-3

Sustainability

Sustainability is the key to success and longevity in any significant emerging market expansion. Sustainability is not just a responsibility but a global necessity.

The world economy is twisting and turning as it caters to a rising population. Former U.S. Vice President Al Gore famously summarized the situation in these words: "We are facing a planetary emergency. The choices we make in the next decade could determine the future of life on Earth" (Gore, 2006).

> *Sustainable development is development that meets the needs of the present without compromising the ability of future generations to meet their own needs.*

This quotation is from the Brundtland Report (World Commission on Environment and Development, 1987). It encompasses the "triple bottom line" – people, planet, and profit (Elkington, 1997).

Emerging markets are home to more than 68% of the world's population. While they are challenged by infrastructure gaps and resource limitations, they have the potential to implement and follow sustainable practices on a very large scale. Examples of sustainability needs include addressing urbanization, reducing dependence on resources, and shoring up institutional weakness. The best-run enterprises in emerging markets look for opportunities to run with advanced technology, find community-driven solutions to widespread problems, and convince global financiers that it is worthwhile to invest in them.

The United Nations Global Compact

In 2000, the United Nations (UN), led by Secretary-General Kofi Annan, established a voluntary initiative to encourage businesses to act in a sustainable and socially responsible manner. It has over 25,000 signatories from 167 countries, yet it is voluntary and has no legal force (UN Global Compact, n.d.). It encourages businesses to integrate environmental, social, and governance (ESG) principles into their operations and offers resources and reporting frameworks. Its ten principles summarize the key sustainability activities toward which businesses should strive. They are as follows:

Human Rights

Principle 1: Businesses should support and respect the protection of internationally proclaimed human rights; and
Principle 2: make sure that they are not complicit in human rights abuses.

Labour

Principle 3: Businesses should uphold the freedom of association and the effective recognition of the right to collective bargaining;
Principle 4: the elimination of all forms of forced and compulsory labour;
Principle 5: the effective abolition of child labour; and
Principle 6: the elimination of discrimination in respect of employment and occupation.

Environment

Principle 7: Businesses should support a precautionary approach to environmental challenges;

Principle 8: undertake initiatives to promote greater environmental responsibility; and

Principle 9: encourage the development and diffusion of environmentally friendly technologies.

Anti-Corruption

Principle 10: Businesses should work against corruption in all its forms, including extortion and bribery.

(UN Global Compact, n.d.)

The United Nations Sustainable Development Goals

The *United Nations Sustainable Development Goals (SDGs)* tower over discussions of sustainability, providing a vision or blueprint for everyone, from the most powerful government to the weakest individual, to achieve meaningful outcomes. They are universal, not business focused.

The SDGs were adopted in 2015. They are integrated: "They recognize that action in one area will affect outcomes in others, and that development must balance social, economic and environmental sustainability" (United Nations Development Programme, 2015). They are set out in Table 3.1.

Table 3.1 United Nations SDGs

Group	*Goals*
Basic Human Needs	1. No poverty. 2. Zero hunger. 3. Good health and well-being. 4. Quality education. 5. Gender equality. 6. Clean water and sanitation.
Economic and Environmental Progress	7. Affordable and clean energy. 8. Decent work and economic growth. 9. Industry, innovation, and infrastructure. 10. Reduced inequalities. 11. Sustainable cities and communities. 12. Responsible consumption and production.
Planetary Health	13. Climate action. 14. Life below water. 15. Life on land.
Enabling Concepts	16. Peace, justice, and strong institutions. 17. Partnership for the goals.

Each of the goals is expanded to include policy guidance.

The impressive global ideas of the SDGs do not fulfil business requirements for targeted guidance. This is where the environmental, social, and governance (ESG) framework comes into its own. ESG breaks sustainability impact into measurable chunks, which addressed together help achieve those global goals.

Environmental, social, and governance

Sustainability has a broad reach. *ESG* is a measurement framework used to manage, track, and report sustainability efforts. Sustainability goals and ESG are further distinguished by timeframe: sustainability is about long-term vision, while ESG measurements focus on short- and medium-term aspirations, particularly reduction of harmful practices. The intended audience is different: sustainability is a global ambition, for everyone, while ESG reporting speaks to investors, organizational boards, and regulatory authorities.

The ESG pillars provide businesses with a methodology for planning, measuring, and reporting, under three headings. The *environmental pillar* relates to the impact of activities on the planet. The *social pillar* envelops impact on people. The *governance pillar* focuses on how a business is managed and how its leaders perform their responsibilities toward stakeholders.

Not all ESG efforts are genuine. We must constantly be on guard to detect companies which abuse ESG metrics as a marketing tool, rather than genuinely embracing change. When companies exaggerate or falsify their ESG claims to convince investors or customers, it is known as *greenwashing*.

What is contained within each pillar, and what are the implications for businesses active in emerging markets?

The environmental pillar

A frightening statistic: we are losing the battle to reduce global emissions of CO_2 and other greenhouse gases. In 2023, emerging markets accounted for nearly two-thirds of global emissions growth (International Energy Agency, 2023).

Commitment to compliance with environmental regulations is part of a holistic ESG-aligned strategy. Emerging markets are especially vulnerable to climate change and other environmental damage. Every business in an emerging market must consider its environmental impact: if it creates harm, it must obviate or at least mitigate it. Investments in sustainability projects like renewable energy and recycling have a positive impact; investments which consume energy or non-renewable resources can have a lasting negative impact. It is too easy to think about today's profits and forget tomorrow's losses.

The Harvard *Oral Histories* project, from which we draw many times in this book, contains impressive examples of successful emerging market organizations portrayed through the words of their leaders. A pervasive theme of contributors is commitment to sustainable agriculture, mining, and manufacturing processes. Sanjay Bansal of Darjeeling Organic Tea Estates, Rosario Bazán of Danper Trujillo, Alberto de la Quintana of Buenaventura, and Federico Braun of La Anónima are just a few examples. They demonstrate convincingly that sustainability goes hand in hand with ethical business practice, a long-term view, and global recognition.

SEKEM

SEKEM, founded by Ibrahim Abouleish, is a beacon literally in the desert for the sustainability movement. It is named for an ancient Egyptian hieroglyph, representing "vitality from the sun." The Abouleish family left a comfortable life in Austria to establish a reclamation project outside Cairo, turning wasteland into farmland. Its emphasis on avoiding chemicals and pesticides and cultivating organic products protected Egyptian exports to Europe at a critical time. Over a quarter century, its network of biodynamic businesses grew to encompass pharmaceuticals in addition to food and textiles and then added education and healthcare as part of its commitment to community building.

SEKEM's outstanding contributions to social entrepreneurship and sustainability have gone far beyond agriculture. They demonstrate that sustainability and holistic human development can overcome the short-termism and volatility that characterize emerging market economies. SEKEM has earned global recognition and inspired many similar projects around the world (Abouleish, 2022).

Methods to achieve and monitor net effects vary. For large physical projects, governments will normally mandate the production of environmental impact assessments and may impose terms and conditions for commencement or continuation. It borders on cynicism, however, to expect government to mandate, then comply with only the minimum requirements. Throughout the life of a project, proactivity will yield far greater benefits, including improved stakeholder engagement and support.

When entire local business or social communities are implicated, engagement with local partners, interest groups, and even competitors is healthy and productive. A business does not want the neighbors to find out what's going on when it impacts them – it wants them to be involved in the decision-making and sign up for the mutual benefits, be they employment, investment, community resources, or just compensation.

The three largest considerations within the environmental pillar – climate change, resource management, and pollution – present the most serious threats and the greatest opportunities.

Climate change

No country is immune to the long-lasting damage which flows from climate change. Emerging markets suffer disproportionate vulnerability as extreme weather events impact (among other things) agriculture, crops, access to water, shelter, health, workforce availability, mortality rates, and infrastructure. When considering a new business venture in an emerging market, businesses must be extremely mindful of the risk of exacerbating these threats.

Emerging markets have significant demand for initiatives which add to the available pool of *renewable energy*. Renewables are energy sources which are constantly replenished by nature, are clean, and consequently have less environmental impact. They contrast with fossil fuel energy sources such as burning coal, oil, and gas. The major renewable energy sources are solar (from the sun), wind, hydro (from falling or flowing water), geothermal (from beneath the earth's surface), biomass (burning organic materials like wood), and ocean (from tidal flows).

In 2023, more foreign direct investment went into renewables than any other sector in Europe, Asia-Pacific, MENA, and Latin America (Dettoni, 2024). Aside from specific opportunities, however, considering climate change as part of the suite of development goals within a business leads to more responsible plans, drives innovation, and may result in job creation. Any initiative to reduce emissions while creating an economic opportunity will attract strong governmental interest in most emerging markets. A dramatic example of the potential role of renewables is Madagascar's Volobe hydroelectric plant, set to increase the country's overall electricity supply by 20% (Africa50, n.d., Payton, 2024).

Most publicity about efforts regarding climate change emphasizes attempts at reduction and mitigation. However, adaptation in the face of its inevitability is also important. Adaptive initiatives include installation of flood-resistant barriers in coastal areas, replacing vulnerable crops with drought-resistant strains, and recovery financing to rebuild communities after natural disasters. Businesses venturing into emerging markets must include plans for adaptation in their long-term vision.

d.light

California manufacturer d.light is a shining example of how to address climate change. It makes and sells solar-powered lighting systems and appliances, aiming to replace harmful use of kerosene with clean use of renewable solar energy. It has sold over 25 million devices, reaching over 193 million people, primarily in emerging markets in Africa. Sales in India experienced 73% growth in 2024. It estimates that it has prevented the release of over 23 million tons of carbon dioxide.

d.light has partnered with pay-as-you-go providers in several developing countries, allowing low-income households to acquire its products using small installment payments (The Earthshot Prize, 2024).

Resource management

New industrial development implicates competition for resources, especially water and land. This poses difficult questions about trade-offs between economic growth and food security. If water is scarce, industry may reduce the amount available for agriculture, reducing food availability and increasing health risks, including malnutrition. Similarly, if land is scarce, urban development also reduces agricultural use. Which is more important? Economic development, or long-term sustainability and community well-being? Are there solutions which accommodate both?

Large-scale energy demands may drive increased production of fossil-based fuels. Manufacturing implies an increased demand for minerals; irresponsible procurement or exploitation can cause lasting environmental and reputational damage. Competition for resources in extreme cases can lead to civil unrest and even war.

However, recognizing resource scarcity creates the potential to develop, deploy, and/or sell new processes which optimize use and reduce waste. As government and industry increase their awareness of resource depletion, they are incentivized to invest in technologies and businesses that make more efficient use of resources and recapture valuable materials.

More than 40% of the population of Africa has no access to electricity (United Nations Sustainable Development Group, 2025). Many countries, including Nigeria and South Africa, are plagued by uneven distribution and systemic failures (Baskaran & Coste, 2024). Their power generation is largely dependent on fossil fuels – coal for South Africa and natural gas for Nigeria. This creates huge opportunities for exploiting vast resources of solar and wind power, reducing dependence on finite fossil fuels. The energy destiny of Africa, however, is closely tied to the ability to store electrical power once it is generated. BESS – battery energy storage systems – have a crucial role to play in the World and African Development Banks' plan to provide electricity to 300 million more people by 2030 (Nyanga & Osinbajo, 2024).

The largest resource opportunity lies in recycling, which has led to the conceptual development of the *circular economy*. This concept is so important to global sustainability that it deserves its own subsection.

The circular economy

It may be surprising to realize that the seeds of the circular economy concept were first sown within living memory, in 1966 when American economist Kenneth Boulding published a colorfully titled paper *The Economics of the Coming Spaceship Earth*. Although he did not use the term "circular economy," Boulding contrasted the traditional idea of a "cowboy economy" with a linear take-make-dispose model with a "spaceship economy" with finite resources and a need for a regenerative system to manage resources within a closed-loop economy.

Instead of extracting, using, and wasting resources, the circular economy "is one that is restorative and regenerative by design, and which aims to keep products, components, and materials at their highest utility and value at all times, distinguishing between technical and biological cycles" (Ellen MacArthur Foundation, 2013).

Emerging markets resonate strongly with two core principles of circularity: closed-loop production systems and waste valorization. Closed-loop systems ensure that at the end of life, the materials contained within products become inputs for new processes. Waste valorization recasts by-products and waste materials as resources which enter the production cycle instead of being discarded. Informal recycling networks, community-based projects, and a familiarity with shortages all create an ideal environment for the promotion of circularity.

Nigeria, Ghana, and Brazil demonstrate promising examples of the circular economy in action. Ghana's Agblobloshie scrapyard employs clean recycling technologies to recover valuable minerals, particularly metals, from 30 to 40 metric tons of discarded electronics from Europe and the Americas every day (Grant & Oteng-Ababio, 2019). In Brazil, an emphasis on reducing, rather than recycling, pollutive plastic products has spawned remarkable developments of plant-based materials for packaging. The Brazilian government offers significant tax credits and grants for sustainable businesses (Froehlich & Vieira, 2020).

Project Reflex

Dow Chemical Company, one of the three largest chemical producers in the world, exemplifies circularity with a flagship initiative in Africa. Project Reflex, which partners Dow with local recyclers such as Mr. Green and Wecyclers, is designed to divert 75,000 metric tons of plastic per year from landfill to reuse. In Nigeria, Egypt, and Guinea, the Wecyclers partnership is estimated to have created up to 50,000 jobs (Dow Africa, 2024).

Regulation plays an important role in promoting circularity. In India, the *Plastic Waste Management Rules, 2016*, revised in 2022, place responsibility for products after their consumer lifecycle back with manufacturers and brand owners. China's *Circular Economy Promotion Law, 2009*, is a comprehensive framework which orders resource efficiency in both manufacturing and distribution and gives tax reductions and grants to companies which transition from linear to circular resource use. China's 2021 *Five-Year Plan* added extensive further circular economy goals. *Brazil's Política Nacional de Resíduos Sólidos (National Solid Waste Policy), 2010*, imposes mandatory recycling targets, builds waste management infrastructure, and supports research and development of circular technologies.

While circular economy principles are attractive and may appear obvious, their growth has not been as strong as environmentalists have hoped due to several limitations. They rely on a waste management and recycling infrastructure, which is often deficient. The informal nature of many waste collection networks, including the Ghanaian facility mentioned above, has led to criticism over safety standards, local environmental impact, and quality inconsistencies. There is a need for increased public awareness of the long-term value of circular products, which is often at odds with shorter-term commercial interests (Bocken et al., 2016).

The ongoing digitalization of global business holds great promise for circularity. Contributions come from blockchain technology, improving traceability of materials, AI-powered waste sorting and recycling, and the Internet of Things' capability to extend product lifecycles (Antikainen & Valkokari, 2016).

Pollution

Because of poor regulation, some emerging markets are attractive to large-scale polluters wanting to reduce the expense of mitigation or amelioration. These two terms have common goals but refer to different approaches. Mitigation is proactive; amelioration is reactive.

For example, consider a power plant which burns fossil fuels to generate electricity. When it installs scrubbers in its smokestacks to reduce sulfur dioxide emissions, it is attacking the problem at source – this is mitigation. However, it still emits excess carbon dioxide and causes acid rain. To address this, it plants thousands of trees in the area around its operation-this is amelioration.

While most emerging markets have regulatory standards for pollution, scope, effectiveness, and enforcement vary widely. We emphasize that mere compliance with minima does not demonstrate a commitment to sustainability. At the planning stage of a new venture, businesses must consider how to reduce pollution of air, water, and soil (U.S. Environmental Protection Agency, n.d.). Financial considerations mandate this, but reputational damage from an environmental disaster can persist for decades and do lasting harm to a business's image and legacy.

Exploitative industries, especially mining and logging, have strong potential to cause lasting environmental damage, particularly if they pollute or deplete rivers where damage can run hundreds of miles downstream. Agricultural or infrastructural improvements can imply deforestation and loss of habitats. Every initiative includes a balancing exercise, and every solution must consider the long-term effects of today's actions.

The larger cities in many emerging markets are home to pervasive pollution problems. Jakarta, Indonesia, has extraordinary levels of fine particulate matter in its air, leading since 2019 to its classification as "unhealthy for sensitive groups" (IQAir, n.d.). In 2024, air pollution caused approximately 12,000 deaths; 10.7 million people have their life expectancy reduced by 2.4 years due to particulate exposure (Abdillah et al. 2024).

The Bhopal Disaster

Pollutive damage can flow not just from ongoing operations but also from single incidents. In December 1984, the Union Carbide pesticide plant in Bhopal, India, released a quantity of highly toxic gas. Between 3,000 and 4,000 people were killed immediately. Around 15,000 more died within a brief period, and over half a million were injured. Hundreds of thousands of people suffered health consequences, and many lost their livelihoods. Later, unborn children whose mothers were pregnant at the time of the disaster were born with defects and health issues caused by the release. The investigations and lawsuits which followed severely damaged the reputation of Union Carbide throughout the world. It paid US$470 million to settle the subsequent litigation (Chatterjee, 2023).

Market opportunities are created on a large scale by the need to ensure that past abuses do not continue or replicate. Waste collection and disposal systems require continuous improvement as the world population grows; an entrepreneur who can efficiently convert waste into a usable product (typically energy) is likely to enjoy global success. There is a massive market worldwide for pollution control systems, sustainability consulting, and the promotion of sustainable agricultural solutions. A recent estimate puts the global value of the e-waste management market at US$80 billion, growing at 11% per year (IMARC Group, 2024).

Ghana, where the government has engaged strongly in promoting recycling and recovery efforts, is flooded with second-hand electronic goods from the rest of the world. It has turned *e-waste*, a relatively new global problem, into economic opportunity. By 2015 the global electronics recycling industry was estimated to be valued at US$52 billion; valuable minerals like gold, copper, and platinum are recoverable from discarded devices, and high market prices encourage and reward recovery efforts. Ghana has moved strongly to formalize the industry and remove fragmentation and barriers, becoming recognized as a leader in Africa (Grant & Oteng-Ababio, 2021).

Green Hydrogen

The field of green hydrogen[1] illustrates a large-scale, global initiative to reduce pollution, replacing fossil fuels in areas where decarbonization is difficult, such as steel, shipping, and aviation. *Decarbonization* is a key environmental goal for the entire world. A chain reaction from the war in Ukraine has caused an imbalance between global supply and demand for energy, resulting in increased use of liquefied natural gas and negative climate change (Iberdrola, n.d.).

Green hydrogen is obtained by electrolysis of water (H_2O), separating hydrogen from oxygen. When the electrical current required for the process is generated from a renewable source such as solar or wind energy, no carbon dioxide is produced, and the world is a cleaner place. The World Hydrogen Council predicts that the cost of producing green hydrogen will fall by 50% by 2030 (Hydrogen Council, n.d.).

Hydrogen is easy to store; it has a wide range of uses to power vehicles and aircraft or produce other energy-based resources like light and heat. One manageable disadvantage is that being highly volatile, it takes great care to avoid leakage and/or consequent explosions.

In Egypt's New Administrative Capital outside Cairo, Magnom Properties is planning to build a New International Tower, demonstrating the potential of green hydrogen. Not only is the building being constructed from materials with low-embodied carbon, but it will also have water recycling and treatment on site. The 240-meter-tall building will be powered 75% by hydrogen and 25% by photovoltaics (sunlight), meaning it has no need for connection to a traditional power grid and will have a zero carbon footprint throughout its lifecycle (Page, 2024).

While innovative solutions such as hydrogen fuels reduce pollution, clear metrics are necessary to quantify their effectiveness. Measurement of real progress earns regulatory approval and stakeholder trust and makes the case for long-term viability.

Metrics for environmental impact

Evaluative processes are necessary from the initial planning of a new venture to future restorative processes when it comes to an end. Impact assessments form part of the planning process, based on prior materiality assessments, asking which risks are most important. Continuous measurement and assessment with transparent reporting will earn increased trust with stakeholders. Environmental risks should not just be known but also be actively managed.

Each business will design its own metrics for assessing environmental impact, according to the features of its business or activities. These are the principal headings to consider:

1. Carbon emissions – climate change.
2. Energy use – consumption, percentage of renewables, and efficiency.
3. Water management – use, reuse, recycling, and pollution.
4. Waste management – waste generated, diverted from landfill, recycled, and safe disposal of hazardous waste.
5. Air quality – particulate emissions, noxious gases generated.
6. Biodiversity and land use – land affected, deforested, mined, and restored.
7. Product sustainability – impact of the product, use of sustainable raw materials.
8. Environmental compliance – the number of violations or penalties paid.

Regional institutions such as the African Development Bank and Asian Infrastructure Development Bank play a key role in promoting environmental responsibility. Both have prioritized funding renewable energy projects and heavily endorse the transition to low-carbon economies. Public–private partnerships (PPPs) also play an important role. Kenya's Lake Turkana Wind Power Project, to which we will return later, draws these two themes together as the government utility constructed transmission lines, private investors financed the construction, and the African Development Bank provided both loans and technical expertise.

Environmental stories, positive and negative, are often the most visible aspects of sustainability. However, as business does not operate in a vacuum, it is noticeable that they always have social impacts – environmental impacts affect people and communities. In the next section, we'll look more deeply at the human dimensions of sustainability.

The social pillar

Human rights considerations are a great umbrella to start thinking about social impact, from which we can drill down further to specific cultural and labor issues. UN SDGs 8, 5, 1, 10, and 16 collectively address this progression, to which we can then add 12 for ethical supply chains and 17 for global collaboration. Human rights, labor practices, and community engagement are not segmented there are many fine examples of businesses which integrate them holistically. For example, Grameen Bank, which we mentioned earlier, in empowering women through the provision of microcredit, has woven together human rights, labor practices, and community engagement.

No business today should benefit from labor practices which involve discrimination, child labor, or slavery. Many prominent global businesses have suffered from accusations of child labor in their supply chains, including IKEA (Rao, 2023), Nike (Conway, 2019), and Apple (Sonnemaker, 2020).

Human rights

There is frequent scrutiny of the human rights practices of businesses operating in foreign markets. Investors, regulators, consumers, and the press all expect companies to observe international standards and conform to local practices. Incorporating best practices into business policies mitigates risk and supports the longevity of overseas ventures.

Discrimination exists in overt and subtle forms. It is frighteningly easy to fall into the trap of supporting discrimination without intending any harm. A notable example occurred in the case of Beiersdorf, a German personal care (cosmetics) manufacturer. Its Indian subsidiary, Nivea India, was strongly criticized for promoting "colorism," a form of discrimination based on relative lightness of skin tone. In response, Nivea removed all references to "whitening" and "fairness" in its advertising and packaging. Major competitors L'Oréal and Unilever did the same within days (Singh, 2020). Nivea was rewarded for its market-leading effort when it was ranked in 2022 as the most trusted skincare brand in the entire country (PTI, 2022).

Diversity, equity, and inclusion (DEI). Although DEI frameworks have become common in western society, the campaign for their universal adoption is not over, as some notable companies are being forced to reconsider their policies to respond to consumer opinion (Riedel, 2025). Not so much so in emerging markets, where racial and class differences and enmities often still exist, are tolerated, and are sometimes supported and enforced by governments.

A business looking to expand into a new market walks the proverbial tightrope to promote its global DEI policies while respecting local culture. Entrenched social norms and gender roles can create strong resistance to gender quotas or diversity hiring practices. Many emerging markets have not yet developed strong anti-discrimination laws, making it more difficult for inward investors to align their policies. Informal labor markets are just one example of a prevalent practice largely untouched by formal regulation. Inclusivity policies supporting members of the LGBTQ2S+ community can be a particular touchpoint in several emerging markets, at the extreme in Saudi Arabia, where homosexuality is punishable by death under Sharia law.

Businesses must make a careful examination of the similarities and differences in company expectations and those of the target market, then make policy decisions. If it is not possible to enter a market and retain core values, this can be a showstopper. On the other hand, it is possible that local anti-discrimination laws go beyond existing company policies, which must be adapted to comply with local standards. South Africa's *Employment Equity Act, No. 55 of 1998*, for example, goes far beyond typical policies found in most companies.

Freedom of speech may not be the most obvious human rights challenge for expanding global businesses. Yet it has been a significant issue for Netflix and Amazon Prime as they expanded into India. A fundamental conflict arose between governmental views on what is appropriate for a national audience and the streaming services' views on free speech. Debates over film content became so animated that death threats were directed toward actors, necessitating a succession of changes to national law and censorship (Mukherjee, 2021).

In August 2024, Elon Musk engaged in a censorship feud with Brazilian Supreme Court Judge de Moraes after a court order to block certain X accounts accused of disseminating misinformation and hate speech. The fight resulted in the closure of X's office in the country (Tangalakis-Lipert, 2024).

Tesco

You might be surprised to find the number of policy publications by Tesco, one of Britain's largest retailers, relating to modern slavery and human trafficking. While it is rare for an international business to suffer direct accusations of human trafficking, much more care is needed with the supply chain. Tesco, in its 2017 report, identified several areas of high risk and singled them out for attention, in addition signaling that it was starting intense efforts to assess labor providers in Thailand and Malaysia (Tesco plc, 2016).

Tesco identified at-risk workers in construction, distribution and logistics, security, and its franchised car wash supplier. Isolating these areas framed the risk of inadvertent involvement in human trafficking; they are manually intensive divisions which can involve long hours, limited skills, and have no great demand for language proficiency. Migrant and illegal workers are particularly exposed to exploitation where work is done out of sight of the public.

Tesco buys significant quantities of seafood from Thailand. Fishing and harvesting are other industries where workers can be subjected to long hours and harsh conditions, far from public view. Not only Thai workers but also migrants from nearby countries, including Myanmar, Cambodia, and Laos, have historically been attracted to Thailand by work opportunities but then severely abused, trapped in debt bondage, and virtually imprisoned by restriction of their documents, movements, and communications (Murphy, 2018).

Indigenous rights

Indigenous rights increasingly demand respect from growing organizations. A lengthy history of colonialism and dispossession shines an even brighter light on oppressors who, in today's world, continue a practice of marginalizing Indigenous communities, disrespecting their culture, or appropriating their lands. Modern views of land ownership and use may be sharply at odds with traditional systems, and valuable minerals may be located beneath land occupied since time immemorial by Indigenous communities. Invasive business interests risk breaching Indigenous rights, reducing self-determination, and damaging fragile economic systems in the pursuit of western style profits. Businesses embarking on new ventures on Indigenous lands or among Indigenous communities have a strong moral, and often legal, responsibility to respect Indigenous rights and protect them from encroachment.

Five key practical actions are implicated in the need to respect indigenous rights.

- Consultation with affected communities must be undertaken to ensure that free, prior, and informed consent (FPIC) is obtained (United Nations Declaration on the Rights of Indigenous Peoples, Article 32).
- Impact assessments should involve Indigenous groups and integrate traditional knowledge (International Association for Impact Assessment, 2012).
- Fair agreements should ensure that affected communities receive real economic benefits from exploitation of resources (International Labour Organization, 1989).

- Cultural sensitivity training should be required by internal policies (United Nations Global Compact, 2013).
- Continuous monitoring and grievance resolution should be maintained throughout the project lifecycle (Equator Principles Association, 2020).

The Pascua-Lama Mining Project

Toronto's Barrick Gold, the world's second-largest gold miner. Its difficulties with the Pascua-Lama Mining Project, located on both sides of the Argentina-Chile border, demonstrate the simultaneous dangers of damaging the environment and Indigenous communities.

In 1994, Barrick took over LAC Minerals, another Canadian precious metal miner. LAC owned the Pascua-Lama project, which became Barrick's property and problem. The potential rewards were an estimated 21 million ounces of gold and 736 million ounces of silver.

Barrick needed environmental permits to conduct its open-pit operations and was required to comply with pollution prevention conditions in an impact assessment. Water running off glaciers in the region feeds tributary rivers, relied on by some 70,000 farmers in the Huasco River basin. The basin is home to Indigenous groups, including the Diaguita, who took successful legal action against Barrick and achieved a ruling from Chile's Supreme Court bringing a complete stop to the project. Contemporary estimates suggested that an investment of US$7.5 billion was stranded by Chile's order to close the project (CDP, n.d.). In early 2024, Barrick committed a further $136 million to remedial action to return the watercourse to its original state (Jamasmie, 2024).

The employment environment, including wages, hours, ages, and safety, can be an enormous source of concern and possible reputational damage.

Employment standards

Employers must monitor treatment of all workforces, whether employed directly or by suppliers. Labor conditions include wages, working hours, health, and safety. An attraction of employees in an emerging market is that they will work for less; this is acceptable, provided that local standards are met. It is advisable, however, to subscribe globally to a whole enterprise standard for hours and safety. There is no morally correct argument that workers in North Africa should be forced to put in 60 hours a week, while their colleagues in France are paid more money for a 35-hour week.

Unilever's Fair Wage initiative is spread across all the emerging markets in which the business operates (Ecclissato, n.d.). It guarantees that all employers and contractors receive a living wage. Unilever assembles cost of living data from each country and ensures that compensation reaches the benchmarks which it establishes. Stakeholders who benefit from the initiative include workers, the company, and local economies, where increases in disposable income generate increased sales for other retailers and service providers.

The concept of a *living wage* is fundamental. A living wage is

> the remuneration received for a standard workweek by a worker in a particular place sufficient to afford a decent standard of living for the worker and her or his family. Elements of a decent standard of living include food, water, housing, education, health care, transportation, clothing, and other essential needs including provision for unexpected events. (Global Living Wage Coalition, n.d.)

UN SDG 8, Decent Work and Economic Growth, contains two subtargets 8.5 and 8.8, which promote equal pay for work of equal value and safe working environments. Article 23 of the Universal Declaration of Human Rights states that "everyone who works has the right to just and favorable remuneration ensuring for himself and his family an existence worthy of human dignity" (United Nations, n.d.).

A forward-thinking investor in a growing market has a strong interest in retaining good workers; it may have more money available to boost their rewards and differentiate itself as an employer. This is good policy but may lead to a situation in which it becomes more desirable to work for a foreign employer than a domestic one, leading to a talent drain on locally based businesses. It is hard to view a long-term policy which damages local enterprise in this way as socially responsible.[2]

One method for an inward investor to make a strong positive impact is by building community engagement into its plans. In 2010, Unilever launched the USLP – Universal Sustainable Living Plan – with ambitious, measurable initiatives "woven into the fabric of the company's operations" (G, S. 2024). One of the many initiatives was the use of the Lifebuoy soap brand to deliver a hygiene improvement by promoting handwashing. Other large multinationals have entire programs or foundations devoted to community projects, such as the Fundación PepsiCo in Mexico (PepsiCo, 2023).

Detailed guidance on key areas, including core labor standards, governance conventions, and technical conventions relating to occupational safety and health, is available in the conventions of the International Labor Organization (ILO) (n.d.). Eleven fundamental conventions cover essential principles relating to labor forces, which are legally binding international treaties. Among emerging nations, Brazil, Mexico, and South Africa have ratified all 11, India six, and China four.

Cobalt mining

Cobalt is an essential component in lithium-ion batteries, which are used in products as diverse as mobile phones and electric cars. Electric vehicle manufacturers consume 40% of the entire global production. Cobalt is also used to make superalloys, metallic components in jet engines which can withstand extreme temperatures.

74% of all the cobalt produced in the world comes from the Democratic Republic of Congo. That amounts to over 170,000 tonnes (metric tons) annually, dwarfing production from otherwise significant producers (Venditti, 2024). Up to 20% of the DRC's annual production is from ASM – artisanal and small-scale mining (Campbell, 2020).

"Artisanal labor" is often a euphemism for forced and child labor. The use of unethically sourced cobalt, whether intentional or accidental, creates an enormous reputational, legal, financial, and political risk for manufacturers and demands firm governance to avoid it. Tesla, for example, has worked hard to ensure due diligence in supply; it tracks cobalt from mine to battery, regularly audits its suppliers, and has a strict policy against using conflict minerals. More forward-looking, however, are its initiatives to promote responsible mining and research spending on new battery technologies which might eliminate the need for cobalt altogether (Dollaride, 2024).

Among the best-known examples of reputational damage is that suffered by Nike before the millennium due to accusations of forced labor in its overseas supply chain. Two decades later, however, Nike is facing a fresh investigation in Canada over its alleged use of forced Uyghur labor in China (Commonshare Editorial Team, 2023).

In 2013, the Rana Plaza factory building in Savar, Bangladesh, collapsed. 1,134 people died, and thousands more suffered injuries. There are gruesome reports of people who escaped only by amputating their own limbs. It was the worst ever disaster in the garment industry. At least 29 global brands, including Benetton, Joe Fresh, Mango, Matalan, and Primark, had current or recent orders with factories in Rana Plaza. Each of these brands, alleged a pressure group in the campaigns which followed, "was a complicit participant in the creation of an environment that ultimately led to the deaths and maiming of thousands of individuals" (Clean Clothes Campaign, 2023). The global press took notice; damaging articles were published by *The Guardian*, *Al Jazeera*, and *The New York Times*.

Such events bring extraordinary opprobrium onto the brands and businesses that are affected, particularly if they delay or fail in making restitution and paying compensation. The correct response is to display leadership and responsibility in planning and sourcing supply chains; closing eyes and hoping nothing bad will happen is never a solution. Loss of integrity is not justified by any amount of profit. Integrity is essential to success: it requires adherence to a code of values (Lidsky, 2023).

Community engagement

Companies expanding into new markets do not only need to guard against negative social impacts: positive community engagement strengthens social capital, reducing social risks.

In emerging markets, *community engagement* initiatives are frequently focused on education, healthcare, economic empowerment, and cultural preservation. They go beyond philanthropy, however, looking for projects that are mutually beneficial. Nestlé, for example, provides training and resources for coffee farmers in Colombia and nine other countries who want to engage in sustainable production; the result is a better crop for both the farmers who learn and the company which buys the beans (Nestlé, 2014).

Today's forward-thinking businesses integrate community involvement, ensuring that they make a positive contribution to the societies within which they operate. PepsiCo is a shining example.

In 2006, Indra Nooyi was appointed CEO of PepsiCo. Under her leadership, the business strengthened its position as a global behemoth in the food and beverage industry.

She recounts in her autobiography (Nooyi, 2024) that her leadership period is viewed by posterity as characterized by great strategy, innovation, and her commitment to the business's social responsibilities. Among successful policies which she championed, improving products, tailoring them to local tastes, and a commitment to sustainability exemplify the messages we emphasize throughout this book.

Empowering women

The empowerment of women is a deep underlying factor in promoting sustainable economic growth and social stability. Enabling more women to engage in employment and leadership improves educational achievement, household incomes, health levels, and community resilience. There are many examples of successful models across diverse regions.

The Kantha project, headed by Shamlu Dudeja, sought to provide economic and psychological independence for women in rural Bengal. Today it employs thousands of women; it started with just a few. The women involved in the project were enabled to earn a living from home, which elevated their social and familial status. As a bonus, the project brought together Hindu and Muslim women to work in collaboration, reducing cultural division (Dudeja, 2018).

Sylvia Escovar of Terpel, a leading fuel and service distributor in Colombia, is a noted thought leader in the gender equity arena. Within her company, in front of a wider audience, she broke new ground in highlighting productivity gains which can be earned with women in leadership positions. She has long addressed the need to question deep-seated stereotypes regarding the roles of men and women. Under her leadership, Terpel made notable strides forward in gender equity, aiming at education and professional opportunities as the vehicles (Escovar, 2019).

These examples demonstrate that empowerment of women in emerging markets has desirable impacts reaching far beyond individual advancement. Business outcomes are strengthened, and a contribution is made to inclusivity and the reduction of systemic inequality.

Metrics for social impact

When developing community engagement initiatives, measurability is an important consideration. Promoters will be interested to see numbers which indicate improvements, for example, in job creation, crop yields, access to services, or public health. Such advances directly support broader ESG goals, including economic empowerment, reducing inequality, and improving health and sanitation facilities.

Four data-driven tools are widely acknowledged as informative measurements of social impact and DEI initiatives:

- Social Return on Investment (SROI) places a financial value on positive social outcomes (Nicholls et al., 2012).
- B Impact Assessment (BIA) evaluates business performance with respect to governance, workers, community, environment, and customers.
- United Nations Development Programme (n.d.) Gender Equality Seal is a certification that an organization meets high standards of gender equality.

- Impact Reporting and Investment Standards Plus (IRIS+) is a framework for assessment of impact strategies, stressing real-world outcomes (Global Impact Investing Network, 2023).

Following are the main categories of measurable impacts in the social sphere.

- Employee welfare – satisfaction, turnover, diversity and inclusion, and health and safety incidents.
- Community engagement – investments in community projects, volunteer hours committed, local hiring.
- Product/service accessibility – affordable access provided, or underserved communities reached.
- Supply chain impacts – labor practices, living wages paid, and elimination of slave and child labor.
- Education – training hours, certifications, employee advancement.
- Human rights – complaints received, resolved.
- Philanthropy – donations, impacts of giving (time and money)
- DEI – percentages of employees at all levels representing diverse groups, including all those entitled to protection from discrimination.

Some emerging markets are characterized by large informal economies with unregistered businesses, gig workers, unprotected employees, and cash-based remuneration systems outside the purview of taxation authorities. ESG reporting frameworks have no established method of recording informal activities, yet they can be substantial. An example is the plastic waste recycling industry in Lagos, Nigeria, which employs thousands of workers with no accounting for their contribution to sustainability.

The governance pillar

Some companies pay lip service to social initiatives yet fail to deliver on their promises. Governance principles hold business leaders accountable for their performance. Rules, audits, regulations, oversight, and reporting standards all serve to ensure that ESG policies are implemented, monitored, and measured, rather than simply expressed.

Governance refers to both the overarching and detailed sets of rules and procedures which specify how executives and senior management are to run a business. The governance framework starts at the top with strategic decision-making, moves through risk management and compliance, and defines who is responsible for achievement and accountable for failure. Good governance is essential to building trust and frequently benefits from external advice, especially in family-owned businesses. A reluctance to engage in artificial, government-influenced ventures is a hallmark of integrity (Von Appen, 2008).

In 2010, *Time* Magazine recognized Kiran Mazumdar-Shaw, founder of Biocon Limited, as one of the 100 most influential people in the world. Biocon is a global biopharmaceutical business and a leading presence in its native India. Besides being known for her efforts to deliver affordable healthcare to emerging markets, Mazumdar-Shaw is a prominent advocate of governance reform, arguing that it is not only a challenge but also an opportunity. In the healthcare sector, trust and reliability are paramount; strong governance creates the opportunity for first movers to build an enviable reputation (Mazumdar-Shaw, 2018).

Governance models

Governance is not static. Neither is it a homogeneous term. It breaks down into three principal models: Anglo-American, European, and Japanese. The first two create the greatest tension in emerging markets. Anglo-American governance is rooted in entrepreneurship and private property, viewing the shareholder as the principal beneficiary, while management are agents acting to promote shareholder primacy. In continental European governance, other stakeholders, especially labor, have a much stronger input to decision-making; it is explicit that companies do not have an exclusive duty to promote the interests of shareholders (Renou, Carraz, & Burger-Helmchen, 2023).

Applying western notions of proper governance in emerging markets can be a complex challenge. The Anglo-American model assumes dispersed ownership. It may appear to be dominant due to the heavy influence of the United Kingdom and the United States in foreign direct investment (FDI), promotion of the model by the IMF and World Bank, and a history of colonization in large markets like India, Nigeria, and South Africa. Franklin Ngwu, a prolific author on this topic, argues that the model has not been successful and does not underly the successes achieved in China or the East Asian economies (Ngwu, 2017).

Rahim and Kuruppu, reflecting on the Indian experience, go so far as to say:

> [A]n overarching tendency to concentrate on the principal-agent relationship and "shareholder centric" perspectives in mainly Anglo-American contexts have constrained our understanding of corporate governance ... India suffers from an overburdened legal system which has resulted in a lack of oversight, rife corruption and limited transparency due to the concentrated ownership structures prevalent in India.
>
> *(Rahim & Kuruppu, 2017)*

In major emerging markets like India, China, and Nigeria, ownership is much more concentrated. The failures of rule-based systems and strength of vested interests, coupled with weakness in bureaucracies and legal systems, all militate against success for traditional governance models and create needs for bespoke local solutions (Osuji, Ngwu & Stephen, 2017).

Many emerging markets have hybrid governance models with strong family controls, for example, in Southeast Asia and Latin America. China's governance is heavily state-driven. The most dramatic rejection of the Anglo-American model has occurred in South Africa. Following centuries of colonialism and racial discrimination, the new ANC government from 1994 mandated fundamental governance changes to reflect the participation of environmental, affirmative action, employment, and Black Economic Empowerment interests (Mthanti & Ojah, 2017).

A strong corporate governance model is essential in emerging markets. By demonstrating transparency and accountability, a business can make itself attractive to investors and suppliers, reduce operational risks, and strengthen its competitive position. With stakeholder trust well established, long-term prospects for success improve as the business secures better terms in capital markets, reduces labor problems, and avoids becoming embroiled in corruption and/or other illegal practices.

However, it can be deeply challenging to implement good governance. Weak regulation, endemic bribery and corruption, and social expectations often stand in the way.

Corruption, bribery, and transparency

Corruption can exist from the lowest levels in society to the highest echelons of government. It can rise to the level of a systemic barrier to market entry and ethical governance. It distorts competition, makes investors very nervous, and erodes trust in government. Expanding businesses are faced with a difficult question: how do they operate ethically in a region where bribery is still considered a normal cost of doing business?

The global coalition against corruption, Transparency International, publishes an annual *Corruption Perceptions Index* (Transparency International, 2023). The index demonstrates the tenacity of corruption in most of the world. Using a scale from 0 to 100, where 0 is highly corrupt and 100 is very clean, over two-thirds of countries score below 50: they have serious corruption problems. The global average is 43. In 2023, 23 countries achieved their worst-ever score.

Figure 3.1 shows the individual scores of emerging markets, which average 41. Black bars are those below the world average; corruption is more of a problem in emerging markets than in the world at large.

Large-scale corruption continues to exist even among global giants who work closely with developed-world governments. Staggering amounts of money are involved.

In 2010, BAE Systems paid a $400 million criminal fine to the United States after pleading guilty to conspiring to make false statements about its anti-corruption compliance programs.

> Through [its] BVI entity, from May 2001 onward, BAES made payments totaling more than £135 million plus more than $14 million, even though in certain situations BAES was aware there was a high probability that part of the payments would be used to ensure that BAES was favored in foreign government decisions regarding the purchase of defense articles. According to court documents, in many instances, BAES possessed no adequate evidence that its advisors performed any legitimate activities in justification of the substantial payments .
>
> *(United States Department of Justice, 2010)*

BAE is not a small, shadowy criminal organization operating in secret; it is a major, world-renowned provider of fighters, bombers, missiles, and spacecraft to the American, European, and other governments. Yet it had paid massive bribes to government officials in the emerging markets of Saudi Arabia, South Africa, Romania, the Czech Republic, and Hungary, demonstrating how government procurement in emerging markets is

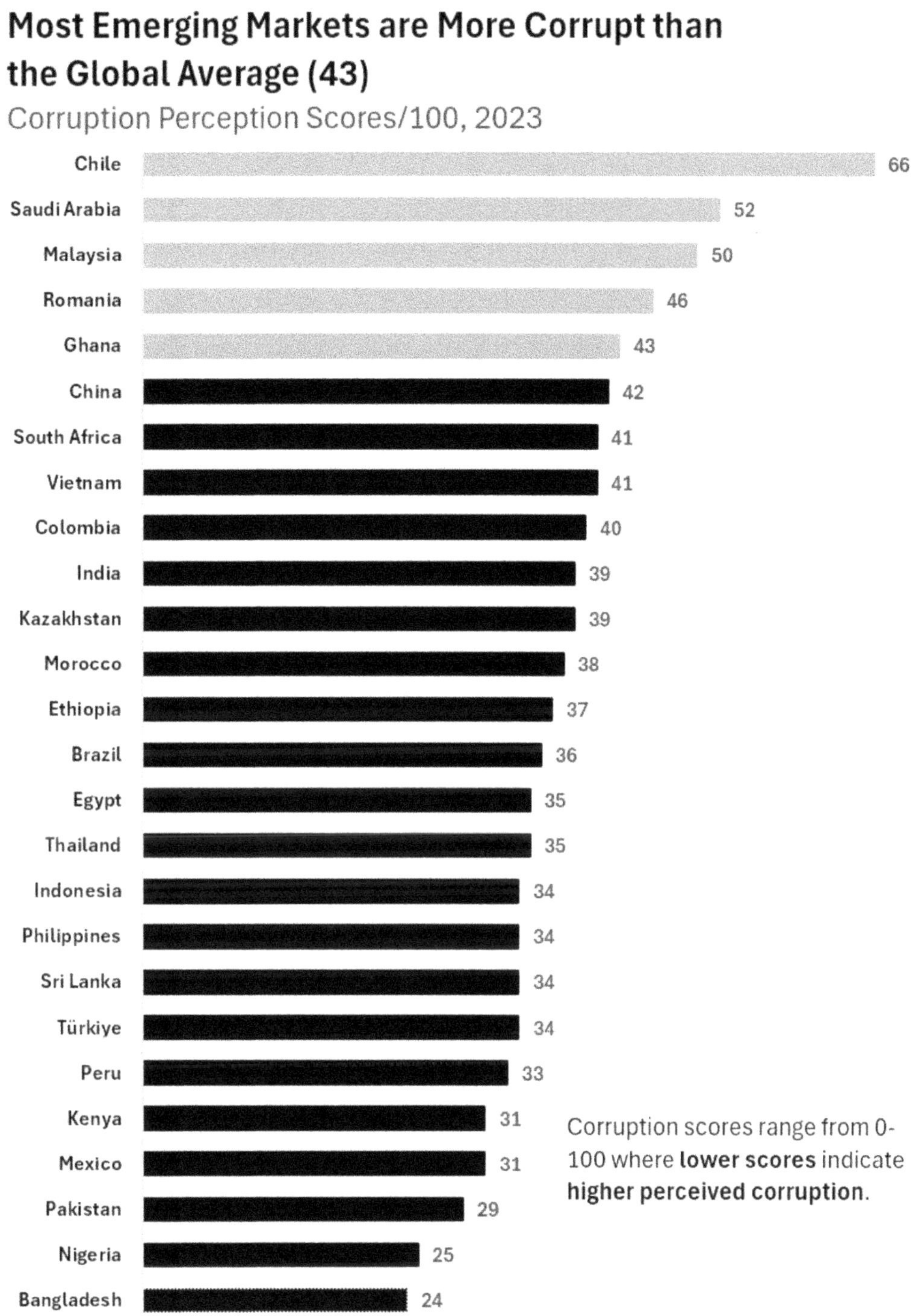

Figure 3.1 Corruption Perceptions Index 2023

particularly vulnerable to bribery and corruption. The consequences can be far-reaching in the home base of the corrupting company.

The lesson is that multinationals operating in emerging markets simply cannot assume that corrupt practices, even if they appear acceptable overseas, will go undetected or unpunished at home.

Operation Lava Jato

The world's largest-ever bribery scheme (US$5 billion) took place in Brazil. Its investigation, *Operation Car Wash*, exposed the participation of high-ranking politicians, government employees, and business executives. Petrobras, the state-owned oil company, was central; politicians and company executives received eye-watering bribes for awarding overpriced contracts to construction companies. Even the President of Brazil, Luiz Inácio "Lula" da Silva, was implicated (Watts, 2017). In 2020, Odebrecht, a massive construction company which was involved, changed its name to Novonor, attempting to disassociate its name from years of damaging scandals (Agence France-Presse, 2020).

While billion-dollar schemes are recounted in the global press, endemic corruption takes place every day in small, routine transactions. Author Paul recounts a petty problem:

> We hoped to obtain a local driver's license in Jakarta, Indonesia, for an expatriate employee and visited the licensing office. There was a two-year wait for the driving test. However, with a payment of 20,000 Rupiah (about $2 at the time) in cash (no receipt available), the license could be issued immediately. The clerk was offering us a 60% discount because our local agent went to school with her! 40% of a bribe is still a bribe, and we went away without the license.

He encountered a larger problem in India.

> Over 15 years ago, I represented an Indian subsidiary of a multinational company. A client of a client defrauded a single Indian consumer, who complained to the Chennai police. I arranged for the consumer to receive a full refund. The police officer handling the case then asked me to pay him a similar amount, as my client could afford it. I responded that paying him would be a crime in my own country, and in India.
>
> The police officer then fabricated a court application for freezing of my client's bank account, which contained hundreds of times the amount disputed. Subsequently, he telephoned to suggested that he would resolve the problem if I showed up at his office with a "gift" for him in my briefcase. I declined again.
>
> We filed an application with the local court for release of the funds in 2015. The court listed the case for hearing in 2024; when it finally came up on the court's calendar, the judge adjourned it until 2029.

The solution to corruption and bribery issues does not lie with one business alone, though collective refusal to engage is part of the solution. Correction must come from the strengthening of government institutions (difficult if stakeholders depend on corruption to bolster their incomes), the promotion of transparency, and international initiatives.

Despite the apparent importance of the global fight against large-scale corruption, some western governments recognize that there are parts of the world where even simple transactions cannot happen unless "facilitating payments" or "grease payments" are made.

The United States (in the *Foreign Corrupt Practices Act, 1977*) (n.d.) is remarkable in allowing such payments under certain conditions. A payment is not regarded as a bribe, and thus not illegal, if it is necessary (required to obtain a routine government action that would be performed anyway), small, and not intended to influence a decision on a non-routine matter.

The United Kingdom is more circumspect. Under the *Bribery Act* of 2010, a facilitating payment must be "reasonable" rather than "small" (though neither government gives clear definitions of what those terms mean). Menacingly, criminal liability in the United Kingdom can fall on businesses which fail to prevent bribes, as well as those who pay them.

Although there are places where it seems almost impossible to function without engaging in a form of financial persuasion, there are many examples of successful businesses in emerging markets which have a firm stance. Manu Chandaria, CEO of Kenya-based Comcraft Group, heads a business with a century of history, which has grown to operate in some 45 countries. He has a simple and straightforward policy in this respect:

> If we can't do something in the simplest and the most straightforward manner, we'll not do it. Many times, we find that our growth gets retarded. But we believe that it is not the way to do it. As a family, the philosophy has always been that you must remain consistent in your core values. You cannot just play around with them.
>
> *(Chandaria, 2014)*

The topic of bribery, corruption, and facilitation is a minefield where any business should tread with great caution. There are very subtle distinctions across legal systems; some, for example, only penalize paying, while others penalize even an offer to pay. Then there are the murky boundaries of preferential treatment and other favors; if governmental officials from one country visit another and receive lavish entertainment, that might fall under the heading of "business development." But if it goes too far and involves valuable gifts, it can easily bear the hallmarks of corruption.

Siemens AG

The history of anti-corruption practices at German company Siemens AG is a classic poacher-turned-gamekeeper story. In the mid-2000s, Siemens was punished for giving billions of Euros and dollars to influence decisions on large contracts. It suffered immense financial penalties and set out to demonstrate a transformation.

Siemens launched its *Integrity Initiative*. This involved setting up advanced digital tools for detecting suspicious activities and tracking supplier transactions through a digitized procurement process. Third-party vendors are assessed using algorithms on their structures, financial histories, and compliance records. All this was complemented by delivery of employee training programs and beefing up of whistleblower protections.

Through the World Bank and other global organizations, Siemens channeled over $100 million into worldwide anti-corruption programs. The journey from crime to ethical leadership remains a model for corporate behavior, and Siemens' tools are widely deployed in both government and private sector offices. They have enabled Siemens to enjoy a strong competitive advantage in sensitive markets (Siemens, n.d.).

State capture, often hidden but a massive menace to sustainability, occurs when elite persons or businesses use legal but unethical practices to control state resources or decision-making. Well-known examples include the Gupta family's influence over resources in South Africa and, in Russia, the inversion of control where energy and mining businesses control the very regulatory policies which should govern them.

The Cost of Governance Failure

Vale S.A., based in Rio de Janeiro, is a global mining behemoth. In January 2019, weak regulatory oversight and corporate negligence combined to produce one of the worst disasters in environmental history. 272 people died; entire communities were destroyed.

A tailings dam at an iron mine in Brumadinho, Brazil, failed. Millions of cubic meters of toxic waste were released into a mudflow which contaminated rivers and destroyed the entire ecosystem of the region. Subsequent investigations revealed severe failings in environmental consideration, an absence of risk reporting for local communities, and an absence of effective regulatory oversight. Deficient in E, deficient in S, and hopeless in G.

The people who died were not the only victims. Survivors of the disaster, many of whom lost family members, report psychological and economic distress that is ongoing. Company executives were charged with homicide, the company was fined $7 billion, its stock price declined by over 25%, and major investment funds withdrew their support. There was evidence of inappropriate pressure on regulators to issue certifications and prioritization of profit over safety. Cutting ESG corners created immeasurable risk for the company and permanent social and environmental damage for the Brumadinho communities.

Metrics for governance

Governance outcomes are often the most difficult to measure and the most varied between different industries. The following are the main headings which assist with preparing assessments.

1. Board metrics – percentage of independent directors, representatives of minority groups, frequency of meetings, and attendance levels.

2. Executive compensation – alignment with performance, pay equity.
3. Ethics – reported violations, trainings completed.
4. Risk management – assessments completed, breaches discovered.
5. Transparency – alignment with reporting frameworks, reporting deadlines, and audits.
6. Anti-corruption – effectiveness of policies, incidents reported, and suppliers audited.
7. Data protection – breaches, audits, and compliance level reports.
8. Legal compliance – fines, penalties, and outcomes of audits.

The corporate path to sustainability

Sustainability expert Dr. Simon Zadek, writing in the Harvard Business Review in 2004, produced a seminal article which mapped out the typical path of businesses as they realize their corporate responsibilities. The article has stood the test of time and clarifies why companies adopt sustainability as a core value at different paces. The five evolutionary stages are as follows:

1. **Defensive.** Businesses deny responsibility and view sustainability concerns as a threat. They strategize to avoid liability or loss.
2. **Compliance.** Reactively, they take minimal steps to meet basic legal requirements.
3. **Managerial.** Sustainability becomes an operational issue but is still regarded as a separate function. At this stage, businesses may create a responsible department.
4. **Strategic.** The business realizes that sustainability leads to competitive advantage, aligned with long-term profitability and resilience. It becomes part of their business model, product design, and supply chain decision-making.
5. **Civil.** Leaders within the business become industry advocates, support stronger regulation, collaborate with external forces such as governments and NGOs, and look to transform the markets where they have influence.

It follows that there should be an economic business case for sustainability. And here it is.

The business case for sustainable strategy

There is always a trade-off between long-term sustainability and short-term economic gains. The Chief Executives Council, the leading community and platform for CEOs, presidents, founders, and related senior executives in the United States and globally, is outspoken on the need to balance instant gratification with long-term goals. The Council points out that "eco-friendly decisions … tend to produce the greatest long-term savings considering time and money" (Chief Executives Council, 2024).

Because it can be hard to justify increased expense today by talking about a better world tomorrow, some ESG strategies are exclusively focused on keeping regulators or investors happy. However, a holistic commitment to sustainability requires embedding environmental, social, and governance principles into a business's very core. Incorporating ESG principles, however, does not only satisfy moral principles and support sustainability goals. There is a solid financial case. Companies with deep ESG consciousness consistently reap benefits which contribute to outperformance of competitors. A strong body of academic evidence supports this claim.

- Focus on optimizing resources and waste reduction lowers costs. Unilever's Sustainable Living Plan saved the group over €1 billion by reducing water use and waste (Unilever, 2021).
- Sustainable brands command premium prices from consumers (Nielsen, 2015).
- Companies focused on sustainability reduce capital costs based on reduced risk and consequent favorable loan terms (Global Sustainable Investment Alliance, 2021; Kotsantonis, Pinney & Serafeim, 2016).
- ESG focus aids risk management, especially regulatory actions and consequent reputational loss (Eccles, Ioannou, & Serafeim, 2014).
- With ESG focus, shareholders receive higher returns based on sustained growth (Khan, Serafeim, & Yoon, 2016).
- Diversity initiatives, creating inclusive workspace cultures, improve productivity, and reduce staff churn (Deloitte, 2021).

Studying emerging market companies from 2016 to 2020, Boston Consulting Group demonstrated that companies in the top 20% of ESG scores outperformed those in the bottom 20% by 2.2% (Tansan et al. 2023).

MSCI, Inc., is a widely respected independent research company with nearly 6,000 employees worldwide. It maintains several indices which measure the performance of companies, including its *Emerging Market Index*. In 2021, MSCI reported that companies with high ESG performance outperformed the complete Emerging Markets Index by 54%.

Fortunately, there is rapid advancement in the technologies and practices that reduce damaging activities. They demand upfront costs and may produce slower returns, but the future belongs to businesses which take a long view of their responsibilities.

Sustainability principles add significant value to risk management. They reduce the risk of negative events, reputational damage, or government penalties. They reduce financial risks such as rising costs of non-renewable resources, operating losses, fines, and difficulty in securing or maintaining investor interest. Simply put, addressing vulnerabilities in a sustainable manner helps build business continuity and resilience.

IKEA

An outstanding example of a major corporation which has shifted wholly into a sustainability business model is IKEA. It launched a strategy in 2012 and has since updated it; it aims to be "climate-positive" by 2030. Its entire business strategy integrates sustainability across all aspects of its operations:

- It is committed to generating more renewable energy than it uses.
- It is committed to making all its products recyclable or reusable.
- It procures 98% of its wood and 100% of its cotton, from sustainable sources.
- It is committed to selling environmentally friendly products at low prices.

The test of IKEA's resilience came with the COVID-19 pandemic, and it passed with flying colors. While competitors faced severe supply chain disruptions and resource shortages, IKEA suffered less than most, enhanced its position as a thought leader in environmentally conscious retailing, and lowered its operating costs simultaneously with reducing its carbon footprint (IKEA, n.d.).

Because sustainability is both financially and strategically important, businesses need metrics and communication methods for ESG performance. Recognized reporting frameworks exist for precisely these purposes.

Global reporting frameworks

While it is easy to propound the idea of sustainability, putting principle into practice is complex. Sustainability as an aspirational toolset addresses "Why?" ESG takes us closer to "how?" Reporting frameworks have evolved to measure achievement in a standardized manner; internally, they empower identification of issues and target-setting; they then equip businesses to tell the world how they have met those targets. Reporting frameworks are not all the same; their diversity reflects the differing needs of those receiving information about performance.

The practical benefit of a solid framework is that it translates abstract ideas into actionable steps and achievements into measurable results. The principal frameworks in use today are the Global Reporting Initiative (GRI), Sustainability Accounting Standards Board (SASB), and Integrated Reporting (IR).

Global Reporting Initiative

The GRI sets out modular standards for comprehensive reporting of organizational impacts. Universal standards apply to all organizations and prescribe formats for general disclosures on governance, strategy, and ethics; sector standards are focused on unique topics for certain sectors, and topic-specific standards are set for specific areas such as energy, emissions, and diversity (Global Reporting Initiative, n.d.). The GRI addresses the concept of *double materiality*, integrating financial and impact materiality to move beyond mere financial disclosures.

Among the most important standards are the following:

- GRI 102 General Disclosures. Governance, strategy, and organizational profile.
- GRI 200 Series Economic Standards. Economic performance, anti-corruption, and procurement practices.
- GRI 300 Series Environmental Standards. Energy consumption, emissions, and waste.
- GRI 400 Series Social Standards. Labor practices, diversity, and community engagement.

Sustainability Accounting Standards Board

The SASB focuses on financially material sustainability topics that could affect financial performance and influence investment decisions, thus being more focused than GRI. The SASB standards, which are set up for 77 different industries in 11 sectors, aim at relevance for investors and other financial stakeholders. They change emphasis with the nature of the business. For example, in renewable energy businesses, the standards have more focus on emissions, while for clothing businesses they give more attention to labor conditions (Sustainability Accounting Standards Board, 2025).

Integrated Reporting

The Integrated Reporting (IR) framework aims to be holistic, embracing financial and non-financial information. Its focus is on value creation over time, connecting financial performance with ESG achievements. It employs a *six-capital model* which asks businesses to view and model their impact on financial, manufactured, intellectual, human, social/relationship, and natural capital. It stresses a theme which is common to all thought leaders in this space – the necessity of looking after all stakeholders in an enterprise, not just the shareholders.

Table 3.2 contrasts the key aspects of GRI, SASB, and IR.

While adherence to recognized schemes is deeply valuable to a business's brand, the benefits go far beyond product reputation. Today most governments offer financial incentives to companies that demonstrate sustainable practices. There is even legislation that mandates the devotion of percentages of profits to socially responsible activities, such as the *Companies Act* of India (Government of India, 2021).

Sustainability certification

The growing pressure from all stakeholders for businesses to demonstrate their commitment to sustainability creates a compelling case for measurability. It opens the door to certification and other schemes which allow businesses to signal compliance and social responsibility.

Table 3.2 Global reporting frameworks

	GRI	*SASB*	*IR*
Audience	All stakeholders	Investors	Executives & Boards of Directors
Alignment	Global sustainability frameworks	Financial reporting standards (e.g., IFRS)	Value creation
Focus	Comprehensive reporting	Specific industries	Integration of ESG and Financial reporting
Intention	Broad accountability	Financial materiality	Holistic decision-making
Purview	Global across all sectors	Issues specific to 77 industries	Large public corporations

Fairtrade[3] is cooperatively owned by more than two million farmers and bills itself as the most recognized and trusted sustainability label in the world. It focuses on sustainable agriculture and improving the lives of small producers. It is popular in sectors like bananas, coffee, and cocoa, and with its provision of minimum prices, it helps to smooth out income volatility. The *Rainforest Alliance*[4] also concentrates on sustainable land use and the treatment of workers, adding biodiversity and conservation to the mix. It has a broad reach, including forestry and tourism in addition to agriculture.

Sustainability planning

Business policies are formal, usually written, guidelines that specify how decisions are to be made and how everyone is to act within a business. Planning a new venture into, or within, an emerging market requires consideration of sustainability goals aimed at balancing economic growth with environmental stewardship and social responsibility.

Businesses must write their policies with practical application in mind, not in flowery terms which aspire to lofty ideals. They should give clear guidance as to expectations and how to satisfy them. They will determine accountability, and if well-crafted, they will allow for adaptation as challenges or opportunities emerge.

A business planning to integrate ESG into its business strategy for the first time is contemplating a large-scale change management project. Assistance may be drawn from one or more of the several well-known models for change management; we suggest it is very likely that Kotter's eight-step model (1996) will be a strong candidate.

Following the Kotter model, the following roadmap may assist in planning integration:

1. Identify the ESG issues which are relevant for the business.
2. Engage with key stakeholders and opinion leaders to gain support for integration.
3. Use frameworks to assess the most relevant issues, set goals, and establish KPIs.
4. Ensure alignment of ESG goals with strategic planning.
5. Write policies and plan initiatives.
6. Start pilot programs, learn from successes and failures, and communicate progress.
7. Closely watch progress and report successes, failures, and metrics.
8. Showcase success and emphasize the value of continuous improvement.

Conclusion: The future of sustainability

Sustainability is not an optional business strategy. In this chapter we showed why it matters: it is a fundamental driver for long-term profitability and success. We introduced ESG, made the business case, and explained the role of international institutions and reporting standards in the governance of expanding businesses. We outlined the strategic considerations necessary to build sustainability into corporate policy and the methods of measuring and reporting success.

Businesses of every size are increasingly strategizing to conform to sustainability expectations. At the grassroots level, local cultural and environmental constraints have primacy.

At the cutting edge of technology, renewable energy, digital platforms, and artificial intelligence (AI) are increasingly employed to advance sustainability goals. Ironically, the processing power to use AI is highly demanding, and there are questions about whether there is truly a net contribution to sustainability (Berreby, 2024).

Frugal innovation, the design process which underlies the circular economy concept, is making its mark on resource protection, while circular economy models are minimizing resource waste. These changes are scalable and benefit not only the businesses that employ them but also the communities they serve.

Sustainability in these dynamic markets is not just about managing corporate risks. It drives competitive advantage. Businesses that incorporate sustainability in their central strategies mitigate risk, drive innovation, and reinforce investor confidence. They hold the best cards to play in the future global economy.

Armed with these insights, we are primed to research and select emerging markets for business expansion. The next chapter identifies the key sources of data and knowledge, guides you through the evaluation process, and equips you with practical methods to find and evaluate market opportunities with confidence.

Notes

1 Why do we refer to "green" hydrogen when it is colorless? The hydrogen industry uses a color-coding system for hydrogen, which refers not to its nature but to its origin. There are nine colors in the scale, from white to black. Blue (produced from natural gas, with some CO_2 as a by-product) and gray (produced from methane or natural gas but without capturing any carbon) are the most important from a sustainability point of view. Gray is currently the most common production method; pink hydrogen is made using nuclear energy as the source of electrical energy, and a refinement named yellow describes green energy exclusively when the source of electricity is solar power (National Grid, 2023).

2 Although we have indicated that the CSR – Corporate Social Responsibility – concept has largely been superseded by ESG, social responsibility is still a useful concept to describe a general commitment to ethical behavior, sustainability, and the well-being of all stakeholders. It is enshrined in ISO26000, Guidance on Social Responsibility.

3 https://www.fairtrade.net/.

4 https://www.rainforest-alliance.org/.

References

Abdillah, H., et al. (2024, October 7). Understanding Jakarta's air quality. https://www.cleanaircatalyst.org/news/understanding-jakartas-air-quality

Abouleish, H. (2022, August 22). Interview by G. Jones. *Creating Emerging Markets Oral History Collection*, Baker Library Special Collections, Harvard Business School.

Africa50. (n.d.). Volobe Hydropower Plant. https://www.africa50.com/investing-for-growth/projects-investments/volobe-hydropower-plant/

Agence France-Presse. (2020, December 18). Brazil's Odebrecht changes name after years of scandals. https://www.voanews.com/a/americas_brazils-odebrecht-changes-name-after-years-scandals/6199737.html

Antikainen, M., & Valkokari, K. (2016). A framework for sustainable circular business model innovation. *Technology Innovation Management Review 6(7)*, 5–12. https://www.timreview.ca/article/1000

Baskaran, G., & Coste, S. (2024, January 31). Achieving universal energy access in Africa amid global decarbonization. https://www.csis.org/analysis/achieving-universal-energy-access-africa-amid-global-decarbonization

Berreby, D. (2024, February 6). *As use of A.I. soars, so does the energy and water it requires.* Yale Environment 360. https://e360.yale.edu/features/artificial-intelligence-climate-energy-emissions

Bocken, N. M. P., de Pauw, I., Bakker, C., & van der Grinten, B. (2016). Product design and business model strategies for a circular economy. *Journal of Industrial and Production Engineering, 33(5)*, 308–320. DOI: 10.1080/21681015.2016.1172124

Boulding, K. E. (1966). The economics of the coming spaceship Earth. In H. Jarrett (Ed.), *Environmental quality in a growing economy* (pp. 3–14). Johns Hopkins University Press.

Campbell, J. (2020, October 29). Why cobalt mining in the DRC needs urgent attention. *Council on Foreign Relations*. https://www.cfr.org/blog/why-cobalt-mining-drc-needs-urgent-attention

CDP. (n.d.). *Pascua-Lama Gold Mine*. CDP North America Inc. https://www.cdp.net/en/articles/water/pascua-lama-gold-mine

Chandaria, M. (2014, June 13). Interview by H. McGee. *Creating Emerging Markets Oral History Collection*. Baker Library Special Collections, Harvard Business School.

Chatterjee, R. (2023, November 22). The world's worst industrial disaster harmed people even before they were born. *NPR*. https://www.npr.org/sections/goatsandsoda/2023/06/17/1181244389/the-worlds-worst-industrial-disaster-harmed-people-even-before-they-were-born

Chief Executives Council. (2024, May 6). Balancing short-term gains with long-term sustainability. https://chiefexecutivescouncil.org/balancing-short-term-gains-with-long-term-sustainability/

Clean Clothes Campaign. (2023). Rana Plaza. https://cleanclothes.org/campaigns/past/rana-plaza

Commonshare Editorial Team. (2023, July 12). Canada investigates Nike for alleged use of forced Uyghur labor in China. https://news.commonshare.com/blog/canada-investigates-nike-for-alleged-use-of-forced-uyghur-labor-in-china

Conway, N. (2019, September 27). Sweatshops almost killed Nike in the 1990s, Now there are modern slavery laws. *RFL*. https://www.thefashionlaw.com/visibility-is-central-to-a-successful-supply-chain-heres-what-brands-need-to-know/

Deloitte. 2021 Diversity, equity, and inclusion (DEI) transparency report. https://www2.deloitte.com/content/dam/Deloitte/us/Documents/about-deloitte/dei-transparency-report.pdf

Dettoni, J. FDI recovery? (2024). *The devil is in the data details. The FDI Report 2024*. Financial Times.

Dollaride. (2024, June 10). The road to ethical EV sustainability. https://www.dollaride.com/blog/ethical-ev-sustainability-cobalt-mining

Dow Africa. (2024). Circular economy. https://africa.dow.com/en-us/science-and-sustainability/circular-economy.html

Dudeja, S. (2018, April 27). Interview by G. Jones. *Creating Emerging Markets Oral History Collection*. Baker Library Special Collections, Harvard Business School.

Eccles, R.G., Ioannou, I., & Serafeim, G. (2014). The impact of corporate sustainability on organizational processes and performance. *Management Science*, 60(11), 2381–2617. https://doi.org/10.1287/mnsc.2014.1984

Ecclissato, R. (n.d.). How to advance inclusion and tackle inequality across your value chain: Unilever's living wage initiative. https://www.sustainablebusinessnow.org/posts/unilevers-living-wage-initiative

Elkington, J. (1997). *Cannibals with forks: The triple bottom line of 21st century business*. Capstone Publishing.

Ellen MacArthur Foundation. (2013). *Towards the circular economy: Economic and business rationale for an accelerated transition*. Ellen MacArthur Foundation. https://www.ellenmacarthurfoundation.org/publications/towards-the-circular-economy-vol-1-an-economic-and-business-rationale-for-an-accelerated-transition

Equator Principles Association. (2020). The Equator Principles IV. https://equator-principles.com

Escovar, S. (2019, November 28). Interview by A. Lluch. *Creating Emerging Markets Oral History Collection*. Baker Library Special Collections, Harvard Business School.

Foreign Corrupt Practices Act, (n.d.), 15 U.S.C. §§ 78dd-1 to 78dd-8.

Froehlich, C. G., & Vieira, M. G. A. (2020). The role of Brazilian policies in promoting sustainable bioplastics from renewable resources. *Journal of Cleaner Production, 258*, 120658.

G, S. (2024, March 8). How Unilever is winning with sustainability: A case study in purpose-driven profit. https://www.linkedin.com/pulse/how-unilever-winning-sustainability-case-study-purpose-driven-g-msd6c/

Global Impact Investing Network. (2023). IRIS+ system: The generally accepted system for measuring, managing, and optimizing impact. https://iris.thegiin.org/

Global Living Wage Coalition. (n.d.). What is a living wage? https://www.globallivingwage.org/about/what-is-a-living-wage/

Global Reporting Initiative. (n.d.). The global standards for sustainability impacts. https://www.globalreporting.org/standards/

Global Sustainable Investment Alliance. (2021). Global Sustainable Investment Review 2020. https://www.gsi-alliance.org/wp-content/uploads/2021/08/GSIR-20201.pdf;

Gore, A. (2006). *An inconvenient truth: The planetary emergency of global warming and what we can do about it*. Rodale.

Government of India General Circular No. 14/2001. (2021, August 25). Frequently asked questions (FAQs) on Corporate Social Responsibility (CSR).

Grant, R., & Oteng-Ababio, M. (2019). E-Waste Circuit: Unregulated E-Waste Recycling and Environmental Health in Accra, Ghana. *Urban Geography*, 40(9), 1276–1296.

Grant, R. & Oteng-Ababio, M. (2021). Formalizing E-waste in Ghana: An emerging landscape of fragmentation and enduring barriers. https://www.researchgate.net/publication/349557037_Formalising_E-waste_in_Ghana_An_emerging_landscape_of_fragmentation_and_enduring_barriers

Hydrogen Council. (n.d.). There's no climate solution without clean hydrogen. *And there's no clean hydrogen without action*. https://hydrogencouncil.com/en/

Iberdrola (n.d.). Green hydrogen: an alternative that reduces emissions and cares for our planet. https://www.iberdrola.com/sustainability/green-hydrogen

IKEA. (n.d.) The IKEA Sustainability Strategy. https://www.ikea.com/us/en/this-is-ikea/climate-environment/the-ikea-sustainability-strategy-pubfea4c210/

IMARC Group. (2024). *E-waste management market: Global industry trends, share, size, growth, opportunity, and forecast 2024-2032*. IMARC Group. https://www.imarcgroup.com/e-waste-management-market

International Association for Impact Assessment. (2012). Respecting Indigenous peoples and traditional knowledge: Principles for impact assessment. https://www.iaia.org

International Energy Agency. (2023). CO2 emissions in 2023. *International Energy Agency*. https://iea.blob.core.windows.net/assets/33e2badc-b839-4c18-84ce-f6387b3c008f/CO2Emissionsin2023.pdf

International Labour Organization. (1989). Indigenous and tribal peoples convention (No. 169). https://www.ilo.org/global/topics/indigenous-tribal/WCMS_503321/lang--en/index.htm

International Labour Organization. (n.d.). ILO conventions and recommendations. Retrieved January 9, 2025, from https://www.ilo.org/dyn/normlex/en/

IQAir. (n.d.). Air quality in Jakarta. https://www.iqair.com/indonesia/jakarta

Jamasmie, C. (2024, January 31). Barrick to spend $136 million on failed Pascua-Lama project. https://www.mining.com/barrick-to-spend-136-million-in-failed-pascua-lama-project/

Khan, M., Serafeim, G., & Yoon, A. (2016). Corporate sustainability: First evidence on materiality. *The Accounting Review*, 91(6), 1697–1724. https://doi.org/10.2308/accr-51383

Kotsantonis, S., Pinney, C., & Serafeim, G. (2016). ESG integration in investment management: Myths and realities. *Journal of Applied Corporate Finance*, 28(2), 10–16.

Kotter, J. P. (1996). *Leading change*. Harvard Business Review Press.

Lidsky, O. (2023, March 14). Why integrity is an essential virtue for business leaders and entrepreneurs. https://www.forbes.com/councils/forbestechcouncil/2023/03/14/why-integrity-is-an-essential-virtue-for-business-leaders-and-entrepreneurs/

Mazumdar-Shaw, K. (2018, June 4). Interview by T. Khanna. *Creating Emerging Markets Oral History Collection*. Baker Library Special Collections, Harvard Business School.

Mthanti, T., & Ojah, K. (2017). Institutions and corporate governance in South Africa. In Ngwu, F.N., Osuji, O.I., & Stephen, F.H. (Eds.). *Corporate governance in developing and Emerging Markets*. 125, Taylor & Francis.

Mukherjee, T. (2021, September 20). The slow death of artistic freedom in India. *Future Tense*. https://slate.com/technology/2021/09/india-censorship-films-freedom-netflix-amazon.html

Murphy, D. (2018). *Hidden chains: Rights abuses and forced labor in Thailand's fishing industry*. Human Rights Watch.

National Grid. (2023, February 23). The hydrogen colour spectrum. https://www.nationalgrid.com/stories/energy-explained/hydrogen-colour-spectrum

Nestlé. (2014, April 30). First harvest for Colombian Nestlé Plan coffee farmers. https://www.nestle.com/media/news/colombian-nescafe-plan-coffee-farmers

Ngwu, F.N. (2017). Development of the Anglo-American Model of corporate governance in developing and Emerging Markets. In Ngwu, F.N., Osuji, O.I., & Stephen, F.H. (Eds.). *(2017) Corporate Governance in Developing and Emerging Markets*. Taylor & Francis.

Nicholls, J., Lawlor, E., Neitzert, E., & Goodspeed, T. (2012). *A guide to social return on investment (2nd* ed.*)*. The SROI Network. https://socialvalueuk.org/resources/a-guide-to-social-return-on-investment-2012/

Nielsen. (2015, October 12). The sustainability imperative. https://nielseniq.com/global/en/insights/analysis/2015/the-sustainability-imperative-2/

Nooyi, I. (2024). *My life in full*. Little, Brown.

Nyanga, J., & Osinbajo, Y. (2024, September 10). Bess key to Africa controlling its energy destiny. *FDI Insights*. https://www.fdiintelligence.com/content/opinion/opinion-bess-key-to-africa-controlling-its-energy-destiny-84068

Osuji, O.K., Ngwu, F.N., & Stephen, F.H. Corporate governance in developing and Emerging Markets. In Ngwu, F.N., Osuji, O.I., & Stephen, F.H. (Eds.). (2017) *Corporate governance in developing and emerging markets*. Taylor & Francis.

Page, T. (2024, September 4). Hydrogen-powered skyscraper set for Egypt's new capital. https://www.cnn.com/style/cairo-forbes-international-tower-hydrogen-nac-spc/index.html

Payton, B. (2024, October 28). Madagascar strives for renewables revolution. *fDi Intelligence*. https://www.fdiintelligence.com/content/feature/madagascar-strives-for-renewables-revolution-84144

PepsiCo. (2023, December 4). Fundación PepsiCo y su compromiso con las comunidades de México. https://responsabilidadsocial.net/fundacion-PepsiCo-y-su-compromiso-con-las-comunidades-de-mexico/

PTI. (2022, March 12). NIVEA India Ranked as India's No. 1 Trusted Brand in the Skin Care Category in 2022 by TRA. *The Times of India*. https://timesofindia.indiatimes.com/nivea-india-ranked-as-indias-no-1-trusted-brand-in-the-skin-care-category-in-2022-by-tra/articleshow/90164972.cms

Rahim, M.M., & Kuruppu, S. (2017). Corporate governance in India: The potential for Ghandism. In Ngwu, F.N., Osuji, O.I., & Stephen, F.H. (Eds.). (2017, pp.92–93). *Corporate governance in developing and Emerging Markets*. Taylor & Francis.

Rao, Y. (2023, August 14). IKEA Case: One company's fight to end child labor. *Markkula Center for Applied Ethics*. https://www.scu.edu/ethics/focus-areas/business-ethics/resources/ikea-case-one-companys-fight-to-end-child-labor/

Renou, R., Carraz, R., and Burger-Helmchen, T. (2023). Japan's corporate governance transformation: Convergence or reconfiguration? *Adm. Sci.* 2023, 13(6), 141.

Riedel, S. (2025, January 15). 12 Companies that caved to the right's anti-woke agenda and rolled back DEI programs. https://www.them.us/story/dei-rollbacks-which-companies

Siemens. (n.d.). Collective Action. https://www.siemens.com/global/en/company/about/compliance/collective-action.html

Singh, N. (2020, June 30). Nivea to review its products, marketing amid movement against racism. *The Times of India.* https://timesofindia.indiatimes.com/business/india-business/nivea-to-review-its-products-marketing-amid-movement-against-racism/articleshow/76699097.cms

Sonnemaker, T. (2020, December 31). Apple knew a supplier was using child labor but took 3 years to fully cut ties, despite the company's promises to hold itself to the 'highest standards,' report says. *Business Insider.* https://www.businessinsider.com/apple-knowingly-used-child-labor-supplier-3-years-cut-costs-2020-12

Sustainability Accounting Standards Board. (2025). SASB standards. https://www.sasb.org

Tangalakis-Lipert, K. (2024). X closes office in Brazil amid Elon Musk's censorship feud with Supreme Court judge Alexandre de Moraes. https://www.msn.com/en-us/money/other/x--closes-office-in-brazil-amid-elon-musks-censorship-feud-with-supreme-court-judge-alexandre-de-moraes/ar-AA1oZ0K9

Tansan, B., et al. (2023, March 14). The sustainability imperative in emerging markets. https://www.bcg.com/publications/2023/the-importance-of-sustainability-in-business

Tesco plc. (2016). *Modern slavery statement.* Tesco plc.

The Earthshot Prize. (2024). 2024 Finalist d.light. https://earthshotprize.org/winners-finalists/d-light/

Transparency International. (2023). Corruption Perceptions Index, 2023. https://www.transparency.org/en/cpi/2023

Unilever. (2021, March). Unilever Sustainable Living Plan 2010 to 2020. *Summary of 10 years progress.* https://www.unilever.com/files/92ui5egz/production/16cb778e4d31b81509dc5937001559f1f5c863ab.pdf

United Nations. (n.d.). Peace, dignity and equality on a healthy planet. https://www.un.org/en/about-us/universal-declaration-of-human-rights

United Nations Development Programme. (2015). The SDGs in action. https://www.undp.org/sustainable-development-goals

United Nations Development Programme. (n.d.). *Gender equality seal for public and private enterprises.* UNDP. https://www.undp.org/gender-equality-seal

United Nations Global Compact. (2013). A business reference guide: United Nations Declaration on the Rights of Indigenous Peoples. https://www.unglobalcompact.org/library/3061

United Nations Global Compact. (n.d.) The Ten Principles of the UN Global Compact. https://unglobalcompact.org/what-is-gc/mission/principles

United Nations Sustainable Development Group. (2025, January 27). *Decoding Africa's energy journey: Three key numbers.* United Nations. https://unsdg.un.org/latest/stories/decoding-africa%E2%80%99s-energy-journey-three-key-numbers

United States Department of Justice. (2010, March 1). BAE Systems PLC pleads guilty and ordered to pay $400 million criminal fine.

United States Environmental Protection Agency. (n.d.). Pollution Prevention (P2). https://www.epa.gov/p2

Venditti, B. (2024, May 31). Visualizing cobalt production by country in 2023. *Visual Capitalist.*

Von Appen, S. (2008, May 28). Interview by A. Lluch. *Creating Emerging Markets Oral History Collection.* Baker Library Special Collections, Harvard Business School.

Watts, J. (2017, June 1). Operation Car Wash: Is this the biggest corruption scandal in history? *The Guardian*. https://www.theguardian.com/world/2017/jun/01/brazil-operation-car-wash-is-this-the-biggest-corruption-scandal-in-history

World Commission on Environment and Development. (1987). *Our common future*. Oxford University Press.

Zadek, S. (2004). The path to corporate responsibility. *Harvard Business Review*, *82*(12), 125–132.

CHAPTER 4

Emerging market macroeconomics and analysis

Learning outcomes

After studying this chapter, you will be able to do the following:

1. Critically evaluate the role of thorough research as a necessary first step in emerging market entry.
2. Find, assess, synthesize, interpret, and evaluate reliable data sources for secondary research.
3. Analyze macroeconomic data to derive market indicators.
4. Find information to support evaluation of the political, legal, and regulatory environment of a potential target market.
5. Design a research plan to arrive at preliminary market selections for an expanding business.

Introduction: Why conduct research?

How should businesses conduct the analyses that will underpin future success? What exactly do they need to know?

It would be naïve to start from the proposition "We will now expand into growth markets," then choose countries from a shopping list. Many factors, ideally logical but often emotional, drive decisions about expansion. We should not overlook the reality

DOI: 10.4324/9781003638490-4

that smaller businesses often choose among various markets simply because they seem sensible. Consider a business in the southern United States which has saturated demand in neighbors Canada and Mexico. Influenced by geographical proximity and language, it is likely to look directly south, and when deciding which Latin American nations to target first, it may well settle on those with characteristics which closely match those of its existing territories.

Businesses which are not global behemoths may be beguiled by the apparent ease of narrowing down the list of countries to just a handful of candidates. They often select a product, think about language, distance, transportation, and culture, and non-contenders based on these criteria. Only a few markets will typically remain. These are valid considerations but should not override the compelling need to base decisions on data-driven research.

A common early reaction is to see widespread poverty as a showstopper. Conscientious investment in an opportunity to serve extremely poor consumers can still produce both financial and social rewards. Professor C.K. Prahalad, the groundbreaking thought leader on this subject, demonstrated convincingly in 2004 that very low-income populations can benefit from innovative entrepreneurship and provide substantial profits as a by-product. Prof. Prahalad coined the phrase *bottom of the pyramid* (BoP) to describe the billions of people who survive on incomes under $2.50 per day. Collectively, their demand is still substantial; businesses which cater to their needs by thinking carefully about packaging, sizes, pricing, and distribution can improve their lives immeasurably.

We are already aware of the major challenges that confront the aspiring emerging market investor. Venturing into a new market must be grounded on solid information and analysis. We cannot overstate the value of fully understanding, on every level, what may lie ahead if an expansion is attempted. Proceeding without thorough analysis invites failure, financial loss, and missed opportunity. Thorough research reduces the risks of overestimating the market or underestimating the challenges. This chapter will provide a roadmap for remote assessment and identify the key techniques and sources of information.

Boyner Holding

Cem Boyner, chairman and former CEO of Boyner Holding, readily admits that research shortcomings led to the failure of his company's expansions into Russia and Egypt. After enjoying significant success in Türkiye, based on customer-centric innovation, in the early 2000s the company assumed that entry into Russia would be simple because it was just another emerging market. It misread product requirements, consumer demand, and infrastructure issues, even locating its store in an inaccessible place.

In Egypt, Boyner opened a luxury department store shortly before the political disruptions and changes of regime that began with a revolution in 2011. Tourist and local demand for luxury products evaporated, destroying the company's market position and precipitating a second financially damaging withdrawal (Boyner, 2014).

Desk-based research: Sources

Mathematician Clive Humby's 2006 observation that "data is the new oil" is often repeated to the point of cliché but remains relevant: while data are abundant, they require discovery, refinement, and treatment before they become valuable (Arthur, 2013). Information may be in the public domain, but despite the explosive growth of the internet, it remains hidden behind layers of complexity and obscurity.

Despite its name, *secondary research* is conducted first. Secondary, because it is the collection and consideration of data published by someone else. With internet access, you can do this work remotely.

The goal is to gather foundational data and insights and then create a broad understanding of potential markets: to identify macroeconomic data and trends, measure size, and assess competition. This enables a business to identify target markets which align with its strategic direction and rule out those that don't.

Current macroeconomic data are the easiest to find; trends should be extracted and predictions of the future reviewed. The four traditional levels of analytics – descriptive, diagnostic, predictive, and prescriptive – are useful headings to organize results of the work. Broadly, these levels address what has happened in the past, why, what is likely to happen next, and what the business should do in light of its knowledge.

Understanding trends, risks, and opportunities at this level enables the first round of informed decisions which rely on well-founded analysis, not surface-level indicators. Fortunately, advancements in AI-powered analytics are transforming some aspects of the process. Today businesses can extract insights from vast troves of data and uncover trends which humans might overlook.

After assembling as much relevant information as possible, it is necessary to engage in critical thinking, reviewing all data with a skeptical eye. Consider whether any political, commercial, or methodological biases may affect the conclusions. Glean all the insight you can from the publicly available information and exploit private resources for added depth.

A simple internet search will produce a wealth of data. *Government and international body publications* such as census data and statistical bureau reports are readily available. Consider both locally and internationally produced reports. Take a skeptical approach, especially when considering data that may have been manipulated for political purposes. For example, China has often been suspected of misreporting GDP growth rates to meet political goals, resulting in discrepancies between official rates and constituent data which can be independently verified (Zhang, 2020).

U.S. Government

The Central Intelligence Agency's *World Factbook*, published online and containing statistical information about every country in the world, is an excellent resource (Central Intelligence Agency, n.d.). It provides country profiles, demographics, and infrastructure data.

The U.S. Department of State publishes annual *Investment Climate Statements* for several countries; they contain a useful summary of quantitative and qualitative data (U.S. Department of State, 2024). The statements review investment conditions, political risks, regulatory politics, business transparency, and investment barriers.

Another strong governmental resource is the website of the International Trade Administration.[1] The ITA's stated and only purpose is to help American businesses succeed in global endeavors. It publishes a wealth of information about foreign markets. A search for almost any country in the world from the home page will reveal an extensive list of articles and resources for business analysis. They cover trade and export data, market trends, and regulatory requirements. There is a strong focus on American businesses looking outward.

Local government

National statistical agencies typically produce large volumes of data, including census and labor force surveys. The researcher can draw conclusions from these data regarding population growth and composition, demographic analysis, and consumer spending.

Local trade associations and chambers of commerce, where they exist, are great sources of information about specific industries, financial incentives, and legal challenges.

International organizations

The Organization for International Co-operation and Development (OECD) publishes valuable studies on policy, economics, tax, regulation, and macroeconomic trends.[2]

The International Monetary Fund (IMF) website contains reports on economic outlooks, stability measures, currencies, exchange rates, and debt sustainability.[3]

The United Nations World Investment Report contains valuable data on foreign direct investment flows, investment policies, and insights relating to cross-border trade.[4]

International businesses

Market research and *statistical reports* emanate from a host of reputable companies and other organizations. German company Statista produces a vast database of historical, current, and predicted information for many fields of endeavor. Global market research companies such as Nielsen,[5] Gartner,[6] and Ipsos[7] publish a wide range of industry reports, from which valuable insights can be gleaned into specific markets, trends, and competition. Business consultants like McKinsey[8] and Boston Consulting Group[9] also generously publish many reports on trends, sector growth, and consumer preferences; management insights are a bonus.

Local advertising and research companies often publish detailed market-specific data, insights, and advice for public education. Examples are RedSeer Strategy Consultants in India,[10] Nielsen Admosphere in the Czech Republic,[11] and Kantar TNS in South Africa.[12] At a later stage, such agencies become a valuable sounding board for ideas and initiatives and can help guard against cultural errors while honing locally relevant messaging.

Active monitoring of *newspapers and trade journals* supports complete currency. While they are not as authoritative as refereed academic papers, they provide insights into historical and current events in a geographical or product area. Online versions have the advantage of making the latest information available in a matter of hours or even minutes. At the planning stage of any new venture, automated daily searches on

Google or another search engine should be set up to alert the planners of any new developments that might affect their initiative.

Academic research

Academic books and articles are plentiful and have the advantage that if published in a refereed journal, an individual scholar has less opportunity to assemble misleading or incorrect data for a political purpose. Local academic institutions themselves may be worthy sources of information or even business partners; their geographical situation in the market may equip them to provide deep insights on entry barriers, regulation, and local cultures. Microsoft sets a global standard in this respect, having forged partnerships with universities all around the world. In India, for example, it leverages its relationship with universities to understand needs, usage, and affordability issues for its software sales models.

Evaluating macroeconomic indicators

Macroeconomic data provide a high-level view of a market's potential, economy, and long-term prospects. The past is informative; the future is of even more interest.

GDP growth rates

GDP growth rates are not only a major factor in determining emerging market status but also an important indicator of the probability of market growth for a product or service. Securing relevant data is a simple process. To illustrate, imagine that a business is considering entry into Bangladesh.

An online search for "Bangladesh GDP growth" will provide instant access to the latest statistics, predictions, and several interesting charts and comparisons. The browser will probably produce a headline message with the latest available annual rate, followed by links to several organizations that provide historical and predicted data. Several reputable forecasters compete for attention. It is advisable to compare their conclusions and draw your own.

Bangladesh

The World Bank and Macrotrends provide reliable historical data, showing sustained growth rates above 5%. Statista provides a projected growth rate of 6.6% for 2025, then 6.5%–7.7% for the next four years (Statista, 2024). The Asian Development Bank is slightly more cautious, predicting 6.1% for 2024 and 6.6% for 2025 (Asian Development Bank, n.d.). Both predictions, however, indicate confidence that GDP growth above the global average is likely to continue for several years.

Market size and potential

At this stage, the high-level macroeconomic analysis includes summary data on population, demographic composition, and infrastructure. However, the detailed analysis of these properly belongs to consumer and supply chain analyses, which are addressed in later chapters.

Market readiness and business climate

Forward-looking governments in emerging markets *want* entrepreneurship, whether native-born or imported. As a result, they are keen to create conditions which encourage international entrepreneurs to choose their country. A recently published study which used advanced analytics to measure relationships between business creation and critical factors strongly supports the position that internet connectivity and infrastructure, availability of digital skills, and rapid response to technological development are the modern keys to attracting new investment. The creation of innovation hubs is central to the effort of filling development gaps; technological development drives the development of industrial efficiency (Biancone et al., 2022).

However, despite the hopes and desires of politicians, an expanding business must understand whether a target market is truly ready for its arrival.

The World Bank's *Business Ready* ("B-READY") report may be a valuable resource, though it presently covers only 50 countries, of which nine are emerging markets. The 2024 edition was released late in the year, after a pause of five years in its production. It is a valuable source of analysis on three topics: regulatory framework, public services, and operational efficiency. Ten topic scores are organized beneath these headings:

1. Business entry
2. Business location
3. Utilities
4. Labor market regulations
5. Financial services
6. International trade
7. Taxation
8. Dispute resolution
9. Competition
10. Insolvency frameworks.

The work combines data gathered from thousands of experts and businesses operating in each economy. The bank plans to increase the number of economies covered in future years; this will be a resource which grows in value.

The Global Entrepreneurship Monitor, GEM, provides valuable research every year on the state of entrepreneurship in 115 economies. From this, we can gain insights which are critical in assessing new propositions, including market gaps and the overall business environment. There is a direct relationship between entrepreneurial activity and the opportunities and difficulties of expanding into a specific market.

Figure 4.1 shows GEM's highly instructive 2023 spider chart for Brazil (Global Entrepreneurship Monitor, 2023). It clearly contrasts the readiness of the private sector with the unreadiness of public authorities; it creates a picture of the private and public environment in which a new venture might operate. A rating of one is "highly insufficient," while five is "highly sufficient."

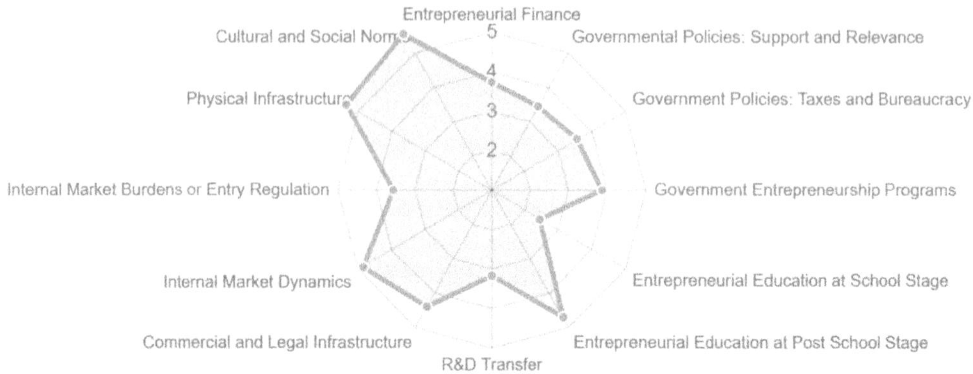

Figure 4.1 Spider chart

Each country chart provides a snapshot of the market situation. We can see from this chart that in Brazil we could expect strong entrepreneurial networks but weak government support, indicating potential difficulties with compliance requirements. The absence of skewness in a chart shows a supportive environment, while strong skewness points to risks.

The categories in the chart can be matched to factors critical for a business model, as a perfect score on all counts is rare. A highly technical business would pay more attention to infrastructure, technology, and education. If funding is needed, availability is important; if government support is essential, public policy will be a strong factor. Having identified priority categories, comparisons between countries become possible based on relative scores in those areas.

Beyond economic data, businesses must also consider the potential impact of regulatory environments on their planned operations.

Political and regulatory environment

Considering the political and regulatory environment of any country selected for potential expansion usually involves retaining trustworthy, competent professionals (lawyers and accountants) to ensure that there are no surprises. Examples include unexpected new taxes, compliance hurdles, or political risks. Local professionals are in the best position to assess future possibilities and will advise on the laws and regulations, existing or planned, which apply to a product or service.

When entering highly regulated markets, foreign businesses typically face three challenges: regulatory uncertainty, ownership and investment barriers, and sector-specific regulations.

Regulatory uncertainty and policy shifts are extraordinarily difficult to manage. Authorities in emerging markets are notorious for frequent changes of tax laws and investment incentives, often with a protectionist intent. Vodafone's headaches in India are a prime example, where the government even attempted to change tax rules retroactively.

Vodafone in India

British telecom operator Vodafone entered the Indian marketplace in 2007 by acquiring a controlling interest in Hutchison Essar. It then fell into a ten-year dispute with national tax authorities, which demanded over $2 billion in taxes based on a retrospective statute. Vodafone invoked the protection of a bilateral treaty with the Netherlands, compelling arbitration which Vodafone won. Increasing complexity and government interference limited Vodafone's scaling, which it addressed by a strategic merger with local giant Idea Cellular.

The Vodafone case highlights the importance of understanding tax policy and the usefulness of international tax treaties and their role in dispute resolution. It demonstrates the importance of contingency planning for regulatory changes.

Tesla's expansion into China demonstrates an approach to foreign ownership and investment barriers. China has strict rules; it is noteworthy that all other foreign car manufacturers have entered joint ventures with Chinese companies to gain permission to operate there. Tesla, amidst a trade war between the United States and China, convinced the government to allow it to operate a wholly owned vehicle factory in Shanghai – the only one in the country (Crider, 2020).

Saudi Arabia's new Investment Law of 2024 illustrates reforms being implemented by a country looking for external investment. The fundamental principles are non-discrimination and fair competition (Ministry of Investment, 2024), messaging that foreign investors will receive treatment on the same footing as locals. Saudi Arabia is seeking to boost progress toward its $100 billion foreign direct investment target. The country now allows 100% foreign ownership of domestic corporations and has a bankruptcy regime which conforms to international standards (Myles, 2024).

Sector-specific regulation is a further specialized area requiring detailed attention. Tesla's experience with China's strong data protection rules is instructive. Tesla faced strong regulation with respect to data collected and used, especially by self-driving cars (Zhang, 2024), in addition to firm vehicle safety rules with rigorous testing procedures. To comply with these laws, Tesla engineered local adaptations of vehicle design and manufacturing processes (Nicholas, 2021).

Sustainability considerations require special attention. The World Bank publishes a set of useful tools, including its *Climate Risk Country Profiles*, on the Climate Change Knowledge portal.[13] They evaluate environmental vulnerability, renewable energy policies, and human rights performance. Evaluating a target country's sustainability status helps researchers to identify risks, address investor expectations, and look for opportunities for responsible growth.

Many governments in emerging markets incentivize green investment, making environmental sustainability an increasingly important factor in target selection. Sustainable businesses may earn carbon credits, enjoy lower tax rates, and receive subsidies. India's Production-Linked Incentive (PLI) scheme encourages domestic production of solar energy components (Raj, 2024).

Consumers, too, particularly if they are young and urban, are increasingly interested in eco-friendly products and brands. IKEA's engagement in India is an outstanding example of a large multinational improving its market share by leveraging environmentally friendly policies – building solar-powered stores, sourcing locally, and eliminating plastic packaging (Wentworth, 2018).

Businesses can address political and regulatory risks through appropriate strategic responses. Strong relationships with local stakeholders provide a flow of information; legal protections are sometimes available from bilaterial investment treaties or similar agreements.

Conclusion

This chapter outlined the role of desk-based research in selecting and understanding potential target markets. We provided lists of significant sources of information and intelligence which might be used.

The sources which we described above will provide a comprehensive historical and predictive dataset. It is not enough, however, to simply identify a growing market. The fit of a product or service will be a critical factor underlying possible success: the focus sharpens, to question the existence and value of potential customers. Despite the economics, do the people in a target country constitute a viable market? Gaining deeper knowledge of those consumers is the focus of the next chapter.

Notes

1 https://www.trade.gov/
2 https://www.oecd.org/en/publications.html
3 https://www.imf.org/en/Countries
4 https://unctad.org/topic/investment/world-investment-report
5 https://www.nielsen.com
6 https://www.gartner.com/en
7 https://www.ipsos.com/en-us
8 https://www.mckinsey.com/featured-insights
9 https://www.bcg.com/publications
10 https://redseer.com/
11 https://www.nielsen-admosphere.cz/
12 https://www.kantar.com/locations/south-africa#_=
13 https://climateknowledgeportal.worldbank.org/country-profiles

References

Arthur, C. (2013, August 23). Tech giants may be huge, but nothing matches big data. *The Guardian*. https://www.theguardian.com/technology/2013/aug/23/tech-giants-data

Asian Development Bank. (n.d.). *Bangladesh: Economy*. Asian Development Bank. https://www.adb.org/where-we-work/bangladesh/economy

Biancone, P., Calandra, D., Lanzalonga, F., & Sadraei, R. (2022). Emerging markets and multiple sectors for entrepreneurship. In Jafari-Sadeghi, V., & Dana, L.-P. (Eds.), *International entrepreneurship in emerging markets: Context, behaviours, and successful entry* (pp. 7–28). Taylor & Francis.

Boyner, C.. (2014, September 16). Interview by F. Oberholzer-Gee. *Creating Emerging Markets Oral History Collection*. Baker Library Special Collections, Harvard Business School.

Central Intelligence Agency. (n.d.). *The World Factbook*. U.S. Government. https://www.cia.gov/the-world-factbook/

Crider, J. (2020, September 27). Tesla's 100% American owned factory In China is a big deal. *CleanTechnica*. https://cleantechnica.com/2020/09/27/teslas-100-american-owned-factory-in-china-is-a-big-deal-heres-why/

Global Entrepreneurship Monitor. (2023). Entrepreneurial framework conditions. https://www.gemconsortium.org/economy-profiles/brazil-2

Ministry of Investment. (2024). *Executive summary profile for Updated Investment law 1446H-2024G*. Ministry of Investment.

Myles, D. (2024, September 12). Saudi's new Investment Law promises FDI level playing field. https://www.fdiintelligence.com/content/news/saudis-new-investment-law-promises-fdi-level-playing-field-84079

Nicholas, K. (2021, June 28). In latest blow to Tesla, China orders safety fix to all its cars. https://www.aljazeera.com/economy/2021/6/28/in-latest-blow-to-tesla-china-orders-safety-fix-to-all-its-cars

Raj, P. (2024, April 16). PLI scheme. *All about Production Linked Incentive*. https://www.clearias.com/pli-scheme/

Statista. (2024). Gross domestic product (GDP) growth rate in Bangladesh 2029. Statista. Retrieved March 7, 2025, from https://www.statista.com/statistics/438214/gross-domestic-product-gdp-growth-rate-in-bangladesh/

U.S. Department of State. (2024). *2024 investment climate statements*. U.S. Government. https://www.state.gov/reports/2024-investment-climate-statements

Wentworth, A. (2018, August 16). IKEA's first store in India will run on solar power. https://www.climateaction.org/news/ikeas-first-store-in-india-will-run-on-solar-power

Zhang, F. (2020, February 11). Study suggests that local Chinese officials manipulate GDP. *Yale Insights*. https://insights.som.yale.edu/insights.study-suggests-that-local-chinese-officials-manipulate-gdp

Zhang, M. (2024, May 9). Tesla clears hurdles in China's electric vehicle market. *China Daily*. https://www.chinadaily.com.cn/a/202405/09/WS663bf65aa31082fc043c602f.html

CHAPTER 5

Emerging market consumers

> **Learning outcomes**
>
> After studying this chapter, you will be able to do the following:
>
> 1. Analyze the role of cultural factors in market selection.
> 2. Critically assess the use of market segmentation to refine business strategies.
> 3. Use case studies of market successes and failures to extract key insights for strategic decision-making.
> 4. Apply knowledge of pricing policies and payment preferences to optimize product and service sales in emerging markets.

Introduction

In Chapter 4, we discussed how to create and execute a high-level economic and market research plan to identify potential targets for expansion. That, we said, can be accomplished remotely. Next, to prepare final recommendations, we need to build a detailed understanding of the consumers in each target market. We want to answer questions about the size and potential of the opportunity, the fit for a product or service, and the challenges that exist due to the characteristics of potential consumers. Who are they? How do their behaviors and cultures define the success of a product or service? What research methods will uncover those insights?

Digital research

Artificial intelligence (AI) and big data analytical tools have profoundly increased the value of desk-based research. *Social media sentiment analysis* is among many powerful

DOI: 10.4324/9781003638490-5

tools that have emerged since the millennium. It enables manufacturers and distributors to understand how their brands, competitors, and industries are perceived in real time. You may consider using Brandwatch,[1] Hootsuite,[2] Meltwater,[3] or Talkwalker[4] for this purpose. Webscrapers and aggregation applications such as Google Trends and SEMrush[5] analyze consumer interest based on search behavior and online demand. In addition, powerful AI-enhanced mechanisms provided by IBM Watson Discovery[6] and Tableau[7] are increasingly able to compile and process vast amounts of unstructured data, extracting analytical results and insights that were unachievable only a few years ago. Used together, these tools make a significant contribution to understanding and mitigating the VUCA risks elaborated in Chapter 2. Watson deploys AI to process large amounts of data, clarifying ambiguities, identifying patterns and trends, and predicting possible outcomes. Tableau has powerful abilities to translate raw data into visualizations that help decision-makers understand complex relationships and changes. Armed with clearer insights, decision-makers can act with more confidence.

Desk-based research and big data analytics, as we discussed in the previous chapter, provide a partial foundation for analysis of proposed new markets. But there will remain gaps in understanding consumer habits, preferences, and behaviors.

Primary digital research, using electronic media to gather data from potential customers, is always biased against non-digital consumers (who may be the majority in an emerging market) and toward urban residents. In emerging markets, there is a risk that digital research captures only input from the privileged few – members of the informal economy who are unbanked and unconnected can make up more than half the population and be a significant potential consumer pool.

This is where primary research is essential. Direct interaction will fill in the gaps and show true consumer behavior derived from real-world observation.

Consumer analysis

Expansion from a developed market into an emerging market involves a wealth disparity between investor and investee. The former typically has significant capital, technology, and international connections. The latter is usually constrained with respect to all three. The imbalance plays into the very nature of the relationship, often affecting bargaining power, risk allocation, and benefit distribution.

Dr. Reuel Khoza, chairman of Dzana Investments, highlights that some businesses expanding within Africa have unintentionally exhibited a condescending attitude. This has particularly been the case with companies led by white C-level executives. Such an attitude creates a barrier to relationship-building and can undermine success. Dr. Khoza wisely suggests that investors should regard local partners in target emerging markets as hosts, not subordinates, to avoid alienation (Khoza, 2023).

This is just one aspect of cultural sensitivity, which is a key element of a successful market strategy. It must include deep cultural understanding: economic viability alone will not drive consumer interest. Having identified *where* opportunity exists, cultural insight determines product design, pricing strategy, marketing messaging, and payment system selection. We will next consider the role of consumer segmentation in market planning and see that cultural understanding is an essential ingredient.

Consumer segmentation

In emerging markets, segmentation involves dividing a consumer population which is rapidly expanding and evolving into distinct groups. Marketers must deal with issues that are not present in advanced economies – rapid social change, underground economies, widening income disparities, and an exaggerated digital divide. The most important characteristics are typically income, urban or rural location, purchasing behavior, and religious/cultural considerations. Cultural and societal pressures influence purchasing behavior in ways which are different from developed markets (Gupta, 2014).

If marketers do not uncover segments, they are likely to miss opportunities and may promote products which appear to appeal to many consumers but in fact appeal to few. Some goods are susceptible to customization for every individual consumer (cars and footwear); others are mass produced for large market segments.

Kotler and Keller's *Marketing Management*, now in its 16th edition (2022), is the standard, most trusted treatise on segmentation. The authors point out several ways to segment a market; no one method will necessarily be used by all sellers in the same market. Modern marketing analysis emphasizes the critical importance of going beyond demographic segmentation, to include behavioral and psychographic measurements. However, it is critical to adapt developed-world models to the realities of emerging markets, as Prof. Chattopadhyay's team emphasizes:

> [W]hich customers to serve – in which countries – is the most fundamental strategic decision that an expanding EMNC needs to make, as all other business decisions are contingent on this ... *Choose Segments First, Then Countries*
>
> *(Chattopadhyay et al., 2012, p. 27)*

The authors point out that many companies have not done this, and they then make the valuable observation that

> [w]hen using country characteristics as a proxy for segment attractiveness, countries that may appear unattractive (or attractive) may actually be very attractive (or unattractive) if one were to consider the attractiveness of the target segment directly.

Segments are not static. Especially in emerging markets, volatility can lead to rapid change. Large, unforeseen economic or political shifts demand agility in re-segmenting. An entire segment can vanish almost overnight.

Events in Argentina over the last 35 years dramatically demonstrate continual shifts in segmentation. Prior to the millennium, an expanding middle class was segmented using aspirational consumption, focused on income and prosperity. Then the economy collapsed. The peso dropped in value by more than half, unemployment rates soared, and poverty increased exponentially. Consumers simply had no money to spend. Segmentation overnight shifted to economic groups with low to no income, low-cost products, and smaller packages. After 2006, a modest recovery led to the emergence of a new middle class, but inflation and new currency crises made consumers increasingly cautious. Marketers had to deal with a decline in brand loyalty, the growth of informal markets, and a widening gap in digital inclusion.

It is hard to imagine a more dramatic change than one where more than half the population moves from looking for ways to enjoy their wealth to looking for ways to save money. It was essential to re-tool even geographic segmentation as formerly wealthy city dwellers increasingly moved to lower-cost areas.

Segmentation requires six characteristics to be useful (Brookmark, n.d.). The segments must be:

1. **Identifiable.** The segments must clearly identify customers and their characteristics. These will include their interests and buying habits, which influence which media will reach them. As traditional customer relationship management (CRM) systems are rare in emerging markets, businesses may rely on proxies such as mobile phone usage to identify segments. Early in 2024, Pizza Hut launched a new brand in Indonesia, Ristorante, specifically aimed at two segments: young families and Gen Z/millennials. Business projections suggested that a combination of premium menu, adaptations to local tastes, and discounts would appeal specifically to these demographics (Staff Reporter, APAC, 2024). It is too soon after the launch to find any meaningful, publicly accessible data on the success of this venture.
2. **Substantial.** The segments must be large enough that marketing is worthwhile. Size, however, is relative to the product. The small gulf country of Qatar has one of the highest percentages of high-net-worth residents in the world among a population of around three million. Bentley cars, with a starting price of close to one million ryals, around US$270,000, have annual sales only in the hundreds. Qatar's population of 36,000 millionaires comprises the segment that might buy a Bentley in any given year – but the segment is still substantial enough to be worth marketing to, because the product is high value and highly profitable.

   A motorcycle producer, on the other hand, would need to find a much larger segment to justify marketing in Qatar. In 2018, there was a year-on-year increase of over 55% in new motorcycle registrations due to the demand for last-mile deliveries by retailers, especially restaurants. To make marketing a motorcycle worthwhile, with its lower price and margin, a much larger segment would be necessary.

   Do we measure segments in dollars? Not necessarily, if our object is merely to describe them. But for business planning, financial measurement is essential; we cannot decide how much to invest in a segment if we don't understand its overall value, what customers are worth, or what individual consumers in a segment can afford.
3. **Accessible.** There must be viable communication and distribution channels to reach the members of the segment. If they do not exist, the incomer may need to create them as part of the entry strategy. Coca-Cola faced difficulties in African rural communities where there is poor infrastructure and retail distribution. It reached low-income consumers through its Manual Distribution Center (MDC) model, relying on people with bicycles and pushcarts instead of trucks and supermarkets. The solution, which created many jobs and helped local economies, turned a serious obstacle into a competitive advantage (International Finance Corporation, 2009).
4. **Stable.** There must be sufficient stability in the segment so that the sales effort enjoys longevity. This is a significant challenge in growth markets and even harder to find in emerging markets. It is newsworthy when segments traditionally felt to be stable experience change. As we write early in 2025, for instance, China is reported to be

entering a "new normal" as flat sales are expected in the dependable luxury goods market among the urban wealthy (Hall, 2025). The complete collapses of middle-class segments in Argentina, Syria, Ukraine, and Venezuela are well-known examples of the disappearance of an entire market segment.

5. **Differentiable.** Closely related to identifiability, the business must be able to delineate segments from each other based on differences. If it cannot, there is no point in trying to address them individually. Tata's Nano story illustrates that segments appearing to be different at first sight may actually behave in a similar way and not need delineation. Tata believed it had two segments – money-conscious car buyers and people upgrading from motorcycles. In fact, both groups identified the Nano's message – the world's cheapest car – as a detriment to their status symbol aspirations and equally rejected the car. Differential targeting made no difference (Pepper, 2022).
6. **Actionable.** The business must be able to identify or create products specially for individual segments and design marketing efforts specifically for them. If this is not possible, the segmentation has no value. In India's low-income rural market, Unilever has achieved great success by designing packaging and quantities small enough to distribute, stock, and use without large financial outlays.

Stanbic Bank Kenya

Stanbic Bank has successfully used segmentation based on psychometric testing of loan applicants. It applies a range of tests, going far beyond normal credit scoring to examine motivation and reasoning (Hatch et al., 2011). Having identified relevant segments, it deploys matching strategies to ensure cost-effective messaging. It modifies the marketing message to fit the audience characteristics; it combines media channels in an integrated campaign. It achieves none of this in a vacuum; local expertise and experience are invaluable in designing campaigns to be successful in distinct markets.

This creative work demonstrates how segmentation methodology can be profoundly more innovative than the exploration of traditional demographics, especially in emerging markets.

Segmentation is the key to realistic assessment of potential market size. No business will ever sell to every prospective consumer. A hypothetical example will illustrate.

A ridesharing service wishes to launch in a territory. It determines that the service will be of interest to tech-savvy mobile phone users, aged 18–40, employed and with disposable income. The country's population is 20 million; however, the population is young; people under 18 constitute 40%, and over 40 constitute 10%. Fifty-five percent of the population live in rural areas, and urban unemployment is at a staggering 30% in the target age group. The country is "dry," that is, the population consumes no alcohol, so one of the principal drivers of ridesharing in "wet" countries is not present. Car or motorbike ownership, estimated at 40% in the target population, is a key limiting factor. Positively though, mobile phone ownership in urban areas is at saturation point, close to 100%.

From the original 20 million people, half are removed on age grounds; 55% of the remainder are in the countryside; 30% of the remaining 4.5 million people are removed for employment; an employed person is assumed to be more likely to own their own vehicle than an unemployed person. The remainder is depleted by another 50% as a conservative final filter for unknown factors (cultural attitudes, alternative transportation systems, affordability). A potential 1.575 million people remain, if the service launches in all the urban populations in the country; if the test market is a smaller number of cities, there will be further discounting to downscale for the proportion of the population which lives in those cities. That produces an estimate of what proportion of the target population is likely to use the service before considering the effect of potential competitors and whether that number is sufficiently large to generate the revenues needed to justify investment.

After quantifying segments, a business must consider competition and the distribution landscape. Is there a need for the product or service? This may not always be apparent; sometimes populations do not know that they "need" something until they can purchase it. If a strong competitor is already in the market or about to enter, that will change costs such as advertising, promotions, pricing (with lower returns), and sales volumes (due to market sharing). Can the market grow if presented with an attractive product or service which was previously unknown to the population? If the population wants the product, is safe and efficient delivery possible with the existing network, or will it be necessary to build a new one?

Even in fast-growing economies, supply chain and distribution issues can reduce market potential. In Brazil, for example, it is unusually difficult to deliver products securely to customers. High rates of theft and loss, caused by poverty and organized crime, plague the postal delivery system, especially in rural areas. Even addressing of packages is an issue, as rural populations are often unaware of the necessity for complete, accurate details. The country is huge, with challenges created by climatic conditions and limited competition. In developed areas, particularly major cities, traffic congestion is omnipresent. Cargo theft is rife, especially on major highways (Wrobleski, 2024).

The assessment does not stop at the potential for the launch of one product or service. If the initial foray is successful, what is the potential to add other products or services? If the first launch is ridesharing, can food delivery be added later? If life insurance proves successful, is there scope for medical or dental coverage? If worthwhile business grows in laundry products, is personal hygiene the next frontier? If the business builds prefabricated houses, can it also sell offices or factories?

Quite beside quantitative assessment, understanding consumer culture is a large task but one which must be thoroughly explored and executed.

Consumer culture

The following are the principal cultural elements requiring consideration.

Values and beliefs are the bedrock of consumer choices. Not only choices, but also the ways of making those choices, vary widely between cultures. A practical example is the preferred packaging of food products for different societies. Some Asian societies are collectivist in nature, meaning that families tend to shop for shared use.

Family-sized packages of staple food are common and easy to sell. In western societies, however, individualism is more common, with the result that single servings, convenience foods, and time-saving products find greater traction.

Decision-making practices differ widely between cultures. A vendor planning to sell solar panels and energy systems in rural India, for example, would need to understand that organized family meetings typically make such significant decisions as these. Messaging to sell such systems needs to emphasize the shared financial burden, recognize the energy consumption of an extended family, and engender a shared understanding across generations about benefits and sustainability. Older family members who recall early solar products which were unreliable and of inferior quality will need additional coaxing to remove their entrenched beliefs.

A car-buying decision would be a family matter in some cultures. In Mexico, however, it will often be the domain of the male head of household. With its strong macho culture, where men have been the primary earners for centuries, patriarchal structures are common. The dominant male often has great authority but also the perceived responsibility to provide for the family by owning a car. The type, size, and quality of car are likely to serve as status symbols as much as a means of transport. Messaging in such an environment will be markedly different from messaging to a collectivist society.

Language is critically important. Local marketing expertise is essential, from product naming to advertising and messaging design. Language and culture entwine inextricably. It is impossible to develop a full appreciation of a culture without immersing oneself in the language (Talotta, 2020). Language does not stop at words. Non-verbal aspects, particularly in advertising, can be compelling in one country and offensive in another.

An advertisement for Pond's body lotion, showing an attractive lady with her back exposed and looking directly at the viewer, won accolades in India and was widely used in training materials as an example of great design. Yet there are other cultures where the direct eye contact of the model with the viewer is at best inappropriate and at worst provocative; for several Middle Eastern countries, the lady's attire is immodest and offensive. Even though beauty products are intensely personal, this product would benefit in such countries from the removal of the direct gaze, a modestly dressed model, and a family setting.

Adapting communication to cope with local nuances requires further consideration. IKEA's global vision is "to create a better everyday life for the many people" (IKEA, 2024). Expanding into India, while the vision remained constant, IKEA understood that the Indian market would require smaller products due to limited living space, brighter colors, lower prices, and an emphasis on sourcing local products. Advertising campaigns, store design, customer service, and product demonstrations all adapted to the communication strategy, reinforcing the global vision in a uniquely Indian way (Sree, 2024).

Religious beliefs and taboos are extremely powerful governors of consumer behavior and choices. There are the obvious and widely known, such as the requirement of meat to be halal in Islamic communities and the prohibition of *haram* foods (such as pork). McDonald's in Dubai and throughout the United Arab Emirates scrupulously avoid any presence of pork in their menu items (Thomas, 2014). Jewish dietary laws stipulate that only certain animal-based foods are kosher. Traditional Catholic communities abstain from eating meat on Fridays, which is good news for fishmongers but bad for butchers.[8] India's rich mixture of cultures, religions, and regions gives rise to a complex map of favored and forbidden foods, requiring restaurants to use culturally sensitive menus and food choices, supported by government labeling regulations (Paro Indian, 2023). Religious beliefs go beyond food and may extend to clothing, interpersonal practices, and methods of transport. Beliefs and taboos are neither a reason to avoid nor to enter a market but an aspect of society which must be carefully considered in product planning, advertising, and consumer-facing practices.

Traditions, in contrast to taboos, tend to be positive and supportive of consumerism. Rather than being traps for the unwary, traditions of gift-giving, sacrifice, or festive consumption can create a commercial opportunity. Throughout Asia, for example, the association of a new year with new beginnings leads to increased spending on home improvement products and electronics. In 2023, Vietnam saw an increase of 8.1% in total retail sales, driven by frenzied shopping in anticipation of Tết, the Vietnamese New Year (Nguyen, 2024).

Product design rounds off the list of planning activities, which must be fully aware of cultural preferences. A color that is positive in one culture may have special significance in another (Eriksen Translations, 2020). Recall that in the previous chapter we drew attention to the importance of doing thorough desk-based research before entering a market? Online sources are packed with readily available cultural analysis and information, yet marketing history contains many stories of corporate failures. Writing for the BBC, Ellen Nguyen (2024), for example, says:

> In 2019, Dolce & Gabbana faced widespread backlash for an advertising campaign that featured a Chinese model struggling to eat Italian food with chopsticks. The controversy escalated quickly, as many consumers perceived the advert as mocking Chinese culture. It led to the cancellation of a highly anticipated fashion show in Shanghai as well as mass boycotting. The mistake has left lasting consequences: the brand's reputation is still shaky in the massive Chinese consumer market.

You might well wonder how such a well-heeled and mature brand as Dolce & Gabbana could make such horrendous mistakes when venturing into an emerging market.

Cultural and social contexts drive not only consumer choices and actions but also behavior. That is the next essential analysis.

Consumer behavior

"Consumer behavior explores how individuals and groups make decisions to purchase, use, and dispose of goods and services" (Radu, 2024).

It is impossible to overestimate the importance of understanding the unique blend of customer behaviors in each target market. To survive and prosper, a business needs to sell: whether the plan is to launch a product or service, whether it is to come from outside or inside the market, without sales the venture is for nothing.

Do not make any assumptions about consumer behavior in one market, based on knowledge about another.

There are, however, core concepts regarding consumer behavior that apply with great vigor in emerging markets, especially for a vendor planning to offer a new alternative in an established market. They are *status quo* bias, framing effects, and decision-making complexity.

New entrants in all markets face the problem of *status quo* bias, also known as *resistance to change* or *consumer inertia* (Gourville & Norton, 2014). Psychological forces encourage potential buyers to stay with the known product, even when a better alternative is presented.

A dramatically successful example of overcoming inertia is the rapid rise of mobile payments in developing economies. Cash has been the trusted, familiar, and default medium of exchange for decades; to introduce mobile payments, providers faced an extreme case of deeply entrenched behavior. In Kenya, for example, Safaricom established its M-Pesa product through a combination of trust-building through partnerships, education campaigns, simplifying the service, and addressing security concerns in plain public view (Lopokoyit, 2022).

The contribution of M-Pesa to Kenyan society is immense. In 2006, financial inclusion was extremely low. Only 26.7% of Kenyan adults had bank accounts. With the introduction of M-Pesa and mobile banking, that number had risen to 75% by 2014 (World Bank Group, 2024) and 79% in 2021. Of that 79%, 98% held mobile money accounts (Business Reporter, 2022). In 2023, the mobile ecosystem contributed Ksh 1.2 trillion (US$348 million) to the country's GDP (CA News, 2024), carrying transactions valued at US$55 billion, 47% of GDP.

Framing effects are a marketing technique used to avoid direct confrontation with an established product or practice. A classic success was Nestlé's positioning MAGGI noodles in India as a two-minute meal. Convenient, quick food preparation was valuable to busy families but was not a feature of advertising of competing products. Noodles were not, at the outset, a staple food in India, but after years of emphasizing convenience, they became one (Tagare & Anand, 2023). Nestlé reframed noodles in customer perception by removing focus on what they *are* and stressing how they fit into busy people's lives.

Product launches in new markets must avoid decision-making complexity, also known as choice overload. Unilever, introducing Dove to the Indian market, found consumers overwhelmed by the range of options and product features for soaps, shampoos, and skincare products. Dove presented only one product, the Dove bar, emphasizing quality over quantity, with clear messaging focused on "real beauty" and "skin nourishment." The roots laid down with easy-to-understand, straightforward benefits and one product enabled Unilever to expand within a few years to many other products under a now-trusted brand (The Brand Hopper, 2024). It is not necessarily the case that a market entrant must arrive with only one product, but it must avoid overwhelming consumers with too broad a range of choices.

These three psychological effects have varied importance and impact between market segments. Price-sensitive customers are more vulnerable to choice overload, while aspirational, middle-class consumers require more attention to framing and premium positioning.

Nokia – China

In July 2011, Finnish multinational IT business Nokia released its quarterly results. Its mobile phone shipments to China were down 52 percent over the previous year (Rein, 2011). That was just part of the story. China was the last major market in the world where Nokia still had a strong position. Yet by this point, it had retained only 10% of the market with wealthy Chinese citizens, down from more than 50% three years previously. Worldwide the figures are even more dire: Nokia had a dominant 49.4% share of the world's mobile phone market in 2007, yet by 2013 had just 3% and was trying to leave the market altogether (Ettinger, 2023).

It was not a single mistake that led to Nokia's dramatic fall but a succession of errors. Specifically with respect to mobile phones, Nokia failed to monitor market sentiment and consumer behavior. At a time when Chinese consumers were moving away from price sensitivity and the mobile phone was becoming the third most important symbol of status after a house and car, Nokia dropped its prices. The status value of its product, at all levels of Chinese society, dropped as loyal customers perceived that their staff members all had cheap Nokia phones; meanwhile, the less wealthy customers did not want the inferior Nokia phones because they lacked functionality comparable to the iPhones that wealthier Chinese customers were buying.

Nokia refused to evolve, continuing with its outdated technology while iPhone and Android devices bit into their market. Nokia's loss of the entire Chinese market due to a failure to read changing conditions and understand its customers may be the most dramatic emerging market failure of all time.

Consumer psychology

An understanding of consumer psychology is especially critical in emerging markets, where the key elements in buying decisions are cultural norms, informal networks, and economic constraints. Here is a summary of the principal elements.

Perception describes how consumers interpret and interact with the messages they receive about a product, based on their own pre-existing conditions and the nature of stimuli that they receive. Externally, advertising and brand messaging may provide inputs to all the five senses. They then interpret these according to their cultural, social, and individual experiences, accumulated over a lifetime. These may include preconceived notions about products, brands, people, or sources. Negative preconceptions can require serious work and investment to correct. When Japanese carmakers first ventured into the world market, their early products were small, underpowered, and prone to breaking down. The perception that they were inferior and unreliable took years to shift as the manufacturers focused on quality and reliability (Cole & Flynn, 2009). Electric vehicles have suffered a similar image problem as an early perception was that they had limited range, were expensive, and had performance shortcomings compared to gasoline vehicles.

Japanese carmakers rebuilt consumer perception with a combination of relentless focus on quality, long warranties, careful targeting of economy-conscious segments, and third-party endorsements. The electric vehicle manufacturers have taken a similar path. These are strong lessons for emerging markets, where perception management is especially important. First impressions, as new products are introduced, can last a long time among risk-averse consumers, particularly if they manifest biases against foreign products. Negative impressions require these same techniques to build trust – quality, well-designed products, economic relevance, and locally tailored advertising and endorsements.

Motivation refers to the internal processes that lead consumers to act in a particular way – what makes them purchase, or not purchase a product, or select a specific product. It has several aspects, including needs (things one needs for survival, like food and shelter), wants (things one would like to have, for various reasons), goals (outcomes that one wants), drives ("urges" which are difficult to explain but arise from unmet needs), and incentives (external forces which drive behaviors).

Maslow's (1943) famous hierarchy of needs, a pyramid with basic physiological needs at the bottom, peaking with transcendence, is a useful tool for marketers to understand human motivation.

Designing a venture into a new market, it is critical for the marketing department to understand local consumer motivations specific to that market – it will help identify the target audience, assist with product development, and dictate marketing and promotional messages and strategies. Uniquely, emerging markets exhibit strong aspirational drivers for modernity, status, and opportunity, combined with practical economic constraints. Xiaomi, entering the Indian smartphone market, understood the Indian preference for physical stores and service centers. To accommodate this, it expanded its offline operations by establishing "Mi Home" stores and selling through local retailers.

Learning is an ongoing factor. It refers to how consumer behavior changes over time, as customers gain new knowledge which drives purchasing decisions. A market entrant needs to learn how to condition consumers by, for example, associating their product with a popular cultural element; it needs to understand how rewards and punishments can be incorporated into a business model (e.g., introduction of loyalty cards); it needs to understand how observational learning is applied in the market – how do consumers react to seeing a friend or role model buying or using a product?

Consumer learning in emerging markets is accelerated compared to developed markets. There are many examples of technological leapfrogs, like the move from cash straight to mobile banking. Consumers learn rapidly from peers and influencers, more than from deliberate product education. In rural and low-literacy communities, product discovery can be largely driven by community-based sharing of knowledge by word-of-mouth. The door is wide open for marketers to deploy demonstrations, trial offerings, and community influencing as inexpensive and powerful techniques.

Belief is an aspect of perception. Consumer beliefs often flow from early encounters with a product or service. First impressions linger. When instant noodles first entered the Chinese market, consumers regarded them as junk food, fried, and with low nutritional content. Manufacturers required considerable effort to improve the product and then change consumer beliefs (Yingqun, 2019).

Attitude comprises aspects of the above elements but adds the notion of consistency. An attitude will lead a consumer to act in a predictable and consistent manner toward a brand or product and may be positive or negative. As with belief, building of positive attitude is critically dependent on positive early experiences.

Personality refers to the traits of consumers, which may affect buying behavior and choices. The marketer needs to understand how diverse types of consumers respond to different messages and how traits may interact with brands. In emerging markets, segmentation by personality type often requires increased emphasis on collective norms, for example, emphasizing that a choice is smart for a family or community in contrast to the individual.

Social factors

Social factors which partially determine consumer behavior describe how individuals "fit in" to society and their interactions. Primary reference groups (family and friends) and secondary groups (clubs, professional associations) have strong influences on individuals. The role played by a person in society (teacher, student, friend, parent) and the status enjoyed because of that role are also influential. Social class, which exists in all societies, can influence buying choices and brand loyalty.

India, which still has a strong class structure, provides a clear example of market segmentation along class lines. The upper class is the primary consumer for luxury brands, while the growing middle class tends to look for a more balanced combination of brand, affordability, and quality. The lower classes tend not to be interested in brands, as they are primarily concerned with basic needs and a lack of disposable income; price and availability are paramount. A similar, though less rigid, segmentation exists in Brazil, Mexico, and Indonesia.

While consumers' characteristics and psychology govern what they buy, payment preferences are deeply engrained in their minds, habits, and financial behavior. It is important to understand why consumers buy: it is just as important to understand how they pay. Payment systems simply must align with local expectations.

Payment systems

Payment systems and practices are not universal. A plan to sell into an unfamiliar market must include acquiring granular knowledge of payment preferences and payment service providers. Emerging markets have an extraordinary variety of innovative, locally relevant alternative pricing and payment models. Failure to adapt to well-established consumer habits can severely impair market penetration and competitive advantage.

Local adaptations of traditional payment systems characterize some markets.

Cash-on-Delivery (COD). In India, Indonesia, and Pakistan, cash-on-delivery is used for a large percentage of e-commerce transactions.

Installment Payments. In Brazil, for example, installment payment is so prevalent that it dictates marketing content, product pricing, and sales strategy. Consumers *expect* zero-interest credit to the extent that many stores don't even display the full price of merchandise, only the installment values.

Sachet Strategy and Micropayments. Low-income consumers need to buy very small units of some products for only a few cents. Ultra-low prices in turn need micropayment facilities to control costs.

New solutions based on digital technology have created whole new financial ecosystems.

Mobile Money and Digital Wallets. In Africa and Asia, mobile wallets and money have brought banking to massive unbanked populations, bypassing entry into traditional banking arrangements. Mobile payment systems are highly integrated with mobile-first marketing strategies.

QR Code and Unified Payments Interface (UPI). QR code payments, usually linked to digital wallets, have enormous traction in China, India, and some other parts of Asia. UPI is instant and free and has revolutionized the digital payments landscape in India.

Cryptocurrencies (especially stablecoins). These are seeing increasing adoption where local currencies are unstable, banking is unreliable, or cross-border payments are expensive. Cryptocurrency is enormously attractive to consumers in countries with high inflation, with very high activity, for example, in Venezuela and Nigeria. El Salvador's legalization of Bitcoin, making it legal tender, indicates the growing importance of cryptocurrency transactions; they are also prevalent in Kenya and the Philippines.

Social Commerce. Sales via social media, especially WhatsApp, are common, for example, in Indonesia, India, and Brazil, followed by fast, low-cost local money transfers.

The evolution of multiple alternative payment systems creates a complex task for businesses entering these markets. They need to understand which payment methods are relevant, which are growing, how pricing and sales models need to adapt, and what risks they import. Costs of individual payments may be reduced; the cost of multiple implementations may be significant. Fraud is an omnipresent threat, and disappearance or impairment of technology providers in digital currencies is commonplace. Clearly understanding who is going to pay, how much, for what, and how is an essential planning element.

Digital-first strategies

E-commerce and mobile payments have become the preferred solution in many emerging markets. Explosive growth has been achieved by Alibaba in Southeast Asia and Jumia in Africa. Mobile payment systems are often the essential underlying technology that enables phenomenal levels of adoption. Localization of a digital-first strategy involves the following:

- Mobile-first design (typically, smartphone ownership far exceeds computer ownership).
- Integrating local payment preferences.
- Considering super apps which bundle several services (Didi Chuxing, the world's largest ridesharing service, also offers financial services including loans on its app (Manky & Mogollon, 2024).

Primary research methods

Assembling all the above analysis is the role of *primary research*, the collection of original, firsthand data directly from real-world sources. Primary research builds on the secondary research described in the previous chapter, where we assembled data from other people's work. On-location experience of the target market delivers enormous value.

This quest may take one of several directions. For businesses with a narrowly defined business model, the focus is on how to enter identified markets. If the only thing a business does is stream movies, then there is less to decide about the service, and the question is where to launch it next. If, however, a business manufactures 1,000 different household cleaning products, it will look not only for target markets but also for enlightenment as to which products are suitable for which markets. The third possibility is a business which has clearly identified a market but needs to refine product ideas to make them fit. If the business makes aircraft in North America and is convinced that the future lies in India, almost all its effort will go into determining what aircraft can be sold in India.

Quality primary research, almost by definition, is conducted inside the target market. While it is true that expatriates and a handful of consultants can provide information about country X from their offices in country Y, the best concrete knowledge needed to ensure success is found through being on the ground.

Which types of primary research will blend to produce the necessary data? There are three main categories: qualitative-, ethnographic-, and survey-based.

Qualitative research

Interviews may be conducted. Consider talking to knowledgeable consultants, industry experts, and academics. But most of all, make sure someone talks to potential consumers! In a large business, there may be expatriate employees who come from the new target market. Market research companies may be hired to interview relevant consumers from their panels. As you conduct physical forays into the target area, you may start to talk with potential suppliers, distributors, and employees. Local advertising or marketing agencies which are in scope to become suppliers can provide valuable insights into culture, preferences, and traditions.

Focus groups which bring together stakeholders and representative consumers are an excellent means of gathering information; they have the advantage that they enable researchers to observe body language and other visceral reactions to a product or idea.

Focus groups are also valuable forums to check for language errors (such as a product name that is offensive or a script that contains mistakes); it is surprising how often we see expensive signs like the one in Figure 5.1 or advertisements which would never have existed if a native speaker were consulted.

Ethnographic research

Enormous value can be drawn from spending time with potential customers in their normal environments. For consumer goods, grassroots-level work in their homes is invaluable, especially when secondary data are unreliable, of limited scope, or of poor quality. Nestlé, planning its expansion in India, sent researchers to sit with families at

Figure 5.1 Airport sign

(Credit: P Davis)

mealtimes and help in meal preparation to determine the taste preferences, package sizes, and product options most valuable to retail consumers.

Author Alym underlines the value of primary research.

> One of the courses that we teach includes an exercise, over six weeks, in which student groups select a start-up business, plan and model it, then submit a complete business proposal with a five-year financial model. Early in the project, we talk through the initial proposal with participants and later review their schedules of core data. We are constantly surprised by the massive improvements that result when students visit an operating business and observe customer behavior just for an hour or two. We've seen all sorts of wild projections of the number of cupcakes which consumers might buy or the number of coffees a barista might make in a day; an hour's personal observation in a bakery or coffee bar offers more realistic insights and enlightenment than any other form of research.

Further product-acceptance data can be obtained from observing consumer interactions with prototype products. The range of possibilities is as wide as life itself; if the proposed service is air travel, researchers observe passengers in airports and on board flights; if it is a children's toy, they give samples to children and watch their play activity; they also consider parental interactions with the toy, as parents hold the purse strings.

A limitation of ethnographic research is that it is vulnerable to power imbalances and cultural distance. It is highly dependent on the researcher's ability to interpret what they see, especially regarding linguistic, social, and cultural dynamics. An international business must not make the mistake of sending in an outsider who misreads cues or reaches incorrect conclusions due to a lack of familiarity with local culture, beliefs, or language. Outsiders can find it difficult to gain the trust and familiarity essential for authentic results to flow and are sometimes perceived as intrusive. Good ethnographic work typically relies on engagement with local researchers and community leaders.

Survey-based research

Consumer surveys gather information directly from potential customers and clients. Formats vary; it is possible that in some areas online surveys can be conducted by providers like Decision Analyst;[9] be aware, though, that the medium through which the survey is conducted may exclude certain demographics within the target market. An online survey will gather the opinions of people with access to the internet who can read and write; it will not tell you what illiterate farm workers in a rural community think. Postal surveys are a possibility, if there is a reliable postal service; in other circumstances, it may be necessary to identify places where potential customers gather, paying researchers to cajole attendees into giving their opinions verbally. Surveys conducted via mobile phone are an increasingly attractive option for developing economies.

Embassies, high commissions, and trade missions are a superb local resource. At home, if starting from a developed country, there are officials who maintain a watch on business opportunities overseas and are in regular contact with diplomatic representatives overseas. They are a useful source of introductions; however, within the foreign country, the embassy or high commission of your home country will usually have trade specialists whose entire job is to facilitate domestic and multinational businesses with international expansion. Quite aside from the reams of valuable data to which they have access, they will also have experience, contacts, and emergency procedures that will prove invaluable.

Being there

An executive tasked with an expansion into a new market really, really must spend time there.

They must get to know the people and gain firsthand knowledge of the infrastructure, transportation, the people, and the language (remember, language gives unique insights into culture). Fluency is not required; it is not essential to "go native." However, a person or team with no firsthand knowledge simply cannot effectively manage an expansion into an unfamiliar territory.

Case studies: Success and spectacular failure

Unilever's success in India demonstrates the importance of weaving consumer analysis into business strategy. Entering the Indian market in the early 2000s, Unilever was aware of the diversity of income groups, elevated risk of inflation, and exchange rate volatility.

It addressed income disparity by introducing different packaging sizes and offering premium products to the growing middle class, dynamically pricing small packages so that inflation did not drive low-income consumers out of the market. It localized its supply chains to insulate costs from exchange rate fluctuations.

One of history's costliest failures (US$4.5 billion), that of Walmart in Brazil, was almost entirely caused by a failure to conduct effective research and interpret the results.

Walmart – Brazil

Walmart's utter failure in Brazil, due to a fundamental misunderstanding of consumer behavior, is a cautionary tale for anyone who assumes that consumer behavior in one market will translate directly into another. Somehow the company missed the point that "everyday low prices" which drive sales in the United States do not resonate with Brazilian consumers, who prefer promotions and bulk discounts. At the same time, building hypermarkets on the edge of major cities was a misreading of a trend toward shopping at convenient, local markets (Picasso, 2023).

After a decade-long attempt to expand and improve, by 2018, Walmart had only "poor locations, inefficient operations, labor troubles and uncompetitive prices." It sold 80% of its operations and booked a loss of US$4.5 billion (Bose & Bautzer, 2018). By 2020, the name Walmart no longer appeared on any Brazilian store; a new brand, Grupo BIG, had been evolved to play into the fast-growing cash-and-carry trend, but it was purchased and absorbed into Carrefour, the top retailer in Brazil and Walmart's nemesis. Sadly, the only "BIG" thing about Walmart Brazil was its losses.

The contrast between lower prices and promotion shopping is neither easy to explain nor to understand, for non-Brazilians. But let's visit Artur Nogueira, a quiet and affluent town of around 55,000 inhabitants, in the orange-growing interior of Sao Paulo state.

There has never been a Walmart in Artur Nogueira. The food retail landscape is characterized by three elements: a weekly local market where farmers bring fresh food to the streets, several small local supermarkets, and four larger businesses, including Pague Menos (translated as "Pay Less"), a Fortaleza-based conglomerate with 1,000 stores and over 24,000 employees. Everyone knows that food prices are cheapest in the farmers' market, where goods are sold by the basket, moderate at the local supermarkets, and highest at Pague Menos. The price difference is so well known that locals jokingly refer to the store as "Pague Mais" – Pay More! Yet the aisles of Pague Menos are crowded every day, while the local stores are not so busy.

Pague Menos, thoroughly understanding the Brazilian consumer, constantly engages in "promotions." It encourages the population to buy much larger quantities of products than they ever buy from the market or a small store. Buy ten bottles of dishwashing liquid for the price of eight. On the day this description was written, a single bottle of Plax mouthwash had a regular price of Rs. 18.89, a 7% discount for loyalty card holders to Rs. 17.49, while a customer buying three bottles would pay only Rs. 11.66 each. Limit 50 bottles per customer!

Every day there is a promotional price in one department or another. One day it is the butchery; another, the bakery. Every week there is a day of discounts on fruits and vegetables. Quantity discounts are available for staples like milk and flour. Pague Menos started as a pharmacy business, and its online pharmacy app continuously runs promotions of its products: "It has the widest variety of products with special offers. Because at Pague Menos we also love a promotion."[10]

The promotional practices work because shoppers, attracted by the reduced-price items, also pick up full-priced products. Having bought copious quantities of the promotional products, they have no need to go to other stores where they might be cheaper at single prices. Finally, because of the large volumes of sales, Pague Menos can buy in larger quantities and leverage discounts at the wholesale level.

Beyond misunderstanding consumers, Walmart failed to leverage strong local partners and failed in risk management. It could not compete on price, quality, location, or concept. It missed one final trick. Because of its emphasis on low prices, despite the size of its stores and the range of merchandise, upper middle-class shoppers shunned it because "where you shop" is a status symbol. The newly rich would pay higher prices, in return for the image of being able to shop at a premium store.

Conclusion

This chapter showed how understanding a target market starts with macroeconomic data and drills down to market potential and cultural nuances. The perspective is both data-driven and culturally sensitive.

Market viability first depends on economic conditions, but infrastructure, regulation, and consumer segmentation require deep consideration. Cultural adaptation, on many levels including pricing and payment structures, is crucial. It must be proactive, not reactive. Conditions will often dictate that a digital-first strategy is most likely to succeed. The significant costs of a wholly new venture in an unfamiliar market may be greatly reduced by integrating sustainability principles and leveraging government incentives. Eco-friendly initiatives are likely to win support from both governments and consumers. Ultimately, success belongs to businesses that integrate economic analysis, deep cultural appreciation, and strategic adaptability.

After conducting these studies, businesses are ready to tackle a fundamental strategic decision: what mode of entry will they deploy for the new market? That is the entire focus of the next chapter.

Notes

1 https://www.brandwatch.com/p/social-analytics/
2 https://www.hootsuite.com/
3 https://www.meltwater.com/en
4 https://www.talkwalker.com/
5 https://www.semrush.com/
6 https://www.ibm.com/products/watson-discovery
7 https://www.tableau.com/
8 In 1966, Pope Paul VI removed the universal requirement to abstain from meat on Fridays, but many Catholics continue the practice voluntarily.
9 https://www.decisionanalyst.com
10 https://play.google.com/store/apps/details?id=br.com.paguemenos.anjodaguarda&hl=en_CA&pli=1

References

Bose, N., & Bautzer, T. (2018, June 4). Walmart sells majority of Brazil unit, takes $4.5 billion charge. https://www.reuters.com/article/business/walmart-sells-majority-of-brazil-unit-takes-45-billion-charge-idUSKCN1J02F3/

Brookmark. (n.d.). Six criteria to ensure an actionable and effective segmentation. https://brookmark.com/six-criteria-for-effective-segmentation/

Business Reporter. (2022, July 5). Kenya stands out in the 2021 Global Findex. *The Kenyan Wall Street*. https://kenyanwallstreet.com/kenya-stands-out-in-the-2021-global-findex/

CA News. (2024, January 11). Kenya's digital economy to contribute over Ksh. *660 billion to GDP by 2028, GSMA report shows*. https://www.ca.go.ke/kenyas-digital-economy-contribute-over-ksh-600-billion-gdp-2028-gsma-report-shows

Chattopadhyay, A., Batra, R., & Ozsomer, A. (2012). *The new emerging market multinationals: Four strategies for disrupting markets and building brands*. McGraw-Hill.

Cole, R.E., & Flynn, M.S. (2009, November 1). Automotive quality reputation: Hard to achieve, hard to lose, still harder to win back. https://hbsp.harvard.edu/product/CMR441-PDF-ENG

Eriksen Translations. (2020, February 3). How translating colors across cultures can help you make a positive impact. https://eriksen.com/marketing/color_culture/

Ettinger, G. (2023, August 18). What happened to Nokia? The rise and fall of a tech giant. https://www.cnbc.com/2011/07/25/rein-why-nokia-falls-in-china-but-apple-soars.html

Gourville, J.T., & Norton, M.I. (2014, June 30). *Consumer Behavior and the Buying Process*. Harvard Business Publishing.

Gupta, S. (2014, June 30). *Segmentation and targeting*. Harvard Business Publishing.

Hall, C. (2025, January 21). China enters 'new normal' for luxury market with flat sales expected in 2025, report says. https://www.reuters.com/business/retail-consumer/china-enters-new-normal-luxury-market-with-flat-sales-expected-2025-report-says-2025-01-21/

Hatch, G., Becker, P., & van Zul, M. (2011, September 7). The dynamic African consumer market: Exploring growth opportunities in sub-Saharan Africa. *Accenture plc*.

IKEA. (2024, May 27). How we work. https://www.ikea.com/global/en/our-business/how-we-work/

International Finance Corporation. (2009, July 19). Developing inclusive business models: A review of Coca-Cola's Manual Distribution Centers in Ethiopia and Tanzania. https://www.ifc.org/en/insights-reports/2000/pub-005-developing-inclusive-business-models-a-review-of-coca-colas-manual-distribution-centers-in-ethiopia-and-tanzania

Khoza, R.J. (2023, October 11). Interview by M. van Waijenburg. *Creating Emerging Markets Oral History Collection*. Baker Library Special Collections, Harvard Business School.

Kotler, P., & Keller, K. L. (2022). *Marketing management* (16th ed.). Pearson.

Lopokoyit, S. (2022, June 29). Driven by purpose: 15 years of M-Peso'a evolution. https://www.mckinsey.com/industries/financial-services/our-insights/driven-by-purpose-15-years-of-m-pesas-evolution

Manky, O. & Mogollon, N. (2024, October 23). How Didi Adapts to Latin America's Era of Digital Platforms. https://latinvex.com/how-didi-adapts-to-latin-americas-era-of-digital-platforms/

Maslow, A. (1943). A theory of human motivation. *Psychological Review*, 50(4), 270–396.

Nguyen, E. (2024, February 9). It's easy to enter the Asian market during Lunar New Year. It's hard to get it right. *BBC*. https://www.bbc.com/worklife/article/20240208-lunar-new-year-advertising-in-asian-markets

Paro Indian. (2023, September 30). Exploring India's cultural and regional influence on cuisine. https://paroindian.com/2023/09/30/exploring-indias-cultural-and-regional-influence-on-cuisine

Picasso, A.P. (2023, July 24). The Walmart journey in Brazil: A tale of rise, decline, and acquisition. *Emerging Markets Today*. https://emergingmarkets.today/walmart-journey-brazil-rise-decline-acquisition/

Radu, V. (2024, June 4). Consumer behavior in marketing. *Patterns, types & segmentation. Omniconvert.* https://www.omniconvert.com/blog/consumer-behavior-in-marketing-patterns-types-segmentation/

Rein, S. (2011, July 25). Why Nokia falls in China but Apple Soars. *CNBC Markets.* https://www.cnbc.com/2011/07/25/rein-why-nokia-falls-in-china-but-apple-soars.html

Sree, A. (2024, January 9). Ikea's winning strategy in India: affordability, design, and local touch. *LinkedIn.* https://www.linkedin.com/pulse/ikeas-winning-strategy-india-affordability-design-local-anu-sree-vbb9c/

Staff Reporter, APAC. (2024, January). Pizza Hut Indonesia's Ristorante concept features diverse menu at reasonable prices. *Retail Asia.* https://retailasia.com/stores/news/pizza-hut-indonesias-ristorante-concept-features-diverse-menu-reasonable-prices

Tagare, S., & Anand, S.V. (2023, February 13). Maggi's two-minute strategy and how convenience and comfort combined. *Forbes India.* https://www.forbesindia.com/article/storyboard18/maggis-twominute-strategy-and-how-convenience-and-comfort-combined/83129/1

Talotta, M. (2020, August 20). Why language and culture are inseparable. *Medium.* https://matteotalotta.medium.com/language-and-culture-are-inseparable-707cc51c136b#

Team Pepper. (2022, May 5). Marketing case study: The story behind Tata Nano's failure as a brand. https://www.peppercontent.io/blog/why-tata-nano-branding-was-a-failure/

The Brand Hopper. (2024, January 6). Case study: Dove's "real beauty" brand campaign. *The Brand Hopper.* https://thebrandhopper.com/2024/01/06/case-study-dove-real-beauty-brand-campaign/

Thomas, B. (2014, April 23). No pork in McDonald's meals, official UAE tests confirm. https://www.arabianbusiness.com/gcc/no-pork-in-mcdonald-s-meals-official-uae-tests-confirm-547664

World Bank Group. (2024, April 17). Financial inclusion in Sub-Saharan Africa – Overview. https://www.worldbank.org/en/publication/globalfindex/brief/financial-inclusion-in-sub-saharan-africa-overview

Wrobleski, A. (2024, January 18). Logistics is now and the challenges of the Brazilian market require attention. *Associação brasileira das empresas de software.* https://abes.com.br/en/logistica-e-o-agora-e-os-desafios-do-mercado-brasileiro-necessitam-de-atencao/

Yingqun, C. (2019, December 4). *Instant noodles steaming back to life.* China Daily. https://www.chinadaily.com.cn/a/201912/04/WS5de6be22a310cf3e3557bbc7.html

CHAPTER 6

Market entry modes

Learning outcomes

After studying this chapter, you will be able to do the following:

1. Compare and assess the advantages, disadvantages, and implications of the four major groups of market entry modes.
2. Explain why the correct choice of mode(s) is a critical strategic decision for expanding businesses, acknowledging the roles of risk, control, cost, distance, and regulation.
3. Analyze and compare the trade-offs between cost, local control, and risk for each mode, applying them to examples for specific industry and country contexts.
4. Analyze how global companies, other than those identified in this chapter, have selected and implemented different market entry strategies.
5. Discuss the role of Special Economic Zones (SEZs) in creating opportunities for inward investment.
6. Compare the "waterfall" and "sprinkler" approaches to expansion, showing the advantages and disadvantages of each.
7. Apply decision factors and frameworks to recommend the best mode(s) for a business considering entry into a new market.

Introduction: Market entry modes

This chapter organizes market entry strategies into four principal groups: exporting, foreign direct investment (FDI), licensing/franchising, and joint venturing. Choosing between them involves trade-offs between cost, risk, and control. The expanding business considers its own resources, industry features, and the target market's characteristics. For

DOI: 10.4324/9781003638490-6

Table 6.1 Control, risk, and cost by modes of entry

Mode of Entry Group	*Level of Local Control*	*Risk*	*Cost*
Exporting	Low	Low	Low
Foreign Direct Investment	Very High	Very High	Very High
Licensing/Franchising	Moderate	Moderate	Moderate
Joint Venture	High	High	Moderate

emerging markets specifically, decisions about mode of entry require careful attention to addressing voids in institutions and infrastructure and all the VUCA factors we have already identified. Consideration of how to leverage local partnerships, SEZs, and other safety nets is critical.

The choice determines how a business will leverage market dynamics, navigate regulatory and legal landscapes, and build local partnerships. It must accommodate the culture(s) of the target market, manage its competitive positioning, allocate resources, manage risks, and support continued growth. This lengthy list hints at the grave consequences of a wrong decision.

Traditional analysis of market entry modes places decision-making focus on the characteristics of the target market and their relationship with the expanding business. However, a growing body of literature, which has given more attention to NTBFs – New Technology-Based Firms – suggests that the size and capabilities of the entering business have powerful influence. This makes intuitive sense: a large business with 10,000 employees can easily afford to place 100 of its people in a foreign market for an extended period; a software developer with a staff of 50 would find this impossible, physically and financially (Mokhtarzadeh, Jafarpanah, & Mahdiraji, 2022).

Table 6.1 summarizes the levels of local control and risk. VUCA challenges can doom an expansion which chooses the wrong mode. There is a close relationship between entry mode, risk, cost, and potential reward.

While most market entry initiatives fall into one group, a large, complex project may cross boundaries. Tesla, for example, employs simultaneous modes. Its early operations focused on making cars in the United States and exporting them to other countries, but it soon moved to building wholly owned manufacturing plants in Germany and China. It also has joint venture arrangements, such as with Swiss semiconductor company Annex (Global Times, 2022).

Let's get familiar with each mode in more detail.

Exporting

An export strategy involves producing at home while selling in a foreign market. Sales can be direct to consumer, using media like e-commerce and interactive TV, or indirect (through agents or distributors). In direct export sales, title to goods passes directly from the exporter to the consumer. In indirect exports, title passes first to a domestic reseller or trading business and from that entity to the consumer.

Exporting is a lower-risk option for entry into a foreign market, as it does not involve significant investments in foreign production, staff, or property (Ordorica, 2019). However, exaggerated difficulties like inefficient ports and transportation, opaque or corrupt customs procedures, and unstable currencies add back to the risk calculation.

For some business types, export is the natural choice. Consider Airbus and Boeing, massive enterprises which build commercial aircraft for the world market. Respectively, their main manufacturing centers are in France and the United States. They sell only a fraction of their production domestically, but given the huge investment in plant and equipment and the transportability of the product, there is a compelling business case for keeping most production at home.

At an early stage, exporting is a low-risk method of testing foreign appetites. An initial export project might demonstrate demand on a scale that leads to a more participatory exercise in the target market or region – or not.

However, moving product across borders introduces risk and cost issues such as transportation, logistics, storage, and taxation. Product tariffs or quotas may exist or be imposed; understanding foreign trade policies and license requirements can be difficult. What appears to be a straightforward process may be complicated by non-tariff barriers, including documentation red tape and customs delays.

It is only on a case-by-case basis that a business can decide whether it wants to send out its products from home base or manufacture them closer to its markets. This can change over time, and sometimes the best option is a hybrid model in which the manufacturer produces parts in one location and then assembles them in another location.

A decision to export has inbuilt financial protection: it does not involve the exporter in significant purchases of plant, property, or equipment in the target market area. However, it creates the possibility of increasing sales of products or services when the home market is saturated and gaining benefits of scale as a result.

A global brand may choose the export model to leverage an association between the home base and perceived quality. Rolex, which leverages its impressive brand reputation to sell luxury watches worldwide, manufactures only in Switzerland. The country name is synonymous with production of top-quality timepieces. In this way, Rolex keeps quality control in its own hands and in a narrowly defined location (Millenary Watches, n.d.).

A subcategory of exporting, colorfully named *piggybacking*, is useful for businesses with limited resources and experience in the new target market (Terpstra & Yu, 1990). The "rider" is a small business wishing to sell into a foreign market; the "carrier" is a larger business, already established in a foreign market, willing to sell on behalf of the small exporter.

Since the millennium, the digital age has engendered rapid growth of a new form of exporting, leveraging e-commerce and cloud-based technologies to enter new markets without a physical presence. Amazon, Alibaba, Shopify, Jumia, and MercadoLibre are well-known examples of businesses which have successfully tested and implemented digital sales from global centers or regional marketplaces. Netflix, Spotify, and Zoom, whose products are purely digital, have proved successful at making content, pricing, and user experience relevant for distinct markets while delivering from a single global platform.

Potential exporters to emerging markets must also determine whether *countertrade* will play a role in their plans. Countertrade involves the exchange of goods or services partially, or wholly, without cash involvement. It is prevalent where a country's foreign exchange reserves are low, the local currency is not widely accepted, or governmental restrictions apply to currency transactions.

The main forms of countertrade are as follows:

- Barter. The direct exchange of goods or services with no cash involvement.
- Counterpurchase. The exporter receives payment but is obligated to spend it on goods from the purchasing country. Defense and transportation sectors are extensive users of counterpurchase, especially for large government contracts, as they stimulate domestic production.
- Buyback. The exporter supplies equipment or technology and is paid with output from its use. Buyback in emerging markets is popular in petrochemical and large infrastructure industries.
- Offset. Also common in defense contracts, in an offset contract the exporter agrees to invest some of its proceeds in the buying country or source part of its supply there.
- Switch trading. A third part assists with the sale of surplus goods from a barter arrangement.

Countertrade is an important element of exportation to emerging markets and can make a significant contribution to the economic well-being of the buying country. A truly amazing countertrade deal from a then emerging market was PepsiCo's $3 billion barter trade deal in 1990 to swap soft-drink concentrate for Russian Stolichnaya vodka and merchant ships (Dahlburg, 1990).

A business with a higher risk appetite, wishing to produce closer to market and have more control over local operations, may instead choose to invest directly in the target region.

Foreign direct investing

Foreign Direct Investment (FDI) is the most capital-intensive and usually the riskiest form of expansion. It involves the parent company setting up a wholly owned subsidiary in the target market. If the enterprise is brand new, like Tesla's ventures in China, it is a *greenfield* investment. Entering a market by a merger or acquisition, like Tata's purchase of Jaguar-Land Rover, is a *brownfield* investment.

Governments in many emerging markets set strict rules around FDI, managing a perception of exploitation, shifts in economic control, or national interests. FDI in key, large sectors like telecommunications and mining often requires partial ownership to satisfy laws that forbid exclusively foreign control.

FDI is not a one-way street. Governments and organizations situated *within* emerging markets are major investors in other countries. In 2023, the world's biggest foreign investor by dollar value was Mubadala, based in the UAE (Dettoni, 2024, p. 3). India's developing market status is increasingly insufficient for the expansion plans of growing domestic companies who looked overseas (Irwin-Hunt, 2024).

The second-largest destination for FDI in 2022, after the United States, was China; China was also the fifth-largest source of outward FDI (World Population Review, n.d.). Between 2003 and 2022, China invested $187.5 billion U.S. dollars in Latin America and the Caribbean, with 42% of the money going to Brazil (Stott, 2024). China has sought not only to leverage Mexico's access to the North American market but also to secure long-term mineral rights and expand its information technology capacity (Interesse, 2024). Meanwhile, foreign investment *into* China has fallen off the proverbial cliff as shown by Figure 6.1.

FDI flows not only to the emerging world but also to developed countries. In 2023, the United States was not only the top source of FDI for other countries but also the top destination for FDI *from* other countries. Of 179 projects worth over $1 billion, 20 of them were *into* the United States.

Growth in investment, influence, and market position of multinational businesses *from* emerging markets has changed the commercial picture of the entire world. Brennan and Bakir (2019), in an important work, argue that such companies have strengths which distinguish them from developed market competitors. They have greater ability to compete in difficult environments, work around institutional voids, and have strengths in cost leadership and innovation. These companies often practice frugal innovation, further leveraging cost as a driver of expansion in both emerging and developed markets.

Acquiring a controlling interest in an established business, short of 100% ownership, is a type of FDI. Acquisitions are a risky first step in internationalizing a business; buying a business in a new market requires considerable experience, management skill, money, and credibility. It typically occurs when the expanding business has already achieved significant size and presence in its own market.

Speaking specifically of Chinese FDI but capturing a useful analytical lens, Professor Panibratov of St Petersburg State University explains the three main motivations: resource seeking, market seeking, and technology seeking. Discerning how different countries make investments, and why, gives insight into their strategic plans and partially explains why different nationalities are active in distinct sectors. China's industrial productivity

Figure 6.1 Chinese Inward FDI 1990–2023 (Macrotrends, 2025; Ministry of Commerce, 2024)

contrasts with India's presence in technology markets; Chinese businesses are actively pursuing very long-term investments in resource-rich African nations, while Indian investors are acquiring technology-based companies in richer nations. To the list of the big three motivators, Professor Panibratov adds *efficiency seeking* (for countries whose businesses look for less cumbersome procedures than they must cope with at home) and *strategic asset acquisition*. The last appears to be a hybrid of resource and technology acquisition (Panibratov, 2017).

The direct investor has the advantage of complete control over its foreign operations, brands, and presence. However, it loses the benefits of shared decision-making with local partners and exposes itself to risks like expropriation, which can result in the loss of the entire operation. FDI, among entry strategies, is the most vulnerable to political instability. Investors turn to political science to quantify political risks, and there is a strong correlation between them and poverty, literacy, and low incomes. Charlie Robinson (2024) sums it up this way: "It's one reason why few investors build factories in the Sahel region of Africa, and the vast majority of FDI flows from rich countries into other rich countries."

Compared to exporting, FDI is advantageous if being present permits the use of local resources, direct employment of local labor, and on-site development of technology. These operational gains can turn around and benefit the home operation.

Because FDI is long-term and demonstrates commitment, negotiations with national governments and local authorities can be easier; locally produced goods will not be subject to tariffs or quota restrictions. Local consumers who see the business's commitment to the country, job creation, and local spending on infrastructure may develop greater loyalty to brands and products. FDI has the potential to earn more profit and a higher return on the original investment than exporting.

Developing countries typically devote significant effort to attracting FDI, though its level can vary with changing conditions. Mexico is currently riding a wave of success, with a record high of almost US$33 billion in the first nine months of 2023 (MND Staff, 2023). While India's great successes in attracting FDI are partially attributable to its size and demographic strengths, low operating costs, and highly educated English-speaking population, the government actively encourages FDI with tax incentives, exemptions from compliance with certain local laws, and slashing of tariffs. In the 2024 budget, foreign companies received a corporate tax reduction from 40% to 35%, abolition of the 2% equalization levy, and removal of the angel tax, which investors had to pay if they acquired interests in a start-up at over market value (McBirnie & Das, 2024).

Many countries have created Special Economic Zones (SEZs) to attract FDI. Nigeria, for example, although limited by difficulties with both soft and hard infrastructure, has announced *digital* free zone plans to attract established and startup technology investors. In 2023, local business Itana gained Africa's first digital free zone operating license and has commenced development of a tech campus in Lekki, Lagos (Nwokoma, 2024). The list of successful SEZs is dominated by emerging market locations, including Shenzhen and Suzhou (China), Dubai International Financial Centre in the United Arab Emirates, Tanger Med in Morocco, NOIDA in India, and Lekki in Nigeria.

Singapore and Malaysia have commenced an interesting two-country experiment with the New Johor SEZ of over 3,570 square kilometers. The area is four times bigger than Singapore itself. Inward investors can set up head offices in Singapore but manufacture in Malaysia. The promise of a 5% corporate tax rate for 15 years, coupled with competitive personal tax rates, is attractive to large, technologically oriented companies. The area is notable for its ability to attract and retain skilled workers (Saieed, 2025).

While SEZs offer significant tax, rent, and regulatory concessions, there are risk considerations. They are vulnerable to sudden changes in government policy (as has occurred in India), isolation from global supply chains (common in Africa), poor infrastructure (e.g., in Nigeria), and environmental concerns. Over-reliance on one sector may expose an entire SEZ to economic changes. In some countries, such as the Philippines, SEZs have suffered from accusations of smuggling and customs fraud. Creating financial favors for powerful inward investors creates a vulnerability to corruption of local officials.

A business wishing to sell its product or service into a new market but unwilling to export or engage in significant FDI may instead consider licensing or franchising its capabilities to third parties with in-country expertise and experience.

The Tata Group's FDI Success

The fabled history of the Tata Group shows the progress of an emerging market business from local (in 1868) to global through FDI.

India gained its independence from Britain in 1947, which heralded a rapid expansion for the group under J.R.D. Tata. Like a spreading vine, the conglomerate grew and grew – then at the millennium, Tata began its diversification into international markets.

In 2000, a foothold was gained in the global tea market with the purchase of British powerhouse Tetley Tea Company. The price, £271 million, was the largest overseas purchase to date by any Indian business. In 2007, however, the record was shattered by the £6.2 billion paid for steelmaker Corus. The following year, the Jaguar and Land Rover brands were purchased from Ford, and U.S. business General Chemical Industrial Products was added to its earlier (2006) acquisition of Brunner Mond.

Not yet satisfied with massive industrial expansions across a broad range of industries, Tata Consultancy Services set up offices in three continents and rapidly became one of the world's largest IT service providers.

Ratan Tata succeeded JRD in 1991, serving until 2012, and returning for a brief period in 2016–2017. Since then, Natarajan Chandrasekaran has occupied the chair. Ratan Tata's leadership led the business through a major shift of mindset as innovation was increasingly stressed as key to the future, ethical business practices were even more keenly sought, and corporate social responsibility gained prominence. This sowed the seeds for the current chairperson to focus the group on clean energy (including electric vehicles), the digital economy, and customer centricity.

The Tata story underlines the importance of vision, focus, strategy, resilience, and long-term planning. It is a global player yet has never lost its interest in nation-building and the welfare of its home population. Jamsetji Tata started the business with 21,000 rupees – about US$250, which today would still be the equivalent of less than $10,000. He is affectionately known to history as "the giant who touched tomorrow" (Tata Group, n.d., para. 1).

Licensing and franchising

In a licensing or franchising arrangement, a business in the target market is allowed, for a fee, to use intellectual property owned or developed by the licensor. This is often a quicker route to market, carrying reduced risks of losses for the licensor; however, transfer of intellectual property (IP) to a foreign operator has its risks and requires careful "what-if" consideration. We will address the difficulties inherent in transferring IP to an overseas partner, including the risk of "gray markets," in more detail in a later chapter. What will happen if the foreign partner does not honor its contractual commitments? Will courts in the foreign country enforce the contracts between the parties?

In a licensing arrangement, the licensee pays a fee, royalty, or commission to operate its business independently, using the IP of the licensor. Pharmaceutical companies, for example, commonly license their formulae to manufacturers in emerging markets.

Licensing can be a method of addressing currency risk, depending on the currency for royalties and fees. However, the licensor may lose all or part of its control over product and service quality, distribution, and even pricing. To support longevity, the licensee will need to retain part of the profits from sales, leaving less for the licensor. In the long term, if contracts run out or intellectual property rights expire, the investor may turn out to have trained and enabled a credible competitor.

Franchising involves the use of an entire business model by the franchisee, who is required to operate within strict guidelines and is subject to greater control by the franchisor. The world's most recognizable franchising model is McDonald's. The behemoth fast-food chain primarily uses franchising to local entrepreneurs, allowing them to use the McDonald's name, restaurant design, menu, and business processes in return for a fee and/or percentage of turnover. McDonald's has franchisees in over 100 countries (McDonald's Corporation, 2018).

While franchising covers a wide range of business types, it is notable that most published lists of global franchises heavily feature food businesses in their annual top ten rankings. *Entrepreneur Magazine*'s 2023 list, for example, awarded the first six places to restaurant chains and the seventh to a convenience store (Entrepreneur, 2023).

Intellectual property protection is a major concern when either licensing or franchising into emerging markets. Local registration is highly advisable, and it should be completed as early as possible; most emerging markets have a "first to file" system which disregards the timing of creation. There are international treaties in place which may allow registration in multiple countries: for example, the TRIPS Agreement provides minimum standards across World Trade Organization members. Strong drafting of contracts and licenses, which should be locally enforceable, is mandatory; the licensor should try to keep particularly valuable information or processes under its own control. The licensor should perform regular monitoring and enforcement of IP rights, and IP owners should not be shy to use technology such as encryption to further protect trade secrets.

Licensors and franchisors retain only partial control over operations in foreign markets but reduce other risks. A business that wants to share risk and decision-making authority with a competent local partner may instead opt for joint venturing.

Joint venturing

Both sharing risks and costs and acquiring local knowledge and talent can be achieved by forming a joint venture with a local partner in the target market. This might be by the establishment of a new company, or by partial merger or acquisition. The involvement of a local player can be reassuring to governments and regulators and open doors within the supply chain. Joint venturing may be essential to securing government contracts or doing business with sensitive sectors like defense or healthcare. PepsiCo's successful expansion into emerging markets has largely been conducted through joint ventures, which have preserved the brand identity and operational control while leveraging local knowledge of government policies, regulations, and market entry barriers (Livewell, 2024).

In emerging markets, joint ventures are sometimes the only viable route to cope with local elite networks, massive family-owned enterprises, or other powerful vested interests. It's crucial, naturally, to select the right partner and avoid being drawn into local feuds or political power struggles. It's essential to examine the credentials of potential partners and ensure that they are not engaging in regulatory capture, overly controlling or influencing the governmental authorities that are supposed to regulate them.

We regard joint venturing as a separate category of entry strategy, as there are profound differences between complete control and shared decision-making. Not all analysts agree with this categorization; an article recently published in Livewell's Finance section defines FDI but goes on to say: "This physical presence can take various forms, such as acquiring assets or shares of foreign companies, setting up subsidiaries or branches, or entering into joint ventures with local businesses" (Livewell, 2024).

From the point of view of the company within an emerging market, while bringing in a strong foreign partner can help or even save a domestic operation, it can also invoke the sharp tension between globalization and national economic sovereignty. This has been a deep concern in certain Mexican sectors, particularly beer production. Business leaders like Alberto Baillères, CEO of Grupo Bal, whose family has a deep love for the country, struggle with ethical dilemmas around giving up local control to foreign investors (Baillères, 2013).

As with licensing and franchising, clear, enforceable contracts are essential. The aspiring joint venture participant must be confident that if the local partner behaves badly, courts will support the legitimate claims of the inward investor. Conflicts can arise over decisions, and if there are sharp differences in business cultures or management styles, these will damage the effort. A serious risk exists with respect to intellectual property. When a business transfers IP into a joint venture which anticipates shared rewards and then fails, the former partner may end up in a position to compete strongly with its erstwhile ally.

There is a rich treasury of success stories respecting joint ventures in emerging markets. The following case studies illustrate several key insights.

While the concept of merger or acquisition may conjure up images of a large fish gobbling up a smaller one, there can be clear advantages to the smaller business.

Acindar (Argentina)

Acindar is a business that has survived extreme economic volatility and multiple regime changes. It is primarily a producer of non-flat steel products – steel other than in sheets or strips. At times government regulation constrained its growth; at others it had to compete with government itself. A liaison with West Germany's Thyssen group in 1962 strengthened Acindar; it bought out the German partner after ten years. It then grew by absorbing local competitors, which improved its market position but saddled it with large debts. A financial recession and the collapse of the Argentinian Peso then had devastating effects not only on Acindar but also on its main customers in construction, automobile manufacturing, and farming. At the millennium, the Acevedo family sold part of its shareholding to Belgo Companhia Siderúrgica of Brazil (Belgo-Mineira); Belgo was at the same time merging with Union Sidérique du Nord (Usinor), a French company, to form Arcelor, which became the world's largest steelmaker.

Today, ArcelorMittal Acindar is alive and well; it remains the market leader in Argentina. Despite a long series of partnerships and mergers, dilutions and changes in shareholding, the business has survived a brutal journey in a challenging global market. Clearly the company itself has been a major beneficiary of its minority status in the many liaisons (Acevedo, 2008).

Suspicion and economic resistance to outside control are powerful business blockers. Strategic joint venturing can overcome both regulatory and economic barriers.

Embraer (Brazil)

If you have commuted on a regional jet between two points served by an airline, you have probably travelled on an Embraer. You may have noticed how smooth and comfortable your flight was, despite the small size of the plane. Embraer jets operate on a vast number of routes worldwide, including journeys with large, well-known carriers like American Airlines, Delta, British Airways, Emirates, and KLM. Yet Embraer started building aircraft only in 1969 and was originally a government business.

Ten years later, Embraer had privatized in a wave of government dispositions in Brazil and had joint ventures with two Italian manufacturers. It gained the knowledge and experience that enabled it to compete with existing players in the regional jet business. It continued to supply security and defense markets at the same time. It is one of Brazil's top ten exporters; around 80% of all its sales are outside Brazil.

Embraer has always stressed innovation, trying to build better products at lower costs than competitors. Since 1981, it has pursued an aggressive policy of FDI, joint ventures, and acquisitions. The company has a significant manufacturing, R&D, and service presence in the United States but built its first non-Brazilian assembly facility in China in 2002, made possible by a joint venture with Chinese manufacturer Harbin. It began operating its first wholly owned facility inside China in 2010 to provide after-sales support to owners of its business jets. Achievement of a wholly owned manufacturing operation inside China is a rare feat: Tesla is almost unique in this respect, as all other auto manufacturers seeking access to the Chinese market have proceeded through joint ventures.[1]

Today, Embraer holds the third position in the world table of commercial aircraft suppliers (Gabruno & Mitchell, 2023).

By forging the right partnerships, it is possible to penetrate near-impossible markets.

MTN (Africa)

MTN is the largest telecommunications operator in Africa. Until August 2020, it was a major provider in the Middle East; it then sold most of its holdings as the region was providing less than 4% of its global income. Since then, its focus has been almost exclusively African. It has displayed extraordinary resilience in emerging and least developed markets.

Founded in South Africa in 1994, MTN has the largest market share in its home base. It is the largest provider in Nigeria. It has significant market share in Benin, Botswana, Cameroon,[2] Côte d'Ivoire, Congo, Eswatini, Ghana, Guinea, Guinea-Bissau, Liberia, Rwanda, Sierra Leone, Sudan, South Sudan, Uganda, and Zambia.[3] Some of these countries have been war-torn, wracked by poverty, and among the most difficult in the world, yet MTN has found a way to do business in them. In the Middle East, its historical success list consists of Afghanistan, Iran, Syria, and Yemen. Many of these countries are synonymous with civil war, human rights abuses, and human suffering.

To create success, MTN has added to its joint ventures a combination of recognizing high growth potential, command of its own infrastructure, and culture-sensitive customer focus (MTN, n.d.).

Making the choice

Beyond quantitative analysis, comfort levels may drive emotions and appetite. A framework for analysis of past decisions was proposed in 2001 by NYU Stern's Professor Ghemawat. It identifies the intuitive factors in such decisions. Distance is the overarching factor, but not a physical measurement of kilometers or miles. There are four dimensions: geographical, cultural, economic, and administrative/political distance.

- **Geographical distance** includes climate, presence or absence of common borders, cost and time of travel, communication capacity, and the presence or absence of foreign bank subsidiaries. Where geographical distance is great, exporting is often the favored mode of entry, though cooperative methodologies may bring advantages. According to Gibbs (2014), in Nissan's first venture into the Brazilian market, it chose to export due to the geographical distance and high costs of setting up local production. Subsequently, however, it moved to FDI.
- **Cultural distance** refers to differences in ethnicity, religion, language, and social elements. Where cultural distance is great, cooperation with local partners, such as joint ventures, is preferable to exporting or FDI. Statistical analysis shows that the relationship between cultural factors and FDI has a strong influence on locational decisions by multinational corporations (Silajdzic & Mehic, 2021). McDonald's' major menu modifications in India, excluding beef and pork while adding vegetarian options, were accomplished in collaboration with local partners. They demonstrate the significant cultural distance which was addressed.

- **Economic distance** looks at disparities in income levels, physical and human costs. It may consider the degree of openness to global markets and quality of exports. Economic proximity supports the case for FDI; establishment or acquisition of subsidiaries also finds favor where growth potential, infrastructure, or quality local labor are abundant. Walmart's entry into South Africa by acquiring a majority shareholding in local retailer Massmart demonstrates attention to the supply chain and distribution challenges in the target market.
- **Administrative/political distance** measures the extent of historical associations between countries, the level of protectionist regulations, and the perception of institutional voids. Emerging markets tend to have more pronounced instances of opaque regulation and state interference, coupled with more extreme institutional voids. The greater the administrative or political distance, the greater the preference for cooperative modes of entry. Vodafone's entry into India, accomplished by acquiring a controlling stake in Hutchison Essar, demonstrates an attempt to cope with administrative distance, although subsequent tax difficulties went on to illustrate the risks.

Analyzing market distance helps refine entry strategy and long-term objectives. As we have seen, the path to choice starts with considering the "fit" of a market for a business's internal strengths and motivations. Risk appetite, financial, reputational, and environmental, will be a major factor. This points toward the most suitable initial entry mode.

However, this is not a one-time decision. The business will determine its performance metrics and continually seek to improve its operations and presence in the target market. It must regularly review the entry strategy. An initial attempt at exporting, for example, may result in worthwhile returns and increased company knowledge, such that direct investment becomes more attractive. Or the exporter might find greater demand than it expected but experience unsolvable logistical problems, indicating that a local partnership is the better way.

How many markets?

Having deeply studied the countries or areas which exhibit potential, several possible target markets may remain. Is it best to proceed one market at a time or to take on several? For larger businesses, there are competing arguments for and against several *parallel expansions*. The debate is known as the waterfall versus sprinkler approach. Dilution of focus suggests that not too much should be taken on. However, given the higher levels of risk, diversification across several markets can also be a sound strategy. The middle ground may be parallel entry into several markets in the same region, although thought must be given to the risks encountered when several countries move in a similar direction which is averse to investors' interests.

There *are* examples of large businesses that have made conscious decisions to expand globally and seek world domination. Coca-Cola and PepsiCo have made a success of this (Belluz, 2016); British clothing retailer Superdry, on the other hand, engineered its own near demise by pursuing an over-ambitious expansion into developed and emerging markets in too short a timeframe (Wright, 2023).

Conclusion: Emerging trends

This chapter reviewed the four principal groups of market entry modes. We saw that selecting the right entry mode is fundamental to the success of any expansion and considered the concept of "distance" in relation to this choice. We saw the trade-off between risk and control, which determines the best mode of entry for any new venture into an emerging market.

As we write, there are three major shifts taking place which may strongly influence choice of mode:

Digital expansion is dramatically reducing the need for traditional entry modes, even in businesses which have traditionally relied on a form of physical presence.

Geopolitical changes are highly visible as changing American policies cast doubt on the future of free trade agreements. Political tension between China and America affects FDI decisions far beyond their respective borders, for example, in Mexico's near-shoring position for the American market. Beyond the United States, however, the 12-country Comprehensive and Progressive Agreement for Trans-Pacific Partnership (CPTPP) and 45-country African Continental Free Trade Area (AfCFTA) greatly simplify cross-border movement of goods and services. They encourage FDI and support the establishment of subsidiaries.

ESG considerations are increasingly important in the choice of mode and detailing of entry strategy. Unilever is a thought leader in this regard, integrating environmental and social priorities in its choice of new markets and local sourcing practices. For example, it prefers partnerships with local farmers and smallholders to importation of agricultural products and supplies. Patagonia refuses to license or franchise so that it can maintain control of supply chain decisions, refusing to enter markets unless ethical manufacturing is viable.

Regardless of the form chosen, it is important to define the corporate identity which will underlie every key decision. The proposition must resonate with local markets while aligning with the long-term objectives of the business. In the next chapter, armed with an understanding of options for market entry, we will explore the formation of a mission, vision, and value proposition, which will allow creation of a competitive advantage there.

Notes

1 For example, SAIC Volkswagen's factory in Shanghai (Volkswagen Group China, 2018).
2 Demonstrating one of the heightened dangers of doing business in LDCs, MTN has been suffering since 2002 from seizure of its bank accounts in Cameroon because of a court dispute between a local entrepreneur and South Africa's First National Bank (Atabong, 2024).
3 Talks are often reported regarding sales of low-profit markets such as Liberia, Guinea-Bissau, and Guinea-Conakry (O'Grady, 2023).

References

Acevedo, A. (2008, August 29). Interview by A. Lluch. *Creating Emerging Markets Oral History Collection*. Baker Library Special Collections, Harvard Business School.

Atabong, A.B. (2024, September 4). MTN says it won't exit Cameroon market amid prolonged funds seizure. https://www.reuters.com/business/media-telecom/mtn-says-it-wont-exit-cameroon-market-amid-prolonged-funds-seizure-2024-09-04/

Baillères, A. (2013, April 15). Interview by Cuéllar, R.G. *Creating Emerging Markets Oral History Collection*. Baker Library Special Collections, Harvard Business School.

Belluz, J. (2016, May 6). How Coca-Cola and Pepsi achieved global domination. *Vox*. https://www.vox.com/2015/9/25/9396859/soda-politics-nestle

Brennan, L., & Bakir, C. (2019). *Emerging market multinationals: A new perspective*. Routledge.

Dahlburg, T. (1990, April 10). Pepsico to swap cola for Soviet vodka and ships. https://www.latimes.com/archives/la-xpm-1990-04-10-mn-1040-story.html

Dettoni, J. (2024). *FDI recovery? The devil is in the data details. The FDI Report 2024*. Financial Times.

Entrepreneur. (2023). 2023 top global franchises ranking. https://www.entrepreneur.com/franchises/directory/top-global-ranking

Gabruno, D.M., & Mitchell, A. (2023, September 10). How Embraer was born – the story of a Brazilian startup. https://simpleflying.com/embraer-start-up/

Ghemawat, P. (2001). Distance still matters: The hard reality of global expansion. *Harvard Business Review*, 79(8), 137–147.

Gibbs, N. (2014, September 1). Nissan's bold new beginning in Brazil. https://www.automotivemanufacturingsolutions.com/nissans-bold-new-beginning-in-brazil/33653.article

Global Times. (2022). Tesla joins semiconductor JV in China as demand soars. https://www.globaltimes.cn/page/202211/1280646.shtml

Interesse, G. (2024, November 11). China-Mexico economic relations: Trade, investment, and opportunities. *China Briefing*. https://www.china-briefing.com/news/china-mexico-economic-relations-trade-investment-and-opportunities

Irwin-Hunt, A. (2024, December 4). India Inc flexes muscles on global stage. *fDi Intelligence*. https://www.fdiintelligence.com/content/data-trends/india-inc-flexes-muscles-on-global-stage-84445

Livewell. (2024, January 15). Why was PepsiCo's direct foreign investment primarily in joint ventures? https://livewell.com/finance/why-was-PepsiCos-direct-foreign-investment-primarily-in-joint-ventures/

Macrotrends. (2025). https://www.macrotrends.net/global-metrics/countries/chn/china/foreign-direct-investment

McBirnie, D., & Das, N. (2024, December 11). How India is using its legal system to attract foreigninvestment.https://www.dentons.com/en/insights/articles/2024/december/11/how-india-is-using-its-legal-system-to-attract-foreign-investment

McDonald's Corporation. (2018, May 21). What countries does McDonald's operate in? https://www.mcdonalds.com/gb/en-gb/help/faq/what-countries-does-mcdonald-s-operate-in.html

Millenary Watches. (n.d.) Is a Rolex Swiss made? https://millenarywatches.com/rolex-swiss-made/

Ministry of Commerce of the People's Republic of China. (2024). *Statistical bulletin of FDI in China 2022*. Ministry of Commerce, People's Republic of China. https://fdi.mofcom.gov.cn/resource/pdf/2024/03/14/564085296c88430c98e426696f3751e1.pdf

MND Staff. (2023, November 10). Foreign direct investment in Mexico hits record high. *Mexico New Daily*. https://mexiconewsdaily.com/news/foreign-direct-investment-record-high-2023/

Mokhtarzadeh, N.G., Jafarpanah, I., & Mahdiraji, H.A. (2022). The influence of organisational capabilities on international entrepreneurship performance. In Jafari-Sadeghi, V., & Dana, L.-P. (Eds.). *International Entrepreneurship in Emerging Markets. Context, Behaviours, and Successful Entry* (pp. 256–273). Taylor & Francis.

MTN. (n.d.). Leading Digital solutions for Africa's progress. https://group.mtn.com/who-we-are/strategy/

Nwokoma, C. (2024, September 27). Itana and AFC look to create Africa's Silicon Valley with Nigeria's first digital economic zone. https://techpoint.africa/2024/09/27/itana-and-afc-partnership

O'Grady, V. (2023, November 8). MTN Group still on track to exit multiple markets. https://developingtelecoms.com/telecom-business/operator-news/15762-mtn-group-still-on-track-to-exit-multiple-markets.html

Ordorica, S. (2019, October 19). International market entry strategies for businesses. *Forbes*. https://www.forbes.com/councils/forbesbusinesscouncil/2023/10/19/international-market-entry-strategies-for-businesses/

Panibratov, A. (2017). *International strategy of emerging market firms*. Routledge.

Robinson, C. (2024, October 28). Today's coups must learn from Arab spring. fDi Intelligence. https://www.fdiintelligence.com/content/opinion/opinion-todays-coups-must-learn-from-arab-spring-84141

Saieed, Z. (2025, February 4). Malaysia unveils tax incentives for companies and workers in Johor-Singapore SEZ. https://www.straitstimes.com/asia/se-asia/malaysia-unveils-tax-incentives-for-companies-and-workers-in-johor-singapore-sez

Silajdzic, S., & Mehic, E. (2021). Institutions, culture, and foreign direct investment in transition economies: Does culture matter and why? In Bobek, V., & Quah, C.-H. *Emerging markets*. Intech Open. https://www.intechopen.com/chapters/74641. DOI: 10.5772/intechopen.95326

Stott, M. (2024, January 22). China shifts Latin American investment to compete with west. *The Financial Times*. https://www.ft.com/content/5858a9e9-b063-40f6-afd6-e35f1ceeb6d1

Tata Group. (n.d.). *Our timeline: The early years (1868-1917)*. Tata Group. https://www.tata.com/about-us/tata-group-our-heritage/Our-Timeline-The-Early-Years-1868-1917

Terpstra, V., & Yu, C.J. (1990). Piggybacking: A quick road to internationalisation. *International Marketing Review* 7(4). https://doi.org/10.1108/02651339010000299

Volkswagen Group China. (2018). SAIC Volkswagen Automotive Co., Ltd. https://volkswagen groupchina.com.cn/en/partner/saicvolkswagen

World Population Review. (n.d.) FDI by Country 2024. Retrieved March 7, 2025 from https://worldpopulationreview.com/country-rankings/fdi-by-country

Wright, G. (2023, May 4). Superdry: What's gone wrong and how can it bounce back? *Retail Gazette*. https://www.retailgazette.co.uk/blog/2023/05/superdry-wrong/

CHAPTER 7

Formulating vision and mission statements, value propositions, and gaining competitive advantage

Learning outcomes

After studying this chapter, you will be able to do the following:

1. Craft a vision statement for business expansion into or within an emerging market, incorporating sustainability principles and ESG practices.
2. Add a mission statement that supports the vision, incorporating medium- and long-term SMART goals, and allows for adaptability to emerging market conditions.
3. Create a value proposition that identifies customer needs, distinguishes unmet from latent needs, and integrates sustainability principles.
4. Analyze competitive advantage strategies in emerging markets, applying frameworks like Porter's Five Forces and the resource-based view (RBV).
5. Assess and integrate cultural, social, and economic factors into strategic decisions regarding business expansion, market positioning, and competitive strategy.
6. Critically evaluate the translation of sustainability principles into vision, mission, value propositions, and pricing decisions.
7. Use real-world examples of market-leading businesses to demonstrate how they maintain leading market presence in the emerging world.

Introduction

So far, we have examined big picture concepts: potential markets, their characteristics, and ways to understand them. We now turn to entrepreneurs and businesses. They will conduct an incisive examination of how their business is going to fit into a new market. What values do they hold? How does the business want to present itself to the new market?

DOI: 10.4324/9781003638490-7

What does it do best? How will it bring that as value into a new market? What result does it want to achieve? Having settled its identity, it will proceed to define its value proposition for the new market, to achieve competitive advantage.

In forming a clear view of strategic direction, ESG considerations are not optional. Integrating sustainability principles and ESG metrics into business philosophy is essential to gain consumer preference, regulatory compliance, and long-term success.

Vision

Organizational vision focuses on future goals rather than immediate priorities. A vision statement expresses what a business strives toward – what it ultimately wants to become or achieve. In the developed world, mere aspiration may be enough, describing what a business wants to become in the long term. When entering an emerging market, more is needed: there may be an opportunity to shape the market and build trust by embedding sustainability principles; growth built on sustainability actively contributes to markets instead of simply exploiting them (Porter & Kramer, 2011).

While some vision statements remain purely aspirational, more evolved statements go further. Compare these two examples:

> To lead the way in sustainable transportation and energy solutions, driving innovation and excellence in the industry.
>
> *(BYD, China: CBM, 2024)*

> To address the Climate Crisis and protect the Amazon, to defend Human Rights and to be Human-Kind, to embrace Circularity and Regeneration.
>
> *(Natura & Co, n.d.)*

The Natura & Co statement is strategic, actionable, and context aware. It explicitly links sustainability to concrete actions – environmental protection, actively defending human rights, and embracing circularity. It states *how* the business is going to achieve its vision. Natura has made enviable progress in achieving its vision, with strong results in Amazon conservation, gender equality, and product biodegradability. Its financial performance is equally enviable; the company is a global leader in demonstrating the success of integrating environmental and social goals into a successful business strategy.

Sustainability themes and ESG-aligned goals are almost omnipresent in the vision statements of leading businesses in emerging markets. It is desirable that such goals genuinely come from within. However, there is also plenty of external pressure: consumers are increasingly attracted by sustainable concepts, more investors are insisting on them, and governments perennially increase regulation.

When considering redevelopment of its vision statement for a new market, a business may benefit greatly from engaging potential customers, suppliers, and community leaders in the discussion. Listening and adapting earns credibility and enhances reputation. An outstanding example of such engagement is Gap, Inc.'s decade-long cultivation of close relationships with labor groups, human rights activists, and governments. Through its stakeholder engagement policy, Gap fundamentally reconstructed its ethical sourcing and sustainability policies (Smith, Ansett & Erez, 2011).

Because emerging markets move and change rapidly, vision must incorporate flexibility. Vision may not change regularly, but it is critical to frame it in a way that does not inhibit agility. It must also be open to introduction of new ideas in response to unforeseeable developments. Nokia's fall from grace in emerging markets demonstrates the fallibility of an inflexible vision. The guiding vision of merely "Connecting People" led to a narrow focus on feature phones with durability and long battery life but with only basic features. It simply aimed at selling more phones to more people. The approach did not equip Nokia to anticipate rapid rise of touchscreen technology, apps, and cheap smartphones, which redefined what "connection" meant to consumers. Samsung and several Chinese manufacturers adapted, supplying vast numbers of inexpensive and superior smartphones to emerging markets. Nokia's market share became an empty wasteland (Doz, 2017). Samsung and the Chinese providers may appear to have been opportunistic, but while they were not directly driven by sustainability, they aligned better with the evolving market and made a better contribution to long-term digital inclusion.

The company's vision must be apparent to the world. Open, clear communication about the business's essence is essential, and it must synchronize vision, mission, and values. Next, let's consider mission.

Mission

A mission statement is present-focused. It captures the activities that will be performed today to achieve the vision of tomorrow. Good mission statements are not lengthy or complicated; they are clear and concise. Their magic is that, in very few words, they capture the very essence of the business's current purpose and operations, communicating it to stakeholders and the outside world. That essence includes contributing to environmental and social goals. This is especially important in emerging markets, where rapid business development poses enhanced threats to people and their environment.

A mission statement which works in a developed market is not guaranteed to translate well into the emerging sector; however, the general practice of large businesses is to make the mission broad enough to cover worldwide operations, then focus their strategies and operations on local requirements. Consider these examples:

> To re-imagine global agriculture and food systems.
>
> *(Olam International, 2023)*

> To continue growing as a responsible organisation that enriches lives, while striving for economic and ecological sustainability.
>
> *(Reliance Industries Limited, 2025)*

> Operate in a safe and profitable manner in Brazil and abroad, with social and environmental responsibility, providing products and services that meet clients' needs and that contribute to the development of Brazil and the countries in which it operates.
>
> *(Petrobras, Brazil) (Comparably, n.d.)*

The pervasive themes of ecological and social responsibility are notable. However, a grand purpose is not enough: second thought is needed for new ventures. Walmart's "saving people money so they can live better" is just eight words yet dramatically illustrates the possible consequences of failure to adapt. Walmart's failure in Brazil had many causes, but it is clear in retrospect that deep thought about whether the price-driven promise was viable in that complex environment might have prevented a sizeable financial misstep.

Once the philosophical underpinnings of a business are clear, it must give careful thought to establishing a set of specific goals to add detail and direction.

Organizational goals

Writing in 1981, George Doran introduced the concept of SMART goals. While the acronym has been tinkered with over the 40+ years since then, his framework still provides a workable set of criteria for long-term planning. In emerging markets, SMART goals keep businesses realistic and focused by setting measurable benchmarks, even in the face of multiple VUCA challenges.

Doran's framework stipulates that management goals and objectives should be the following:

Specific. A specific goal is clear and does not contain ambiguity. "Improve road safety in Manila" is non-specific, unactionable, and provides no direction. "Reduce peak period accidents by 5% next year by deploying 20 uniformed officers in marked vehicles on the approaches to hotspots from 7 to 10 each morning and from 4 to 7 each afternoon" is specific; it identifies what is to be achieved, which is measurable, how it will be done, who will implement it and when the goal should be achieved.

Measurable. The example just given demonstrates measurability because it incorporates a statistical goal. Measurement can be as straightforward as counting or timing something (e.g., patient wait times in a clinic), but it can be more esoteric, for example, increasing customer satisfaction (measured by questionnaires using a Likert scale).

Achievable. Best practice is to set a goal which stretches and challenges the business, its resources, and staff but is realistic and achievable. Over-ambition will lead to disappointment and resentment. eBay set an arguably unachievable goal when it tried to capture the Chinese online market; after a few years of intense competition, it lost the battle to Alibaba and sold its business to its main rival (Wang, 2010).

Relevant. Relevance requires that a goal align with the broader mission and values of the business. That does not imply that every effort should be exclusively aimed at increasing profits for shareholders. Any new effort must align clearly with overall organizational goals. Relevance means having a positive impact for all stakeholders.

Time-Bound. Doran concluded by stipulating that clear target dates should be set – not just end-dates but milestones. This not only enhances measurability but also calibrates progress tracking, helps establish priorities, and allocates accountability for achievement or failure.

Core competencies

To be successful in any competitive marketplace, a business must possess core competencies. These are the skills, knowledge, and abilities that it possesses, making it capable of creating superior value for its customers. One widely recognized framework for understanding core competencies is the RBV, introduced by economist Birger Wernerfelt in 1984. The RBV postulates that a business's likelihood of success in an emerging market depends on its ability to leverage its own resources and capabilities, rather than on external opportunities or the market. Resources can be tangible or intangible; they must be valuable, rare, inimitable, and non-substitutable (VRIN). In emerging markets, companies can differentiate themselves if they have resources that satisfy VRIN and are a fit for the unique local conditions. These might include abilities in working with informal regulatory systems, frugal innovation, and building trust with local stakeholders. The RBV predicts success for a business with dynamic capabilities to create or change resources when there is rapid change in the local environment.

The RBV also provides an explanation for the success of large businesses, such as Tata Group and Natura, who have VRIN resources and deploy them in new markets. The focus on internal strengths allows them to overcome institutional voids, compete with (other) global giants, and drive innovation. This century, businesses that lead the way by incorporating ESG-driven sustainability initiatives into their practices create VRIN assets which competitors cannot easily replicate.

The RBV has some limitations. Unique resources may be copied or reverse-engineered by competitors or become obsolete in the face of rapid technological advancement. Internal resources may be difficult to scale up for growth. If there is over-reliance on a model where a business is the market leader, this can delay necessary changes or inefficient investment in a dying technology (such as film-based photography).

In emerging markets, the triple threat of institutional voids, weak regulatory enforcement, and informal economies can fundamentally alter how resources qualify as VRIN. For example, in a market with uneven regulation, ability to navigate unpredictable government interference can be a VRIN resource; so too can creative distribution models based on mobile phones or informal gig work.

Jim Collins' (2001) famous *hedgehog concept* is a more recent application. It helps businesses to focus on their potential for uniqueness. Just as a hedgehog does one thing really well (rolling into a ball), businesses need to determine what they can do best in the world, what they are passionate about, and how they make money. When these three areas are aligned, the business has sufficient strength for success and longevity. In emerging markets, simplicity and clear messaging are often key strategic advantages; hedgehog logic returns focus to core propositions even in fragmented, unstable market conditions.

If a competency is easy to copy (especially by competitors), it is of limited value. If only one or two departments or individuals hold the competency, it does not support cross-functional progress. If it is not customer-focused, it is of no long-term commercial value (Prahalad & Hamel, 1990).

Lean manufacturing, which optimizes production while eliminating waste, is a classic core competency. Mastery of lean principles is a flagship competency of Toyota, which has simultaneously increased product quality and reduced costs. Today the Toyota Production System (TPS) is used as a benchmark in many industries besides automobile manufacturing (Toyota, 2024). Lean techniques are especially valuable in emerging markets, because production models are constantly challenged by resource scarcities and infrastructural deficiencies.

Lean is not only a manufacturing technique. In African healthcare, for example, lean methodology is used to improve patient intake processes in clinics and hospitals, building capacity in the face of severe resource limitations (Naidoo & Mahomed, 2016).

Contextual exploration of core competencies is critical when venturing into a new market. Will this competency translate well into the new market? What adaptations must be made to achieve that translation?

McDonald's core competencies, developed in the United States, have always been efficiency, standardization, predictable food quality, and successful franchising. Branching out internationally, it could not simply replicate the American model in over 100 countries with varied tastes, cultures, and business practices. While keeping some core menu items, McDonald's has localized menus, adjusting food tastes, types, and origins, to cater to regional preferences (Sheldon, Awati, & Pratt, 2024).

Another example of regional adaptation is Nestlé's approach in India. Nestlé identifies its core competencies as "Innovation and Renovation," "Wherever, whenever, however," "Consumer engagement," and "Operational efficiency." Translated from the catchphrases and blended with other corporate goals, Nestlé strives to capitalize on its reputation for good, nutritious products, deliver them to entire populations, satisfy customer needs, and operate the best possible supply chain (Nestlé India Limited, 2024).

In India, the first competency resonates with the growing population, especially in urban areas. However, especially in rural areas, there is a massive low-income population. Nestlé introduced smaller packages at very low prices to cater to quantity needs, expanded its own distribution network to reach remote rural areas, and incorporated local flavors into its products (e.g., a Masala version of Swiss MAGGI noodles).[1]

The quest for local relevance brings with it an essential requirement of developing local expertise within the business. Nestlé and Unilever are both renowned for the strength of their decentralized approaches. Some analysts suggest that they epitomize businesses where local employee development is so strong that it weakens global leadership (Levenson, 2020).

Values

Values held by a business typically fall into two categories: core values, which apply across the enterprise, and focused values, which apply to specific areas within the business such as people, finance, or the environment. Like a mission statement, they are deeply held beliefs which can transcend national boundaries, are susceptible to minor adaptations, and speak volumes not only to the business but also to the people who own and manage it.

Patagonia has for years built its entire brand around its *core values*: quality, environmental stewardship, and social responsibility. Patagonia's customer base expects to see these values played out in every initiative and decision taken by the business.

People-based values are necessary to build loyalty and growth in the workforce. A business that embraces diversity, equity, and inclusion will not only experience lower turnover and better morale but will also be viewed more favorably by governments, suppliers, and customers. A challenge arises when an investing business with strong traditions of equality proposes to operate in an area where there is a rigid class structure or other social inequality. If insisting that race, lineage, or gender be disregarded is going to cause unresolvable conflicts, the business may reconsider expanding into that market. It is hard to conceive of a business case that would legitimize abandoning fundamental values.

Identity

Identity is how a business is perceived by the public, whether that is the entire world or a small local population. It must be driven by ethical decision-making and is the product of the business's mission and values. Corporate identity today starts with visual and verbal elements (logos, mottos, and advertising messages), runs through the business's culture and values, incorporates its ethics and sustainability, and culminates in how it is perceived by stakeholders and the public.

Nike is a universal example of a business with a strong identity. It is known everywhere for its dedication to inspiring athletes and achievement. "Just do it," in hundreds of languages, is synonymous with the company itself. It is not just a shoes-and-sportswear business but an international symbol of winning (Hashem, 2024).

Sustainability concepts are foundational in defining the identity of an enterprise and ensuring long-term success. They shape operations, garner stakeholder trust, and support brand positioning. Effective alignment with ESG pillars helps a business to meet society's expectations and identifies its management as thoughtful, innovative leaders. In emerging markets, visible social contributions are an extremely powerful way of building identity, far beyond mere product features or marketing spend. Natura & Co's stewardship of the Amazon is an outstanding example.

Itaú Unibanco is another world-class example of integration of ESG with core strategy. It is highly involved in financing renewable energy projects across Latin America and focuses on financial inclusion in its home market of Brazil. Its Board of Directors includes a dedicated ESG committee, tasked with continuous oversight of sustainability and risk management (Itaú, 2024).

Tentree

While not based in an emerging market, Canadian apparel company Tentree International Inc. is widely regarded as a model for embedding sustainability into identity. With a mission to inspire a generation to embrace sustainable living, its vision is grounded in environmental restoration for future generations. Its core values focus on environmentally friendly sourcing of materials, transparency, and the impact of its practice of planting ten trees (hence the name) for every product purchased. It leverages its strong value-driven identity into competitive advantage (Tentree, n.d.).

A thorough evaluation of a business's mission, vision, values, and identity sets the stage for building a market strategy, clarifying how it will make customer centricity the core of its value proposition.

The customer value proposition

A customer value proposition (CVP) has three essential elements: a description of what problem or need it addresses, identification of the benefit(s) it delivers, and the unique aspects which differentiate it from alternatives. In an emerging market context, especially when targeting underserved or price-sensitive segments, the CVP typically embraces accessibility, affordability, customization to local needs, and cultural adaptation.

We intentionally use the word "customer" in this definition to emphasize its customer-centric nature. While academic literature often abbreviates this to "value proposition," doing so can lead to confusion with the general value proposition, the broader set of benefits a company promises to deliver to all stakeholders (Payne, Frow, & Eggert, 2017).

Value proposition as a concept first appears in an internal McKinsey paper by Lanning and Michaels in 1988, titled *A Business Is a Value Delivery System*. Since then, scholars in marketing and customer experience management have greatly expanded on the original ideas.

Osterwalder's *value proposition canvas* (VPC) is a practical tool to design and refine a CVP (Osterwalder et al., 2014). It has two elements:

- The customer profile (referred to as the "right side").
- The value proposition map ("left side").

The customer profile identifies customer needs in terms of "jobs-to-be-done." They further break down into functional, social, and emotional jobs. For example, in an emerging market context, a functional job might involve accessing affordable products or reducing reliance on environmentally inefficient services. A social job might point toward supporting local businesses with ethical supply chains. An emotional job could include trusting that the supplier is committed to the local community, not just exploiting its resources.

To create an effective CVP, a product or service must address these needs. In this example, it might offer an environmentally friendly alternative to existing options, address pain points (affordability) by adding an installment plan for payment, and partner with a trusted NGO operating in the area to show commitment. If well-designed, the CVP will ensure that products and services are attractive, provide real value, and stand out from the competition.

Unmet and latent needs

CVP analysis benefits from a further distinction between unmet needs and latent needs.

Unmet needs are those which flow from a gap between the desires or requirements of a population and the existing solutions available. Populations, whether of individuals or businesses, can articulate and are conscious of them. Often, the solutions are readily identifiable. Rewards are available to entrepreneurs who develop them.

Latent needs, while they also represent a business opportunity, are not readily identifiable by consumers. Potential customers may be completely unaware of the improvement that a new product or service might bring to their lives until the solution is presented to them. There is a greater role for innovation and creativity in addressing latent needs; they often exist because consumers are unable to think of solutions outside their current experience. Addressing latent needs often requires innovators to think far out of the box, beyond what consumers express or can even imagine.

Latent and unmet needs are not always completely distinct. As latent needs enter consumer consciousness, they transition toward unmet status with a period of overlap. While potentially more profitable, latent needs are initially more difficult to address, requiring greater investment in innovation, consumer education, and marketing. Unmet needs will find early demand more easily but more readily invite competition. Latent needs are likely to start slowly but secure advances over potential competitors.

Selçuk Yaşar's impressive business empire in Türkiye, Selçuk Holding, is built on the identification of unmet needs. In 1954, the business established the first paint factory in Türkiye; ventures into milk and meat followed in response to the inability of the state's distribution system to supply customer needs. The constant search for unmet needs led to the establishment of the first fish farm in Türkiye in 1985; this was the seed of Türkiye's significant role in the world seafood market today (Yaşar, 2014).

As a first step in building a value proposition, expanding companies will develop a business proposition which addresses either unmet or latent needs. The entrepreneur wishing to find opportunities in a chosen market, as opposed to having a product and looking for new markets, will employ a variety of techniques to identify them.

There is considerable commonality to the areas of unmet need across most emerging markets. Low-income areas typically have restricted access to goods and services regarded as essential in developed countries. These include social necessities such as education and healthcare. Infrastructure deficiencies are common, creating both a barrier and an opportunity. Technologies that are widely available in the developed world may be inaccessible in an emerging market, or the population may not have the ability to use them.

Infrastructure shortcomings are often found at a continental level. This opens possibilities of expanding a successful initiative into several countries connected within the same landmass. The African continent faces an annual infrastructure deficit estimated at $95 to $100 billion annually; across many countries, there is a need for regulatory reform so that pension and sovereign wealth funds can bring international capital into solutions. This is inextricably linked to the wider need for Africa's relationship to the world to move away from government and aid solutions toward trade and investment (Danso, 2015).

The following case studies illustrate the role of the value proposition.

MineSense

We are going to spend a little longer than usual on the Minesense[2] case, because it is a clear example of a large-scale value proposition satisfying a latent need, with profound sustainability benefits for the business and customers. It also demonstrates a real contribution to sustainability in resource extraction, a critical industry in many emerging markets.

The mining industry is a huge consumer of water, which it needs for everything from ore processing to air quality control and miners' hygiene. Mining is a dirty business! However, decent quality deposits of many ores are in dry or semi-arid areas where there is a severe shortage of water. There is a pressing and obvious need for new processes to find water, use less, and recycle it after treatments. This is an unmet need and a significant opportunity in several emerging markets.

MineSense Technologies supplies a new product and accompanying technology. Mining has always been an inefficient process. The percentage of a mineral like chalcopyrite (which contains copper) or argentite (which contains silver) in a quantity of rock, even from a rich vein, is exceedingly small. Veins are narrow and often irregular, so vast quantities of waste rock (known as overburden) are blasted, extracted, and discarded in the quest for the small quantities of ore which will produce profitable yields. How much mineral is potentially lost, however, when apparent overburden which contains worthwhile quantities of mineral is discarded as waste?

MineSense's signature product, ShovelSense®, is shown in Figure 7.1. It is a robust scanning system with accompanying software to analyze the mineral content of every bucketload of material as it is removed. The operator is instantly notified if a bucketload of previously classified waste contains ore above the cutoff grade, and the corresponding

Figure 7.1 ShovelSense® at work

truck is re-rerouted into processing. The reverse also occurs; bucketloads of ore that are waste are rerouted to the waste piles.

Because the software also knows where every bucketload of rock came from, the enhanced analysis of waste product also allows better mapping of the orebody itself. Not only is more mineral recovered from each mine, but the quantity of resources used (water, energy, and reagents) is reduced, as less but higher-grade materials are processed.

More accurate mining means less disruption of habitats and ecosystems, lower carbon emissions, and smaller footprints for mining operations. The ultimate removal of overburden is less, meaning less tailings and cheaper reclamation. Finally, the full circle comes back to water – if there is better classification of extracted rock, then less water is wasted in the extraction process.

The dramatic increase in profitability and sustainability of mining operations in the emerging markets of Chile, Peru, Brazil, and Indonesia have won the company many awards, massive acclaim from cleantech experts, and tens of millions of dollars in new investment.

ShovelSense® is a superb example of a latent need. Most users had no idea they needed such a product, until the solution was presented to them. Mining operators may have believed, before the solution was conceived and presented, that previous inefficiencies were inherent and unsolvable. Emerging markets, by their very nature, are filled with opportunities to turn waste into value.

VietJet

In 2007, Vietnam passed Decree 76, which permitted private sector participation in the airline business. Nguyen Thi Phuong Thao, CEO of VietJet, recounts how prior to the airline's launch, only 1% of the local population had even potential access to air travel. VietJet's story is a classic example of *market creation* – identifying a segment with a latent need and building a service model which fits the segment's economic and social requirements.

Thao reviewed global operating standards, then adapted them to the resource-constrained local context, advocating to break state monopolies with the addition of more fuel suppliers and overcoming supply chain bottlenecks. VietJet then targeted first-time flyers with educational marketing, simplifying processes and making flights accessible to low-income and rural populations.

Based on these successes, Thao points to the importance of technology (such as internet and mobile check-in) to efficiency in a resource-constrained environment. She leveraged her global expertise into locally relevant solutions, reducing costs, increasing capacity, and advocating for improved air traffic control. She successfully positioned VietJet as a global player while strategizing for local expansion (Thao, 2017).

Unlike many low-cost carriers in Europe, VietJet also carries cargo; along with ancillary revenue from meals and merchandise, it accounts for 40% of its revenue (Doran, 2024). Strategic expansion of the route network has built up capacity to 400 flights per day, with 82 aircraft by the end of 2023. It is presently adding ten more (Reuters, 2024). Its 2023 passenger count was

25.3 million, an increase of 183% over the previous year. It also became profitable, earning over US$25 million in a significant turnaround (TTR Weekly, 2024). All of this is the result of a clear focus on cost leadership, market expansion, and brand differentiation.

By operating primarily newer Airbus 320 and Airbus 321 aircraft, VietJet emits less carbon dioxide per passenger than airlines with older models. Its high load factor contributes to an enviable emission per passenger. It has introduced waste reduction measures like a prohibition on single-use plastics and paperless ticketing. Its ground operations increasingly engage with renewable energy providers. It invests in community development, with workforce training for underprivileged young recruits. Each of these activities support VietJet's commitment to sustainability, reducing costs while strengthening stakeholder relationships (VietJetAir.com, 2023).

Adapting to regional markets

We emphasize again the critical importance of understanding specific cultures, values, and languages in the market to be entered. No assumptions can be made based on what happens at home – anything from a social taboo to an unusual government regulation can doom an enterprise. Adaptation brings with it several necessary strategies.

Coca-Cola in Asia

The century-old story of Coca-Cola's Chinese naming is amusing but instructive.

> Coca-Cola first entered the Chinese market in 1927, but it wasn't initially known as kě kǒu kě lè. Instead, it was translated as kē kē kěn là. This translation aimed to mimic the English pronunciation but ended up with a bizarre meaning: kē means tadpole, kěn means to nibble, and là means wax. Chinese consumers envisioned tadpoles gnawing on wax, no metaphor for an appetizing beverage. As a result, unfamiliarity with the taste and the strange name led to dismal sales.
>
> *(Bielewicz, 2024)*

Localization for tastes and preferences is also crucial. Coca-Cola's diverse product offerings in regional markets show how much variety is possible. The trademarks and names may be the same, but the drinks are not. "Soy-milk-based variants were launched in Asian countries to cater to dietary preferences. Coca-Cola offers fruit juice blends in Europe, dairy-based fusions in Latin America, and lower-sweetness dry drinks in Japan based on regional taste inclinations" (The Strategy Institute, 2024). Kasa masala and nimbu pani, for example, are both Coca-Cola products created for the Indian market.

This tale illustrates a fundamental truth: successful entry to an emerging market requires not just product availability but relevant messaging. Coca-Cola's early misfortunes in China show how badly a product can fail if its name, advertising, branding, or taste do not appeal to consumers. Coca-Cola made the product successful, ultimately, by tailoring its products using deep localization. Meaningful consumer messaging is a cost, but one well spent to build connection and trust.

Volkswagen in India and Brazil

The popular Volkswagen Polo car was a larger vehicle in India than in Europe. It was discontinued in India in 2022. Volkswagen established that Indian consumers would prefer a larger car; they tended to have larger families traveling together than Europeans. The new design had a higher roof and more legroom. Yet another version went to market in Brazil, the Polo Robust, with off-road adaptations. Volkswagen is now hinting that the Polo may return to India in an all-electric version (Athul, 2024).

To thrive in a new market, a business must deliver a compelling value proposition to potential customers. This requires understanding what customers trust, how they evaluate quality, and what unmet or latent needs they have. The value proposition is not shaped by the product or the developed-world messaging it carries, but by asking a simple question – "Why would a consumer in this market, at this time, choose our product?" The Coca-Cola story, which we just recounted, shows a progression from complete failure to answer this question, to the achievement of a successful understanding.

The business must also position itself effectively in relation to its competition. The next section explores how businesses achieve and sustain competitive advantage.

Gaining competitive advantage

Competitive advantage occurs when a business performs better than others in a market by delivering greater value to its customers. It is created either by *cost advantage* (lower costs) or *differentiation advantage* (better benefits). It is necessary to understand competitors' offerings to assess competitive advantage.

Competitors exist in three areas: existing local competitors, global competitors, and potential future entrants. It is not sufficient to make a successful first penetration of the market; longer-term success planning requires assessment of the competitive threat.

What should be determined about each type of competitor? Their market share is an important statistic which needs analysis in context with their products and pricing strategies. What are their brands – how are they positioned and what is the messaging? How are their products distributed – does this reveal any opportunities? What aspects of their service create an opportunity for competitive advantage – are they weak on public relations or customer service, for example? Are they profitable? If they are not, how long can they cover their losses to maintain their market position – and can the market entrant incur similar losses just to remain competitive? If competitors are highly profitable, can the entrant accept lower margins? How will incumbents react?

A SWOT type analysis – evaluating strengths, weaknesses, opportunities, and threats – is a powerful tool for evaluating internal strengths and external threats. Businesses and analysts frequently use SWOT analysis as an aid to understanding their competitive position and their relationship with the market environment. In emerging markets, SWOT categorization of the myriad potential challenges to a new business helps paint a clear picture their situation and the positions and roles of various risks.

Appendix 1 contains two examples of SWOT tables, one for emerging markets in general and one for a specific business proposition, Hult International Business School's theoretical new campus in Brazil.

Harvard Professor Michael Porter's "five forces analysis" (Porter, 1980) is detailed and directly applicable. This multipronged tool assists in the analysis of profitability and competition. Porter's five forces are the threat of new entrants, bargaining power of suppliers, bargaining power of buyers, the threat of substitutes, and competitive rivalry.

Threat of new entrants – how easy is it for a new player to enter the market and take share? Ease may be influenced by economies of scale (if the existing players are producing large volumes, small entrants will be discouraged); capital requirements (big projects require large amounts of capital which may be difficult to obtain); government regulations (if they are burdensome or lengthy, new entrants will be discouraged); brand loyalty (how difficult is it to persuade consumers to try a new name); and switching costs (what does it cost customers to come over to a new product).

The automobile industry exemplifies these difficulties. To design and build an entirely new car requires an extraordinary amount of investment, which large existing manufacturers can spread over their millions of vehicles sold. Licensing and regulation requirements are stringent and costly. Convincing lifelong brand-loyal consumers to spend significant sums on a new name is no small feat. Only switching costs are comparatively light for consumers when it comes to car brands.

The barriers to entry in the financial services sector have been significantly reduced by the introduction of mobile banking technology. While the original lack of a banking infrastructure was seen as an opportunity by companies like Safaricom, they in turn are now continually challenged by fintech start-ups (European Investment Bank, 2024).

ESG compliance frameworks and sustainability regulations are a formidable barrier to entry. Compliance is expensive for new entrants, giving a first-mover advantage to incumbents who have stayed "ahead of the curve" and incorporated best-in-class ESG practices into their supply chains and operations.

Bargaining power of suppliers – Suppliers, whether of raw materials, manufactured components, or logistics, are typically few but can control essential inputs. Their pricing significantly impacts profitability. India and China dominate the global supply of pharmaceutical ingredients, for example, making manufacturers around the world highly sensitive to their demands. The dual risks of price volatility and supply reliability are intense. The social impact pillar of ESG can play a powerful role in supply management – a commitment to ethical sourcing of materials or labor decreases dependency on risky sources which can lead to supply chain disruptions or severe reputational damage.

Bargaining power of buyers – Porter points to the level of ability possessed by consumers to influence price and conditions. The smartwatch market in China exemplifies such power, flooded with products from domestic and overseas manufacturers, while online marketplaces give consumers easy ability to compare prices and features. Any new manufacturer seeking to enter the market will have little price-setting power, given the need to compete with existing offerings. In another example, strong price sensitivity has emerged for consumer electronics in Indonesia due to the ease of switching to competitor products (Kadence International, 2024).

Threat of substitutes – Porter underlines the competitive threat from similar, or alternative, products that could satisfy the same consumer need. The smartphone market in East, West, and South Africa demonstrates the challenge: while exporters make budget-friendly phones to sell in those markets, they must compete directly with products like Tecno and Infinix, by Transsion.[3] The Transsion phones are produced in Ethiopia, to reduce importation and transportation costs, with very similar features and strong local tailoring of marketing strategies.

Competitive rivalry – How heated is competition, already? It is likely that with more competitors, lower growth rates, little product differentiation, and low switching costs, rivalry will be more intense. Mobile payment technology in Kenya is a field which displays intense competition; a dominant market position held by M-Pesa[4] is constantly challenged by Airtel Money,[5] Equitel,[6] and T-Kash.[7] The level of competition has led to rapid enhancements of the product offerings and made Kenya, which has high mobile phone penetration and low banking penetration, the leading zone for mobile payments innovation on the African continent. Ride-hailing services in India suffer fierce competition due to the number of players in the market and the creation of localized service types (Shankar, 2017).

While it seems logical to analyze the five forces individually, in practice they interact. A strategic decision may shift the balance between two forces, evidencing that there are trade-offs at play. For example, a business which decides to focus on the highest quality products in its range will increase differentiation but may also increase its dependence on suppliers. If those suppliers increase prices, profit margins are reduced. Maintaining competitive advantage while business evolves requires understanding these interdependencies.

The traditional assumptions underlying Porter's model are often distorted in emerging markets, making the interplay dynamic even more complex. The difficulties of market entry may be compounded by weak enforcement of legislation lowering barriers, only for politics or corruption to present their own barriers. Supplier power can be increased by infrastructure deficiencies or limited options for supplies, while informal economies may rapidly present substitutes. Emerging market conditions cause the five forces to interact in less predictable ways, meaning that businesses need more localization in their strategies to maintain competitive advantage.

Holding competitive advantage is of no value if it is transitory. Keeping hold of competitive advantage is deeply dependent on pricing, which is particularly complex in emerging markets. In the next section, we will explore pricing models which may be appropriate to maintain the value of a competitive advantage after launching a new product or service.

Pricing models

Correct pricing of products and services, which requires continuous monitoring and adaptability, is critical to long-term success. In emerging markets, *penetration* or *economy pricing* (to gain market) and value-based pricing (selling based on benefits) are the most frequent launch models. *Cost-based pricing* (adding a percentage to the cost of production) is virtually never appropriate at launch, as it doesn't account for local demand elasticity or competitor positioning. Although eventually the selling price must be higher than the cost of production and delivery, in the early days flexibility and responsiveness have high priority over cost recovery.[8]

The foundational choice is between economy pricing (supported by cost leadership) and value-based pricing (particularly for premium products). Will the business compete on price and keep costs down or offer a superior version of a product, relying on perception of value to support a higher price? In traditional microeconomics, this distinction is seen slightly differently: price takers are in a competitive marketplace, with other providers and substitute products, and thus are compelled to compete on cost. Unique products with few competitors or subjects make the offeror a price setter, allowing more flexibility and higher prices (Perloff, 2020).

As *cost leadership* (low pricing) is the dominant model in new markets, competitive pricing is crucial. An entry is much more likely to enjoy success if initial prices are lower than competitors, although one might usually expect a counterattacking move by established providers. When Chinese smartphone producer Xiaomi launched in India, it quickly captured market share by offering feature-rich models at much lower prices than the incumbent providers. Samsung's introduction of the Galaxy M series, a very low-priced version of its smartphone, was a direct response to the Xiaomi pricing and triggered a price and feature war across the country. It shows no signs of abating (Ingelido, 2023).

A business which is a cost leader in a developed country cannot simply replicate its model in an emerging market. Although cost leadership is the dominant model, this is a result of six distinct factors: wage costs, logistics, regulation, consumer behavior, competition, and technology.

Wage costs are typically lower in emerging markets, allowing lower costs of labor. In developed markets, production savings are usually made from automation. Underdeveloped logistics in emerging markets typically raise costs, whereas good infrastructure in developed markets reduces them. The regulatory environment is typically less stable, resulting in lower compliance costs but a greater need for vigilance. Consumers are more price-sensitive in emerging markets, lessening the opportunities for brand differentiation. Competing low-cost producers, often small firms, dominate emerging markets, while larger businesses are more easily able to dominate cost leadership in developed markets. Finally, technological development in emerging markets tends to focus on distribution issues, while in developed markets there is more focus on production.

Dr. Raghunath Mashelkar, former Director General of India's CSIR, is widely credited with popularizing, or maybe even creating, the concept of *affordable excellence*. Emerging markets, he argues, need products which are affordable for large populations, but they must be created without compromising quality. He points to several famous examples, including the Tata Nano (the world's cheapest car), Aravind Eye Care (low-cost cataract surgery), and the Jaipur Foot (a prosthetic limb produced at a fraction of the cost of traditional devices). The guiding principles that make affordable excellence possible include radical reengineering, scalability, and cross-subsidization (where wealthy customers pay more than disadvantaged people for the same product).[9] Mashelkar's views and speeches have had a profound effect in emerging markets and are partially responsible for the emergence of a new generation of social entrepreneurs and socially responsible capitalists (Mashelkar, 2022).

Value-based pricing, also known as premium positioning, can be established in emerging markets. Value-based pricing includes *green premium pricing*, also known as *ESG premium pricing*, a relative newcomer with an attractive future. Consumers can be convinced by companies like Tesla to pay more for products with sustainability deployed as a differentiator. The growing middle class in emerging markets is moving away from price sensitivity, placing more value on ecologically responsible brands.

Natura, based in São Paulo, Brazil, has carefully cultivated a perception that its products are based on advanced science and sustainable sourcing from the Amazon region. This image successfully supports premium pricing. Natura also offers an example of bundled pricing, bringing the Brazilian love of promotions to the rest of the world.[10] Remarkably, Natura enjoys successful sales of its "50% off summer mystery box" – an unusual methodology for a premium brand.

Adaptive pricing models are particularly effective (Hutchinson et al., 2017). The business may wish to consider *penetration pricing*, in which a low initial price is used to gain market share, followed by later increases, or *dynamic pricing*, where demand, competition, seasonality, and other inputs determine optimal prices. Dynamism may also include different prices in distinct locations.

The opposite of penetration pricing is *skimming*, where new products, such as iPhones, gaming consoles, or drugs, are introduced at high prices to recoup research and development costs or maximize profits before competitors catch up. Skimming works for premium brands and helps with market segmentation but limits the potential size of the early market. The profits attract the attention of competitors who are likely to emulate products at a lower price, forcing eventual price reductions. Apple's iPhone sales in India have historically followed skimming paths; the iPhone 15 Pro Max was introduced in India at a price more than 50% higher than in the United States.

Dynamic pricing in response to demand and competition is particularly prevalent in e-commerce in emerging markets, as exemplified by Flipkart and Amazon in India (Flipkart Commerce Cloud, n.d.).

Neither sellers nor markets invariably hold the power to dictate pricing and conditions. Government may intervene. For example, patents and other intellectual property rights may empower pharmaceutical businesses to dictate prices to governments and consumers, especially for essential medicines with no competing products, yet regulation of pharmaceutical markets has become an important government strategy, for example, in South Africa, which in 2004 implemented a single exit price policy for generic medicines (Moodley & Suleman, 2019).

Table 7.1 summarizes key pricing strategies.

As a business from a developed economy contemplates emerging market entry, it must also assess the possible impact of **consumer bargaining**. It is much more prevalent in emerging markets and can have an impact on pricing strategy, sales methods, and product positioning. Bargaining, negotiating the final price with the seller, is an essential part of many transactions and can directly affect how consumers finally feel about their purchase. If the product is subject to a high degree of consumer bargaining, then the choice of sales channel will be critical; the business may attempt to establish fixed prices but may also prefer to work with local vendors who are familiar with the culture. You may be surprised to learn that although some brands like Walmart and McDonald's have been successful in establishing fixed pricing everywhere they go; in Asia, even some e-commerce platforms, such as Taobao, are designed to accommodate bargaining.

There are serious risks if inappropriate pricing models are deployed. Underpricing can damage the perceived value of a product, while overpricing can alienate customers,

Table 7.1 Key pricing strategies

Strategy	*Description*	*Practitioners*
Cost Leadership	Offering low prices enabled by reducing costs.	Walmart, Xiaomi
Value-based pricing • Sustainability-driven pricing	Creating perceived value to support higher pricing. Leveraging environmental friendliness as a justification for higher prices.	Natura, L'OréalPatagonia, Tesla
Dynamic Pricing • Penetration • Skimming	Adjusting prices in response to demand, seasonality, region, or competition Initial offering of products at very low prices, possibly at a loss Introduction at high prices to maximize early revenue, gradually lowering to attract price-sensitive customers	Amazon Reliance Jio (Indian Telecom) Apple (India)

especially in price-sensitive and low-income markets. Dynamic pricing, making continuous adjustments in response to market conditions, is increasingly used in emerging markets and may be highly effective.

Mindray

Mindray is a premier example of a business which started with a home focus and then made great inroads into developed markets by securing a competitive advantage through cost leadership. Founded in Shenzhen in 1991, it first developed products for domestic Chinese markets, where hospitals needed low-cost medical equipment, such as patient monitoring systems, to cope with rapid increases in demand after economic reforms.

Mindray's management, when first looking outside China, made a shrewd decision to explore other emerging markets. They rapidly gained market share elsewhere in Asia and in Latin America, where needs were similar but market conditions were different. Mindray built an impressive knowledge bank for managing diverse international operations.

After the millennium, Mindray moved to take on powerful global competitors in developed markets. It made serious investments in research and development centers in America and Europe, leaping into the U.S. market through an acquisition, Datascope. Its investment in R&D gave Mindray the technological edge it needed to compete with the established giants, expertise in satisfying regulators, and the ability to continue with cost leadership. Today Mindray holds a strong competitive position inside the world's most advanced healthcare systems and in its original markets (Zhang, 2020).

Conclusion: Joining theory and practice

This chapter reviewed a series of key concepts which support a business's desire for long-term success. In emerging markets, there are unparalleled opportunities for sustainable growth and inspired leadership. Vision and mission provide strategic direction, while strong value propositions are supported by localization. To secure market entry advantage, the newcomer must identify unmet or latent needs. Market entry advantage is gained through either cost or value leadership, then retained through sophisticated pricing practices. One consistent theme permeates these strategic efforts: sustainability. The application of ESG practices to core business philosophies inspires customer, investor, and regulator confidence. The result: when flexible, nimble policies are combined with cultural insight, businesses create winning strategies that are deeply meaningful to millions of consumers and other stakeholders.

The next chapter will take all this foundational knowledge and use it to explore the next step: how to effectively market or service a product to new customers in emerging markets.

Notes

1 https://www.amazon.com/Maggi-Minutes-Noodles-Masala-grams/dp/B07B4KQRZG
2 MineSense Technologies Ltd. https://minesense.com
3 www.transsion.com
4 https://www.safaricom.co.ke/main-mpesa/m-pesa-services/
5 https://www.airtelkenya.com/about_money
6 https://equitel.com
7 https://telkom.co.ke/t-kash/
8 We encounter cost-plus pricing in emerging markets in government contracts where cost control and transparency are priorities. In commercial settings, competition, low margins, and consumer awareness virtually always dictate that cost-plus is the wrong approach.
9 Affordable excellence has been a powerful concept in healthcare; another example is Prathap Reddy's Apollo Hospitals. See Reddy (2014).
10 https://www.naturabrasil.com/

References

Athul. (2024, March 25). Volkswagen Polo may return to India: All details here. DriveSpark. https://www.drivespark.com/four-wheelers/2024/volkswagen-polo-possible-return-india-011-045213.html

Bielewicz, M. (2024, June 16). *Cracking the code. How global brands woo Chinese consumers with clever name creations*. Part 1. Chinese Leleland. Trademark Partners. https://trademark.partners/en/what-chinese-character-is-frequently-used-in-marketing/

CBM. (2024, October 2). Mission, Vision & Core Values of BYD Company. https://canvasbusinessmodel.com/blogs/mission/byd-company-mission

Collins, J. (2001). *Good to great: Why some companies make the leap… and others don't*. HarperBusiness.

Comparably. (n.d.) Petrobras Mission, Vision & Values. https://www.comparably.com/companies/petrobras/mission

Danso, H. (2015, April 17). Interview by E. Akyeampong. *Creating Emerging Markets Oral History Collection*. Baker Library Special Collections, Harvard Business School.

Doran, M. (2024, February 1). Vietjet moves 25.3 million passengers on its airbus fleet in 2023. https://simpleflying.com/vietjet-253-million-airbus-fleet-2023/

Doran, T.T. (1981). There's a S.M.A.R.T. way to write management's goals and objectives. Management Review. 70(11), 35–36.

Doz, Y.L. (2017, November 23). The strategic decisions that caused Nokia's failure. *Insead Knowledge*. https://knowledge.insead.edu/strategy/strategic-decisions-caused-nokias-failure

European Investment Bank. (2024). EIB Finance in Africa 2024: Fintech transforms African financial services but high funding costs hinder climate and digital transitions. Retrieved from https://www.eib.org/en/press/all/2024-435-eib-finance-in-africa-2024-fintech-transforms-african-financial-services-but-high-funding-costs-hinder-climate-and-digital-transitions

Flipkart Commerce Cloud. (n.d.). Improve Your top and bottom line with smarter, faster dynamic pricing. https://www.flipkartcommercecloud.com/retail-dynamic-pricing/

Hashem, H. (2024, February 7). 5 things we can learn from Nike's brand identity and advertising strategy. *Kubbco*. https://www.kubbco.com/blog/5-things-we-can-learn-from-nikes-brand-identity-and-advertising-strategy

Hutchinson, R., et al. (2017, March 7). *A pricing playbook for Emerging Markets*. Boston Consulting Group. https://www.bcg.com/publications/2017/marketing-sales-pricing-playbook-emerging-markets

Ingelido, M. (2023, November 6). Xiaomi 14 vs Samsung Galaxy S23: Specs Comparison. https://www.gizmochina.com/guides/xiaomi-14-vs-samsung-galaxy-s23-specs-comparison/

Itaú. (2024). ESG highlight. https://www.itau.com.br/relacoes-com-investidores/en/itau-unibanco/know-more/esg/

Kadence International. (2024). Indonesia market research: Key consumer trends you must know. https://kadence.com/indonesia-market-research-key-consumer-trends-you-must-know/

Lanning, M. J., & Michaels, E. G. (1988). *A business is a value delivery system* (McKinsey Staff Paper No. 41). McKinsey & Company.

Levenson, A. (2020, October 2). Decentralizing your operating and talent models the right way. *MIT Sloan Management Review*. https://sloanreview.mit.edu/article/decentralizing-your-operating-and-talent-models-the-right-way/

Mashelkar, R.A. (2022, June 30). Interview by T. Khanna. *Creating Emerging Markets Oral History Collection*. Baker Library Special Collections, Harvard Business School.

Moodley, R., & Suleman, F. (2019, July 31). The impact of the single exit price policy on a basket of generic medicines in South Africa, using a time series analysis from 1999 to 2014. *PubMed Central*. https://www.ncbi.nlm.nih.gov/pmc/articles/PMC6668780/

Naidoo, L., & Mahomed, O. H. (2016). Impact of Lean on patient cycle and waiting times at a rural district hospital in KwaZulu-Natal. *African Journal of Primary Health Care & Family Medicine*, *8*(1), e1–e9. https://doi.org/10.4102/phcfm.v8i1.1084

Natura & Co. (n.d.). Commitment to Life. *Sustainability Vision*. https://www.naturaeco.com/sustainability-vision-2030/ Nestlé. Roadmap to good food, good life. https://www.nestle-caribbean.com/aboutus/strategy

Nestlé India Limited. (2024, April 8). *Nestlé India – Presentation – 1-2-1 investor meet* [PDF]. https://www.nestle.in/sites/g/files/pydnoa451/files/2024-04/Nestle%20India%20-%20Presentation%20-%201-2-1%20investor%20meet.pdf

Olam International. (2023). Our Purpose. https://www.olamgroup.com/about-olam/our-purpose..html

Osterwalder, A., Pigneur, Y., Bernarda, G., & Smith, A. (2014). *Value proposition design: How to create products and services customers want*. Wiley.

Payne, A., Frow, P., & Eggert, A. (2017). The customer value proposition: evolution, development, and application in marketing. *Journal of the Academy* of Marketing Science, 45(4), 467–489. https://doi.org/10.1007/s11747-017-0523-z

Perloff, J. M. (2020). *Microeconomics: Theory and applications with calculus* (5th ed.). Pearson Education.

Porter, M. E. (1980). *Competitive strategy: Techniques for analyzing industries and competitors.* Free Press. See also his later article, (2008). *The five competitive forces that shape strategy.* Harvard Business Review Press.
Porter, M. E., & Kramer, M. R. (2011). Creating shared value. *Harvard Business Review*, 89(1–2), 62–77.
Prahalad, C.K. & Hamel, G. (1990). The core competence of the corporation. *Harvard Business Review* 68:3, 79–91.
Reddy, P. (2014, April 29). Interview by T. Khanna. *Creating Emerging Markets Oral History Collection.* Baker Library Special Collections, Harvard Business School.
Reliance Industries Limited. (2025). Growth is Life. https://www.ril.com/
Reuters. (2024, August 8). Vietnam's VietJet to take delivery of up to 10 Airbus jets this year. https://www.reuters.com/business/aerospace-defense/vietnams-vietjet-take-delivery-up-10-airbus-jets-this-year-2024-08-08/
Shankar, S. (2017, May 24). Uber is no match for auto-mated Ola here. https://economictimes.indiatimes.com/small-biz/startups/uber-is-no-match-for-auto-mated-ola-here/articleshow/58817104.cms
Sheldon, R., Awati, R. & Pratt, M.K. (2024, July). Core competencies: What they are and how they lead to success. TechTarget. https://www.techtarget.com/searchcio/definition/core-competency
Smith, N.C., Ansett, S. & Erez, L. (2011, June 22). How Gap Inc. engaged with its stakeholders. *MIT Sloan Management Review.* https://sloanreview.mit.edu/article/how-gap-inc-engaged-with-its-stakeholders/
Tentree. (n.d.). We believe big change starts small. https://www.tentree.ca/pages/about
Thao, N.T.P. (2017, December 12). Interview by L.P. Sawyer. *Creating Emerging Markets Oral History Collection.* Baker Library Special Collections, Harvard Business School.
The Strategy Institute. (2024, April 19). Coca-Cola's global dominance – Decoding the beverage giant's business strategy. https://www.thestrategyinstitute.org/insights/coca-colas-global-dominance-decoding-the-beverage-giants-business-strategy
Toyota. (2024). Toyota production system. https://global.toyota/en/company/vision-and-philosophy/production-system/
TTR Weekly. (2024, April 16). Vietjet: A turnaround profit in 2023. https://www.ttrweekly.com/site/2024/04/vietjet-a-turnaround-profit-in-2023/
VietJetAir.com. (2023). *Business performance results.* VietJet Air.
Wang, H.H. (2010, September 12). How eBay failed in China. https://www.forbes.com/sites/china/2010/09/12/how-ebay-failed-in-china/
Wernerfelt, B. (1984). A resource-based view of the firm. *Strategic Management Journal*, 5(2), 171–180.
Yaşar, S. (2014, April 24). Interview by A. Colpan. *Creating Emerging Markets Oral History Collection.* Baker Library Special Collections, Harvard Business School.
Zhang, M. (2020, June 24). Mindray, the dominant a-share medical device maker: Not a COVID-19 speculator. https://equalocean.com/analysis/2020062414140

CHAPTER 8

Branding and marketing for emerging markets

Learning outcomes

After studying this chapter, you will be able to do the following:

1. Analyze the roles of branding and marketing in emerging markets.
2. Prepare critical explanations of how marketing strategies differ between developed and emerging markets.
3. Evaluate the effectiveness of global brand adaptations for local cultures and conditions in emerging markets.
4. Analyze quantitative data on media penetration and explain their implications for marketing in emerging markets.
5. Examine case studies of brands leveraging sustainability for competitive advantage in emerging markets.
6. Define black and gray markets, discuss the role of counterfeiting, and explain other types of illegal competitive practices and their effects on legitimate brands and businesses.
7. Develop marketing strategies that include digital and influencer marketing, contextualizing them with regional media consumption habits.
8. Recommend technological solutions to address risks to valuable brands.

Introduction

In emerging markets, unique branding and marketing challenges are presented due to differences in infrastructural development, rapid change, and increasingly because of vastly different levels of digital access. This chapter is an overview: for a lengthier,

DOI: 10.4324/9781003638490-8

Table 8.1 Branding and marketing

Aspect	*Goal*	*Time*	*Activities*
Branding	Build brand identity and emotional connection	Long term	Define vision, mission, identity; publish and promote
Marketing	Drive product and service revenues	Shorter term, can be limited to one campaign or product	Advertising, promotions, events, digital outreach, and influencer engagement

excellent exploration of the finer details, we recommend Sheth, Sinha, and Shah's *Breakout Strategies for Emerging Markets: Business and Marketing Tactics for Achieving Growth* (2016).

Branding and marketing are separate but closely related concepts. Branding is about a business's identity: its name, values, and emotional connections. Branding defines who a business is and what it means to its customers or clients. Both companies and products are branded. Unilever, which we have mentioned several times, has a strong corporate brand in emerging markets. It is known for sustainability and quality. People trust the company. It has also successfully branded a range of products, such as Dove, Lifebuoy, and Surf, each of which has a separate way of appealing to customers. Sometimes the same product is given a different brand name in different markets. Surf Excel, for instance, is also known as Persil and OMO.

Marketing is the practical activity of promoting the brand so that customers hear about products and purchase them. Marketing activities include advertising, online content, sales promotions, and campaigns. Marketing aims to convert customers to drive revenue. Table 8.1 summarizes the key factors which distinguish branding from marketing.

In emerging markets, we must devote particular attention to brand protection, as some areas remain hotbeds for counterfeiting, black and gray operations, and intellectual property infringements. In their media landscapes, traditional channels exist alongside rapidly developing digital platforms. While urban populations may exhibit consumer behavior that is closer to Western patterns, many rural populations rely on legacy channels like radio and television. Influencer engagement and trust are higher, while brands which are universally known in a large city may be unknown and untrusted in a rural community. Sustainability is a strong branding and marketing advantage. Powerful customer connections can be built by brands which represent ethical businesses. Let's start with a walk through the key elements of branding.

Brand concepts

Approximately half of Chattopadhyay, Batra, and Ozsomer's (2012) excellent book *The New Emerging Market Multinationals* is devoted to a detailed exposition of the importance of brands. The chapters have timeless relevance, and we highly recommend them.

In keeping with the emerging nature of markets themselves, media landscapes and marketing trends are undergoing rapid change. For example, the sustainability of products has immense value as a marketing tool. Many emerging market businesses focus on environmentally friendly materials, ethical sourcing, green certification, and impact assessments. Businesses should never disregard the rich connection between modern populations and Indigenous cultures which treasure their connection with the earth. A narrative that truthfully emphasizes respect for nature and its resources can build a very authentic connection with products and services. Brazilian company Natura, a flagship for corporate success based on its earth-friendly image, has long emphasized the natural origins and biodegradability of its cosmetic products. It has been carbon neutral since 2007, achieved through the purchase of offset products to counter emissions it cannot eliminate (United Nations Climate Change, n.d.).

The following is a summary of branding concepts with strong relevance to emerging markets.

Discount brands are brands that appeal to customers because of affordability and thus become almost synonymous with saving money play a huge role in emerging markets. It is tempting to believe that only discount brands will succeed in markets where price sensitivity is high. However, the most successful discount brands, such as Xiaomi, work to build a perception of smart value and reliability, not just low price. In most emerging markets, discount brands exist alongside mid-range and premium products, demonstrating that brand strategy must be aligned with segmentation.

Brand identity is a broad term which refers to the visual, verbal, and conceptual elements which work together to present the business to the world. It can include the brand's name, logo, colors, typestyle, messaging, values, and more. It is a source of success, a matter of pride, and a symbol of identity. The overriding concern, however, is to strike the right balance between global consistency and local relevance. Indomie, for example, has a strong brand value in Indonesia and Africa. It has maintained a consistent brand identity while tailoring its products to align with local cultural factors. Although the markets are very different, the local strategy has built deep emotional loyalty with diverse consumers.

Brand values should not be abandoned, but they may require adaptation. Local variations must be faithful to the corporate brand but relevant to local consumers. McDonald's adapts its menu items to suit local tastes but never abandons its brand values of delivering fast, accessible food.

Brand messaging is a subtle add-on to the broader matter of brand values. The communication of brand values must respect the nature of local audiences; cultural insight is required to ensure that messages are relevant. Just how badly this can go wrong is exemplified by H&M's disastrous "coolest monkey in the jungle" advertisement released in South Africa in 2018. Widespread outrage in social media and elsewhere resulted in mobs trashing outlets of the store and consequent police actions to restore calm (Guardian Staff and Agencies, 2018).

Cultural heterogeneity can be challenging. Large countries like India, Nigeria, and Indonesia have extreme regional diversity, which can require carefully differentiated marketing messages and strategies. Linguistic diversity can be a strong indicator of wider differences – Nigeria, for example, has over 500 languages, while Indonesia has over 700. A further refinement of the local language challenge is script diversity, as packaging and advertising design may need to cope with Arabic, Latin, and Devanagari characters, for example. Areas of low literacy will need attention to visual messaging, icon development, and delivery of messages by voice rather than in writing.

Brand features must be carefully considered. The product or service itself may require adaptation to fit the local requirement. Getting this right can become an immense competitive advantage.

Pizza may appear at first to be a uniform product. But on the Pizza Hut Kenya menu[1] you will find flavors unfamiliar to non-African consumers – nyama choma (barbecued meat, typically goat) and chicken choma sausage (which is highly spiced).

McDonald's, synonymous in North America with the beefburger, invites local customers in India to enjoy the McAloo Tikki (McDonald's Corporation, 2018) and Veg Maharaja Mac (McDonald's Corporation, 2021). These are brand features.

Brand strength should be sought after by applying the above. Relevance and resonance will build identity. Unilever Hindustan provides a compelling example: advertising for its Surf Excel detergent leverages family values, learning, friendship, and motherhood to make the case for its use.

> Surf Excel believes that dirt and experiences are a gateway for unleashing human potential and encourages mothers to push their children to learn by experience, while Surf Excel takes care of the dirt and tough stains.
>
> *(Hindustan Unilever Limited, n.d.)*

Brand economics are the financial value and business impact aspects of a brand. While a business's brand may appear intangible, it is an asset, sometimes one of the most valuable. What price would someone pay to use, buy, or copy the brand?

Brand economics are also applied to consumer analysis. The financial situation of target segments may deeply influence the content and delivery of messaging. A poor segment may appreciate the stress on affordability, while the same message could be disastrous in a segment which regards a product as a status symbol. In India, Bajaj Auto produces low-cost motorcycles and promotes their low cost heavily in low income segments (Shastri, 2024). In the same market, Royal Enfield, a British-owned manufacturer, promotes its high-end motorcycles to aspirational buyers with a premium brand strategy (Shastri, 2023).

Brand awareness considerations govern many marketing selections. There are markets where general messaging will promote long-term sales; there are others where it will waste resources which could have been better devoted to single products or product groups. Marketing and promotional strategies must be carefully selected according to the branding goal. Unilever in Nigeria sells toothpaste in regions where Colgate has high market share. It produces very intense product-specific campaigns for its Close-Up product, informing customers why this particular toothpaste is "better" (Marketing Edge, 2015).

Brand storytelling is a powerful technique. Careful evaluation of the segment's appetite for stories and the types of stories which resonate can pay huge dividends by engaging consumers' emotions. Patagonia employs storytelling masterfully to the point of

Table 8.2 Brand storytelling

Element	*Developed Market*	*Emerging Market*
Emotional Connection	Weak: consumers are individualistic in brand choices	Strong: collectivist cultures emphasize roles of family, tradition, and community.
Trust	Easier to establish due to regulatory oversight and consumer protection.	Must be built due to fears of fraud and counterfeits.
Cultural and Religious Narratives	Branding often centers around convenience and lifestyle.	Essential to align with local traditions, religious beliefs, and national pride.
Social Validation	Celebrity endorsements play a large role.	More trust is placed in micro-influencers, using local languages.
Mobile-first Engagement	Less important. Consumers are accustomed to traditional narratives.	Critical. Short, engaging videos work best, due to prominence of TikTok and gamified promotions.
Price Sensitivity	Strong mix of price-based and value-based positioning.	Price sensitivity is far higher thus brands which emphasize value-for-money and durability.
Social Responsibility	While important, sustainability does not resonate as strongly with consumers.	Consumers expect brands to contribute to society.

having a "Director of Philosophy" who also serves as chief storyteller (Browness & Kurtz, 2022). There are profound differences between the effective use of storytelling in developed and emerging markets. They are summarized in Table 8.2.

Brand collaboration asks what opportunities are there to involve local partners, influencers, or even consumers in the marketing effort? Could a joint venture or strategic alliance increase the acceptability of the brand? In Egypt, Unilever creates joint campaigns with retailer Carrefour for its soaps, which emphasize sustainability and environmental benefits while leveraging the strong Carrefour presence. With over 400 brands in its house, Unilever is an extremely valuable partner to thousands of retailers worldwide.[2]

Brand performance is the ultimate measure of strategic success. Will the business recognize it when it sees it? Will it know it has found it? From the very beginning, relevant key performance indicators (KPIs) for marketing campaigns must be established and then measured.[3]

Brand equity assessment is a sophisticated but essential exercise. How has the message resonated, and what brand loyalty has been created in the target segments? Ongoing market research is essential to understand how the brand is performing and find the negative areas that require attention (Taylor, 2023).

Brand protection

Brand protection and counterfeiting are serious challenges in many emerging markets. Black markets, gray markets, supplier theft, and corporate espionage are grim realities,

Viña Concha y Toro

Rafael Guilisasti Gana, the vice chairman of Viña Concha y Toro, is well positioned to share his knowledge of branding. He stresses the importance of the distribution network and strong alliances with distributors while clearly communicating a message of quality to customers. At the millennium, Concha y Toro was acutely aware of the fragmentation of the wine market and chose to focus on Casillero del Diablo as a flagship brand. It was not new but had the ability to resonate empathetically in new markets. The expansion of markets, however, brought with it the challenge of balancing scale and exclusivity. The winemaker was able to achieve one of the highest recognizabilities among global wines by strategic brand identity development, focused on quality perception and global reach (Gana, 2008).

especially where supply chains are not well organized and intellectual property rights are weakly enforced.

Supply is only half of the problem. All over the world, black markets supply plentiful consumer demand for cheap branded goods, whether counterfeit or stolen. Many emerging markets have a reputation for being sources of counterfeit goods. These reputations are not undeserved – any foreign visitor who has walked the streets of Hong Kong will have encountered offers of fake Rolex watches several times each hour, while the street markets of some Southeast Asian nations seem to have nothing but knockoffs for sale. Sometimes the goods are simply blatant copies; sometimes they are off-hours extra runs by licensed manufacturers who risk their trade relationships for a few extra dollars.

Gray markets are established when genuine goods are sold through unauthorized channels, typically at large discounts. Arbitrage is a related complication; branded goods intended for a low-income market may be resold into a higher-priced market in competition with authorized distributors.

The damage to brand reputation is obvious. If the brand emphasizes quality, counterfeit goods erode customer confidence. Where customers would have bought a genuine article but are satisfied with a copy, revenues and profits are lost. Some counterfeit products, especially in electronics and health markets, are simply dangerous.

Competitor espionage is widely practiced in emerging markets due to weak regulation and poor legal enforcement of agreements. It comes in many forms, including workforce infiltration, unauthorized data use by partners, and reverse engineering (Federal Bureau of Investigation, 2015).

Best practices to protect brands often only dent the operations of counterfeiters. Registration of patents, trademarks, and copyrights is essential, though enforcement may be difficult. A more controllable area is the supply chain; manufacturers and processors should be contractually bound to regular audits to ensure that all their production goes to the brand owner. Some developing technologies show promise in stemming the growth of counterfeit products, such as blockchain and AI-based authentication techniques to reassure consumers that they have bought genuine branded products. These protections are more feasible for high-value products than inexpensive merchandise.

With an understanding of branding and marketing concepts, we can turn to an examination of how businesses in emerging markets reach consumers. The choice of media is today highly data-driven and varies greatly by country, region, and segment. Many businesses develop omnichannel marketing plans, using online and offline media to maximize customer reach. Strong retail brands like Jumia and Reliance Retail exemplify the use of online communications to complete sales but direct consumers to their physical stores for deliveries.

The media landscape

While internet and mobile penetration are today's trending themes of the marketing world, legacy channels are still remarkably relevant in emerging markets. Media reach and trends are different in every market; they often vary widely in regions of the same country. Television may be old news among younger populations in urban centers yet be a recent development in rural communities or under-developed cities. Just a few examples of rapidly developing cities where television ownership is a notable upward trend are Lagos, Nigeria; Pune, India; Belo Horizonte, Brazil; and Qingdao, China.

Cable and satellite are rapidly supplementing terrestrial broadcasting, providing a much wider choice of channels. In Indonesia, while internet access increased for the three years to 2022 by 20% and TV declined by 10%, TV remained "king of reach." Nielsen data released in December 2022 showed that the average consumption of streaming was 9 hours per month, while the average consumption of TV remained at 80 hours per month (The Feed, 2022). This presents a targeting challenge: different segments increasingly view different media, so brands must make difficult decisions about how to allocate marketing budgets between TV and digital. Compounding the difficulty, data and analytics on media consumption may be of limited quality.

Across vast tracts of remote rural land, electronic media penetration is poor; internet access may be severely limited, leading to the dominance of physical media. Some emerging markets, including China, Egypt, Saudi Arabia, Türkiye, and Vietnam, also suffer from strong government censorship (Human Rights Watch, 2020).

Many people, when surveyed, will state that they never listen to radio. AM and FM may be declining. But in areas with severe traffic congestion, drivers may have several hours per day of exposure. The Philippines' capital Manila comes easily to mind; workers traveling into and out of the center may spend as much as 4 hours per day in their cars. While dated, a Kantar Media Habits survey in 2018 found that the average Filipino listens to 2.5 hours of radio per day (Lasco, 2021). In rural India and Kenya, northern Nigeria, the Brazilian interior, and rural Indonesia, news-hungry communities listen avidly to radio channels, often in local languages, due to limited availability of TV signals or internet penetration. A high percentage of listeners access radio channels through mobile phones. Therefore, a company looking to expand in an emerging market must resist the temptation to overlook radio as it assesses media consumption habits. Radio remains an effective and inexpensive way to address large audiences, especially when local languages and cultural considerations are paramount.

Print media – newspapers and magazines – face severe challenges in the age of digital delivery. Newspapers themselves are moving in many markets to purely digital delivery. Bangladesh's Daily Star, for example, is now exclusively an *ePaper*.[4] Circulation and readership require good quantitative research if print is still contemplated.

Digital media demand quantitative assessment. What are the depth and rate of internet penetration? What factors are affecting these metrics? Which demographics within the market are using which social media? They are all extensively used for advertising; some are fading, and some are growing. How do their user populations match with the target segments for each product or service to be sold? Mobile marketing must be considered separately from social media, despite the mobile phone being the primary vehicle for social media. SMS, mobile app, and web marketing may all be in scope. Only excellent quantitative research can establish the best media mix.

Within digital media, further trends are rapidly emerging. For example, in Brazil and India, WhatsApp marketing and other messaging apps are rapidly overtaking traditional digital advertising. Approximately 60% of small businesses in Brazil use WhatsApp for marketing; it is the leading communications application in the country (Goyal, 2023). Mobile internet penetration is growing rapidly in Nigeria, increasing the use of SMS marketing and influencers (Olamide, 2024). For much of Latin America, Facebook is the dominant social media platform, while WhatsApp and Instagram are making huge advances in replacing traditional media (Sinch, 2025).

India's marketing landscape can be quantified for illustration. In 2024, Statista estimated that internet penetration in India reached over 52% – rapidly approaching one billion users (Basuroy, 2024). Mobile penetration is even higher, with over a billion subscribers communicating on 660 million smartphones (Singla, 2024). The implications for marketing are clear: many Indians today use mobile devices as their main channel for finding information, goods, and services. A successful mobile campaign has the potential to reach two out of every three consumers in the world's largest population.

Influencer marketing has risen rapidly in importance everywhere, but especially in emerging markets where there is a significant demand for influential figures to set an example (Rahmayanti, Reyta, & Wijaya, 2019). Within emerging markets, trust in influencers is higher than in traditional advertising, while return on investment is higher than in developed markets due to relatively lower costs (Ernst & Young, 2024). Because of the typical high rates of social media penetration, influencer marketing is increasingly effective and relevant.

It's important not to apply a developed-economy mindset to influencer selection. While marketing in developed markets is often highly polished, emerging market consumers tend to prefer authentic, relatable content. This contributes to a relatively lower cost and the ability to partner with many smaller influencers simultaneously. Social media has the additional attraction of limited regulation compared to traditional media. A common downside, however, is that tracking results can be more difficult in emerging market conditions.

There are many examples of successful micro-influencer campaigns in emerging markets. The following are some examples:

- In Kenya, Instagram and TikTok are heavily used to promote skincare products that work well with East African skin tones and climate concerns. Mwende Frey, @mwendefrey, for example, has over 83,000 followers on TikTok.
- In Indonesia, halal cosmetics brands and Islamic clothing are promoted by hijabi influencers who are trusted by young people with strong religious beliefs. Aghnia

Punjabi, @emyaghnia, has 2.6 million Instagram followers and over two million TikTok followers.

While large-scale influencers are relevant, micro-influencers with smaller and more focused followings are often more relatable and thus perceived as trustworthy. Influencers provide a valuable method of embracing local cultures if they are deeply embedded. They are a priceless sounding board for ideas which risk breaching social norms; a quality influencer will not risk damaging their own reputation by messaging inappropriately for a "foreign" product. The risk of language errors is also reduced when local influencers are trusted to deliver messages.

The rapid rise of the influencer on the marketing scene calls for some basic rules. At the outset, it is necessary to measure influencer values, audiences, and content to ensure that they align with the business. Good influencer campaigns will keep an eye on the future and look for long-term engagement. Influencers should not be encouraged to spawn artificial content, as genuine resonance with followers will flow from authenticity – messaging that aligns with the personal values and qualities of the influencer. At the design stage, it is also useful to consider measurability: will the business be able to track the effect of influencer campaigns and identify opportunities for improvement or disengagement?

Few businesses will embrace all media types. It is necessary to select those that fit with target segments. With that selection in mind, every business must give serious attention to the possibility of regulatory constraints and consumer privacy protection. A broad range of prohibitions and restrictions can be found across emerging markets, including bans on alcohol or tobacco promotion or use, restriction on foreign media, and sometimes mandatory influencer disclosures.

Nykaa

Nykaa, India's leading e-commerce beauty retailer, sells online and in physical stores, offering domestic and international brands. Its success derives from the "Nykaa Army" of Instagram influencers, YouTubers, and beauty bloggers. Its marketing campaigns are conducted in multiple regional languages by locally recognized personalities, reaching diverse demographics and promoting its role in ethical production. Nykaa is a textbook example of the success of a *digital-first marketing* strategy.

Conclusion

Successful marketing campaigns have simple goals: persuading consumers to make their first purchase and encouraging repeat purchases. Building long-term relationships with consumers depends on delivering products and services in a timely, safe, and efficient manner. This chapter reviewed the fundamental role of branding. We examined the media landscape, which is essential for getting the brand's message to consumers. We saw how marketing media are evolving rapidly and have a different shape than we might find in a developed economy.

Marketing creates demand, which in turn drives supply chain and distribution requirements. Where there is demand, companies must procure materials and supplies, position them for manufacturing or distribution, and then deliver them. The right products must reach the right hands at the right time. Effective management of the supply chain and distribution channels, which form the focus of the next chapter, is essential to capitalize on the marketing effort.

Notes

1 https://www.pizzahut.co.ke/order/pizzas
2 The specific web pages promoting Unilever products in Egypt are available only from Egyptian IP addresses; therefore, they are not referenced.
3 It is beyond our scope to explore KPI measurement here. For an extremely useful summary, see Nensee and Bajj (2023).
4 www.thedailystar.net

References

Basuroy, T. (2024, May 15). Internet penetration rate in India 2014–2024. https://www.statista.com/statistics/792074/india-internet-penetration-rate/

Browness, J., & Kurtz, Z. (2022, May 27). The power of storytelling at Patagonia. https://blog.uvm.edu/si-mba/2022/05/27/the-power-of-storytelling-at-patagonia/

Chattopadhyay, A., Batra, F., & Ozsomer, A. (2012). *The new emerging market multinationals*. McGraw-Hill.

Ernst & Young. (2024, May 30). How to reach the independent consumer: The art of persuasion. *EY*. https://www.ey.com/en_gl/insights/consumer-products/the-rise-of-the-independent-consumer

Federal Bureau of Investigation. (2015, July 23). *Economic espionage*. FBI. https://www.fbi.gov/news/stories/economic-espionage

Gana, R.G. (2008, December 18). Interview by A. Lluch. *Creating Emerging Markets Oral History Collection*. Baker Library Special Collections, Harvard Business School.

Goyal, S. (2023, June 21). 51+ WhatsApp Marketing statistics in 2025. https://www.notifyvisitors.com/blog/whatsapp-marketing-statistics/

Guardian Staff and Agencies. (2018, January 14). H&M stores in South Africa trashed by protesters after 'racist' ad. https://www.theguardian.com/world/2018/jan/14/hm-stores-in-south-afrtica-trashed-by-protesters-after-racist-ad

Hindustan Unilever Limited. (n.d.). Surf Excel: Dirt is good. https://www.hul.co.in/brands/home-care/surf-excel/

Human Rights Watch. (2020). In China, the 'Great Firewall' is changing a generation. https://www.hrw.org/news/2020/09/01/china-great-firewall-changing-generation

Lasco, G. (2021, September 10). Listen to the radio. *Philippine Daily Inquirer*. https://opinion.inquirer.net/144039/listen-to-the-radio

Marketing Edge. (2015). Unilever repackages Close-up. https://marketingedge.com.ng/unilever-repackages-close-up/

McDonald's Corporation. (2018, May 4). The wholesome McAloo tikki burger. https://mcdonaldsblog.in/2018/05/the-wholesome-mcaloo-tikki-burger/

McDonald's Corporation. (2021, July 6). Your veg Maharaja Mac is made up of these. https://mcdonaldsblog.in/2021/07/your-veg-maharaja-mac-is-made-up-of-these/

Nensee, K., & Bajj, A. (2023, March 16). How to measure the success of marketing campaigns. *Startup Talky*. https://startuptalky.com/measure-success-of-marketing-campaigns/

Olamide, S.K. (2024, December 28). Influencer marketing: Nigeria's opportunity in the global creator economy. https://businessday.ng/bd-weekender/article/influencer-marketing-nigerias-opportunity-in-the-global-creator-economy/

Rahmayanti, R., Reyta, F., & Wijaya, N. (2019, July). Do Indonesian social media celebrity, influencer and opinion leader affect shifting in consumer behavior? *Proceedings of the 5th Bandung Creative Movement International Conference on Creative Industries 2018.*

Shastri, A. (2023, April 13). About Royal Enfield. https://iide.co/case-studies/royal-enfield-marketing-strategy/

Shastri, A. (2024, April 18). Comprehensive Marketing Strategy of Bajaj Auto. https://iide.co/case-studies/marketing-strategy-of-bajaj-auto/

Sheth, J.N., Sinha, M., & Shah, R. (2016). *Breakout strategies for emerging markets: Business and marketing tactics for achieving growth*. Pearson Education.

Sinch. (2025, February 13). The most popular messaging apps in the world by country: Stats, user behavior, and more. https://sinch.com/blog/most-popular-messaging-apps-in-the-world/

Singla, K. (2024, August 20). *India's internet surge: Catalyzing change in the telecom landscape.* Invest India. https://www.investindia.gov.in/blogs/indias-internet-surge-catalyzing-change-telecom-landscape

Taylor, E. (2023, March 15). Measuring brand equity in 5 steps. *Drive Research*. https://www.driveresearch.com/market-research-company-blog/measuring-brand-equity-in-5-steps-with-examples/

The Feed. (2022, December 16). Streaming advances in Indonesia but TV is still king of reach. *WARC*. https://www.warc.com/content/feed/streaming-advances-in-indonesia-but-tv-is-still-king-of-reach/en-GB/7624

United Nations Climate Change (n.d.). Natura's Carbon Neutral Programme Global. https://unfccc.int/climate-action/momentum-for-change/climate-neutral-now/natura

CHAPTER 9

Supply chains and distribution channels in emerging markets

Learning outcomes

After studying this chapter, you will be able to do the following:

1. Evaluate the principal infrastructural, supply chain, and distribution challenges in emerging market conditions, and explain their impact on business strategy.
2. Analyze methods used by successful organizations to overcome gaps in infrastructure of transportation, utilities, digital networks, and logistical systems.
3. Within emerging markets, compare challenges in supply chain and distribution networks.
4. Analyze how supply chain management (SCM) produces competitive advantage and drives expansion in emerging markets, identifying key elements in optimization.
5. Apply ESG and sustainability principles to SCM and distribution strategies and show how they help underpin success.
6. Design KPI frameworks to measure the efficiency and effectiveness of supply chains and distribution channels.
7. Evaluate real-world case studies of successful supply chain and distribution strategies.

Introduction: Perilous travels

A packet of noodles or a jar of cosmetic cream can take a treacherous journey on the way to an emerging market consumer. It may travel along a winding mountain road, cross an insanely busy urban street, or find its way into a remote region with little modern infrastructure. Every step along the supply chain or distribution network is another opportunity for delay, loss, or inefficiency. Addressing the logistical challenge is essential to realizing market potential.

DOI: 10.4324/9781003638490-9

Author Alym lives in Vancouver, Canada, and travels regularly to Seattle, in Washington State. The drive takes just over two hours, and the distance is about 140 miles. He made a similar journey while visiting East Africa: it took more than half a day. Living in North America, we take infrastructure for granted. But this simple example illustrates the profound differences in logistics and infrastructure often found when comparing developed and emerging markets.

The supply chain encompasses all the components of the inward flow of goods, materials, and supply toward a business, enabling it to conduct its operations. It includes people, businesses, processes, activities, and resources. Commencing with procurement, the sourcing and purchasing of supplies or services, the chain may include manufacturing, logistics, and customer service.

Goods and services travel from business to consumer, including other businesses, along routes known as *distribution channels*. Traditional retail, the sale of products in stores, is characterized in most emerging markets by a higher percentage of small, independent stores. E-commerce may account for a smaller proportion of overall retail sales, but the ratio is shifting rapidly.

Both supply and distribution depend on infrastructure, often the biggest obstacle of all in emerging markets. Businesses overcome deficiencies through investment, partnership, and increasingly by using technology-driven solutions. After setting out the fundamental issues, we will explore those solutions, place them in the context of sustainability and ESG, and discuss measurement and KPIs that are relevant. We will discuss infrastructure for both areas together, then move to separate consideration of other aspects of fulfilling supply and demand.

Infrastructure deficiencies

Infrastructure deficiencies are the primary bottleneck in supply chain management (SCM) and distribution planning. They impact transportation, storage, and delivery to consumers. Emerging markets are especially prone to logistical difficulties. Penetrating a new market requires careful evaluation of the challenges that may lie ahead in getting materials into factories, products out to their distribution locations, and delivering orders to customers.

These challenges also present opportunities. Investment is needed to improve the delivery of goods and services but may not lead to immediate economic benefits. If it is left to government to take necessary action, infrastructural improvement may be impeded by budgetary constraints.

Road networks are frequently substandard. Poor roads limit access to essential services, contribute to economic disparity in rural areas where even harvests may be lost, increase the likelihood of accidents, and magnify costs of delivery. In countries with large land areas and disparate populations, this issue is exacerbated. Road transport is an inefficient method of moving goods over long distances; the need for trucks decreases where there is a good rail network.

Railways and roads exist in a cycle of mutual inefficiency. In large countries like Brazil, India, and Nigeria, vast distances need to be covered and maintained. These are just individual countries, located in continents which are even bigger. The inadequacy of the rail network leads to more cargo being on roads, which deteriorate rapidly with heavy truck usage. Poor rail connectivity adds passenger vehicle volume to the roads, increasing travel times and decreasing productivity. The golden age of railway construction (the 19th century) has long passed. Today, land is scarcer, construction is more expensive, and maintenance costs can be prohibitive. While trucks, cars, and airplanes have lessened the importance of railways, improvement of rail services could still enhance logistics in some emerging markets.

Ports and airports have a central economic role in emerging markets. They are the kingpin of connectivity to the rest of the world, making possible the movement of goods, people, and capital.

Port and airport construction and operation on their own tick many boxes in the development checklist. They attract foreign investment, create jobs, and stimulate local industry. At the world's busiest airport, Dubai International (DXB), the airport company alone employs over 8,000 people. Thousands more are employed by the airlines, cargo handlers, retailers, and service providers at the airport. Many hub airports have a larger population than some cities.

The remarkable rise of Turkish group Akfen Holding, led by billionaire Hamdi Akin, illustrates the potential in public–private partnerships for infrastructure development. Akfen built Ataturk Airport in Istanbul and several others; his TAV Airports Holding is one of the world's largest airport management companies. The genius in Akfen's business model is in its provision of capital for projects desired by governments, in return for a promise of future operating income (Akin, 2015).

Warehousing is an important consideration for physical goods. Efficiency in storage reduces lead times and increases customer satisfaction; if products are available when they are needed, stockouts and consequent lost sales are avoided. Storage optimization reduces transport costs; advanced technology and automation techniques can reduce waste and ensure that goods are where they need to be when they are needed. Walmart, in India, provides a large-scale model for building a holistic ecosystem (Walmart, n.d.).

Cold storage, a subsector of warehousing, is particularly important to emerging markets. A high proportion of emerging economies are in areas of high temperature. Perishable goods like fresh fruit, meat, seafood, and flowers last longer and maintain quality in cold storage facilities. Local food security and public health improve, export becomes possible, and higher incomes can be generated for producers. Conversely, a lack of adequate cold storage can disincentivize investment and development.

Recent global developments, including the growth of online food delivery services and demand for storage of vaccines and pharmaceuticals, have accelerated cold storage growth. It involves the use of both static and mobile refrigerated components – in trucks, trains, ships, and planes. Expansion of cold storage capacity correlates closely with the development of emerging markets, especially for food and pharmaceutical industries (Banerjee, 2024).

Vietnam provides an example of the rate of development and the successful leveraging of cold storage facilities, growing its value from US$169 million in 2019 to an estimated $295 million by 2025. The compound annual growth rate is 12%. Cold storage revenue is estimated to reach US$15 billion in 2025 (Pham, 2022).

Telephone network coverage is problematic. It has seen improvements in recent years, but there are still large disparities between urban and rural areas. Mobile phone availability has been the largest growth area, fueled by the development of cheaper smartphones. The divide, and its closure, are fundamentally important in emerging markets because mobile network access is critical to market participation. It enables digital payments, banking, internet purchasing, access to education, and telehealth. Mobile connectivity is nothing short of the gateway to economic inclusion. Uneven network coverage, unfortunately, emphasizes inequalities which need to be addressed.

Mobile phone situation in Nigeria

Business visitors to urban centers like Lagos, Nigeria, are treated to a view of an unusual solution to an even more unusual problem. They may be surprised to see their lawyer or banker settle into a meeting with four or five mobile phones placed on the table.

The explanation for this (and the reason so many used mobile phones are resold in Nigeria) is that there is intense competition for market share between four principal operators (MTN, Globacom, Airtel, and 9Mobile). Each has their own network, and most have their own mobile towers. However, those towers usually rely on the public grid for electrical power; that grid is far from dependable. When one of the frequent power outages occurs, company-owned generators are often insufficient to power all the towers in an area, and the entire network goes down.

Professionals – people who need connectivity 24/7 – solve this problem by having subscriptions to more than one network and different numbers on each. They then carry multiple phones to be able to take and make calls regardless of service interruptions at some carriers. Their business cards may have four telephone numbers or six, including a landline and fax. In addition, people who travel need several phones and subscriptions to ensure that they have connectivity to a provider who has coverage in particular areas – it is not universal.

Lest you think this description lacks credibility, some simple statistics will demonstrate the extent of multiple subscriptions and phone use. Experts at Media Landscapes, a noted telecommunications analyst, believe that approximately 40 million Nigerians do not have access to mobile telephony in any form. The population – from newborn babies to the oldest residents – is around 218 million. Subtraction tells us that the maximum possible number of mobile phone users, assuming every man, woman, and child in the country has one, is 178 million.

Yet there are 189 million subscriptions. Where are the additional millions of subscriptions coming from? They result from multiple subscriptions by the same people (Kolawole & Umejei, n.d.).

Internet connectivity maintains impressive improvement. Mobile internet has become the main channel, while fixed-line infrastructure has receded. While decreases in costs have enabled double-digit growth in most emerging markets, the urban-rural divide is still significant.

Despite the obvious social benefits of market access and education, internet connectivity is also a potential single point of failure. National censorship, including the banning of specific websites, is still prevalent in China and some other emerging markets

(GeeksforGeeks, 2024). Limitation of internet access can occur hand-in-hand with other economic or political disruptions, as was demonstrated in the July, 2024 complete shutdown of the internet in Bangladesh as the government attempted to contain student protests (Zami, 2024). India and Pakistan have both deployed internet interference during periods of insecurity.

Satellite-based services like Starlink have some potential to challenge government interference by offering decentralized internet access. However, in low-income and politically charged environments, affordability, regulation, and infrastructure still limit access. Satellite-driven access is not yet sufficiently widespread to obviate the damage associated with internet interference by governments.

Power outages disproportionately affect any business which is dependent on power supplies to conduct its operations. Any such business needs a thorough assessment of power reliability and a plan to cope with outages. Emerging markets suffer disproportionately from power unreliability, fueled by aging infrastructure, faster growth in demand than supply, corruption, and inefficiency.

The authors have many firsthand experiences of power interruptions. In South Africa, the national utility Eskom euphemistically refers to them as *load shedding* and schedules cuts to manage the imbalance between demand and supply. Above, we mentioned Nigeria's vulnerability and the consequent losses of telephone service. Cuts occur in major Indian cities without warning, sometimes many times in a 24-hour period. On a larger scale, Brazil's electricity supply has a heavy dependence on hydro (water) power but is increasingly experiencing droughts which threaten supply consistency over extended periods. In September 2024, hydroelectric generation in Brazil fell to 28.7 terawatt-hours, a severe fall from the monthly average of ≈40 TWh. In a blow to sustainability goals, this is forcing the country's utilities to return to reliance on fossil fuels (Maguire, 2024).

Businesses which need reliable access to power are directly impacted by energy disruptions. They must establish backup systems, such as generators or battery storage, and need contingency plans for failures of mains supply. More broadly, lack of power reliability is a factor in choice of location, timing of investment, and commitments to sustainability.

Fuel availability may be a concern for some business types, especially those that rely heavily on road transportation or self-generated power. Some emerging markets suffer from insufficient refining capacity, increasing dependence on imports, while the transportation and distribution facilities to deliver fuel to where it is needed may themselves be lacking. The triple factors of exchange rates, government taxes, and subsidies can cause wild swings in prices, causing financial projections to be almost useless. In India, densely populated states like Maharashtra have struggled to cope with demand amid industrial disputes (BL Pune Bureau, 2024).

Complex regulations, especially customs duties and border control, plague businesses that need rapid importation. Brazil is an example with its complex tariff structure, vast documentary requirements, and procedural red tape. Unfortunately, the complexity of import and licensing regulation lends itself naturally to bribery and corruption, which further complicates the processes.

Among emerging markets, Indonesia may be the worst example. Border corruption is widely regarded as the single most problematic feature for international trade. Bribes and favors are routinely demanded by customs agents as a price for clearance, and imposing damaging arbitrary delays is a common way of extorting money from importers. Even doing everything by the book is expensive – the cost of documentary compliance is significantly higher than elsewhere in Southeast Asia and takes twice as long (GAN Integrity, 2020).

Security risks range from piracy and theft to cybercrime and regulatory dishonesty. Supply chains are vulnerable to disruption by political and civil conflicts, sudden changes of government, and even piracy. **Maritime piracy** affects the security of whole ships and their contents; the reality is that it is not the stuff of romantic legends but an ugly crime affecting major markets. The Gulf of Guinea has one of the highest rates of piracy in the world, causing devastating losses to the economies of Nigeria and its neighbors (United Nations Security Council, 2023). Problems off the coast of Somalia are well known, affecting maritime traffic to and from India. Ships on the Red Sea are also vulnerable, despite being on a trade route linking Africa, Asia, and Europe.

It is not only on the high seas that security risks are heightened. A complex interplay of diverse factors, including corruption and bribery, results in limited physical security at warehouses and distribution centers, cybersecurity vulnerabilities, poor control of counterfeiters, and product pirates.

Mo Ibrahim's astounding success in building Celtel in Africa exemplifies the lengths to which an innovator may need to go to build supply chain infrastructure where it is scarce or nonexistent. Professor Clayton Christensen tells the story beautifully in *The Prosperity Paradox*, including this description:

> Where there was no power, he provided his own power; where there were no logistics, he developed his own; where there was no education or health care, he provided training and health care for his staff; and where there were no roads, he either built makeshift roads or used helicopters to move equipment around.
>
> *(Christensen, Ojomo, & Dillon, 2019: 5)*

Without reliable roads, power, logistics, and other aspects of infrastructure, all other challenges in emerging markets are magnified. Infrastructure failures are a barrier to entry, fundamentally affecting how supply chains are created and managed. Businesses in regions with poor infrastructure need to plan around those gaps, investing in their own solutions or establishing relationships that share resources. Improving local infrastructure can earn a significant strategic advantage.

Supply chains in emerging markets

A quick reminder – in this book, we use the term supply chain to mean all the elements of the logistical chain which get materials or goods to a factory or distribution point. Some writers use the term to include what we call distribution channels. Supply chain analysis is most readily associated with manufacturers and service providers. However, retailers, agricultural businesses, technical platforms, non-profits, and non-governmental organizations (NGOs) can all secure benefits by constructing a dependable chain to procure and receive inputs dependably and efficiently.

Table 9.1 Comparison of supply chain characteristics

Aspect	*Emerging Market*	*Advanced Economy*
Infrastructure	Inconsistent, unreliable, under-developed	Consistent, reliable
Costs	Relatively high	Highly optimized
Technology Integration	Low to medium, rapidly developing	High
Visibility and tracking	Limited, inadequate data, latency issues	Advanced, real-time
Regulation	Unstable, unclear	Stable, clear
Informal Economy	Very present	Largely absent
Vulnerability	High	Largely managed

Efficient supply chains are fundamental to economic development. Therefore, they matter immensely in emerging markets, reducing costs, and improving access to materials and goods. Supply chains deliver everything from basic food and hygiene supplies to logs and ore, luxury goods, and designer clothing. They create employment and business opportunities for aspirant workers and entrepreneurs, but when they break down, they can be extremely damaging.

Emerging market supply chains typically have several key differences from those in emerging markets, summarized in Table 9.1.

Sustainability challenges

Designing transportation routes for goods and services with sustainability front of mind is fraught with barriers, yet businesses are under increasing pressure from all sides to do just that. These are the principal difficulties.

- **Carbonization** is a measurable and damaging metric. Many emerging markets still rely heavily on diesel-powered vehicles, aging railways, and inefficient logistics, leading to high emissions. Port congestion and shipping delays add to emissions as ships and trucks sit idle for long periods.
- **Deforestation** on a large scale is linked to agricultural industries and forestry operations. Local sourcing and sustainable land use are ideals, but expense is often an immediate concern.
- **Water** use is frequently inefficient and wasteful.
- **Electricity grids** are often unreliable, causing reliance on diesel generators (and thus increased emissions).
- **Waste management** and limited recycling, particularly for single-use plastics, result in increased landfill and ocean dumping.
- **Ethical labor** practices are difficult to implement in areas characterized by informal markets, weak enforcement, and human rights violations. Child labor and exploitive conditions have not been eradicated; mining and electronics businesses continue to face ESG scrutiny.
- **Urban pollution** and congestion are exacerbated by inefficient last-mile logistics.
- **Governmental priorities** may pay lip service to sustainability but provide insufficient guidelines and facilities.

It is not difficult to work down this list and see what needs to be done or how it might be turned to profit. The low-hanging fruits are green transport and energy, recycling and circular economy development, and waste reduction programs. Reverse logistics, where companies take back used products, is rapidly growing in emerging markets. Dell, for example, has invested heavily in recycling of electronic products in India and Latin America. These expansions formed part of Dell's global circular economy initiatives but demonstrated their commitment to educating customers in emerging economies (Dell Inc., 2006).

Consideration of sustainability in selecting suppliers and supply routes pays reputational and cost rewards. Sustainable sourcing is best practice whenever possible, especially for locally procured raw materials. A preliminary assessment which reports positively on sustainable practices and minimizing environmental impact will cast a favorable light on competing suppliers, while ongoing audits will continue to stress the importance of relevant practices. Certifications, such as Fair Trade, have downstream value in building brand trust.

It is important to include government and NGOs in sustainability initiatives. Limited infrastructure may constrain a business's success, yet local government may have an appetite to engage in partnerships to secure improvements. Equally, NGOs with interests in ecosystems, habitats, forests, or water systems are valuable allies. Other NGOs focus on human conditions – labor, healthcare, and education. Arrangements with such interest groups can build local goodwill and increase interest from ethical investors.

Supply chain challenges

Supply chains take on unique characteristics in emerging markets. Coping with their challenges is a key aspect of gaining and maintaining competitive advantage: beyond infrastructure, which was described earlier, the following may be encountered.

- Lack of reliable suppliers.
- Inconsistent and bureaucratic regulation.
- High delivery costs.
- Adverse weather conditions.
- Labor and skill deficiencies.
- Security risks.
- Unreliable financial systems.
- Localized business practices.
- Corruption and favoritism in supplier selection.
- Digital communications difficulties.

Addressing such challenges requires a clear supply chain management (SCM) strategy. Businesses entering emerging markets will find that cost control, customer behavior, and the regulatory environment all respond to supply chain best practices.

Shoring techniques

Shoring refers to decisions relating to the location or relocation of business activities to different places, almost always to take advantage of local conditions.

Global movements of manufacturing facilities have yielded a rich vocabulary of practices which wax and wane in popularity in response to geopolitical and other seismic events. The earliest manifestation was *offshoring* – moving production to a foreign country to take advantage of lower costs or economic conditions. While offshoring reshaped global commerce, it has engendered massive political and social protest since it first began. Occasionally, the term *farshoring* is used to describe offshoring when the relocation is to a place very far from home.

Its opposite, *onshoring* or *reshoring*, refers to bringing business back home. Onshoring is central to current American government policy yet is not completely supported by American manufacturers.

Since the millennium, Mexico has emerged as a top *nearshoring* destination for U.S. manufacturers and others seeking proximity to the U.S. market. Vietnam and India have gained nearshoring ground from China in sectors like textiles and electronics due to potentially lower costs and less complex politics. Nearshoring moves production closer to consumers and directly impacts emerging markets, with India, Mexico, and South-East Asian countries being the primary beneficiaries in 2023 (Global X Research Team, 2023).

However, the location of a manufacturing facility does not necessarily indicate local sales; for example, Mexico – the largest recipient of nearshoring investment globally – attracts this attention primarily because of its proximity to the U.S. market (Irwin-Hunt, 2024: 20). India also receives significant nearshoring foreign direct investment (FDI), leveraging its position within the subcontinent to serve both domestic and broader South-East Asian markets.

The increasingly uncertain geopolitical environment of 2025 has accelerated the use of *friendshoring*, where investors and manufacturers move their manufacturing and distribution facilities to countries which share political values with the home nation. Examples include the movement of semiconductor manufacturing away from China and the European movement of sourcing operations out of Russia. There is a trade-off involved; reducing vulnerability to political shifts may mean higher financial costs, damaging or losing relationships with the most efficient suppliers.

Greenshoring refers to the selection of manufacturing locations based on their sustainability in preference to other considerations like cost or proximity (Brooks, 2024).

Rightshoring is the omnibus term which refers to optimizing choice of location. It could include all the above types, and its execution is not uniform; it depends on the priorities of the relocating business.

Supply chain management

Successful SCM distinguishes a business from competitors who may suffer from delays, cost overruns, or stockouts. As the following COVID-19 example illustrates, there are cascading risks which start from supply chain disruptions. Especially in emerging markets, with the double liabilities of increased risk of disruption and magnified effects of failures, businesses must design supply chain strategy with these in mind. The more important service reliability is, and the harder it is to ensure it, the more valuable a secure supply chain becomes. Sudden disruptions come in many forms, from pandemics to physical bottlenecks and geopolitical events. The following examples illustrate their diverse effects.

While the COVID-19 pandemic was largely unpredictable and disrupted business on an unimaginable scale, the effect on automakers in India was especially dramatic. Reactive lockdowns in key part-producing states like Maharashtra caused an immediate shortage of components for Hyundai. Production slowed or stopped as the factories waited for transmissions and chips. Alternatives were sourced from outside the country, procured at higher prices with increased shipping costs. Then, port slowdowns led to congestion, and inventories of parts were stuck in logistical limbo. As dealerships could not obtain new cars, customers cancelled orders; financial losses compounded as the just-in-time inventory system failed. Even when the supply of parts resumed, congestion and imbalances still permeated the supply chain (The News Minute Staff, 2021).

COVID-19 was dramatic but far from being the only global risk affecting supply chains. Wars like the Russia-Ukraine conflict create energy shortages and grain distribution; extreme weather like the floods recently experienced in Pakistan damage infrastructure, and geopolitical tensions, such as between the United States and China, result in tariff threats and changes of supply routes. Sanctions and export restrictions can drive decisions on location of manufacturing hubs, as, for instance, U.S. restrictions on semiconductor exports have forced chipmakers to locate facilities in Asia. Western sanctions on Russia have forced rerouting of oil and gas tankers and pipelines, while China's restrictions on rare earth mineral exports have changed the shape of mining investments in Africa.

In March 2021, the *Ever Given*, a massive container ship, ran aground in the Suez Canal and blocked traffic for six days. The extraordinary disruption of global trade underlined the world's reliance on critical shipping routes (Braw, 2021). In direct response to this event, businesses have diversified logistics by setting up overland transport, repositioning supplies to regional hubs, and deploying AI-driven rerouting algorithms.

The competitive effects of good SCM are multiplied when difficulties are overcome. Sourcing materials locally reduces costs, resulting in lower consumer prices. An effective supply chain enables faster response to changing consumer or market demands and reduced risk of damage from geopolitical events. All this leads to improved brand image, enhanced by sustainability and ethical practices.

Technological developments have huge potential to improve SCM. Digital processes, including blockchain supplier verification, demand forecasting using AI, and tracking of deliveries using the Internet of Things, are all growing in use. They can be deployed, for example, to optimize inventory holdings, detect fraud, and anticipate delays.

AI Logistics at Flipkart

Flipkart's Indian operations have integrated AI into all logistics operations. AI forecasts demand before orders are received, stocking warehouses for anticipated deliveries. Delivery fleets use AI-powered traffic analysis to minimize transit times, robotic systems sort packages with an error rate 90% lower than humans, and AI-powered fraud detection tools flag suspicious transactions. The holistic AI-driven approach ensures on-time and correct deliveries, inward and outward, demonstrating convincingly that AI leverage can optimize supply chains and distribution networks to overcome deficiencies.

AI-driven forecasting is not limited to e-commerce. Maersk uses AI to predict port congestion, and Chinese fashion retailer Shein uses AI-driven analysis of big data to design, produce, and distribute new clothing items. This last use shows how technological advances are empowering companies to shorten response times in the quest for optimization of supply and delivery procedures.

Supply chain strategy

Developing and executing a supply chain strategy for operation in an emerging market requires a complex balancing exercise. The business will seek to achieve efficient and effective inflows but will encounter trade-off decisions in the quest. Efficiency and cost considerations must balance and optimize cost, speed, quality, and resilience.

The cheapest supplier in the market may have inferior standards or dependability. The realization that inputs may be unavailable, unreliable, or of insufficient quality tempers the desire to buy local. The preferred system is to have a primary supplier plus a ramping-up agreement with a secondary supplier, who is under contract to provide continuity in the event of a disruption. This is known as *dual sourcing*, widely used throughout emerging markets. In addition, a good failover system to ensure dependable supply will add an importation option.

> Nestlé sells noodle products across India. At a minimum, it has contracts for the supply of every essential ingredient in at least two Indian regions, then adds pre-approved international suppliers from Malaysia and Thailand, thus ensuring two levels of redundancy and enabling continuous production.
>
> *Responsiveness and adaptability* require careful negotiation and consideration of suppliers' abilities and needs. It is important to build strong relationships with local suppliers. Investing time, training, and energy in suppliers can not only help bring them up to international standards but also create loyalties, which can be invaluable in troubled times. The collaborative approach to quality and processes yields an immediate payback when local suppliers struggle to maintain standards. Clear expectations, benchmarking, and sometimes auditing may be beneficial.
>
> Unilever's palm oil suppliers in Indonesia, typically smallholding farmers, enjoy long contracts, co-investment in transport and processing facilities, and access to micro-loans in collaboration with local banks (Unilever, n.d.).

Supply chain risk management

Risk management requires the development of contingency plans and imaginative forethought about business interruptions. Financial risk is highly visible, but other types can be equally damaging and include operational (breakdowns and delays), geopolitical (conflicts, trade barriers, sanctions), cybersecurity, and reputational damage. History contains many examples of large- and small-scale disasters which have exposed weaknesses in risk management, from nuclear plant failures to cyberattacks on global shipping operators, from child labor allegations to contamination of products.

The "tariff wars" that began in late 2024 and escalated in 2025 brought a new dimension to supply chain risk. High, unpredictable import duties, sometimes changing literally day by day, undermined the predictability of sources and routes. Factoring in protectionism forces businesses, at a financial cost, to prioritize resilience over efficiency. Friendshoring and regionalism (the tendency of countries to build stronger trade relations with others in the same geographic area, as opposed to globally) assume greater importance; sourcing supplies in politically aligned countries and/or near neighbors, rather than the most cost-effective, has become necessary.

For businesses in emerging markets that are accustomed to competing on price to build sales, there is an enhanced need to display political alignment and stability. Strategic adjustments include incorporating price adjustment clauses into contracts, diversifying export markets, and even repositioning brands to emphasize stability and alignment with political trends.

Disaster response planning requires consideration of how to build resilience and to find help in extreme adversity. A typical framework for assessing risk involves a linear process – identification assessment, mitigation, and monitoring. Disaster response management is a whole science, to which many books, courses, and advanced educational programs are wholly devoted.

In the quest to develop risk response plans, governments and NGOs are extremely important. Especially in the event of natural disasters, they will be key players and may be key partners. A prominent example of such cooperation is Coca-Cola's partnership with the Red Cross in the Philippines. When typhoons strike, Coca-Cola's distribution network, normally used for soft drinks, pivots to delivering clean drinking water to affected areas (Coca-Cola, 2022).

It is impossible to eliminate all physical risks to the supply chain; thus, strategy must also take account of instruments and products which alleviate financial risks or consequences. Currency and interest rate hedging are commonplace. Commodity hedging, or participating in futures markets, makes costs predictable. It is possible to buy insurance against political risks; the World Bank's Multilateral Investment Guarantee Agency, MIGA, offers highly specialized products for this purpose. Each business must carefully assess its financial risks, then implement appropriate safeguards.

Quality control

Quality has two faces. Internally, every business wants to ensure the quality of products and services flowing in. Externally, it needs to ensure that supply chain components comply with applicable laws and regulations, including environmental standards. Quality control is a vast area mainly beyond our scope; one widely used methodology is TQM, total quality management, which was developed in Japan but has since enjoyed global adoption in many industries. Tata Motors, to whom we refer many times in this book, uses not only TQM but also ISO 9001 (Quality Management Systems – Requirements) certification, Six Sigma (Pyzdek & Keller, 2023) and Kaizen (Imai, 1986). Quality is a fundamental goal throughout the business.

Reputational risk

All participants in the supply chain can damage the reputation of a business. Well-known examples include the sensational news headlines that have plagued fashion companies with manufacturers in developing nations. Every business must ensure that suppliers rigorously follow labor conditions, ESG practices, and legal standards. Community engagement, showing a genuine interest in the welfare of local communities, is a valuable step not only in building loyalty but also in ensuring a flow of firsthand information about working conditions and practices in supplier establishments.

> Dabur India Ltd., well known for its health and wellness products and particularly for its focus on ayurvedic products, exemplifies SCM competency. Wherever possible, it sources its raw materials locally, reducing reliance on imports, securing cost savings, and mitigating risks. It uses SAP Ariba to manage inventory, logistics, and procurement. Because it sells its products across a vast territory of urban and rural places in India, distances matter, while reliability is key. Dabur's maintenance of a best-in-class supply chain, coupled with a robust and durable distribution network, exemplifies adaptation to challenging conditions (Dabur, 2024).

Actionable steps for SCM

We suggest the following steps as a framework for planning a viable SCM system.

1. Conduct a deep assessment of local suppliers, infrastructure, regulatory environment, and logistics.
2. Identify appropriate sources and channels, then plan to build relationships.
3. Consider digital solutions for all aspects of SCM and distribution.
4. Determine measurable KPIs, aligning them with local conditions.
5. Look at each aspect of the system and maximize its flexibility.
6. Develop worst-case scenarios and contingency plans and identify needed failovers.
7. Look at all aspects of the supply chain and distribution channels in the light of sustainability and ESG.
8. Decide how to incorporate feedback loops and how improvements will be made based on the information gathered.
9. Consider whether local suppliers and channels will benefit from partnerships in training, quality control, audits, etc.
10. Set initial benchmarks for supplier, chain, and channel performance and then monitor and adjust as conditions change.

Lessons learned in optimizing supply channels will prove useful as a business turns its attention to delivering goods and services to its customers. Distribution channels are the essential pathways which take the business's offerings out to their final destinations.

Distribution channels

Like supply chains, distribution channels in emerging markets face a significant list of potential challenges. Here are the main obstacles:

- Infrastructure deficiencies.
- Last-mile delivery problems.
- Regulatory and bureaucratic inefficiencies (described in detail in Chapter 10; familiar examples are Brazil's import tariffs and Indonesia's customs delays).
- High costs.
- Inefficient or untrusted payment systems.
- Workforce and training gaps.
- Outdated inventory management systems.
- Environmental threats.

Choosing valid, effective channels can be "crucial to the success of the product or service that a business offers" (Rangan, 2014). A well-designed channel strategy is tailored to work given the infrastructure, culture, and business or consumer practices of the market. Dabur, mentioned above, has maintained its growth with a two-pronged approach: e-commerce for urban and overseas markets and a dedicated sales force visiting remote customers in rural areas (Burman, 2017).

To confront the many challenges, businesses must build a distribution strategy which dovetails with local conditions and consumer expectations.

Building a strong distribution network

Decisions about distribution depend in large part on the target population. It may require one framework to sell to urban dwellers but quite another to sell to rural inhabitants, especially in a large, geographically diverse market. Strategic use of local distributors is the most common solution.

A well-designed distribution partnership will go beyond mere invoice-based payment for services and provide incentives for the partner to meet or exceed expectations. These can include bonus payments, additional business, and other forms of recognition. The objective is to ensure that channel partners see themselves truly in a partnership, not simply selling a service.

Superior design in the distribution partnership bolsters one of the key attributes of long-term success – preserving relationships for the future and building trust within them. There may not be a generous selection of local businesses that can perform to the standard required by the incomer; once found, quality partners must enjoy gold standard treatment, with mutual trust, clear communication, and fair rewards for their efforts. In many large emerging markets, longevity of relationships is highly valued and will often outweigh prospects of a short-term profit or windfall. China and Vietnam have specific names for this: Chinese business draws strong influence from *guanxi*, the emphasis on personal relationship and trust rather than transactional elements. Commitment to a partner's long-term future is far more likely to yield fruitful cooperation than stressing the immediacy of financial gains. Vietnamese business values *nhân tình*, basing decisions not on immediate profitability but how well they know and trust their counterparts.

A hypothetical example will illustrate a feasible approach. Imagine an energy drink manufacturer planning an expansion into Nigeria. Energy drinks are bulky, heavy, and of low value in proportion to their volume. In a developed market, the business might profit handsomely from direct-to-retail channels, cutting out distributor margins to its own benefit. In Nigeria, however, given the infrastructure gaps, success might come more readily through partnerships with local distributors who know the landscape and their populations. Regional rather than national manufacturing might significantly reduce costs and build local ties; established wholesalers are likely to have multifaceted relationships with smaller retailers who have the consumer interface. In this scenario, feedback from local distributors may shape the presentation and packaging of the product. In a developed market, the most frequent purchases may be of 4, 6, or even 12 packs of cans; in a rural area where consumers have limited income, single units may be more popular.

While only very large businesses can build their own complete distribution system, control over the entire supply chain from manufacturing to retail can address weak infrastructure and protect brand integrity. Walmart in India has built a vast network of warehouses, supplied by its own fleet of trucks. Most businesses are, however, at least partly dependent on contracted services from local and international specialists.

Sefam, producer of the luxury fabric Grand Bareeze, began by making embroidered fabric. Its commitment to quality led to large investments in quality control and ultimately to the opening of its own stores. The full integration addressed the lack of infrastructure in Pakistan and positioned Managing Director Seema Aziz first to expand into the Middle East and compete with global brands and then to pay back her community with her leadership of the CARE Foundation (Aziz, 2016).

Technology has a large part to play in enhancing delivery efficiencies. Flipkart, mentioned above, has state-of-the-art GPS-based tracking of packages. It sends real-time updates to customers, including estimated delivery times and interactive query handling. Invisibly to drivers and customers alike, the technology is also constantly monitoring traffic and routes, optimizing them so that the most customers receive the most goods on time or early (Poojary, 2019).

Predictive analytics plays a huge role in distribution channel optimization. Businesses can use a combination of historical analysis, modeling, and machine learning to organize the distribution network based on predicted demand, manage inventory, schedule transportation, and figure out optimal locations for storage of products.

Bancolombia and FirstRand

Bancolombia's success story illustrates key strategic themes. The explanation for its success is its strategy of focusing on emerging markets and technologies which enhance delivery channels.

Colombia has a large rural population where traditional banking has poor reach. However, there is a high penetration of mobile phone usage. The bank was an early investor in digital banking (Genesys, 2024). This, coupled with its energetic pursuit of rural customers through an agent network, produced a meteoric rise in customer numbers (Martinez & Hernandez, 2023). The bank also improved its market share through strategic acquisitions, notably of HSBC Colombia. It prioritizes financial inclusion and is a market leader in microfinance and affordable credit. Sustainability is also high on Bancolombia's agenda, with green financing, renewable energy, and conservation projects receiving special attention. Bancolombia has kept its attention on the moral authenticity of its business, resulting in strong financial performance and market leadership (Grupo Bancolombia, 2023).

This echoes the experience of Sizwe Nxasana, former C.E.O. of FirstRand Bank in South Africa. FirstRand was keen to reach underserved and unbanked African populations, succeeding by offering mobile and digital services without needing physical branches. Partnerships with telecoms helped banking to penetrate on the coattails of mobile telephony, while the introduction of simplified products with minimal fees began to serve lower-income groups (Nxasana, 2017). Another remarkable success story along similar lines is told by James Mwangi of Equity Bank, Kenya (Mwangi, 2018).

As fintech drives mobile banking to deliver services to unbanked populations, it is also removing cash flow barriers for small logistics providers, as digital payments provide supply chain financing and mobile-based credit solutions.

Last-mile delivery

Last-mile delivery is the very last stage of the process, where goods leave a distribution center for their destination. Order fulfillment is a critical operation and can be the most expensive part of the sales operation (Simmons, 2024).

Emerging markets face intensified last-mile challenges, especially for remote populations. E-commerce growth brings increased demand for efficient last-mile delivery services, an opportunity and a challenge. Third-party service providers are frequently less dependable and more costly. DHL might be an effective and safe delivery solution in many difficult environments, but the cost of sending a courier shipment is prohibitive for the average consumer.

While some government-owned distribution networks, such as India Post, have successfully adapted to e-commerce, in other emerging markets they are rarely the solution. An e-commerce merchant selling to Americans or Canadians is likely to consider the national post office as a contender for deliveries; Canada Post is estimated to lose only 0.42% of parcels entrusted to it (Lessard, 2023). There are few published statistics for the postal services of emerging markets, but it is not difficult to find a cacophony of internet complaints, reinforcing the common view that loss rates are much higher in emerging markets. An online forum discussing Moroccan mail, for example, suggests that a regular letter has a 50/50 chance of loss or delivery.

Responses to this need are both physical and technological. Micro-fulfillment places products nearer to consumers in crowded areas; *crowdsourced delivery* is a strong improvement which uses existing service providers in new ways. An excellent example is the leveraging of Uber's driver network to deliver food from restaurants to homes, which gained a massive boost from the COVID-19 pandemic.

Drone delivery is exciting and newsworthy, though in its infancy. Important discussions about airspace congestion and safety lie ahead. A 2019 survey reported that drone delivery operations had become reality in 27 countries (Unmanned Airspace, 2019), although the majority are developed nations. China, the UAE, and Indonesia were named pioneering locations for product deliveries by drone. Drones are effectively used to deliver medical supplies and samples in India, Thailand, and several nations in Sub-Saharan Africa.

Locker systems are growing in utility for last-mile delivery. Goods are placed in lockers from which they can be picked up, usually 24/7, by consumers who are given a PIN or code to open the locker just once. They are highly convenient and much more secure than leaving goods outside homes. China has been the world's leader in locker systems, where they are commonly integrated with e-commerce platforms (Morgan, 2021); however, they are also growing in use in India, Brazil (Baker, 2022), and Mexico, among others.

Serve robotics, the use of autonomous delivery robots, holds promise as a way to overcome last-mile hurdles like traffic congestion and poor infrastructure by using sidewalks instead of roads. They offer potential speed, emissions, and scaling improvements. Their use in emerging markets is very limited, typically expanding from use in developed markets to test cases in emerging markets. Kiwibot, for example, was developed at California universities but now has a flagship project in Medellin, Colombia (Bizkova, 2021).

Last-mile requirements underlie the popularity of nearshoring, discussed above. Last-mile logistics are particularly critical for e-commerce merchants, as fast and reliable delivery drives customer satisfaction. E-commerce has risen so rapidly in emerging markets that we should consider it separately from the mainstream problems previously enumerated.

E-commerce logistics in emerging markets

It is difficult to assemble comparable e-commerce penetration rates for all emerging markets. However, there are some compelling data which we can summarize. Globally, at the end of 2024, e-commerce sales were rapidly approaching 20% of all retail sales (Coppola, 2024). By value, although China topped the list with over $3 trillion in sales (compared to #2, the United States, with only $1.16 trillion), developed countries dominate the top 10 markets worldwide. India and Indonesia are the only two other emerging markets to feature in that list (Buck, 2024).

A table of the fastest-growing e-commerce markets is impactful. In 2023, emerging markets occupied all eight top positions in the world. The Philippines led with a compound annual growth rate from 2019 to 2023 of 28.6% (GlobalData, 2024), while only Mexico at 14.2% (#6 on the list) was not an Asian nation. When e-commerce penetration as a percentage of retail sales is tabulated, China comes out top again with 47%, and Indonesia is in second place with almost 32% (GlobalData, 2024).

As levels of smartphone ownership and internet access increase, consumer behaviors are changing rapidly with e-commerce the fastest-growing source of sales. Logistics for e-commerce are well described as a bottleneck, with unique challenges in emerging markets.

Consumer delivery preferences differ significantly from developed country tastes. There are often trust issues in emerging markets which lead to a preference for physical collection of goods rather than delivery. Trust issues are traditionally addressed by cash-on-delivery systems, in-store pickups, and local courier deliveries. With the improvement of delivery services and increased e-commerce, this distinction is eroding.

Cash on Delivery (COD) is extremely popular in several large emerging markets, including India and Indonesia. However, it invokes a series of risks, including cash-handling issues (theft and robbery), delivery delays due to congestion, and high return rates, because consumers can simply change their minds and refuse a delivery or may not have cash at home to pay when goods arrive. Merchants encourage digital payments by offering discounts or loyalty points, integrating with mobile wallets, and sometimes using partial payments with orders, leaving only a balance for COD.

Inventory mismanagement, possibly partly caused by expensive or poorly located warehousing, can cause stockouts and excesses. Some large e-commerce merchants like Alibaba have found a solution in robotic handling and AI-powered forecasting. Flipkart has deployed a system of smart fulfillment centers, small warehouses in or close to urban areas, to decentralize inventory. These facilities are also known as *dark stores*.

Demand for logistics solutions has led to the creation of several successful start-ups in emerging markets. Examples include Ninja Van,[1] which uses route optimization and real-time tracking across Southeast Asia, and J&T Express[2] which operates in the same area with a heavy focus on e-commerce logistics. Gokada,[3] in Nigeria, was originally an Uber-like system for motorcycles but diverted its fleet of bikes to logistics, coping admirably with traffic congestion, to provide last-mile delivery services for small businesses. Loggi,[4] in Brazil, is also focused on last-mile delivery for e-commerce, while India's Delhivery[5] uses AI and automation to optimize end-to-end supply chain execution.

These solutions will certainly increase in use and utility for the foreseeable future. Tracking and security benefit from the development of AI and blockchain tools, while COD is likely to decrease in popularity as digital payment solutions are developed and encouraged. Last-mile delivery from small, well-positioned warehouses seems to be the solution best positioned to improve last-mile delivery.

Measuring chain and channel efficiency

KPIs and other metrics form an important part of monitoring and analysis. In the emerging market context, the following are of particular interest.

Inventory turnover gives a strong indication of how well storage costs are optimized, whether warehousing is optimally deployed, flags overstocking, and measures efficiency in moving goods out to customers. Turnover rates vary widely by industry, though generally they are much smaller for heavy goods and industrial products than consumer goods like clothing and electronics. Some e-commerce retailers maintain very impressive ratios: for example, Amazon which generally falls between 9.5 and 12 (Alphaquery, 2025), while traditional fast-moving consumer goods vendors often struggle to turn inventory over five times per year.

Supplier lead times may be tracked and compared over time, allowing assessment of reliability and production planning. ERP (Enterprise Resource Planning) and SCM software contain modules to automate these processes; smaller operations without access to such systems may use barcode tracking or manual logs and spreadsheets.

COGS (cost of goods sold) variability is useful wherever a business can quantify the effects of supply chain changes. When costs and prices are subject to strong fluctuations,

COGS monitoring is especially valuable as a means of measuring cost efficiency. Drilling down on the data can be complex, taking account of material efficiency, defect rates, and overall quality of incoming supplies.

After analyzing internal costs related to quality, waste, rework, and defects, the business must also consider any impacts on customer perception or warranty expenses. COGS monitoring ultimately provides assurance that procurement decisions have not compromised quality in pursuit of lower costs.

Environmental measures (sustainability metrics) have immense importance as the world increasingly focuses on impacts. These include carbon fuel usage and carbon emissions, water consumption and wastewater production, waste generation, recycling percentages, energy consumption, deforestation, air quality, and others.

KPI measurement may be deployed not only within the business's own operations but also to the activities of suppliers and distributors.

Conclusion

Organizing and managing the flow of goods and services is a highly rewarding, if complex, task. Success transforms the challenges into unique competitive advantages.

This chapter described infrastructure challenges, identifying them as the root cause of most difficulties in both the supply chain and distribution channels. We discussed some notable solutions, identified the unique issues facing e-commerce merchants in emerging markets, and considered the role of sustainability in supply chain and distribution operations.

The principles and practices outlined in this chapter emphasize the critical roles of partnerships and technology. They underline the need for sustainable solutions. Businesses can leverage these factors in supply chain and distribution strategies, maintaining steady growth in the world's most expansive markets. Technology appears to offer the most promise in overcoming the many barriers that we identified.

While efficient procurement and distribution are key to success, navigating legal frameworks is also critical. Businesses must frequently deal with ambiguous rules, uneven enforcement, and unpredictable changes in policy. The legal environment creates risks and opportunities, as a competitive edge can be gained from knowing how to play the local game. The next chapter will examine legal and compliance challenges in emerging markets.

Notes

1 https://www.ninjavan.co/
2 https://www.jtexpress.com/en
3 https://www.gokada.ng/
4 https://www.loggi.com/
5 https://www.delhivery.com/

References

Akin, H. (2015, February 11). Interview by F. Oberholzer-Gee. *Creating Emerging Markets Oral History Collection*. Baker Library Special Collections, Harvard Business School.

Alphaquery. (2025, March 7). Amazon.com, Inc. (AMZN). *Inventory Turnover (Annual)*. https://www.alphaquery.com/stock/AMZN/fundamentals/annual/inventory-turnover

Aziz, Seema. (2016, October 18). Interview by T. Khanna. *Creating Emerging Markets Oral History Collection*. Baker Library Special Collections, Harvard Business School.

Baker, E. (2022, December 19). Cainiao and Facily to pilot smart lockers in São Paulo. https://www.parcelandpostaltechnologyinternational.com/news/lockers-pudo/cainiao-and-facily-to-pilot-smart-lockers-in-sao-paulo.html

Banerjee, A. (2024, December 9). *Cold storage market size, share & trends analysis report by type (refrigerated warehousing, cold chain logistics), by applications (food and beverages, pharmaceuticals, chemicals, others), by ownership (private, public) and by region (North America, Europe, APAC, Middle East and Africa, LATAM) forecasts, 2025-2033*. Straits Research. https://straitsresearch.com/report/cold-storage-market

Bizkova, T. (2021, December 13). Kiwibot: The Colombian startup charming the world with its cute food delivery robots. https://thebogotapost.com/kiwibot-the-colombian-startup-charming-the-world-with-its-cute-food-delivery-robots/49471/

BL Pune Bureau. (2024, January 3). Rumours of fuel shortage spark crowded scenes at petrol pumps in Maharashtra. *The Hindu Business Line*. https://www.thehindubusinessline.com/news/rumours-of-fuel-shortage-spark-crowded-scenes-at-petrol-pumps-in-maharashtra/article67701403.ece

Braw, E. (2021, November 10). What the Ever Given Taught the World. https://www.aei.org/op-eds/what-the-ever-given-taught-the-world/

Brooks, P. (2024, March 14). Comment: Greenshoring can help manufacturers hit ESG goals. https://www.theengineer.co.uk/content/opinion/comment-greenshoring-can-help-manufacturers-hit-esg-goals/

Buck, A. (2024, September 26). e-commerce Market Size by Country. https://www.mobiloud.com/blog/e-commerce-market-size-by-country

Burman, A. (2017, December 21). Interview by S. Srinivasan. *Creating Emerging Markets Oral History Collection*. Baker Library Special Collections, Harvard Business School.

Christensen, C., Ojomo, C., & Dillon, K. (2019). The Prosperity Paradox. *Harper Business*.

Coca-Cola. (2022, March 2). Bayanihan in the midst of a pandemic: The Coca-Cola Foundation, Coca-Cola Philippines contribute aid to Filipinos impacted by Super Typhoon Odette. https://www.coca-cola.com/ph/en/media-center/bayanihan-in-the-midst-of-a-pandemic

Coppola, D. (2024, May 22). E-commerce as percentage of total retail sales worldwide from 2021 to 2027. https://www.statista.com/statistics/534123/e-commerce-share-of-retail-sales-worldwide

Dabur. (2024). Manufactured capital: Integrated annual report 2023-24. https://www.dabur.com/digital-annual-report/integrated-reports/manufactured-capital.html

Dell Inc. (2006, December 12). Dell Complete Implementation of Global Free Recycling. https://www.csrwire.com/press_releases/26081-dell-completes-implementation-of-global-free-recycling

GAN Integrity. (2020, September 30). Indonesia risk report. https://www.ganintegrity.com/country-profiles/indonesia/

GeeksforGeeks. (2024, February 9). Websites blocked in China. https://www.geeksforgeeks.org/websites-blocked-in-china/

Genesys. (2024, May 14). Genesys recognizes Bancolombia as winner of CX mover award. https://www.genesys.com/company/newsroom/announcements/genesys-recognizes-bancolombia-as-winner-of-cx-mover-partner-award

Global X Research Team. (2023, April 12). Nearshoring and the new countries driving growth in Emerging Markets. https://www.globalxetfs.com/nearshoring-and-the-new-countries-driving-growth-in-emerging-markets/

GlobalData. (2024, May 27). Philippines e-commerce payments to surge by nearly 20% in 2024, reveals GlobalData. https://www.globaldata.com/media/banking/philippines-e-commerce-payments-to-surge-by-nearly-20-in-2024-reveals-globaldata/

Grupo Bancolombia. (2023). *Well-Being for all: Periodic fiscal year-end report 2022*. Grupo Bancolombia.
Imai, M. (1986). *Kaizen: The Key to Japan's Competitive Success*. McGraw-Hill.
Irwin-Hunt, A. (2024). *Global nearshoring FDI proliferates: The FDI report 2024*. The Financial Times.
Kolawole, S., & Umejei, E. (n.d.) Nigeria: Mobile network ecosystem. https://medialandscapes.org/country/nigeria/telecommunications/overview
Lessard, M. (2023, November 11). Q3 2023 Data: What is the percentage of packages that get lost in transit? Data by Province and Carrier. *Buster Fletcher Report*. https://www.busterfetcher.com/en/blog/q3-2023/what-is-the-percentage-of-packages-that-get-lost-in-transit-data-by-province-and-carrier
Maguire, G. (2024, November 6). Brazil lifts coal imports to record as hydro hit lingers. *Reuters*. https://www.reuters.com/business/energy/brazil-lifts-coal-imports-record-hydro-hit-lingers-maguire-2024-11-06/
Martinez, C., & Hernandez, E. (2023, January 19). How did Bancolombia Create a successful rural agent network at scale? *CGAP*. https://www.cgap.org/blog/how-did-bancolombia-create-successful-rural-agent-network-scale
Morgan, E. (2021, March 29). Hivebox case study: How lockers became essential to Chinese e-commerce. https://www.doddle.com/blog/hivebox-case-study-how-lockers-became-essential-to-chinese-e-commerce/
Mwangi, J. (2018, April 24). Interview by T. Khanna. *Creating Emerging Markets Oral History Project*. Baker Library Special Collections, Harvard Business School.
Nxasana, S. (2017, May 23). Interview by J. Macomber. *Creating Emerging Markets Oral History Collection*. Baker Library Special Projects, Harvard Business School.
Pham, X. (2022, March 10). Cushman & Wakefield: Vietnam's cold chain market is expected to boom. https://www.cushmanwakefield.com/en/vietnam/insights/vietnams-cold-chain-market-is-expected-to-boom
Poojary, T. (2019, April). How Flipkart is using automation to delivery your products on time. https://yourstory.com/2019/04/e-commerce-flipkart-automation-logistics-ekart-delivery
Pyzdek, T., & Keller, P. (2023). *The Six Sigma Handbook*, Sixth Edition. McGraw Hill.
Rangan, V.K. (2014, June 30). *Developing and Managing Channels of Distribution*. Harvard Business Publishing.
Simmons, K.-J. (2024, February 14). Order Fulfilment costs: Fulfillment center pricing explained. https://fitsmallbusiness.com/order-fulfillment-costs/
The News Minute Staff. (2021, June 1). COVID impact: Maruti Suzuki, Hyundai, M&M and others see huge decline in May sales. The NEWS Minute. https://www.thenewsminute.com/money/covid-impact-maruti-suzuki-hyundai-mm-and-others-see-huge-decline-may-sales-149927
Unilever. (n.d.). Our palm oil supply chain. https://www.unilever.com/sustainability/nature/deforestation-free-supply-chain/palm-oil-story
United Nations Security Council. (2023, June 21). *Ongoing Decline in Gulf of Guinea's Piracy. Security Council Report 15331*. United Nations.
Unmanned Airspace. (2019, April 7). Drone delivery operations underway in 27 countries. https://www.unmannedairspace.info/latest-news-and-information/drone-delivery-operations-underway-in-26-countries/
Walmart. (n.d.). India. https://corporate.walmart.com/about/international/walmart-india
Zami, T. (2024, July 26). Bangladesh's internet shutdown isolates citizens, disrupts business. *Reuters*. https://www.reuters.com/world/asia-pacific/bangladeshs-internet-shutdown-isolates-citizens-disrupts-business-2024-07-26/

CHAPTER 10

Legal complexity in emerging markets

Learning outcomes

After studying this chapter, you will be able to do the following:

1. Analyze, categorize, and compare legal and regulatory frameworks that present challenges in emerging markets, assessing their impact on operations and strategy.
2. Evaluate the impact of diverse labor, trade, investment, and IP laws and practices.
3. Assess the risks and opportunities which flow from legal complexity.
4. Analyze real-world examples to demonstrate successful approaches to legal complexity.
5. Critically evaluate the role of environmental, social, and governance (ESG) considerations and sustainability principles in responding to legal and regulatory demands.
6. Formulate risk mitigation strategies, including compliance management.
7. Justify retaining legal advisors and local partners to maintain a compliant business, resolve disputes, and adapt quickly to unfolding changes and challenges.
8. Evaluate the ethical aspects of regulatory arbitrage in diverse situations.
9. Determine the possibilities and processes of non-market strategies in emerging markets.

Introduction: Regulation and strategy

Regulatory expansion

In emerging markets, the extent of regulation is expanding rapidly. The forces driving legislative development are both external and internal. Within each jurisdiction, the increasing complexity of business creates a need for improvements in oversight and governance. Global forces, including trade agreements, sustainability standards, and attempts to harmonize legal frameworks, demand ever more, and more sophisticated, rules and

DOI: 10.4324/9781003638490-10

regulations. The World Bank (2020) underlines the necessity of regulatory convergence for developing countries as they seek participation in global value chains. With such breadth of legislation in so many markets, a full analysis would require an entire book. This chapter contains an overview of how regulatory compliance dovetails into business strategy, with illustrative examples.

Strategic implications

Businesses expanding internationally must deal with diverse and often unique regulatory regimes. Understanding legal systems and operating within their constraints are strategic imperatives, made more difficult in emerging markets by VUCA factors and the layering of international, national, state, and local regimes. We will describe how differences in legal systems and history change business behavior. We will examine how regulation sometimes helps, and sometimes hinders, foreign investment. We will look at well-developed and weak legal frameworks and see how bureaucratic inefficiencies, spotty enforcement, and volatile legislators require businesses to be proactive in their legal strategies.

In a dedicated section, we will introduce the concept of non-market business strategies. These are practices which support business development through activities which involve relationship-building with governments, NGOs, and others, with the goal of shaping regulatory and institutional environments in ways that are favorable to business. In emerging markets, as legal systems may be changing rapidly, non-market strategies are particularly relevant to long-term success.

Attracting investment

A quality regulatory framework is essential for any emerging market that wants to attract foreign direct investment (FDI) or encourage domestic investors to put their money to use at home. The World Bank's 2024 *Business Ready* report found a direct correlation between framework scores and net FDI; when it took the connection between public services and FDI into consideration, the correlation was even higher.

The question of whether better regulation *causes* higher investment is complex. Before-and-after studies from the early 2000s showed that removing entry barriers led to greater inflows (Alfaro et al., 2004; Busse and Groizard, 2008); however, more recent research is suggestive of a feedback loop in which an influx of investment leads to improvements in regulation (Jordaan et al., 2020). A more refined view is that it is not regulation itself, but the quality of reporting and transparency, that leads to increased investment. Reliable reporting lowers perceived risk for capital investors, who experience less information asymmetry. The World Bank (2020) concluded that regulatory frameworks prioritizing transparency and investor protection are especially powerful magnets for FDI.

Legal systems

No two legal systems are exactly alike. Even in culturally similar countries, businesspeople are sometimes surprised to learn that "ownership" or "rights" can have fundamentally different meanings. Local differences can mandate a unique way of doing the same business in a new location. For example, while Brazil and Mexico have legal systems heavily influenced by European civil law, India has inherited common law from the British colonial period. Sharia law has a strong influence in the Middle East, while China has a socialist legal system which emphasizes state control. Thailand has a mixed legal system with elements of civil and common law; Indonesia mixes Dutch civil law, customary practices, and Islamic legal principles.

Profound differences in legal systems affect every aspect of business operations. Typically, private (contract, tort, and property) law governs relations between parties, while through public, administrative, and criminal laws, governments regulate relationships between individuals and the state. Importantly for business competition, corporate formation and governance, data protection, environmental protection, intellectual property (IP), investment, labor and employment, and taxation are usually governmental domains. However, the division is not uniform between countries; for example, there are emerging markets where all land is government-owned or IP is poorly defended. We will highlight and illustrate the effects of these differences as we proceed.

The major areas of regulation in emerging markets are much the same as in developed markets. The details, however, can be very different. In the following subsections, we will outline each of the major domains which require deep consideration by expanding businesses.

Regulatory matters typically fall squarely under the "C" of VUCA – they are extremely complex. A broad-brush view of markets in general is insufficient to identify the challenges posed by each specific market. Differences between jurisdictions add operational complexities as a business producing the same product in different locations must cope with different laws and regulations.

Regulation is not static. Daily changes can create new opportunities in hitherto unknown areas where new business models or products can be developed and grown. While unexpected changes can occur quickly, needed changes may take years to implement, requiring businesses to develop adaptive, resilient strategies. Patience and planning for the long term are required.

> Keshub Mahindra, former chairman of the Mahindra Group, returned home to India from studying at the Wharton School of Business (University of Pennsylvania) early in the post-independence period. It was a time of idealism, with many business leaders hoping that the government would allow non-governmental business to flourish. He was to be disappointed; all industries required government permission to operate, and the government heavily dictated the speed and scope of expansion (Mahindra, 2013).

Many emerging markets, even if they have regulatory frameworks, suffer from inefficient processes, bureaucracy, and consequent costs. To compound this, even where clear laws and regulations exist, enforcement is often sporadic or even haphazard; sadly, for some businesses, the lack of consistent enforcement is an attraction. A business which falls victim to the lure of lax regulation may soon come to regret its decisions, as competitors take advantage of that same lawlessness to attack it.

Nevertheless, adept businesses with strong legal expertise can leverage diversity into an advantage, setting up components of their business in jurisdictions most favorable to their operations. In Southeast Asia, for example, many companies manufacture and sell in emerging markets but set up headquarters in Singapore to gain tax and IP protection benefits.

Judicial systems and enforcement

Businesses in developed markets are accustomed to the presence of a court system, largely free of corruption or undue influence, which can be relied on for efficient and fair resolution of contentious matters, either between private parties or between business and government. In emerging markets, it often simply is not so; then there is a compounding of the problem when the laws are strong, but enforcement is weak, corrupt, or nonexistent. Business ventures in unstable, unreliable judicial environments must be ready to absorb the losses that flow from slow processing of disputes, unpredictable outcomes, corrupt judges, and lack of enforcement even after a favorable judgment. Corruption tends to be found most often in the lower courts but can reach the highest levels. Foreign companies can find themselves significantly prejudiced in actions against well-connected local businesses or state-owned enterprises.

A well-known case of judicial corruption occurred in South Africa, running through 13 years of hearings and appeals regarding Judge John Hlophe, the Judge President of the Western Cape High Court in South Africa. Hlophe was ultimately found guilty of gross misconduct in 2021, but then resigned before his impeachment proceedings could be completed. Even though justice finally prevailed in condemning the actions of a corrupted high judicial officer, the delay in determining accountability was of itself a further cause for criticism (Judges Matter, n.d.).

Earlier in this book, we mentioned the extraordinary delays encountered in India, where an inadequate court system has backlogs of years or even decades, clogged by literally millions of pending cases. Brazil has a similar situation. In contrast, some countries such as Malaysia and South Africa have made great leaps forward in the last decade.

A partial solution to these problems, at least in contract matters, is to draft clauses which specify arbitration or some other form of alternative dispute resolution and to agree that resolution argument and decision will take place in a stipulated international center such as London, Paris, or Singapore.

Where businesses are dependent on effective legal protections, they must carefully consider not only legislation but also its enforcement and the institutions which support, or fail to support, the rule of law. Any indication that local processes are inadequate should trigger consideration of moving dispute resolution to another forum, though that is rarely possible when contracting or conflicting with governmental agencies.

Regulatory domains

Market entry and competition law

Competition law, the body of regulation which seeks to keep businesses competitive with each other and prevent abuse of monopoly or price-fixing, is nascent in emerging markets. A merger or acquisition is an attractive way to capture market share, but if government or entrenched commercial interests perceive a threat, new laws may quickly be enacted. An outsider moving into a new market may face political resistance, defensive actions local controlling interests, or both, and a frank assessment of the likelihood of regulatory pushback is absolutely required.

For example, South Africa has strong competition laws: the *Competition Act, 1998* has forceful prohibitions of cartel activity, bid-rigging, abuses of dominant positions, and mergers which reduce competition in the market. The Competition Commission has fearsome powers that can extend all the way to compelling the sale of acquired assets (South African Government, 1998). An inward investor perceived as undermining competitive activities might quite literally be forced to sell up and go home.

By contrast, competition law in the Philippines is weak and ineffective. The Philippine Competition Commission, only established in 2015, lacks resources and the independence to enforce its mandate, to maintain market competition, regulate anti-competitive conduct, review mergers, and ensure a level playing field. In reality, corruption and the extreme power of large conglomerates thrive (Balisacan, n.d.). Major resistance to a new entrant in this market is likely to come from other businesses, not from government.

Businesses entering markets with strong competition laws or entrenched anti-competitive power blocs may use one or more of several strategies, after conducting thorough due diligence to understand the local situation. Strategic partnerships with locally or state owned enterprises may avail of existing consumer bases and avoid the need for new penetration techniques such as aggressive pricing. There may be the opportunity to engage with business associations or government interests to improve legislation. Niche market positioning may help avoid direct confrontation with local interests which feel threatened by new market entrants.

Intellectual property

Intellectual property rights are a monstrous challenge in emerging markets. Weak IP enforcement engenders damaging counterfeiting, trademark violation, and patent infringement, which are widespread in Africa and some parts of Asia. In the pharmaceutical business, counterfeit products can create health crises while undermining revenue and reputation. Market opportunities can be lost while emerging market governments execute slow and cumbersome patent approval processes.

A partial counter to slow bureaucratic procedures would be the availability of patent extensions. Unfortunately, the large emerging markets, which most manifest slow and complex approval procedures, are also often sluggish in granting supplementary protection certificates or patent extensions.

Despite these difficulties, businesses seeking to innovate and expand in emerging markets require the best possible IP protections. They can work closely with local lawyers to optimize registration processes then engage in local partnerships to strengthen enforcement. If they are significant employers or investors, they may be able to work through industry lobby groups or diplomatic means to encourage government reforms. Emerging market governments do have a vested interest in improving registration processes and enforcement – without them, innovation is hindered in key areas like healthcare and technology, which detracts from economic and social development.

Brazil, China, India, and South Africa have all made strong moves to restrict the practice of *evergreening* – extending patents based on minor variations or enhancements to prolong protection against competition (Collier, 2013). Political opinion tends to frown on patent extensions as they run counter to the ideal of affordable public access to essential medicines.

Glivec, by Novartis

Novartis' life-saving leukemia drug, imatinib, was patented in the early 1990s. In 1998, the company applied for an Indian patent for a new form which was more easily absorbed. Litigation around a denial of the Indian patent went all the way to the Supreme Court, which in 2013 upheld the rejection of the patent on the ground that it did not significantly advance therapeutic efficacy. The decision allowed the drug to be sold at $2,000 per year instead of $70,000 per year, delighting generic drug manufacturers and cementing India's stance against evergreening (Supreme Court of India, 2013).

Licensing and franchising agreements require particular care to protect IP rights and manage the consequent revenues. This is especially true where valuable technology or closely guarded trade secrets are to be transferred under a cooperation agreement. Franchised operators are an attractive option to improve the chances of a successful market penetration but carry the risk of loss of trade secrets or technology if not carefully structured and monitored.

Reluctance to transfer, share, or license technology can be a significant barrier to expansion for businesses growing within emerging markets. Gülsüm Azeri, an accomplished Turkish business leader, recalls her early career at Çukurova Holding, one of Türkiye's largest conglomerates. She participated in an ambitious project to develop chrome chemical production; despite approaches to several western countries, she eventually succeeded only in accessing technology from Russia (Azeri, 2014).

Formal strategies for protecting IP are widely employed in emerging markets, albeit with limited success. Local trademark and patent registration is usual, although some companies, notably Coca-Cola, avoid public disclosure of their secrets and formulae, instead relying on secrecy. Licensing and franchising agreements must always include strong clauses protecting any IP being transferred.

The *Paris Convention for the Protection of Industrial Property*, first agreed in 1883 and since revised many times, is one of the most widely subscribed treaties on earth, with 193 member countries. While enforcement is not uniform, it contains several key provisions for the protection of IP, including trademarks, patents, and industrial designs. It has a leveling effect in that each member country must treat all persons and organizations the same way as it treats its own; a filing in one country has priority over later filings by another person in another country. This means that an inventor or creator is not obliged to pursue simultaneous registration in all countries where they might one day seek to profit from it.

The Paris Convention has its own website, which maintains a list of member countries. Every country that we identified as an emerging market is a signatory.

The Trade-Related Aspects of Intellectual Property Rights (TRIPS) Agreement was established in 1994 and is legally binding on all countries which are members of the World Trade Organization. It mandates baseline protections for copyrights, patents, trademarks, and trade secrets. Countries are required to treat domestic and foreign IP holders equally, without discrimination; this is known as granting Most-Favored-Nation (MFN) status. TRIPS requires member nations to grant patents for at least 20 years and allows for compulsory licensing to allow governments to authorize production of medicines without patent-holder consent when there is a public health emergency.

As with the Paris Convention, many emerging markets do not have strong enforcement, and some have argued that TRIPS favors developed nations and creates economic and social distance by restricting access to technology and medicines.

TRIPS-based argument was intense during the COVID-19 pandemic, as India and South Africa led a push for temporary waivers to permit increased production of vaccines. An agreement was reached on a temporary waiver in June 2022, leaving both sides unhappy, as developing countries felt it did not go far enough, while patent holders argued that it undermined their rights without solving the issues (Congressional Research Service, 2022).

Counterfeiting in China

Despite strengthening IP laws under the 2020 Phase One Trade Deal with the United States, enforcement of international protections remains difficult for foreign companies. Luxury brands have undergone decades-long wars against voluminous production of copied products such as Louis Vuitton accessories and Rolex watches. Even Apple suffered losses from widespread production of iPhone copies which flooded international markets.

Data protection and digital regulation

Data protection refers to the body of laws, regulations, policies, and procedures that are designed to shield personal information from loss, misuse, or unauthorized access. Most data protection laws grant individuals control of the collection, processing, and sharing of their data.

Among regulatory areas in emerging markets, data protection has the most disparity; legislators struggle to keep pace with technological change. Some jurisdictions do not yet have a fully developed framework, have weak enforcement mechanisms, and may suffer from technological deficiencies.

Bangladesh, as we write in April 2025, does not have any enacted legislation for data protection, though a draft has been in circulation since late 2023. Brazil has enacted the General Data Protection Law (LGPD), a framework driven by Europe's GDPR (European Union, 2016). China has a framework titled *Personal Information Protection Law*, but its strict measures seem to favor state control rather than individual rights. India's *Digital Personal Data Protection Act*, 2023, has attempted to modernize regulation but has faced severe criticism for supporting invasive governmental powers. Weak enforcement does not equate to safety – businesses may still encounter consumer backlash or international regulatory action.

If consumer data are to be collected in any market, the business must take seriously the application of consent requirements and data security measures. As progressively more complex rules surrounding data transfer are developing all around the world, they are of particular concern to a business operating across borders. A business which is based in one country, collects data on consumers from another, and moves that data across borders or onto the cloud will need to consider at least three regulatory regimes – home, foreign, and transfer rules –to remain compliant. There could be more if the data are hosted on servers in yet other countries.

Corporate formation

Corporate formation, compared to developed markets, is frequently complex, expensive, and time-consuming. The current (early 2025) range of estimates is from six (Thailand) to over 30 (Brazil) days (Expatica, n.d.; TMF Group, 2023). While no period within this range is a serious impediment to doing business, the time taken by the process is a useful bellwether of the level of government efficiency and bureaucracy which might be anticipated throughout the medium-term life of a new subsidiary.

Property and land use

Property ownership and land use laws typically flow from the origins of legal systems themselves, but with some adaptations to economic considerations.

Indonesia, Thailand, and Vietnam all have prohibitions on foreigners owning land. They have workarounds – Indonesia allows leased-use agreements for up to 80 years, while Thailand permits condominium ownership of less than half of a building. Vietnam's leases are for 50 years, but with a possibility of options to extend.

Existence of land registries might be seen as supporting claims of land ownership, as in South Africa. Land redistribution efforts can shake the apparent entitlements of domestic and foreign owners; when big money is involved, as with emergent mineral claims, corruption can emerge in land registry systems.

Vietnam and China have paradoxically simple philosophies on land ownership: everything belongs to the government. China leverages its position by imposing zoning restrictions through a centralized land-use system. We find a contrasting situation in Kenya, where despite the existence of a recording system there is a lack of effective enforcement, leading to unusual development plans and many informal settlements. In some countries with fragile ecosystems, such as the Brazilian Amazon, environmental laws protecting native vegetation are frequently ignored by exploitive businesses.

Nigeria serves as an African illustration. The country's legal system has three main elements: British common law, customary law, and (in some regions) Sharia law. This leads to unusual challenges with property and contractual rights, as there is a mixture of formal and informal title systems. According to the *Land Use Act 1978*, the government owns all land, with legal and natural persons able to hold only leaseholds. Nevertheless, in rural areas, strong customary claims to land rights can rapidly ignite disputes. A new business in the north of Nigeria will need to ensure that contracts, particularly financial contracts, comply with Islamic principles.

Table 10.1 Adverse possession risks in emerging markets

Active Enforcement of Adverse Possession			
Country	*Source*	*Qualifying Period(s)*	
Brazil	Civil Code, Article 1,238	5 or 15 years (can be reduced in case of economic activity)	Squatters may gain full legal title.
Colombia	Law 200 of 1936, Law 9 of 1989	5 (agrarian only) or 10 years	Shorter period requires existence of some document, longer period with no document.
India	Limitation Act, 1963	12 years (private), 30 years (government)	Includes adverse possession against government.
Indonesia	Adat (customary) law	No fixed period	Wide variations among ethnic groups and regions. Prevalent in rural areas.
Mexico	Federal Civil Code, Article 1,152	5 or 10 years	Good or bad faith determines the qualifying period
South Africa	Prescription Act, 1969	30 years	Courts highly sympathetic to long-term informal residents under land reform conditions.

In some emerging markets, there are conflicts between formal ownership ("title") and claims based on long-term continuous possession. Sometimes referred to as *squatters' rights*, adverse claims customs or laws create parallel ownership – the legal owner claims title *de iure*, while the occupier claims title *de facto*. Such conflicts are widely found, for example, in Brazil, India, and South Africa, exacerbated by inefficient, incomplete, or contentious registration procedures. Long-standing informal settlements can create major issues for investors or developers who wish to acquire land. Due diligence on property ownership goes far beyond establishing legal title and must consider the historical and present possessory history of land. A wrong move can cause litigation, delays, financial losses, and even reputational harm if evictions are seen as unfair social impacts. Table 10.1 details the emerging markets in which adverse possession laws are particularly risky.

For any expansion within or into an emerging market, the development of a comprehensive strategy, equipped with full understanding of the local scene, is indispensable. Local partnerships are often a solution but can quickly become a liability if relations sour with the trusted local participant.

Labor and employment

Labor laws vary widely. It is essential to know and follow the laws, and if they are very unfavorable or unfair to workers, it is best practice to go beyond the minimum necessary. Many international businesses have paid a heavy price for labor practices which conformed to local law but were not globally acceptable. Labor laws apply not only to

Brazil's unique land-use model

Henry Eder is the chairman of Inversiones Manuelita, a Colombian-based agribusiness multinational which is a major player in sugar production. It grows sugar cane in Colombia, Peru, and Brazil. Bringing modern techniques and expert management to Peru, Manuelita was able to revive a struggling sector, but in Brazil it had to cope with a unique operational situation. In the Andean nations, large agribusinesses usually own the land they cultivate. In Brazil, however, there is a large surplus of rentable land, and it is often cheaper to rent than own. Thus, more capital remains available for production, but leasing land carries with it the risk of non-renewal, unexpected rent demands, and owner interference with operations. "Ownership" in Colombian agribusiness usually refers to the land and the crop, but in Brazil, it typically attaches only to the crop and is temporary (Caicedo, 2018).

wages and hours, but to the contents of employment contracts and health and safety provisions.

Job security has significantly different meaning across markets. Latin American countries typically have strong worker protection, making dismissal costly in all but the most clear-cut cases. Employers frequently use independent contracting arrangements to circumvent the laws. Southeast Asia is at the opposite end of the scale, with easier layoff procedures and inexpensive severance packages.

Minimum wage provisions are frequently more local than national. In China and India minima vary by state and industry, while Mexico has varying levels roughly in inverse proportion to the proximity of the U.S. border. Union involvement in wage negotiations is significant in South Africa, highly fractionated in India where there are thousands of unions, and nonexistent in China where independent unions are illegal.

A further challenge arises when an inward investor wishes to bring in foreign workers, either from the home base or by recruitment. Southeast Asian governments commonly require proof that no domestic worker is available to fulfil any job, while Saudi Arabia has a requirement for a minimum percentage of Saudi nationals in each workforce. In Latin America there may be strict limits on the percentage of foreign workers permitted: 15% in Chile, 20% in Peru, and 10% in Brazil. Exceptions typically apply for small companies, specialized professionals, and permanent residents.

To understand the scope of complexity, imagine setting up an operation in several cities in India. Several labor codes will apply; regulations will be different between states. It is likely that several unions will be involved in worker negotiations. While complying with current laws, the employer will also need to monitor national activity, as the Indian government is pursuing codification to unify regulations on wages, social security, industrial relations, and health & safety. Local commentators point out, however, that the existing codes are poorly enforced. It may be that consolidation of the rules is nothing more than a paperwork exercise (Iyer, 2024).

In Brazil, a maze of regulations comes from several angles. Trade unions are strong, and wage negotiations may be conducted at an industry or sector level, meaning smaller businesses may have little influence. Brazilian staff have guaranteed employment rights, minimum wage levels, and government-specified social security rights. Lower-level staff are entitled to distribution of food coupons and/or boxes of staple food like rice and oil. One of the many unusual aspects of Brazilian labor law is that the number of days of paid leave each year is based on the number of days of absence in the previous – meaning that paid sick leave may turn out to be unpaid (Marfice, 2023).

Environmental, social, and governance frameworks and regulation

National legislation within emerging markets addresses all three pillars of ESG – environmental, social, and governance, at a local level. ESG is increasingly used as a framework for investors and institutions to assess sustainability and impact. Environmental protection encompasses pollution, waste, and climate impact. Social impact is partially governed by competition law, data protection, labor, and property rights. Governance includes rules and regulations about corporate conduct.

Environmental laws

Environmental laws draw their inspiration from international agreements and domestic policy. The details of the legislative response and its enforcement are often tempered by economic realities, resulting in trade-offs. Ideally, local laws will, at a minimum, lay down standards for pollution control, waste management, protection of biodiversity and resources, climate change, and land use management. Sometimes there is legislation with wide coverage across several areas; at other times specific legislation targets one or two aspects.

Enforcement is practically more important than mere existence of legislation. Many emerging markets are limited by corruption, lack of resources, and limited ability to monitor corporate activities. Governments in economies with high resource dependency may be motivated to prioritize income from extraction over environmental protection, while large corporations may make deliberate plans to exploit resources in markets where regulation is less strict. Nevertheless, all emerging markets have made significant attempts to establish legislation targeting environmental abuses. In Table 10.2, we show the extent of constitutional and legislative environmental protection legislation in emerging markets.

All emerging markets have many legislative instruments related to environmental protection.

A business considering an expansion into an emerging market must carefully review, with legal advisors, the potential application of local or national laws to the proposed activity. However, there are two further steps; the first is to consider the quality of enforcement, including the possibility of corruption in the enforcement system. The second is to understand that mere compliance with legal minima is not sufficient; if the proposed activity has environmental impacts, then the business must consider its own compliance standards and apply those. There is much to be said for being "ahead of the curve" and future-proofing the business from legislation which is likely to be enacted in the future.

In some ways, the blank cells are more interesting than those with check marks. They identify, for example, where the environment has not yet achieved constitutional protection. Sometimes, the blanks reflect a nation's geography; in Egypt, there are no national

Table 10.2 Environmental protection legislation

Country	*In Constitution*	*Broad Environmental Act*	*Specific Legislation*								
			Air Quality	*Climate Change*	*Fisheries*	*Forests*	*Mining*	*Renewables*	*Waste*	*Water*	*Wildlife*
Bangladesh	✓	✓			✓	✓	✓	✓		✓	✓
Brazil[1]	✓	✓	✓	✓	✓	✓	✓		✓	✓	✓
China		✓	✓		✓	✓	✓	✓	✓		
Colombia	✓	✓	✓	✓	✓	✓	✓	✓	✓	✓	✓
Egypt	✓	✓	✓		✓		✓	✓	✓	✓	✓
Ethiopia	✓	✓	✓	✓		✓	✓		✓	✓	✓
Ghana	✓	✓			✓	✓	✓	✓	✓	✓	✓
India	✓	✓	✓			✓	✓		✓	✓	✓
Indonesia	✓	✓	✓	✓	✓	✓	✓		✓	✓	✓
Kazakhstan	✓	✓	✓		✓	✓	✓		✓	✓	✓
Kenya	✓	✓	✓	✓	✓	✓	✓		✓	✓	✓
Malaysia		✓	✓		✓	✓	✓		✓	✓	✓
Mexico	✓	✓	✓	✓	✓	✓	✓	✓	✓	✓	✓
Morocco	✓	✓	✓	✓	✓	✓		✓	✓	✓	✓
Nigeria		✓	✓	✓	✓		✓		✓	✓	✓
Pakistan	✓	✓	✓	✓	✓	✓	✓		✓	✓	✓
Peru	✓	✓	✓	✓	✓	✓	✓	✓	✓	✓	✓
Philippines	✓	✓	✓	✓	✓	✓	✓	✓	✓	✓	✓
Saudi Arabia		✓	✓		✓	✓	✓		✓	✓	✓
South Africa	✓	✓	✓	✓	✓	✓	✓	✓	✓	✓	✓
Sri Lanka		✓	✓		✓	✓	✓	✓	✓	✓	✓
Thailand	✓	✓	✓	✓	✓	✓	✓		✓		✓
Türkiye	✓	✓	✓		✓	✓	✓	✓	✓	✓	✓
Vietnam	✓	✓	✓		✓	✓	✓	✓	✓	✓	✓

forestry laws largely because there are very few forests. We can see that climate change has not been directly addressed everywhere, and that there is much scope for increased attention to renewable energy sources, especially in Asia. Gaps in India and Pakistan are caused by devolution of powers. Some Indian legislation, such as the *Electricity Act, 2003*, mandates the states to legislate for environmental concerns. In 2010, Pakistan amended its constitution to make environmental protection a provincial responsibility.

Social impact

While legislation for social impact is largely contained within the headings of data, labor, and property rights, which we outlined earlier in this chapter, there is a broader theme that businesses must assess their potential negative impact on community well-being, the risk of causing displacement, and the opportunity to enhance digital inclusion.

Businesses which rely heavily on natural resources and/or labor may engender far-reaching changes in long-established communities, for example by uprooting people from their homes during land acquisition or mining development or disrupting labor standards where there is a large informal economy. This has led to the notion of a "social license to operate" – the informal, but powerful, approval of local leadership and power groups. Failure to engage meaningfully with social forces can lead to negative press, organized protest, and even transformation of informal disapproval into regulatory enforcement.

Increasingly, social impact legislation revolves around the rights of marginalized people and may include protection for gender-based and Indigenous groups. Businesses need well-informed local counsel to ensure correct navigation through these challenging considerations.

Kiryandongo Sugar, in Uganda

While Uganda is not one of our emerging markets, this case study dramatically illustrates the effects of failure to take informal ownership and social impact into consideration.

The Rai Group, a Mauritius-based holding company for a Kenyan family, is a major supplier of sugar to international markets. Subsidiary Kiryandongo Sugar Limited leased approximately 6,000 acres of land from the Ugandan government to create a sugar plantation. The land, however, had been occupied for many years by thousands of informal farmers and their families. Many claimed customary rights although they had no title documents.

The company began bulldozing homes and crops in 2017, allegedly using police and private security firms for support. Displaced families, estimated at some 35,000 people, were neither helped nor compensated, and local authorities claimed that de facto rights were ignored. The company pointed only to its formal leases and disregarded local community concerns.

International NGOs and media became involved, leading to worldwide condemnation and reputational damage of the Rai Group, which owned Kiryandongo Sugar. Financiers called for divestment and reform of land acquisition processes throughout Uganda.

Lessons learned: Ignoring informal rights and social impact can lead to litigation, international condemnation, operational disruption, and loss of finance and customers (Alliance for Food Sovereignty in Africa et al., 2020).

Governance

Corporate governance codes

Governance codes may be legislatively imposed by government, voluntary, or commercially required, for example, by stock exchange listing requirements. Voluntary codes often go further than strict legal requirements to establish standards for transparency, accountability, and ethics. Their content typically includes board roles and responsibilities, shareholder rights, certain aspects of risk management, and stakeholder engagement.

The latest edition of the Organisation for Economic Cooperation and Development rules, the 2023 edition, is supported by the OECD Corporate Governance Factbook 2023. It examines alignment by several significant emerging markets, including Brazil, India, and South Africa, concluding that many jurisdictions, particularly these three, have taken significant steps to incorporate the rules into national frameworks.

For example, King IV, the fourth edition of a series of South African governance reports, was published in 2016 by the Institute of Directors in South Africa. It is unique in the world of corporate governance because it is voluntary, yet companies which list on the Johannesburg Stock Exchange are effectively mandated to follow its principles. *In India SEBI LODR*, the Securities and Exchange Commission (Listing Obligations and Disclosure Requirements) Regulations, 2015, exemplify more formal government-backed governance codes as they are issued by the capital markets regulator.

Transparency laws

Transparency laws are designed to reduce corruption and other financial crimes, building trust and improving capital market access. Typical requirements are financial reports, ownership, and conflicts of interest. Disclosures may be required to various government agencies, including anti-corruption bodies or tax departments.

Participation in international markets increasingly requires compliance with global frameworks established by intergovernmental organizations. Examples are the Financial Action Task Force (FATF), OECD, and the Extractive Industries Transparency Initiative (EITI). Of interest in emerging market contexts, Pakistan, the Philippines, and South Africa have all been placed on the FATF gray list in recent years, prompting corrective actions and putting investment flows at risk. Ghana, Indonesia, Colombia, and Nigeria are all EITI-compliant countries.

Shareholder rights, disclosure, and anti-corruption

Reporting requirements directed to supporting shareholder rights have some overlap with more general transparency rules. Shareholders require minority protections and restrictions on related-party transactions. Disclosures which are important to shareholders include financial reports, material events, and executive pay. Anti-corruption provisions form part of good governance but also respect the interests of minority shareholders.

Indonesia is among the countries which have enacted strong laws to protect minority shareholders (Law No. 40/2007). Shareholders with 10% or more of shares can call general meetings and propose agenda items; minority shareholders have the right to see company documents and seek court protection against decisions that harm their interests.

Malaysia's *Companies Act, 2016*, allows derivative actions against directors, by shareholders, on behalf of a company; in cases of fraud or oppression, it allows representative action lawsuits. The Malaysian *Act* is supplemented by a Corporate Governance Code, which seeks to ensure effective participation by all shareholders in meetings.

Board diversity and independence

The last decade has seen greatly increased focus on board composition, in terms of both diversity and independence. Today balanced representation is seen as a key indicator of governance strength.

While board diversity considers personal attributes such as age, ethnicity, gender, and expertise, the presence of independent directors fosters objectivity and reassures minority shareholders. Legislated quotas for both elements are becoming common. India, for example, mandates the presence of one female director on the board of any listed company; Malaysia's code recommends a majority of independent directors and 30% female board membership.

In summary, while all emerging markets have ESG legislation, enforcement is not consistent. Corruption, competing financial priorities, and resource constraints all lessen the intended effects of government control. Businesses must go beyond mere compliance and integrate ESG proactively into their plans, to stay ahead of increasing global strictures. Most significantly, they must avoid greenwashing risks by making genuine commitments and taking actions that go beyond mere words. Here are some steps to address weak ESG enforcement.

- Implement internal ESG audits. To ensure compliance with international standards, consider using external auditors to verify and report labor standards.
- Apply and report based on global ESG frameworks, supplementing local standards.
- Apply rigorous supply chain oversight.
- Engage with local NGOs and fund ESG community initiatives.
- Use market-based ESG incentives and funding.
- Prioritize voluntary ESG reporting, surpassing local requirements.

Finance and taxation

Investment laws address the fundamental reason for most emerging market investments – the prospect of making significant returns. The opportunities come with significant complexity and risk.

Inward investors must consider sector-specific ownership rules and requirements for government participation. Some sensitive industries like banking and telecommunications may require majority local ownership (e.g., in Indonesia), while others, such as technology enterprises, may bear a heavy licensing burden (e.g., in China).

Taking profits out may be equally complex. Some countries give better tax concessions to foreign investors than locals but then restrict repatriation of funds, either by way of absolute prohibition or further taxation. Parallel markets, where the street value of local currency is substantially less than the official value, may create additional challenges, especially if combined with governmental exchange controls.

Tax considerations have a gargantuan role in investment decisions. The percentage of profits that is retained and does not go to governments can have a profound influence on investors, who have a choice as to where to site their expansionary plans and even the choice of market entry method.

Corporate income tax

The principle that income tax should be paid in the country where profits are earned seems simple. If tax has been paid once, the remaining profits should not be taxed again. Many countries, including most developed nations, have double taxation avoidance agreements (DTAAs), which give the benefit of a foreign tax credit to an investing company for the taxes it has paid overseas. If there is no DTAA, the domestic tax laws of each country come into play.

In practice, taxation is anything but simple. A business expanding into a new territory will need sound advice from tax professionals on how to determine its residency for tax purposes and the effect of different structures or levels of ownership in foreign enterprises. Income tax planning heavily implicates transfer pricing, which we will deal with next.

International transfer pricing

Transfer pricing policies have received much publicity and have been the subject of some hefty fines and penalties. The concept refers to the determination of prices for assets or services sold from one part of a multinational corporation to another. The parties are "related," though they may be subsidiaries, joint venturers, branches, or affiliates.

To illustrate, suppose that the basic rate of corporate tax in Switzerland is 12%, and in India, it is 35%. A Swiss business supplies components to its Indian subsidiary; they are then assembled into a final product and sold in India. The components are a significant part of the value of the finished product, but value is added by the assembly. The manufacturing cost of each product in Switzerland is CHF 50 (50 Swiss Francs), the cost of assembly is also equivalent to CHF 50, and the product sells for CHF 200.

The Swiss business must determine what price to charge to India for the components. Table 10.3 shows the tax calculations depending on whether it charges CHF 75, 100, or 125.

The more the Swiss business charges to India for the components, the lower is the total tax paid and the greater the group's profit. The Indian government would benefit more from lower pricing, the Swiss from higher; the business wants the transfer price to be as high as possible.

Transfer pricing is a detailed operation within multinational corporations, performed by specialists who are employed full time to do only this. The objective is plain: a job advertisement for Nestlé in Switzerland, which had a lengthy battle with Indian tax authorities involving just such a scenario, says, "[Y]our responsibilities will include ensuring compliance with tax laws and optimizing tax within business objectives" (Nestlé, n.d.).

Negative press has come from this characteristic: the two parties are in different countries; the price set has the effect of reducing the overall tax liability by increasing profits in the lower tax area. However, this is not the only objective of transfer pricing.

Table 10.3 Tax and transfer pricing

Switzerland			
Revenue	75	100	125
Cost	50	50	50
Profit	25	50	75
Tax 12%	-3	-6	-9
Net Profit	22	44	66
India			
Revenue	200	200	200
Cost	125	150	175
Profit	75	50	25
Tax 35%	-26.25	-17.5	-8.75
Net Profit	48.75	32.5	16.25
Group			
Revenue	200	200	200
Cost	100	100	100
Profit	100	100	100
Tax	-29.25	-23.5	-17.75
Net Profit	70.75	76.5	82.25

It has its legitimate uses; it may genuinely distribute profits among entities within a business according to their contributions, which is important if they have disparate shareholdings. Transfer pricing is also useful in evaluating the performance of business units. If a fair price is set with reference to the external market, the profitability of individual units may be used to assess their efficiency and productivity.

Deliberate misuse or unintentional error in transfer pricing carries substantial risks. Reputational damage is possible; tax disputes, often simultaneous in several jurisdictions, can be inordinately expensive. Fines, penalties, and prosecution can result from abuse.

As a result, international organizations have developed several credible best practice methods of setting prices for transfer methods. Each method has its own acronym:

- CPM – Cost price method starts with the cost of producing the item and then adds a markup for profit.
- CUP – Comparable uncontrolled pricing uses similar transactions between unrelated parties as a benchmark.
- PSM – Profit split method looks at the relative contribution of each party to the value created and allocates profits accordingly.
- RPM – Resale price method uses the resale price of the transferred item (to prevent manufacturing of losses).

Tax authorities examining transfer pricing arrangements will typically look at three sources as fundamental bases for assessment. First, they prefer the arm's length principle (close to CUP) as an independent standard. Second, the business must provide documentation to demonstrate that it has considered and accurately assessed its pricing responsibilities.

Third, for an authoritative reference, they refer to the Organization for Economic Co-operation and Development's (OECD's) published guidelines, which are widely relied upon to establish consistent standards (Organization for Economic Cooperation and Development, 2022). The OECD, based in Paris, is an intergovernmental organization of 38 member countries, which promotes international standards, including for taxation. The last revision was published in 2022.

Taxes on sales

Taxes on the sale of good and services vary in both amount and methodology. All emerging markets except Kazakhstan have value-added taxes, where a government levy is charged to each participant in a chain (raw materials supplier, manufacturer, wholesaler, retailer), with the consumer ultimately bearing the entire tax burden and each intermediary receiving credit for the taxes it paid to the previous party. Complex rules govern whether, when goods or services are exported, input credits are deductible for taxes paid in the country of origin.

In a system that does not operate on value-added principles, governments typically levy taxes at the final provision of a good or service. Here the consumer is the nominal payer of the tax, though if the manufacturer or retailer must adjust prices downward so that the consumer will buy, the tax burden does not fall on the consumer despite the appearance. In such systems, manufacturers and retailers may be exempt from paying sales taxes on goods or supplies which move onward to consumers but not on items which they consume themselves. Nomenclature can be confusing; it is common for a tax to be referred to as a tax on goods but to operate as a value-added tax.

Withholding taxes

Most countries require employers to keep back part of salary and wage payments for remittance to the government. Many emerging market tax authorities, in addition, have complex withholding requirements for payments between businesses. Operating in Brazil, Mexico, Colombia, China, India, Indonesia, Thailand, Vietnam, Poland, Turkey, and South Africa requires careful execution of payment adjustments to satisfy local taxation law.

India, for example, has a complex system designed to collect government revenues at the source of payment. An Indian business making a payment to a foreign company must withhold a portion of the payment and remit it to the government. Royalties, loan interest, fees for services, and dividends are all subject to withholding rules. The Indian organization making the payment is responsible for collection; it will be held liable to make additional payment to the government if it fails this responsibility. To fully understand the complexity of withholding tax systems, it is worthwhile to consult a "simplified" list of taxes and thresholds such as the one published by PWC (PWC, 2024).

Compliance strategies

Effective management of legalities in a new market typically requires three principal activities: engagement with strong local counsel, establishment of an independent compliance department, and proactive compliance. These are mutually supportive practices, not standalone functions.

(1) Contracting with competent, trustworthy local lawyers to provide regulatory guidance (or hiring them, in a large business) shows good faith and a genuine attempt to know the law and follow it. Part of the in-house or external legal mandate should be to maintain a constant watch on all applicable regulations and legislation and to lobby for improvement where there is any proposal for change which may be hurtful.
(2) In all but the smallest businesses, establishment of a compliance department with its own independent mandate, reporting directly to the most senior level in the business. Compliance professionals knowledgeable about the country and the industry must be given clear instructions to safeguard the compliance practices and record of the business; they should report independently to the Board of Directors and never be put under the control of any other department.
(3) Proactive compliance, a forward-looking approach to regulatory adherence. The business practicing proactive compliance will monitor trends, predict new regulations, and prepare for them in advance. It might adopt higher standards than currently required in anticipation of a coming tightening of rules. Proactive compliance is an important factor in the reduction of legal risk and costs.

Compliance demands are not uniform. For a multijurisdictional business, differing standards can cause business interruptions; within supply chains, non-compliance by suppliers can also damage continuity.

When viewed as an opportunity, enhanced compliance can compel innovation and better planning. Non-compliance, on the other hand, risks customer and monetary loss, reputational damage, fines, penalties, and worse. If non-compliance is highlighted outside the business's walls, it can have a deleterious effect on investment, licensing, and permissions and block the ability to secure government contracts. Compliance is here to stay, and the best place to be is ahead of the game.

Regulatory arbitrage

Selection of business location based on differences in regulation is known as *regulatory arbitrage*. It can increase efficiency while reducing costs, accelerate innovation, and enable lower pricing to attract customers away from competitors.

Arbitrage may be ethical or unethical. Ethical arbitrage is exemplified by companies that set up sustainable energy projects, such as battery manufacturing, in countries which have favorable regulatory environments and tax conditions. Siemens Gamesa Renewable Energy is active in Morocco because of the country's plan to produce 52% of its energy from renewables by the end of this decade (Africa Intelligence, 2023).

Unethical arbitrage is illustrated by companies that set up garment manufacturing operations in countries with weak labor laws, enabling them to cut costs and operate in poor conditions. When things go wrong or the media publish damaging reports on such businesses, the reputational damage can be enormous and extend into developed markets where the products are sold.

Market watchers observe that regulatory arbitrage creates an unfair playing field, as businesses in countries with less regulation incur lower costs than those in countries with more. The biggest problem, however, is often uncertainty; legislators tend to trend in similar directions, and an expensive investment in a country based on its loose regulation may prove foolish if local regulation catches up and the advantage is lost.

Non-market strategies

This chapter has considered rules and regulations as they are today or are expected to be in the future, as the product of a third party (government). However, businesses may find themselves in a position to influence the environment within which they operate. Non-market strategies are designed to affect the social, political, and institutional environments which influence a market, rather than to simply enable operations within the existing structure. Non-market strategies address key elements other than competition, including government relations, ESG, partnerships, ethics, and public opinion. A strong combination of market and non-market strategies significantly enhances the probability of business success (Baron, 1995).

Government relations and lobbying. Building relationships with decision-makers and policy champions within government, especially communicating proactively with regulators. Engagement with politicians and their aides can also help manage political risk and establish an early warning system for policy and governmental changes. Chinese company Huawei has engaged strongly with African governments to build telecommunications projects, including the National Broadband Strategy in Kenya, Smart City Solutions in Uganda, and partnership with Ethio Telecom in Ethiopia.

Collaboration with good government as a partner is a valuable extension of a growing business's commitment to sustainability. A working relationship with local and national authorities can be crucial to securing investment, gaining access to many different resources, and navigating regulatory environments.

This said, government can be slow to act and lag private sector development, particularly where technology and social change are implicated. Cas Coovadia, the managing director of the Banking Association of South Africa, had an insider's view of sweeping changes as his country progressed out of apartheid. He strongly argues that in times of change, businesses should not wait for government but need to be proactive in developing their own policies to create a conducive business environment (Coovadia, 2020).

When government has been heavily involved in a business, state protections may have excused inefficiencies. CAP (Compañía de Acero del Pacífico) was a state-controlled business in Chile with a large footprint in the steel business. When CAP was privatized and forced to survive through the economic reforms of the 1970s and 1980s, it was compelled to eliminate waste and become more efficient and competitive in the international market. In the privatization process, workers at the company became its shareholders, an unusual and creative model for aligning employee and employer interests (De Andraca, 2008).

Sistema B

María Emilia Correa is a co-founder of Sistema B, a Latin American organization that promotes the idea of *benefit corporations*. Benefit corporations commit to making positive societal and environmental impacts in addition to profits. They subscribe wholeheartedly to the *triple bottom line* – working for people, planet, and profit.

Government collaboration is central to this work. Correa points out that governments have huge purchasing power, which can be leveraged to promote responsible business practices – in Mendoza, the heart of Argentina's wine-producing region, local government made fundamental changes to its procurement policies to favor suppliers with positive ESG. A continuing theme of her work is that government must see businesses as part of the solution, interdependent parties, not as the problem. The partnership is required not only for local improvements but all the way to addressing global challenges like climate change (Correa, 2019).

Sometimes, the size of a sector and the extent of regulation make government partnership essential to sustainability goals. Aydem Enerji, a leading energy business in Türkiye, has worked closely with the national government to advance renewable energy projects in hydroelectric, wind, and solar plants. The country's objectives of reducing greenhouse gas and improving energy security are supported by Aydem, which gains the benefit of constant dialog with its regulators and improved access to capital markets. "The battle," says Paul Smith of Reuters, "for net-zero emissions will be won or lost in emerging markets." (Smith, 2024) National governments need buy-in from private enterprises for their environmental policies, while few private businesses have access to the heady amounts of dollars required to realize them.

ESG initiatives help businesses build positive reputations and public support while enhancing brands. Examples are investments in education, infrastructure, and healthcare. An outstanding case is Tata Group's $100 million endowment to the Indian Institute of Science.

Partnerships. By creating strategic partnerships with community leaders, NGOs, and local suppliers and distributors, businesses not only engage in community development but can also access a stream of local insights and information. Such partnerships are also enablers for *cultural engagement*, the acceptance and adoption of local preferences, and social rules.

Public relations. PR campaigns and social advocacy can make a huge contribution to a brand or a business's image. Trust and goodwill in the community are great contributors to stakeholder relationships. A well-known and phenomenally successful example is Safaricom's "Transforming Lives" campaign in Kenya, which cemented the role of M-Pesa as a force for social good.

Ethics. Good governance and positive compliance, including anti-bribery and anti-corruption policies, protect the business's reputation, shareholder confidence, and legal status. Unilever's *Global Code of Business Principles* (Unilever, n.d.) has zero tolerance for bribery or corruption in any form and is applied across all its operations worldwide.

Conclusion: Rising to the challenge

Aspiring market entrants often view legal complexity as an obstacle to doing business. Savvy operators, however, realize that it is also an opportunity to gain competitive advantage through sophisticated strategy. Legal mastery is a key differentiator in uncertain conditions and the key that unlocks significant market opportunities.

We saw that regulatory uncertainty demands competence in drafting of contracts and may govern the choice of jurisdiction. Contracts with suppliers and partners should include provision for future changes in regulation; if the first chosen head office location is in an uncertain jurisdiction, multiple residencies may be an answer. Due diligence is critically important in considering mergers, acquisitions, or partnerships; reliable legal advice on contractual provisions and the compliance status of counterparties is essential. We summarized that legal sophistication includes proactive compliance, genuine ESG integration, and reputation management.

We also saw that non-market strategies are powerful tools in the legal arsenal. Large, reputable businesses have the opportunity not only to leverage government relations but also to use them for positive influences on future changes of law. Uber's persuasion of several governments to legalize ridesharing is a leading example of such success.

We are not quite finished with our examination of legal and regulatory environments. Although we explored rules and regulations for labor markets, the human component of business is critical in many ways. Legal and ethical behavior does not occur in a vacuum: people make them happen and respond to changes in relationships and regulation. The next chapter, therefore, will be devoted to the field of human resources and the appropriate ethical best practices.

Notes

1 In Brazil, national policies are usually enacted as laws but retain the name "policy." When formally passed by the Congress they are given a law number and date, confirming their legislative status.

References

Africa Intelligence. (2023, September 11). Siemens Gamesa installs turbines on Jbel Lahdid wind park. https://www.africaintelligence.com/north-africa/2023/09/11/siemens-gamesa-installs-turbines-on-jbel-lahdid-wind-park,110041090-bre

Alfaro, L., Chanda, A., Kalemli-Ozcan, S., & Sayek, S. (2004). FDI and economic growth: The role of local financial markets. *Journal of International Economics, 64(1)*, 89–112. DOI: 10.1016/S0022-1996(03)00081-3

Alliance for Food Sovereignty in Africa, GRAIN, & Witness Radio. (2020, August 25). Land grabs at gunpoint: Thousands of families are being violently evicted from their farms to make way for foreign-owned plantations in Kiryandongo, Uganda. *GRAIN*. https://grain.org/en/article/6518-land-grabs-at-gunpoint-thousands-of-families-are-being-violently-evicted-from-their-farms-to-make-way-for-foreign-owned-plantations-in-kiryandongo-uganda

Busse, M., & Groizard, J. L. (2008). Foreign direct investment, regulations, and growth. *The World Economy, 31(7)*, 861–886. https://doi.org/10.1111/j.1467-9701.2008.01106.x

Azeri, G. (2014, April 29). Interview by A. Colpan. *Creating Emerging Markets Oral History Collection*. Baker Library Special Collections, Harvard Business School.

Balisacan, A. M. (n.d.) *Competition a game changer in PHL economy*. Philippine Competition Commission.

Baron, D. P. (1995). Integrated strategy: Market and nonmarket components. *California Management Review*, *37*(2), 47–65.
Caicedo, H. E. (2018, November 21). Interview by A. Lluch. *Creating Emerging Markets Oral History Collection*. Baker Library Special Collections, Harvard Business School.
Collier, R. (2013, June 11). Drug patents: the evergreening problem. *Canadian Medical Association Journal. 185*(9): E385–E386. https://www.ncbi.nlm.nih.gov/pmc/articles/PMC3680578/
Congressional Research Service. (2022). *World Trade Organization: "TRIPS waiver" for COVID-19 vaccines* (R47231). U.S. Library of Congress. https://crsreports.congress.gov/product/pdf/R/R47231/2
Coovadia, C. (2020, January 13). Interview by E. Naidoo. *Creating Emerging Markets Oral History Collection*. Baker Library Special Collections, Harvard Business School.
Correa, M. E. (2019, May 8). Interview by A. Lluch. *Creating Emerging Markets Oral History Collection*. Baker Library Special Collections, Harvard Business School.
De Andraca, R. (2008, May 27). Interview by A. Lluch. *Creating Emerging Markets Oral History Collection*. Baker Library Special Collections, Harvard Business School.
European Union. (2016). Regulation (EU) 2016/679 of the European Parliament and of the Council of 27 April 2016 on the protection of natural persons with regard to the processing of personal data and on the free movement of such data (General Data Protection Regulation). *Official Journal of the European Union*, L119: 1–88. https://eur-lex.europa.eu/legal-content/EN/TXT/?uri=CELEX%3A32016R0679
Expatica. (n.d.). How to start a business in Thailand. https://www.expatica.com/th/work/self-employment/starting-a-business-in-thailand-2172873
Iyer, A. (2024, March 7). *Employment & labour laws and regulations India 2024*. Global Legal Group.
Jordaan, J. A., Douw, W., Qiang, C. Z. (2020). *Foreign Direct Investment, Backward Linkages, and Productivity Spillovers: What Governments Can Do to Strengthen Linkages and Their Impact*. World Bank Group.
Judges Matter. (n.d.). Judicial Conduct Trial for Judge President John Hlophe. https://www.judgesmatter.co.za/conduct/hlophe-tribunal-2008-2019
Mahindra, K. (2013, July 24). Interview by T. Khanna. *Creating Emerging Markets Oral History Collection*. Baker Library Special Collections, Harvard Business School.
Marfice, C. (2023, March 30). The complete guide to offering employee benefits in Brazil. https://www.rippling.com/blog/guide-to-offering-benefits-in-brazil
Nestlé. (n.d.). Transfer Pricing Specialist. https://jobdetails.nestle.com/job/Vevey-Transfer-Pricing-Specialist/1153643201/
Organisation for Economic Cooperation and Development. (2022). *OECD transfer pricing guidelines for multinational enterprises and tax administrations 2022*. OECD Publishing. https://doi.org/10.1787/0e655865-en
PWC. (2024, May 15). India: Corporate – Withholding taxes. https://taxsummaries.pwc.com/india/corporate/withholding-taxes
Smith, P. (2024, September 12). The battle for net-zero emissions will be won or lost in emerging markets. https://www.reuters.com/sustainability/climate-energy/comment-battle-net-zero-emissions-will-be-won-or-lost-emerging-markets-2024-09-12/
South African Government. (1998). *Competition Act 89 of 1998*. Government Communications.
Supreme Court of India. (2013). *Novartis Ag v. Union of India & Others*. Civil Appeal Nos. 2706-2716 of 2013.
TMF Group. (2023, November 17). Doing business in Brazil. https://www.tmf-group.com/en/news-insights/articles/doing-business-in/brazil/
Unilever. (n.d.). Purpose, values & principles. https://www.unilever.co.uk/sustainability/purpose-values-principles/
World Bank. (2020). *Global Investment Competitiveness Report 2019-2020: rebuilding investor confidence in times of uncertainty (English)*. Washington, DC: World Bank.
World Bank. (2024). *Business Ready 2024*. World Bank. https://doi.org/10.1596/978-1-4648-2021-2

CHAPTER 11

Human resources and talent management in emerging markets

Learning outcomes

After studying this chapter, you will be able to do the following:

1. Analyze the unique human resources (HR) challenges faced by organizations expanding into emerging markets, including talent scarcity, informal employment, and cultural nuances.
2. Assess the effect of cultural and social factors on recruiting, training, and retaining employees, recommending adaptations for specific industry and country contexts.
3. Critically evaluate the roles of training and community engagement in finding and retaining skilled workers.
4. Analyze the effects of cultural differences, language barriers, visa rules, deportation, and discrimination in retaining valuable workers, and propose measures to mitigate their negative effects.
5. Design HR policies that align with corporate values, cultural norms, and sustainability principles, giving attention to ESG, diversity, equity, and inclusion (DEI), and corporate social responsibility (CSR) considerations.
6. Find and perform in-depth analysis of real-world examples to discover methodologies for managing talent in resource-constrained and rapidly evolving business environments.

Introduction

In emerging markets, talent scarcity, informal employment networks, and cultural elements combine to make human resources (HR) management particularly challenging. A business entering an emerging market must decide how it is going to dovetail its people and processes into the local environment. Each stakeholder has specific needs. The incomer has talents, skills, and/or products which are wanted in the local market, while people already in the market have cultural wisdom, local insight, and practical solutions that are essential to the business's success.

DOI: 10.4324/9781003638490-11

Businesses investing in emerging markets can positively invest in all three pillars of ESG – environment, social, and governance. Local employment helps reduce carbon footprint, by minimizing travel. Fair treatment of all workers directly addresses social impact in several ways – it promotes equity and inclusion, improves the well-being of workers and their families, encourages community involvement, reduces social inequalities, and earns public trust. Transparent HR policies demonstrate good governance and accountability.

This chapter will describe the economic and social dimensions of hiring workers in emerging markets and then discuss how businesses attract, hire, and retain workers. We will draw attention to the importance of cultural sensitivity and identify some tools for understanding it. We will then review best practices in HR through the lenses of ESG, diversity, equity, and inclusion (DEI), and CSR. We will use case studies of best-in-class businesses which stand out as models for good HR management.

HR challenges in emerging markets

The arrival of a foreign business or expansion of a local enterprise in an emerging market can have a highly positive impact on the local economy, communities, and government. For example, it might attract migrant workers who become productive and contribute to economic growth of the business and the economy. Businesses which enjoy success have a compelling need to design and structure their recruitment and retention policies to find and keep the right talent.

Businesses operating in emerging markets face several issues: we will discuss the most significant areas.

Migration and labor dynamics

Creating employment opportunities and recruiting workers are positively viewed by governments, local and national. However, when performed on a large scale, there is a danger of accentuating migration problems as listed below, leading to undesirable effects. Migration issues that affect growing businesses globally fall into four categories:

- **Urbanization.** Companies entering emerging markets frequently first establish in urban areas. This attracts talent from rural populations, which can lead to congestion, overcrowding, sanitation, and infrastructure problems. In Lagos, Nigeria, nearly 70% of residents live in informal settlements. Dhaka, Bangladesh, is one of the world's most polluted cities and has one of the worst gridlock problems in the world.
- **Brain drain.** When educated workers leave a developing country for economic gain in a more developed country, a talent shortage is caused. Emigration statistics for India, South Africa, and Romania, for example, all highlight the outflow of skilled professionals to richer countries. A new entrant in an emerging market may struggle to find sufficient technical or managerial staff or draw them from another emerging market where they are equally needed but insufficiently compensated to keep them. Sri Lanka, for example, suffered severe brain drain to India during the 2021–2022 economic crisis. The competitive dynamic between markets is known as *talent siphoning*.

- **Regional inequality.** When inward investors are concentrated in small areas, they attract large numbers of skilled workers who leave other regions. Bangalore in India, São Paulo in Brazil, and Johannesburg in South Africa are all economic power centers which have drained skilled professionals from other regions. The problem is so intense in India, the "Silicon Valley of India," that smaller cities have suffered underinvestment and talent pool shrinkage. The local state government has been forced to apply legislative curbs on in-migration to Bangalore.
- **Labor exploitation.** Unscrupulous local employers who gain lucrative contracts with international companies are incentivized to cut costs. This occurred during construction for the FIFA World Cup in Qatar, 2022, where dealings with immigrant workers (especially from Southeast Asia) led to reports of thousands of deaths from heat exhaustion, unsafe conditions, forced labor, and the extraction of illegal recruitment fees.

Recruiting and retaining talent

Incoming businesses must decide how many local staff they will require and how many workers they will bring in from home or other locations. When Unilever concentrated its East and Central African operations in Nairobi, Kenya, it relocated skilled staff from Uganda, Tanzania, Ethiopia, and Malawi. The drain of talent from those countries caused slow-downs in decision-making and knowledge transfer, leading to increased reliance on centralized management in Kenya.

In assessing local candidates for on-site employment, the business will need to assess their cultural knowledge and fit, language and communication skills, and ability to become loyal and productive in the interests of a foreign business.

Businesses may draw on global talent to supplement, train, or supervise local recruits. Exceptional expatriates who are prepared to move to a new country and work hard to establish a growing proposition are not only valuable but also expensive. They need compelling compensation, support, and resources to help them adapt, and well-designed communication structures so that they stay on-message and in the fold while fostering the local talent they supplement or manage.

For local recruitment, emerging markets have proved fertile ground for the rise of digital job platforms. Online marketplaces like Jobberman[1] in Africa and Naukri[2] in India allow businesses to post vacancies while candidates apply directly. There are, however, concerns that workers dependent on these platforms may be denied valuable social benefits of regular employment and that data-driven selections can suffer from AI bias (Dhar, 2025). AI-driven matching systems offer recommendations and filtering at lightning speed compared with human time and effort. While digital matching of jobs and job seekers appears to be a positive development, many of the positions posted are temporary or freelance and may even be informal.

Technological advancements are invaluable tools in overcoming stubborn recruitment challenges. AI-driven application systems, mobile-first training and engagement apps, and AI-driven HR analytics are impactful additions to the recruiter's toolset.

A useful metaphor when thinking about the employer's interests and needs is to realize that an employer in a competitive labor market is, in effect, selling itself to potential employees. In this respect, the employer has a brand *as an employer*, which it must nurture. The business wants to be known as *the* place to work, *the* place that treats its staff well and cares about their futures. It greatly assists if the business has a positive, inclusive culture and already exhibits a diverse workforce. Upwardly mobile talent – workers seeking educational and career advancement in their roles – are most drawn to businesses that offer opportunities for internal training and promotion.

Cross-cultural management

Throughout corporate history, there have been many missteps based on deep cultural divides – mistaken assumptions that what was considered normal in one country would be acceptable in another. Cultural sensitivity is a large topic which today enjoys the benefit of much scholarship and great resources. Intercultural management embraces the understanding and management of people from diverse cultures. Cultural diversity is best viewed as an opportunity – it "brings different perspectives, experiences and skills to the workplace" (The Culture Factor Group, n.d.).

Styles and expectations in communication can produce surprises. In some cultures, being direct and to the point is an advantage; it can appear rude and confrontational in another. Indirect communication, where speakers imply or suggest meaning rather than saying outright what they want to say, is prevalent, for example, throughout Asia and Latin America. It can be quite unfamiliar to those with a different heritage (Sierra, 2022).

A thought leader in the analysis of multicultural teamwork, Professor Geert Hofstede, proposed a six-dimensional model to understand the culture of a country or group based on its cultural values. The dimensions are as follows:

- **Power Distance** – The extent to which less powerful members accept unequal distribution of power.
- **Individualism** – The extent to which individuals take care only of themselves and their immediate families.
- **Masculinity versus Femininity** – This description has been controversial and is now named "Motivation towards achievement and success." In the old model, masculinity referred to achievement, heroism, and assertiveness, while femininity contrasted these with cooperation, modesty, and a consensus orientation.
- **Uncertainty Avoidance** – The extent to which people try to control the future, as opposed to letting it happen.
- **Long-Term Orientation** – A culture that is suspicious of change and strives to maintain old traditions will score low on this dimension, while a high-scoring society will embrace change and prepare for the future.
- **Indulgence** – The opposite being restraint. In restrained societies, social norms suppress gratification – in indulgent societies, people are freer to pursue their natural drives, enjoy life, and "have fun" (Hofstede, 2010; Hofstede, Hofstede, & Minkov, 2010).

Professor Hofstede's research group makes freely available a cultural comparison tool found at https://www.hofstede-insights.com/country-comparison-tool. There are other, more complex models, including the Global Leadership and Organizational Behavior Effectiveness (GLOBE) Project (GLOBE Project, 2020) and Meyer's "Culture Map" (2014).

These, however, are starting points and never sufficient on their own to be the end of the enquiry.

Across a large country there can be vast differences of culture, as for example between north and south Brazil or India. Understanding cultural dimensions enables employers to customize HR policies, which in turn smooths cross-cultural integration as new markets are entered.

It is not essential that two or more cultures become homogenized. Understanding is necessary; change may not be. For example, consider a local supermarket employee in Nigeria or India, working for a French company. The employee may not need much training to serve customers of the same nationality, but to progress to management in the French-owned chain, they will need to understand more about French management culture, which is much more formal and structured. Without an appreciation of the foreign culture, they may find it difficult to interact effectively with international colleagues.

While there is no universal agreement on an exact list, many training programs, consultants, and international management textbooks highlight three cultural areas – decision-making, authority, and time – as particularly susceptible to wide variation and damaging misunderstandings (Hall, 1983; Hofstede, 2001; Trompenaars & Hampden-Turner, 1997).

Decision-making is a process that may take distinct forms. Consider a hypothetical German business expanding into Brazil. German corporate structures tend to be hierarchical, with emphasis on data-based, risk-averse planning. On arrival in Brazil, it will need to adapt its practices to gain trust; Brazilian business decisions are often made with a view to consensus, broad agreement, and the building of relationships. The German investor might be quite surprised to learn of the changeability of policies in typical Brazilian companies compared to the more rigid following of set guidelines in German contexts.

Authority also takes diverse forms in different geographies. In North American business environments, some degree of skepticism by subordinates is tolerated and/or encouraged, while other cultures are characterized by rigid acceptance of authority and, in government, suppression of dissent. Such cultural inclinations call for careful design of feedback processes to harness the knowledge and skills of local staff. Kilsgård, Nero, and Sundin (2008), in their dissertation *Cultural differences when entering a new market*, provide an excellent example drawn from Swedish companies entering new markets in Eastern Europe.

Time might be considered by an English, German, or Swiss national as an immutable and obvious way to organize activity. Doing business in Indonesia, they might be stunned to learn of *waktu karet* ("rubber time"), a colloquialism which colorfully portrays a relaxed attitude to time, deadlines, and meetings. *Waktu karet* has been made essential by the incredible traffic jams which characterize large cities like Jakarta, but it predates the motor vehicle. Indonesians, in our experience, see time as unpredictable, are patient and understanding, and consider the relationship more important than punctuality. It is not unusual for a meeting place to be arranged, but for the time to be left unclear such as "in the afternoon." Mobile telephony has made this practice more manageable, but it can be severely frustrating for foreigners.

A business entering a market where perceptions of time and punctuality are markedly different will need either to accept the local practices or make its requirements for adaptation very clear to its new workforce, who may not easily accept them.

Accenture

Global consultancy Accenture is present in 18 emerging markets and prioritizes cultural and language skills in hiring (Accenture, n.d.). It favors local talent by recruiting primarily from local labor pools, which strengthens local economies (The Australian, 2025). It then supplements employee knowledge with cultural training, locally and internationally. It is a fundamental requirement of employment in any foreign market that an employee demonstrate proficiency in the local language(s) and that all employees are committed to Accenture's ideals of diversity and inclusion (Accenture, 2024).

Informal and gig work

Although employers from developed markets are today familiar with *gig work* thanks to prominent international success stories like that of Uber, digital platforms have made a more significant impact in emerging markets. The relative informality of gig work has its own challenges, including patchwork labor protections, irregularity of income for participants, and difficulties in establishing training programs.

Informal employment, working in an unregulated, unprotected relationship, is widespread throughout much of Africa and large parts of Asia. This is a significant problem for governments that are unable to collect taxes or offer protections to informal workers. It can also present a barrier to effective recruitment, as work records, references, and trade certifications may be hard to obtain or nonexistent. Large population groups accustomed to being paid in cash without deductions may be difficult to employ in formalized systems, and even more difficult to keep happy, by an employer accustomed to more conventional hiring and payment practices.

The growth of the gig economy is so strong that governments have begun modifying social security provisions to add schemes for freelancers. India's e-Shram portal[3] provides gig workers with accident insurance and pension plans. Businesses have also recognized the potential recruitment channel in the gig economy, offering training programs to improve workers' skills and attract them into permanent employment (Singh, 2024). Mobile payment platforms like M-Pesa[4] and Nigeria's Paystack[5] add some formality to gig contracts by enabling contributions to benefit schemes and tracking compensation. They also facilitate record-keeping and taxation. By integrating such schemes, businesses can move gig workers closer to formal employment while staying compliant with government requirements.

While gig platforms can provide short-term solutions to labor needs, they do not cater to businesses that have long-term plans and require career advancement within their walls. Businesses must invest in workforce training and development to enhance their talent pools.

Developing talent

Having found the right people, a business would be foolish not to retain them by creating career paths and opportunities which are meaningful to them. A workforce without inbuilt training programs is unthinkable; opportunities to travel and interface with employees in other countries can be invaluable, and mentorship programs within the business can pay huge dividends in executive development.

The two main approaches to training are centralized (from head office) and decentralized (developed locally). Inevitably there are trade-offs.

Centralized training delivers benefits in consistency, standardization, economies of scale, and concentration of materials, technology, and resources. However, it must cope with time zone differences or travel and lack of local relevance. If it is delivered in person, employees may need to travel long distances and be away from their families for lengthy periods.

Decentralization assumes particular importance in emerging markets where there is limited access to further education, training programs, or vocational education. There is potential for more local relevance, removal of language barriers and time zone problems, and higher engagement. Despite potentially higher costs and the need to duplicate and customize training materials, the wider the cultural disparity, the more effective local training solutions are likely to be. Localized training usually more than justifies the expense by delivering a valuable return on the investment.

One solution does not fit all needs; businesses must carefully balance the advantages and disadvantages of training locations, perhaps solve some issues through online sessions, and maybe create hybrid solutions.

Siemens, a global engineering leader, has contracted with South Africa's Council for Scientific and Industrial Research to create specialized programs in automation, energy, and manufacturing. These programs benefit workers, communities, and the business itself (Siemens, 2021).

Grassroots innovation – empowering every employee to innovate – is a powerful concept which is especially applicable to emerging markets. This contrasts with traditional top-down or research-and-development-driven innovation; it is particularly effective where resources are constrained. Dr. Raghunath Mashelkar, former Director General of the Council of Scientific and Industrial Research in India, emphasizes that top-down innovation is inadequate when a large percentage of the population lives on very little. He believes that the gap must be filled by practicing *inclusive innovation* – with a focus on products that are relevant to low-income populations. Such communities often harbor the creativity and resourcefulness born of their unique needs and limits (Mashelkar, 2022).

Marico Limited

Harsh Mariwala, chairperson and founder of Marico Limited, entered his family business in the early 1970s. Over several decades, he expanded the business's activities in the fast-moving consumer goods market until it became a multinational with operations in over 25 countries, principally in Asia and Africa. He credits innovation at all levels within the business, decentralized decision-making, and a customer-centric approach for this impressive growth. He argues strongly that his system of recognition and rewards for any employee who contributes a significant idea fosters a sense of ownership and pride among all staff. Freedom to experiment enabled Marico to stay agile, responding quickly to shifts in consumer demand and operational needs (Mariwala, 2019).

Forward-looking practices in HR

Meet Professor Dave Ulrich, of the University of Michigan. Prof. Ulrich is known as the father of modern HR, as his seminal book *Human Resource Champions* fundamentally redefined HR roles, emphasizing strategic alignment in contrast to administrative functions. Ulrich breaks down the key competencies required in HR today, under six headings.

1. **Strategic Positioner.** Prof. Ulrich encourages HR professionals to educate themselves on global business contexts, translating their economic, social, technological, and political knowledge into actions that support the business's goals.

   Earlier, we praised MTN for its navigation of complex environments with volatile currency swings. As part of its strategy, MTN Nigeria has been noted for use of compensation strategies based on keen understanding of local and global economic conditions (MTN, 2019).
2. **Credible Activist.** HR professionals need to be credible and trustworthy. Integrity in the delivery of results builds the ability to influence others effectively. They must advocate for both the business and its employees.

   Tata Steel is a poster case for employee treatment in grievance matters. Its *Code of Conduct* was published in 1988, and its ethics helpline provides workers, even in its most remote locations, transparent dealing with complaints (Tata Steel, 2023)
3. **Capability Builder.** HR must develop and enhance the business's core capabilities, including agility, collaboration, and innovation. HR professionals are responsible for developing a culture that fosters capabilities in alignment with strategic objectives.

   Nestlé's program of assisting coffee growers to adopt regenerative agriculture involves training and support. Farmers – the key human resource – are regarded as partners in the quest for sustainability and contribute to the dependability of the business's supply chain (Nestlé, 2024).
4. **Change Champion.** HR professionals must initiate and sustain positive change efforts. They are critical to keeping the business evolving and relevant.

   YODY, one of Vietnam's foremost fashion retailers, has led the way in digital transformation for employees and customers. According to its public profile and industry commentators, the HR department was tasked to ensure that all employees were trained to handle new technologies as they were implemented (YODY, n.d.).
5. **HR Innovator and Integrator.** Continuing the theme of business alignment, Ulrich stresses that HR practices must support the direction of the business. HR professionals must design and implement performance and development processes that result in continuous improvement.

   WorkPlus HCM, in Kenya, has streamlined payroll and HR software via cloud platforms for Kenya. Automating administrative work aims to engender large increases in productivity (WorkPlus HCM, n.d.).
6. **Technology Proponent.** HR processes must embrace and leverage technology so that they maximize organizational effectiveness. Data analytics is fundamental to this effort.

   Across Africa, the mobile phone has been the driver of improvements in community health, especially in remote areas. The initial take-up appears to have been informal, but great steps have been made by HR administrators to formalize use and ensure that health inequalities are not exacerbated (Hampshire et al., 2021).

Basic HR policies are not sufficient to build workforces for long-term success. Understanding cultural sensitivities is essential, but it must be accompanied by structured, fair policies that promote development of the entire workforce.

A business should never lose sight of culture in its quest to control costs by reducing attrition. Markets where informal labor is the rule require sensitive cultivation of employee expectations and skills, to equip them for formal employment and career-based thinking. Management styles can be very different from those in developed countries, especially in countries like China and Saudi Arabia, where there is deep respect for seniority, regardless of ability.

There are some specific areas that have particular relevance in emerging markets.

Today we can take it as given that HR effectiveness produces desirable business outcomes. Companies that invest in their employees' *well-being* and careers have up to 20% higher talent retention and innovation, according to McKinsey (Hunt et al., 2023). Employee well-being initiatives can not only set a new entrant apart from established employers but also make a valuable contribution to business continuity by retaining valued employees. At leading employers like Tata Group, such programs go beyond salary and benefits to include medical and mental health support, flexible working arrangements, career counseling, and advancement opportunities. Leadership development which creates future managers from within the business is a powerful motivating tool.

DEI initiatives, embedded into business culture, bring the diversity of local labor pools into the workplace. Cultural sensitivity and bias training are important counters to the often-found tendency toward unconscious bias in decision-making. Achieving *equity in employment* requires addressing gender barriers: attention must be devoted to pay gaps, availability of employment, and paths to seniority.

Pay is not everything. **Non-monetary incentives**, such as housing and education provision, help employee perceptions of value. They are especially valuable where public provision is limited. Career development programs reduce attrition as future leaders develop a vision of the future which includes the present employer and personal advancement.

Corporate responsibility is critical to a business's image and ability to attract talent. Anti-exploitation policies are unquestionably required, but simple transparency in hiring, compensation, and promotion practices is also essential. A powerful expression of responsibility is participation in community development, for example, by supporting local educational institutions and programs. Skills development programs which are pertinent to the business's needs can create an enhanced labor pool of more skilled recruits.

Expatriate employees are frequently used by multinationals as a solution to local shortages. However, in the long term, they are usually more costly than developing local leadership. Training local leaders, identifying high-potential employees and accelerating their advancement, paying honest attention to DEI and ESG initiatives, and centralized training programs at headquartered locations are all components of a future-oriented talent management plan.

Tata Group

India's massive Tata Group has long been known for its people-centric culture. It has over a million employees worldwide (Tata, n.d.-a). Tata Steel, a central business within the conglomerate, offers employees health check-ups every two years, first aid centers, and career development programs (Tata Steel, n.d.).

The group is also a world leader in supporting DEI initiatives, as it has progressively introduced paternity leave, menstrual leave, LGBTQ+ support, and financial assistance for gender affirmation surgery (Tata, n.d.-b). Tata Motors takes pains to recruit a multitalented, diverse workforce through in-school programs both inside and outside the motor industry (Jadhav, 2019). Equally, it inspires and develops its management through leadership development programs, attended by over 10,000 people each year (Kumar, 2017).

Conclusion

This chapter outlined the challenges of hiring and managing talent in emerging markets, considered economic, social, and cultural dimensions of workforce management, and laid out best practices for those markets. We examined the nature of employment pools in emerging markets and considered the balancing of local and expatriate workers. We stressed the importance of employer branding.

To understand cross-cultural management and workplace behavior, we introduced Hofstede's six cultural dimensions. We closed with a review of best practices, including DEI, employee advancement programs, and corporate responsibility.

High-quality HR management is essential to business success everywhere. In emerging markets, businesses must not only comply with regulatory and labor market expectations but also learn the nuances of complex cultures, develop and balance local and expatriate talent, and foster sustainable practices that support long-term goals. Businesses which develop facility in dealing with informal labor structures, shallow talent pools, and cultural misalignment gain a valuable competitive advantage.

The complementary human elements, people management, and cultural understanding, are critical to successful operations in emerging markets. HR is not a mere operational function; it is one of the drivers of long-term success.

How do businesses fund start-up operations or rapid growth? The next chapter will explore the options for securing investment and funding, once again revealing unique aspects of the emerging market world.

Notes

1 https://www.jobberman.com/
2 https://www.naukri.com/
3 https://eshram.gov.in/
4 https://www.safaricom.co.ke/m-pesa
5 https://paystack.com/

References

Accenture. (2024). How we foster a culture of equality. https://www.accenture.com/ca-en/about/inclusion-diversity-index

Accenture. (n.d.). Find an Accenture office. https://www.accenture.com/us-en/about/location
Dhar, P. (2025, January 22). AI job-screening tools are very prejudiced, study finds. *Science NewsExplores*. https://www.snexplores.org/article/ai-job-screening-tools-very-biased
GLOBE Project. (2020) GLOBE 2020 study. https://globeproject.com/study_2004_2007.html
Hall, E. T. (1983). *The dance of life: The other dimension of time*. Anchor Books.
Hampshire, K., et al. (2021). Informal mhealth at scale in Africa: Opportunities and challenges. *World Development*, 140, Article 105257. https://doi.org/10.1016/j.worlddev.2020.105257
Hofstede, G. (2001). *Culture's consequences: Comparing values, behaviors, institutions, and organizations across nations* (2nd ed.). Sage Publications.
Hofstede, G. (2010). The 6-D model of national culture. https://geerthofstede.com/culture-geert-hofstede-gert-jan-hofstede/6d-model-of-national-culture/
Hofstede, G., Hofstede, G. J., & Minkov, M. (2010). *Cultures and organizations: Software of the mind* (3rd ed.). McGraw Hill.
Hunt, V., Dixon-Fyle, S., Huber, C., Martínez Márquez, M., Del M., Prince, S., & Thomas, A. (2023). *Diversity matters even more: The case for holistic impact*. McKinsey & Company.
Jadhav, P. (2019, February 1). HR policy and HR practices of Tata Motors. https://www.slideshare.net/slideshow/hr-policies-and-hr-practices-of-tata-motors/130242133
Kilsgård, D., Nero, M., & Sundin, E. (2008). *Cultural differences when entering a new market: A study of Swedish companies entering the Eastern European markets* [Bachelor's dissertation, Kristianstad University College]. DiVA Portal. https://urn.kb.se/resolve?urn=urn:nbn:se:hkr:diva-4825
Kumar, J. (2017, May 25). Nurturing leaders – the Tata way. *The Hindu*. https://www.thehindu.com/todays-paper/tp-features/tp-opportunities/nurturing-leaders-the-tata-way/article12560253.ece
Mariwala, H. (2019, November 6). Interview by J.B. Fuller. *Creating Emerging Markets Oral History Collection*. Baker Library Special Collections, Harvard Business School.
Mashelkar, R.A. (2022, June 30). Interview by T. Khanna. *Creating Emerging Markets Oral History Collection*. Baker Library Special Collections, Harvard Business School.
Meyer, E. (2014). *The culture map: Breaking through the invisible boundaries of global business*. Public Affairs.
MTN Nigeria Communications Plc. (2019). *Listing Memorandum*. The Nigerian Stock Exchange.
Nestlé S.A. (2024). Creating Shared Value and Sustainability Report 2023. https://www.nestle.com/sites/default/files/2024-02/creating-shared-value-sustainability-report-2023-en.pdf
Siemens. (2021, February 3). CSIR and Siemens partners to boost South Africa's 4IR competitiveness. https://press.siemens.com/za/en/pressrelease/csir-and-siemens-partners-boost-south-africas-4ir-competitiveness
Sierra, A. (2022). Rising stars: Understanding differences in cultural communication styles. https://devinepartners.com/blog/understanding-differences-in-cultural-communication-styles
Singh, S. (2024, May 24). Drive growth with purpose-built gig worker training. https://business.adobe.com/blog/perspectives/drive-growth-with-purpose-built-gig-worker-training
Tata Steel Limited. (2023). Business Responsibility and Sustainability Report for FY 2022-23. https://www.tatasteel.com/media/18371/brsr.pdf
Tata Steel. (n.d.). Human resources: Putting employee welfare at the very heart of our growth strategy. Retrieved January 15, 2025, from https://www.tatasteel.com/corporate/our-organisation/hr/
Tata. (n.d.-a). At Home Around the World. Retrieved January 15, 2025, from https://www.tata.com/tata-worldwide
Tata. (n.d.-b). Designing a people philosophy. Retrieved January 15, 2025, from https://www.tata.com/newsroom/careers/tata-steel-people-hr-philosophy
The Australian. (2025, February 3). Accenture embarks on hiring sprees with first regional office. https://www.theaustralian.com.au/business/companies/accenture-to-recruit-more-than-100-people-for-first-regional-office-in-ballarat/news-story/fcc2bb33c92296117ee3bf020cdb54f5

The Culture Factor Group. (n.d.). Intercultural management: What you need to know. https://www.hofstede-insights.com/intercultural-management

Trompenaars, F., & Hampden-Turner, C. (1997). *Riding the waves of culture: Understanding diversity in global business* (2nd ed.). McGraw-Hill.

WorkPlus HCM. (n.d.). HR software in Kenya: Automate HR operations. Retrieved April 8, 2025, from https://workplus.ai/hr-software-kenya/

YODY. (n.d.). *YODY company profile*. LinkedIn. Retrieved April 8, 2025, from https://www.linkedin.com/company/yody/

CHAPTER 12

Financing, fundraising, and investment in emerging markets

Learning outcomes

After studying this chapter, you will be able to do the following:

1. Analyze and evaluate traditional and novel financing routes for business expansion in emerging markets.
2. Critically assess the role of venture capital, private equity, and international development bodies in emerging market expansion.
3. Evaluate the risks associated with investment in resource-constrained or high-risk markets and recommend strategies for mitigation.
4. Develop and justify strategies to align financial structures with corporate goals and emerging market characteristics.
5. Assess the effectiveness of innovative fundraising methodologies in emerging markets.

Introduction: Scope

This chapter explores the challenge of raising investment funds for new ventures in emerging markets, whether the entrepreneur is inside or outside the target market(s).

We will discuss perceived risk and regulatory matters. We will explore traditional and alternative sources of funding, with real-world case studies to illustrate how well-known businesses have coped in complex financial marketplaces.

We know already that emerging markets attract investors due to their rate of economic growth. External funding to take advantage of the opportunities may be difficult and/or expensive to secure. Inside the market, there may be a limited financial infrastructure. In many emerging markets, there are restrictions as to how money can be

DOI: 10.4324/9781003638490-12

transferred from abroad, what can be done with profits, and what can be transferred out, either from profits or a sale or liquidation of a business.

Perceived risk and the cost of capital

The same factors that make emerging markets attractive also create perceived investment risks. We previously identified market volatility, currency risks, political and social instability, bribery and corruption, and regulatory risks.

Investors decide where to commit their money based on the balancing of perceived risk and potential rewards. Businesses assess the viability of propositions by balancing the cost of capital against expected rewards. Risk is the dominant factor in both deliberations, and its role can be quantified.

In developed markets, the Capital Asset Pricing Model (CAPM) quantifies the relationship between risks and costs. In its standard form, investors expect a return on equity (r_e, the money they invest) based on this formula:

$$r_e = r_f + \beta\left(r_m - r_f\right)$$

r_f is the risk-free rate, usually based on government bond interest rates, β (beta) is a measure of the relationship between movements in stock prices and the overall market, and r_m is the expected market return. The calculation in parentheses provides the market risk premium (MRP), the additional return which investors expect for putting their money into equity instead of risk-free government bonds.

In addition to the basic CAPM formula, size premium (SP) *may* be added to account for illiquidity, information asymmetry, earnings volatility, key-person risk, and small firm effects. SP may apply to specific cases in both developed and emerging markets. There are also industry-specific risk premia (IRP) for especially volatile sectors such as agriculture, oil, and fintech.

The CAPM algebra demonstrates that the higher the risk, the higher the cost of capital. However, CAPM assumes stable, efficient market conditions with trustable data and functioning institutions. These conditions often do not exist in emerging markets.

Investors in emerging markets generally believe that CAPM underestimates risk. They point to VUCA conditions to highlight the deficiency – volatility flows from heavy fluctuations in exchange rates and commodity prices, uncertainty from the weakness of legal institutions, complexity from political realities, and ambiguity from inadequate data reliability. These shortfalls are economy-wide, so SP is inadequate, and one of three additional approaches is typically used: adjusted β, country risk premium (CRP), or sovereign default spread.

Adjusted β is depicted as β^*. The formula becomes:

$$r_e = r_f + \beta^*\left(r_m - r_f\right)$$

Adjusting β is often an incomplete approach, as it modifies for systematic risk, but does not take full account of risk specific to a country.

The CRP approach adds a premium to the required return based on perception of additional risks. It can be estimated using economic data such as sovereign bond or credit default swap (CDS) spreads and may also include specific provision for political risk.

With CRP, the formula is instead:

$$r_e = r_f + \beta\left(r_m - r_f\right) + \mathrm{CRP}$$

The sovereign default spread also uses observable data, taking the difference in yield between a country's government bonds and U.S. treasury bonds as a quantification of the additional risk. Then the formula becomes:

$$r_e = r_f + \beta\left(\mathrm{r}_m - r_f\right) + \mathrm{SDS}$$

Several reputable sources regularly publish and update country risk premia tables. Professor Aswath Damodaran of the Stern School of Business is widely known and trusted;[1] accounting firms like KPMG[2] provide their own lists, and countryeconomy.com[3] offers daily updates and functionality for comparisons. Professor Damodaran's website is particularly useful for academic study, as it also maps default spreads, equity risk premia, corporate tax rates, and Moody's ratings. In January 2025, India had 2.18% default spread, 7.26% ERP, and 2.93% CRP; Brazil and Colombia have similar rates, while Egypt's numbers were more than double these. Simply put, perceived risk adds a significant premium to the cost of capital throughout emerging markets.

Cost of capital example

Let's imagine a hypothetical company and calculate its cost of capital. It's based in Colombia, is an unlisted start-up, with low capital, few employees, and plans to explore for oil and gas.

r_f is 4%. *B* is 1.1, MRP ($r_m - r_f$) is 5.5%, the country risk premium is 3%, and SP is 4.0 for a small-cap startup. IRP for oil and gas exploration is 2%. The extended CAPM formula is

$$r_e = r_f + \beta\left(r_m - r_f\right) + \mathrm{CRP} + \mathrm{SP} + \mathrm{IRP}$$
$$r_e = 4.0\% + 1.10\left(5.5\%\right) + 3.0\% + 4.0\% + 2.0\%$$

The result is a conservative, but realistic cost for a high-risk, high-reward investment. We say it is conservative, because using regular β can underestimate risk in volatile sectors – some analysts would multiply the CRP by β to arrive at an even higher cost.

While the CAPM model concentrates on the cost of equity capital, in practice most businesses are financed by a blend of equity and debt (borrowing). A calculation which incorporates the after-tax cost of debt is known as the Weighted Average Cost of Capital (WACC); it provides a broader picture of the cost of capital because it incorporates a proportionate view of interest costs. The extent to which a business is financed by loans is referred to as *leverage*; cost of equity typically dominates in the early stages of a business, but as it becomes established, borrowing may increase and WACC quickly becomes the more relevant metric.

Liquidity risk is an additional concern. Investors sending money into a foreign market need assurance that their capital can be recovered in the future. However, it can be extremely difficult for an investor to find a buyer for a failing business in an immature market. Many examples of this involve large, well-known businesses like HSBC in Argentina or Walmart in Brazil, both of which booked stunning losses as they failed to recoup value from their assets. It is not impossible though: Uber, for example, sold its operations in China to Didi Chuxing rather than abandoning its creation entirely (Abkowitz & Carew, 2016).

Home depot

Home Depot left South America altogether in one move in 2001, selling its nine stores in Chile and Argentina to its local partners. The prices were "undisclosed," but it is widely believed that they were a fraction of the original investment. Home Depot was a giant in the home improvement business with 1300 stores and sales of over US$45 billion, but it revised its expansion plans and pitched its future squarely back into its home ground of North America (Admin1, 2001).

The Home Depot case illustrates the realization of risk from overconfident expansion into a market where it did not fully understand consumer behavior or regulatory systems. Specifically, Home Depot did not have a clear exit strategy to retrieve its investment, which was largely if not completely lost.

If there is also widespread inefficiency in the tax system, investor confidence is further damaged. Author Paul recounts a classic case that ended badly.

> I represented a multinational which contracted with local partners to establish a small subsidiary in Brazil. It was a requirement that local citizens constitute majority shareholders. After several years of successful operation in the medical services field, the subsidiary shut down. It had substantial cash in its bank accounts, and this was transferred back to Head Office. Several *years* later, tax authorities assessed the Brazilian nominee shareholder (a legal representative with no ultimate beneficial interest in the company) *personal income tax* on the value of the funds transferred.
>
> The tax assessment was nonsense; we prepared an extensive package of explanatory documentation. We met with the tax assessors in their offices; they received us respectfully and treated us to coffee and refreshments in their executive suite. We believed everything was on the path to resolution. Then all went quiet, and a new government was elected.
>
> To our surprise, a new tax demand appeared, with interest and penalties almost doubling the original amount. The local tax office sent plain-clothes agents to stake out the home of the local nominee and placed a lien on their *mother's* home. While these tactics were clearly and obviously illegal, the local tax office gained the upper hand with oppressive and threatening behavior.

> Then there was a regime change in the tax office, and assessors received federal government instructions to make settlements that would bring as much money as possible, as quickly as possible, into the dwindling government coffers of the new administration. The local tax office made an offer to "settle" the case for the original illegal tax amount and waive the interest and penalties. To avoid the cost, stress, and expense of litigating the matter, my client agreed to settle the entire original tax assessment.

Since the cost of investment (share) capital is high, there is an incentive to rely on debt; unfortunately, perceived risk also increases borrowing costs. Therefore, the total cost of raising the money required for a new venture is increased by perceived risk; the business requiring capital must either find methods of reducing risk for investors (such as government guarantees) or improve the aspects of the business (such as governance) which affect risk premia, thus reducing the level of investor demands for returns.

Traditional sources of funding

We can group sources of investment in several ways – for example by the type of participation (equity vs. debt), cost, or risk appetite. Broadly, traditional sources are like those in developed markets, but there are newer types which are particularly effective in emerging markets.

Stock exchanges (for equity issues) exist today in all emerging markets. Some, corresponding roughly to a list of countries that were formerly colonies of large empires, have existed since the 1800s. Others did not have their own capital markets until after 1975. In the following 30 years, there was a golden era of new stock exchange creation, with approximately 100 new national exchanges created and beginning operations. During that same period, the capitalization of those exchanges grew at a much greater rate than that of established, older exchanges.

There is a strong correlation between stock market development and economic growth; the opening of a market typically empowers ownership of corporate assets by a much larger number of individual investors (Petraki & Zalewska, 2009). Local stock markets are important as an indicator of regulatory maturity, and garner investor trust.

Nicky Newton-King, former CEO of the Johannesburg Stock Exchange, makes a powerful case for consolidation of financial exchanges in emerging markets. Small exchanges may conduct low transaction volumes, making it difficult to cover fixed costs. Consolidation, such as occurred in South Africa, lowers average cost per transaction to the benefit of all stakeholders. A resultant larger exchange is better positioned to compete for global capital and streamlines compliance procedures and regulatory oversight (Newton-King, 2023).

Establishing a new public company, or taking an existing enterprise public, is a large undertaking and open only to exceptionally large businesses, usually with significant established operations. India has seen several quite recent start-ups proceed to Initial Public Offerings (IPOs) with mixed results; there is a wide range of opinion regarding the current valuations of many. Nykaa,[4] notable for being the first Indian unicorn headed by a woman, increased in valuation from $1.4 billion to $7.4 billion in the first ten months of 2021. Other impressive flotations were achieved by Paytm,[5], Zomato,[6] and Policybazaar[7] in the early 2020s.

Bond issue is a viable alternative for established businesses which have developed sufficient trust to keep interest rates competitive. In 2021 Brazilian cosmetics company Natura, which owns recognizable brands such as Avon and The Body Shop, announced the conclusion of an international fundraising of US$1 billion in bonds linked to sustainability. While the features are complex, the company summarizes them as follows:

> The transaction commits Natura to meet two environmental performance indicators by 2026 year-end: i) reducing Scopes 1, 2, and 3 of relative greenhouse gas ("GHG") emissions intensity by another 13%, and ii) reaching 25% of post-consumer recycled ("PCR") plastic in plastic product packaging. These goals are aligned with the Group's "Commitment to Life, Sustainability Vision 2030" and support Natura & Co's efforts to address the global climate crisis and adopt full packaging circularity.
>
> *(Natura & Co, 2021)*

Borrowing in local currency from local banks can create a natural hedge; if the currency loses value, subject to inflation and interest rates, the debt burden can decrease proportionally. Borrowing in a strong currency to invest in a country with declining currency values creates a significant risk. Walmart, in its successful Indian expansion, borrowed heavily from local banks, in rupees, to execute such a strategy.

The Asian Financial Crisis of 1997 demonstrates the exchange risk. Governments and businesses in several Asian countries found themselves in dire financial trouble as the values of local currencies plummeted on exchange markets (the Indonesian Rupiah, for example, fell to one-sixth of its previous value against the U.S. dollar). Businesses faced bankruptcy, while governments endured balance-of-payments crises as they had borrowed in U.S. dollars to make investments in local currencies. Even the strong economy of South Korea came to the brink of default. The International Monetary Fund and World Bank were only able to stop the contagion with an injection of some $118 billion into Thailand, Indonesia, and South Korea. In Indonesia, the government fell as a direct result of the crisis (Investopedia, 2024).

Bank financing can be exceedingly difficult to obtain in emerging markets, even for domestic companies. Local banks frequently demand heavy collateral, which may limit scaling; this in turn can make it difficult to compete with multinational competitors. Collateralization is an interesting and surprising topic in the emerging market environment. Hanedar, Broccardo, and Bazzana (2018, ch. 17) performed an extensive review and discovered that "the role of country-specific factors in emerging economies is more important than the role of firm-specific factors … however … the country-specific factors are more significant for small- and medium-size enterprises."

Danper Trujillo, a major agroindustry player in Peru, has continually suffered this restriction, solving the problem by entering joint ventures and reinvesting profits (Bazán, 2017).

Supply chain finance, reducing the need for cash by negotiating long payment terms with suppliers, is a common solution to cash flow needs. While it may come at a cost in terms of invoice value, it also places a portion of the financial risk in the same market where products are manufactured or sold. It can be a strong motivator for suppliers to fully support the venture. Where sales are on credit, factoring of invoices is also worthy of consideration to reduce short-term cash flow needs. In the longer term, we would always advocate moving toward a payments model where cash flow is accelerated, thus making cost savings and demonstrating financial strength.

Many forms of **government sources** can be very significant. No stone should be left unturned in the search for governmental incentives and breaks. In emerging markets, we find a mixture of fiscal, regulatory, and trade incentives, including business registration and tax holidays, free trade zones with no corporate tax, and capital subsidies for manufacturing operations. Applying the full range of incentives correctly can move a project into the realm of viability and make a significant difference to profitability.

Vietnam provides an illustration of all these working together: the country has a well-articulated national development strategy which is played out through several channels. The government has selected certain sectors for priority, such as industries defined as "high tech," "large scale," or "socially important." These are encouraged by reduced tax rates, set for certain periods, or absolute tax holidays (Dezan Shira & Associates, n.d.). A deeper dive into Vietnam's encouragements would find special treatment on import duties, rents, free trade agreements, double taxation avoidance, and much more. Vietnam also enjoyed success with the launch of a project to simplify customs procedures using AEO status – Authorized Economic Operator (Torello, 2021).

International institutions may provide loans, grants, or direct investments to ventures that align with their mandates – for example, infrastructure development, sustainability, or the reduction of poverty. The main institutions of interest in emerging markets are as follows:

World Bank – through the IFC, it aims to stimulate private investment in emerging markets by reducing risk. Its preferred vehicles are loans and equity investments.

International Monetary Fund (IMF) – primary focus is on macroeconomic stability, but it has often given financial assistance to initiatives promoting economic development.

African Development Bank (AfCB) – funds projects across the continent in agriculture, energy, and infrastructure.

Agence Française de Développement (AFD) – provides finance and support for work that combats poverty and/or supports sustainable development in developing countries.

Asian Development Bank (ADB) – lends and grants money to projects which promote social and/or economic development.

Inter-American Development Bank (IDB) – funds projects focused on infrastructure development, sustainability, and social welfare across Latin America and the Caribbean.

A consortium including the World Bank, AfDB, and European Investment Bank (EIB) provided US$680 million to build the Lake Turkana Wind Power Project in northern Kenya from 2012 to 2017, with connection to the national electricity grid in 2018. Today, the project supplies 15% of the country's total energy needs and is an important contributor to Kenya's transition to a sustainable energy mix. The domino effects of the project included improvements in local infrastructure and the creation of around 2,000 construction jobs and 200 permanent positions (Lake Turkana, n.d.).

MJ group

Mohamed Jaffer occupies the Chair of MJ Group, based in Kenya. In the mid-1980s, he developed a novel approach to grain shipment based on his international knowledge but initially could not secure local funding. A friend suggested that instead of presenting a Kenya project, he should emphasize its value to the region – Uganda, Rwanda, Burundi, and Sudan. This opened doors to international funding, with the CDC (Commonwealth Development Corporation[8]), IFC and Proparco[9] each investing several million dollars. His success highlights the importance of recognizing regional, as opposed to national, advantages of large development projects (Jaffer, 2019).

Blended finance combines public and private capital with philanthropy to reduce risks for private investors while achieving sufficient financing for large, high-impact projects. Initial funding or guarantees from development banks or governments reduce the level of risk for private investors, making commercial capital available in circumstances where it would otherwise shy away. A successful example is the Ghana Water Project, where the World Bank provided loans and grants to reduce risk for private investors in a large-scale clean water project (Global Partnership for Results-Based Approaches, 2019).

The Aga Khan Fund for Economic Development

Industrial Promotion Services (IPS), an arm of the Aga Khan Fund for Economic Development (AKFED), uses equity investments, joint ventures, and strategic partnerships to stimulate economic growth in many countries. Among emerging markets, it is especially active in Kenya and Pakistan. For example, it participated in the public–private partnership which built the New Bong Hydropower Project, Pakistan's first independent hydropower producer. In Kenya, it was a pioneering investor in the Tsavo Power Plant, leading the private sector investment and ensuring adherence to technical and environmental standards (Eberhard et al., 2016).

Venture capital (VC) has played a significant role in the funding of startups in emerging markets. California-based Sequoia Capital, a household name in the technology sector, has invested in a veritable who's who of successful companies in India, including Oyo, Byju's, Ola, Zomato, MobiKwik, Mu Sigma, and Unacademy (Varun, 2018).

There are venture capitalists whose strong preference is to stay within the bounds of developed markets, such as Andreessen Horowitz. It is easy to identify and qualify them online; pitches directed to VCs which have historically enjoyed successes outside the safe havens will meet with more enthusiastic reactions.

The interests of VCs presage global trends. Preliminary data indicate that in 2024, 50.8% of global VC funding went into AI-focused companies – almost double the share in the previous year (Irwin-Hunt, 2025).

VCs are not only a source of finance but also have deep knowledge and insight into business growth, which is available to collaborators for the asking.

This last aspect contrasts VCs sharply with *private equity establishments*, which typically have less risk tolerance, seek to invest at later stages, and often look for controlling stakes. Private equity cannot be discounted completely, but there are better prospects at VCs with a demonstrated interest in emerging markets.

Private equity participation in the MENA region has increased sharply over the past few years, after a weak start caused by poor returns and well-known misuses of early investments. The digital revolution is the driver, with technology and healthcare being the star performers in attracting investment. In May 2022, Blackstone Group paid $1.1 billion to acquire VFS Global, a technology and visa-outsourcing provider. The level of funding provided to startups, as opposed to established businesses, has underlined the importance of government investment in attracting innovative technology businesses. A 2022 report calculated that startups in the four MENA innovation hubs UAE, Saudi Arabia, Egypt, and Pakistan accounted for 89% of Venture Capital invested in the region in the previous three years. Fintech alone drew between a quarter and a third of this investment (Elgazzar, 2022).

Businesses planning to export to an emerging market will reap rewards from investing time in understanding *export credit agencies* such as Export Development Canada, the Export-Import Bank of the United States, and Brazil's Agência Brasileira Gestora de Fundos Garantidores e Garantias S.A. (ABGF) Backed by the home government, their objectives are to promote export sales by domestic businesses. They typically provide loans, guarantees, and insurance to exporters. Repayment terms are normally very flexible, engendering possibilities that may not be supportable with traditional lenders. They reduce risk and cost for businesses that expand overseas and fill gaps where private lenders are reluctant to participate.

Export development Canada and Bombardier

When Canadian manufacturer Bombardier saw an opportunity to supply electric railway systems and locomotives to the Gautrain project connecting Johannesburg to Pretoria in South Africa, EDC provided a loan guarantee to the South African purchaser, enabling them to raise funds for the purchase. The agency then provided insurance against non-payment risk and political risk for Bombardier. The result was a win-win for all parties as Bombardier won the supply contract and reduced its risk, while local employment increased, and the South African purchaser was able to proceed with its plans.

The Bombardier case illustrates the value of government support for exporters making bold moves into large emerging market projects.

Debt-based alternative sources of funds

Ventures which have difficulty raising sufficient capital from traditional sources may need to combine alternative sources. As traditional funders such as banks, stock markets, and private equity have stringent requirements, alternatives like microfinance, crowdfunding, and peer-to-peer lending are more accessible. Although they may have higher costs, they frequently provide faster access to money, lower demands for collateral or guarantees, and may assume higher risks despite lower assurance of returns.

Businesses looking to start new ventures in several emerging markets, particularly those with significant Muslim populations, may contemplate *Islamic finance* arrangements. The specific rules of Islamic finance require careful observance of several fundamental principles; among them, the charging and paying of interest are forbidden in favor of risk-and-reward sharing arrangements. In Islamic markets, the rule of *gharar* prohibits transactions involving uncertainty or speculation. Certain types of businesses are also outside of scope, including those involving gambling, alcohol, and pork.

There are several sophisticated financial instruments developed within the Islamic framework; they are designed to enable commerce while observing sharia law. If Islamic finance is contemplated and attractive, specialized advice is essential (Obaidullah, 2020).

Microfinance is important and highly visible. It enables people with low incomes or small businesses to access financial services that are not available from traditional systems. These include loans, insurance, and sometimes other facilities. There are many variants on the model, but the common thread is that the numbers involved are small – thousands or even just hundreds of dollars. Repayment terms are usually flexible; lenders have tolerance for elevated risk of default. One remarkably successful development is the *group lending model*, in which similar borrowers join common interest associations and cross-guarantee other members' obligations. The emergence of microfinance, visibly championed by Grameen Bank in Bangladesh and its internationally active foundation, has empowered individuals in approximately 25 emerging markets, created jobs, and significantly reduced poverty. Non-profit organization Accion, based in the United States, was founded to supply microfinance to Venezuelans but has since become a global business.[10] Microfinance businesses make an especially important contribution when they combine educational programs with their lending activities.

The Aga Khan Agency for Microfinance

Since 2005, the Aga Khan Agency for Microfinance (AKAM) has been a major player in the microfinance industry throughout regions underserved by traditional banking. Among emerging markets, it has been very active in Egypt and Pakistan. Its range of financial products include microcredit for small businesses, especially those run by women, housing, education and agricultural loans, and micro-insurance. Setting it apart from many microfinance institutions, AKAM emphasizes sustainability and social impact, measuring its success not in profits but in improvements in clients' lives. In Pakistan, AKAM operates as a licensed, full-service bank; in Egypt, its focus is on the urban poor, especially women in Cairo and Upper Egypt. AKAM institutions to date have helped over half a million clients to better their lives.[11]

Peer-to-peer lending is frequently part of the microfinance environment. Technology platforms which match small lenders to small borrowers take costs out of the lending process, most of the savings being passed back to participants. The technological basis typically speeds up the approval process, also an advantage in fast-moving environments. Because no institution is taking a profit on a spread, both earnings for lenders and costs for borrowers are improved. Most emerging markets have successful P2P platforms: Faircent[12] in India, Yirendai[13] in China, and Modalku[14] in Indonesia are leaders among many.

Growth in the small lending market has been such that the distinctions between types have blurred. Lendingkart[15] has for some years been the leading business loan marketplace in India, with important subdivisions focusing, for example, on loans to women. In August 2024, however, it formed a partnership with international giant Tata Capital to provide unsecured business loans to small business. Peer lending is out of the equation. This looks much more like a microfinance venture – except that the amounts are potentially much larger (Konde & Bajj, 2024).

Participation-based alternative sources of funds

Crowdfunding might be viewed as another extension of the microfinance / peer-to-peer arena. It leverages internet connectivity to bring public attention to projects which require funding to move forward but are not able to secure traditional financing. Crowdfunding platforms have done a wonderful job of building communities around their inventors and manufacturers, with the result that many "lending" participants fund many different projects, each in a small way. Contributors often have first buyer rights to products and the opportunity to try, review, and promote them. Crowdfunding has made a clear contribution to both entrepreneurship and employment in emerging markets.

Crowdfunding platforms are often confined to a single market, evidencing the importance of cultural nuancing. India has Milaap,[16] charging no fees and dedicated to medical emergencies and social causes. Benfeitoria,[17] a Brazilian network, draws in funds to support educational initiatives. Farmcrowdy in Nigeria "connect[s] potential investors to farmers through a sponsorship model to fund higher yields for a share of the returns" (Malabo Montpellier Panel, 2020).

Still fast-developing, crowdfunding has evolved four principal subtypes: equity-based, donation-based, lending-based, and reward-based. Their natures are self-explanatory; reward-based is the only one requiring illustration. In this format, backers contribute money to a project in return for a defined reward or gift – often the merchandise or product, such as a suitcase or music album, which is the object of the venture (Ahmad, Nor, & Kamely, 2022).

Impact investing has gained popularity in emerging markets. It is not truly a separate type of financing, but a distinct investment philosophy, geared to the "double bottom line" – a desire to earn financial rewards while generating positive social impact. Impact investors tend to congregate around predictable sectors: renewable energy, healthcare, and education are strong examples. Impact investors are sharply focused on their public image, with an aversion to very high-risk projects or environmental damage. Impact investing is a well-developed arena with trade associations, non-profit foundations offering guidance to investors, and a large ecosystem of contributors and participants.[18]

Acumen,[19] an American non-profit, exemplifies impact investment. It uses eight guiding principles to deploy capital with the intention of solving problems of poverty and to "build a world based on dignity." Among its many projects are ventures into solar lighting, low-cost foods, and sustainable water.

Revenue-based financing has gained popularity in emerging markets. It starts life as a loan, thus not diluting equity, but repayments are based on revenue streams instead of fixed schedules. It has several challenges, including the difficulty of valuing an unknown revenue stream, securing investors' capital, and an under-developed regulatory framework, but it has gained a footing in financial markets and is expected to grow. Capchase,[20] an American lender, is actively lending to software-as-a-service ventures in Brazil, India, and Mexico.

ESG-driven financing

The rise of ESG-driven financing on world markets is powerful testament to the importance of sustainability in large-scale investment planning. We have mentioned some aspects already, but the field deserves its own focus. Investors of all types are increasingly aware that ESG considerations are not only ethical imperatives, but also important factors to be considered when assessing financial risk. Weakness in environmental stewardship, social awareness, or governance structures all pose direct threats to profitability.

ESG-driven financing focuses the attention of businesses on exposure to such weaknesses, while moving their projects up the priority list with many development banks, institutional investors, and especially sustainability funds. As a result, businesses with ESG-aligned financing are valued at a premium and enjoy greater investor confidence. ESG-based borrowing is not limited to small amounts; we mentioned above, for example, Natura & Co's $1 billion sustainability-linked bond in 2021.

The principal financing models in play as we write are as follows:

- **Green bonds**. Debt instruments issued by companies or governments, to fund environmental projects (e.g., in renewable energy, water conservation, or waste management). Green bond issue has already reached across continents with deployment in many sectors. The first Islamic green bond was Indonesia's Green Sukuk in 2018, worth US$1.25 billion; in 2019, AC Energy in the Philippines raised $410 million for expansion of renewable energy and battery storage across Asia; the City of Cape Town, South Africa, raised $74 million in 2017 for water resilience projects. In 2023, the Government of India's sovereign green bonds, worth approximately $2 billion, were oversubscribed. To be classified as a green bond, a debt issue must typically meet the requirements of a framework such as the International Capital Market Association's (ICMA's) Green Bond Principles.
- **Sustainability-linked bonds (SLBs)**. In contrast to green bonds, sustainability-linked bonds are not restricted in the use of funds but instead tie interest rates to achievement of sustainability goals. In effect, the borrower is penalized if it fails to meet targets. The world's first airline SLB was issued in 2020, tying terms to reductions in carbon emissions.
- **Impact investing**. Impact investment funds seek initiatives which return not only profits but also measurable ESG outcomes. An example is KKR Global Impact's $510 million investment in Ramky Enviro Engineers, an environmental services provider in India (Hurley, 2021).

- **Blended finance.** Exemplified by the Ghana Water Project, blended finance attains extremely large scale by reducing risk and enticing private capital to join institutional funding in large public projects.

Not all ESG-linked financing projects have met expectations. Risks of greenwashing, poor compliance with reporting standards, regulatory incompetence, and high initial costs which bar entry for small to medium enterprises, are all limitations; it is notable that most successful ESG-linked financing projects are very large initiatives. A notable dispute has erupted around Greenpeace's March 2022 report on programs developed in Indonesia and Malaysia for financial institutions to support sustainable palm oil production (MSPO, 2022).

There is a clear path to obtaining ESG-driven financing. A business cannot start without clearly quantifying its ESG goals and metrics; the documentation is strongly supported by certifications such as LEED (green buildings) or Fair Trade. ESG reporting standards must be adopted and detailed. The business can then look to a variety of sources, including development banks, impact investors, and sustainability-linked lenders, while also considering issuing its own green bonds. The field is not open only for established businesses; start-ups like Byju and Ola in India have raised millions of dollars in ESG-driven funding.

We see only growth in the future of sustainability-driven funding in emerging markets. The successive launches of new carbon markets (e.g., China in 2021, India in 2022, and Taiwan in 2023), standardization of metrics, engagement of fintech (with blockchain transparency mechanisms), and evidence of investor pressure for clear ESG strategies all point to the emergence of ESG-driven financing as a fundamental strategy. There are clear benefits to becoming an early mover and aligning financing models with sustainable finance trends.

Investment risk management

Given the inherent risks already discussed, *risk management* is a crucial part of planning an expansion into emerging markets. Insurance, hedging, derivative investment, contingency planning, and relative risk assessment (not putting too many eggs in one basket) are among the techniques to be deployed.

Financial products such as insurance and hedges are often best acquired in developed markets such as Switzerland, the United Kingdom, or United States. In the event of a large-scale disruption, local insurance policies may become worthless. A higher premium may be paid for outside insurance from a major financial center, but it may be justified. Reading the fine print (with competent legal help) is critically necessary; most insurance policies have exclusions for wars, terrorism, insurrection, and the like; these may be the very risks most requiring insurance coverage.

To mitigate currency exposure, sophisticated financial instruments may be used. *Forwards*, or forward contracts, allow businesses to contract for guaranteed exchange rates in the future, protecting against currency declines. *Currency swaps* set up future exchanges of principal and interest payments in different currencies, permitting businesses to synchronize debt repayments with income expectations. *Currency options*, which come in buy and sell flavors, set up rights (but not obligations) to exchange in the future at a rate which his set today. Such instruments are usually arranged through international financial institutions, and often obtained by headquartered offices in stable markets.

Reinvestment and cross-subsidization are often used in developed markets to support struggling units within a business. Cross-subsidization involves taking profits from one unit to cover losses in another. This can mask inefficiencies, allowing component businesses to avoid addressing fundamental issues. In emerging market ventures, over time, it can also inhibit accountability and innovation, as struggling units rely on successful ones instead of resolving their own problems. Self-sufficiency is usually the better policy, because of the volatility and resource constraints encountered.

Other risk management techniques already discussed are not strictly financial but nevertheless help secure the financial position of the business. These include diversification, local partnerships (to mitigate or share risk), and conducting market simulations as part of scenario planning exercises.

Hochschild mining

Eduardo Hochschild, chairman of Hochschild Mining, exemplifies the commitment to independent, self-financing businesses within an emerging market group. Each of his mines is required to generate its own cash flow and remain solvent, which requires financial discipline. He believes that this approach is critical to ensure that a failure in one segment does not drag down the entire company (Hochschild, 2017).

Options Theory, often applied in financial derivative markets, is sometimes useful in decision-making under uncertainty. The holder of an option has the right, but no obligation, to exercise it at a certain price and within a certain period. Options have value because they give the holder the flexibility to exercise them only if conditions make it favorable to act.

Just as with options, businesses operating in emerging markets take large risks but have the potential for high rewards. Principles from Options Theory can be adapted for use in emerging market decision-making.

Staged market entry involves starting with pilot projects or joint ventures. The investor has the benefit of capping potential losses, while the potential for expansion is maintained.

Strategic flexibility applies to operations, distribution, and supply chains. Participation in a local partnership, for example, may enable fast changes to align with market conditions.

Diversification in a stock portfolio has parallels with a business launching in several markets, or pursuing several lines of business, to spread risk instead of concentrating it in one location.

Hedging involves making parallel investments which compensate losses on one with gains on another. Businesses may hedge business risks by identifying products or activities with see-saw relationships. An example would be the launch of a ride-sharing app, where the investors also bought shares in a traditional taxi business.

Because emerging markets frequently suffer from volatility and uncertainty, outside funding obtained for rapid growth can leave companies vulnerable to economic shocks. There is a compelling case for slower, organic growth, which allows businesses to make gradual adaptations without pressure from external investors. Planning to grow slowly using internal resources can build more robust operations, supply chains, and financial structures while avoiding excessive debt. Pressure for rapid scaling can cause failure to learn, adapt, and integrate into the local context (Jodal, 2023).

Investment strategy

Besides considering whether each source of funding is likely to be available, a business entering, or growing within, an emerging market will need a decision-making framework to identify appropriate sources. The three-dimensional matrix will consider the stage of the business, its risk tolerance, and market conditions.

Startups, facing pressure for fast growth and willing to give up a substantial percentage of ownership, will often find the best reception among venture capitalists and angel investors. They may receive substantial government grants.

Early growth companies will continue to be of interest to VCs but are better positioned to look for development bank funding. Traditional debt funding may still be difficult, but crowdfunding becomes a strong contender.

Once the business is established and has demonstrated its viability, many more sources become available, including private equity, trade finance, structured debt, and public offerings.

Once the business is mature, traditional bank loans become more available, public markets will have even greater interest, and the issue of corporate bonds or preferred shares becomes viable.

VUCA factors underlie the third dimension. The business will need to look very carefully at the economic climate in the target market. Interest rates may vary significantly between the home and emerging market; typically, they are higher in unstable countries. However, the business may be willing to pay this price for the natural hedging advantage that comes from borrowing and investing in the local currency, as devaluation risk is intense in some markets. Inflation and capital controls must also be considered.

Whatever the stage, source, and risk, the business is essentially looking to use someone else's money to fund its plans. Investors in emerging market businesses are attracted by several factors. These include the following:

- The business's familiarity with the local market.
- The business's ability to manage local risks.
- ESG factors.
- Quality of business planning.
- Financial projections.
- Availability of collateral.
- Size of owners' stake (equity) in the business.

Giving up

When committing to investment in an emerging market, a long-term perspective is needed. Not all investments pan out, and it can be difficult to know when to give up. There are many examples of large global businesses who did their best then stemmed losses by leaving. Others, though, have retained their commitment, sometimes through decades, before finally seeing success. Coca-Cola invested in the Chinese market in the 1970s but did not see a significant return for approximately 30 years. Halfway through that long waiting period the company had to make significant additional investments, but even they did not pay off for over a decade (History Oasis, n.d.).

Such stories highlight a harsh reality. Investing in emerging markets, despite the pace of economic growth, requires a mixture of patience, resilience, and even stubbornness. Some markets take decades to mature, and interim setbacks can be stepping-stones on the path to eventual success. Regular strategy reviews are required to discern what obstacles or failures are temporary, and which are fatal. Pivoting, further investing, and exiting are all viable choices at any given moment.

Conclusion

Financing in emerging markets is an opportunity and a challenge. Despite significant risks, there are appreciable rewards for businesses that find relevant financing and turn investment into profit. In this chapter we reviewed the entire landscape of financing options, from the most traditional to the most creative new types.

We saw that risk premia drive up capital costs, as investors want higher returns to compensate for uncertainty. Local capital markets still matter; despite the emergence of alternative sources, banks and other financial institutions remain a major source of funding. Profit and purpose walk hand in hand when the innovative solutions so loved in emerging markets bring success to mega-projects like Lake Turkana and financial independence to micro-borrowers. Across all financing types, we noticed the growth of sustainability and ESG-linked financing, including green bonds and impact investment.

Emerging markets are particularly vulnerable to a range of failings; addressing the risks at the financial level positions a business for long-term growth. We saw how multifaceted strategies, which balance risk with opportunity, work best. Decentralization is growing, with agile new models filling gaps created by the preferences of traditional financiers.

The future is filled with promise driven by the digital revolution, explosive fintech expansion, and ESG-driven investment trends. Businesses that pursue opportunities within emerging markets, staying flexible, performing quality research, and having open minds about alternative sources and technology-driven solutions will dominate emerging market commerce for decades to come.

There remains one final chapter. We will explore a vision of the pathways down which emerging markets appear to be headed in 2025.

Notes

1 https://pages.stern.nyu.edu/~adamodar/New_Home_Page/datafile/ctryprem.html
2 https://atlas.kpmg.com/de/en/deal-advisory-services/cost-of-capital-and-multiples/country-risk-premium

3 https://countryeconomy.com/risk-premium
4 www.nykaa.com
5 Paytm is the full name of the company. It stands for "Pay through mobile."
6 www.zomato.com
7 www.policybazaar.com
8 The British government's overseas development agency recently rebranded as BII – British International Investment.
9 Proparco's full name is Société de Promotion et de Participation pour la Coopération Economique, a subsidiary of the French Development Agency AFD.
10 https://aofund.org/
11 https://the.akdn/en/how-we-work/our-agencies/aga-khan-agency-microfinance
12 https://admin.faircent.com/
13 https://www.yirendai.com/
14 https://modalku.co.id/
15 https://lendingkartfinance.com/
16 https://milaap.org/
17 https://benfeitoria.com/
18 See, for example, Calvert Impact (https://calvertimpact.org/). A U.S.-based not-for-profit with a global view, Calvert has been quietly and effectively making a difference for three decades
19 https://acumen.org/investment-principles/
20 https://www.capchase.com/

References

Abkowitz, A., & Carew, R. (2016, August 1). Uber Sells China Operations to Didi Chuxing. *The Wall Street Journal.* https://www.wsj.com/articles/china-s-didi-chuxing-to-acquire-rival-uber-s-chinese-operations-1470024403

Admin1 (2001, October 26). *Home Depot leaves South America*. VMSD News. https://vmsd.com/home-depot-leaves-south-america/

Ahmad, K., Nor, M.N., & Kamely, A.A. (2022). Crowdfunding in the emerging markets. In Rana, S., & Shrivastava, A.K. *Doing business in emerging markets*, pp. 178–205. Taylor & Francis.

Bazán, R. (2017, May 27). Interview by A. Lluch. *Creating Emerging Markets Oral History Collection.* Baker Library Special Collections, Harvard Business School.

Dezan Shira & Associates. (n.d.). Why invest in Vietnam? Retrieved March 9, 2025, from https://www.vietnam-briefing.com/doing-business-guide/vietnam/why-vietnam

Eberhard, A., Gratwick, K., Morella, E., & Antmann, P. (2016). *Independent power projects in sub-Saharan Africa: Lessons from five key countries* (World Bank Report No. 102365). World Bank Group. https://ppp.worldbank.org/public-private-partnership/library/independent-power-projects-sub-saharan-africa

Elgazzar, F. (2022, September 8). MENA private capital industry surges further with tech advancements. https://www.arabnews.com/node/2158911/business-economy

Global Partnership for Results-Based Approaches (GPRBA). (2019). *Blended finance for sanitation: Using results-based approaches to catalyze public-private partnerships in Ghana.* The World Bank. https://www.gprba.org/sites/default/files/publication/downloads/2019-03/blendedfinance_ghana_sanitation.pdf

Hanedar, E.Y., Broccardo, E., & Bazzana, F. Collateral in emerging economies. In El-Erian, M., Boubaker, S., & Nguyen, D. K. (Eds.) (2018). *Emerging markets and the global economy: A handbook*. Academic Press.

History Oasis. (n.d.). Coca-Cola's history in China. https://www.historyoasis.com/post/coca-cola-history-china

Hochschild, E. (2017, May 26). Interview by A. Lluch. *Creating Emerging Markets Oral History Collection.* Baker Library Special Collections, Harvard Business School.

Hurley, M. (2021, August 20). The billion-dollar funds that have changed impact investing. https://www.environmental-finance.com/content/analysis/the-billion-dollar-funds-that-have-changed-impact-investing.html

Investopedia. (2024, April 19). Asian financial crisis: Causes, response, lessons learned. *Investopedia.* https://www.investopedia.com/terms/a/asian-financial-crisis.asp

Irwin-Hunt, A. (2025, January 8). AI dominates venture capital funding in 2024. *fDi Intelligence.* https://www.fdiintelligence.com/content/data-trends/ai-dominates-venture-capital-funding-in-2024-84500

Jaffer, M. (2019, May 15). Interview by T. Khanna. *Creating Emerging Markets Oral History Collection.* Baker Library Special Collections, Harvard Business School.

Jodal, N. (2023, July 24). Interview by A. Lluch. *Creating Emerging Markets Oral History Collection.* Baker Library Special Collections, Harvard Business School.

Konde, N., & Bajj, A. (2024, August 26). Tata Capital and Lendingkart Formed a Partnership to Co-lend Unsecured Business Loans. https://startuptalky.com/news/tata-capital-lendingkart-partnership/

Lake Turkana. (n.d.). The Lake Turkana wind power project. Retrieved March 9, 2025, from https://ltwp.co.ke/

Malabo Montpellier Panel. (2020, September 6). Five start-ups that are transforming Africa's agriculture. https://www.mamopanel.org/news/blog/2020/sep/6/five-start-ups-are-transforming-africas-agricultur/

MSPO (Malaysian Sustainable Palm Oil). (2022). The "Destruction:Certified" report by Greenpeace disregards the efforts and improvements done by the palm oil industry. https://mspo.org.my/collection-stories-from-the-field/the-destruction-certified-report-by-greenpeace-disregards-the-efforts-and-improvements-done-by-the-palm-oil-industry

Natura & Co. (2021, May 4). Natura & Co raises US$1 billion in sustainability-linked bond offer. *PR Newswire.* https://www.prnewswire.com/news-releases/natura-co-raises-us1-billion-in-sustainability-linked-bond-offer-301282631.html

Newton-King, N. (2023, October 4). Interview by M. van Waijenburg. *Creating Emerging Markets Oral History Collection.* Baker Library Special Collections, Harvard Business School.

Obaidullah, M. (2020). *Islamic finance: A global perspective* (2nd ed.). Islamic Development Bank Institute.

Petraki, A., & Zalewska, A. (2009). Growth prospects of new and old Emerging Markets. In *Gregoriou, C.N. Emerging markets: Performance, analysis, and innovation* (pp. 1–20). Chapman & Hall.

Torello, A. (2021). *The simplification of customs formalities: The role of the Authorized Economic Operator (AEO) in Vietnam and in the EU.* In Bobek, V., & Quah, C.-H. Emerging Markets. Intech Open.

Varun. (2018, July 23). Top 10 Sequoia capital investments in India. *The Indian Wire.* https://www.theindianwire.com/startups/top-10-sequoia-capital-investments-india-65486/

CHAPTER 13

Trends and opportunities in emerging markets

Learning outcomes

After studying this chapter, you will be able to do the following:

1. Analyze the most important developing trends in emerging markets, evaluating their implications for business and government.
2. Assess the impact of artificial intelligence (AI), digital transformation, and automation on business development in emerging markets.
3. Critically evaluate the influence of growing middle classes on consumer demand in emerging markets.
4. Apply insights from real-world case studies to formulate strategies for businesses wishing to ride the wave of technological advancements in emerging markets.

Introduction

This chapter will share our view of the most significant trends and developments affecting businesses in, or entering, emerging markets. After describing the role of AI, we will group other trends under the ESG headings of environmental, social, and governance effects, and demonstrate that technology is an overarching theme with profound implications for all three areas. We will then consider supply chain and competition matters before concluding with an engaging case study which demonstrates many themes.

We begin with AI, not because we consider it the most existential challenge, but because it is the disruptive technology with the most potential to address climate change. Emerging markets must engage in some adaptation to the environmental shocks which are increasing in intensity, but their impact may also be mitigated by proactive intervention.

DOI: 10.4324/9781003638490-13

Artificial intelligence

The single most significant area of change is the rapid advancement and deployment of AI. AI is not just another technology or trend – it has already emerged as a transforming force whose impact is being felt across ESG initiatives, throughout emerging markets, and in every field of endeavor. While we can barely contain our enthusiasm for AI-driven advancements, we must preface our comments with an acknowledgment that many of the barriers we have surveyed in earlier chapters – internet infrastructure, electricity, and digital skills, for example – are also hurdles in the path of AI development in many emerging markets.

AI is a broad term that refers to technology enabling machines to do things that are done by humans – speaking, creating art, analyzing data, making predictions, and so on. AI in general is focused on the processing of datasets and drawing insights or predictions from them. One of its most useful features is its ability to handle very large amounts of data and draw insights from them which might not be seen by humans.

Generative AI, however, is the subset which *generates* original content, including written texts, pictures, music, and computer code. Generative AI is based on patterns which it learns from large amounts of data on which it is "trained."

It is easy to confuse AI with robotic process automation (RPA). RPA also takes on human tasks and automates them, saving time and cost. However, it is limited to repetitive, definable tasks. AI allows machines to learn and improve, much as a human mind develops over time. AI has the potential to make new decisions which have not been designed as outcomes by humans while handling many different data types as inputs. AI-based automation can increase productivity and efficiency in agriculture and manufacturing, but it has also proved to be the key to financial inclusion, vast improvements in healthcare, and enormous gains in the provision of education.

AI comes with challenges. Automation is a wonderful tool for the entrepreneur but can displace workers from jobs and make it difficult for them to find new ones. How severe can this be? Although not in an EM, Swedish bank Klarna announced in August 2024 that, after reducing its workforce from 5,000 to 3,800 in the past year, it planned to reduce further to 2,000 by using AI in marketing and customer service. 40% to 60% of all jobs in the company will be eliminated by AI replacement (Gerken, 2024).

However, the very development of robotic processes also creates jobs and profits. Computers need developers, servicing, parts, operators, coders, security, and much more. If automation reduces prices or increases exports, the population has more disposable income to spend on other products and services. It is exceedingly difficult to quantify the net impact of AI as applied to a single industry, let alone an entire economy.

If poorly trained, AI bias can exaggerate social inequalities when used in recruitment, lending decisions, or other discretionary processes. Its ability to access and store vast amounts of data raises a plethora of privacy and security concerns. However, AI can be turned to positive use against bias, as its strong analytical tools can root out patterns which are imperceptible to humans.

While AI has a dominant role to play in the future of emerging markets, it will not be even across continents or countries. Those who invest in AI, support developers, and provide a digital infrastructure to help it grow will gain the greatest rewards for their populations. Qatar, for example, has built a digitally driven AI ecosystem. Underlining the country's ESG commitment, its long-term investment plan is focused on "renewables and green hydrogen, logistics, tourism, sports and AI (Hajhamad, 2024)."

The rapid deployment of these new technologies must take place in a well-regulated, safe marketplace where the digital divide is not further reinforced.

Environmental

Climate change is a significant factor in many emerging markets, some of which are highly vulnerable to floods, fires, and other large-scale disasters. Extreme heat, flooding, rising sea levels, desertification, and more – all these dramatic events occur disproportionately in vulnerable emerging nations. Some are existential threats to countries like Bangladesh and parts of Sub-Saharan Africa. They cause domino effects like migration, infrastructure failures, and social unrest. Climate-induced migration is expected to displace up to 216 million people by 2050, with the majority in Asia, Africa, and Latin America (Clement et al., 2021).[1]

We highlighted earlier that emerging markets, despite movement toward urbanization, remain heavily dependent on agriculture. Climate change threatens complete collapse in parts of Africa and Central and South America, as rising temperatures and fungal pathogens undermine production of staple crops. Food insecurity is increasing; the UN Food and Agriculture Organization's 2023 report estimated that 2.4 billion people were experiencing moderate to severe insecurity, an increase of 500 million people from 2019. Fifty-seven percent of all people in Africa experienced this level of deprivation; in Latin America the corresponding figure rose from 24% to 37% in just three years. Without intervention, it is currently estimated that an additional 70 million people could be pushed into chronic hunger by 2030 (FAO, 2023).

Deforestation and habitat losses lead to more serious threats than simple loss of biodiversity. The pursuit of economic growth at a cost to Mother Nature increases the risk of **zoonotic transmission** – the transfer of animal diseases to humans. Examples (admittedly, subject to some argument) in recent times include COVID-19, HIV/AIDS, Ebola, avian and swine flu, and rabies (Centers for Disease Control and Prevention, n.d.). Emerging markets have enhanced vulnerability to zoonotic outbreaks due to the triple effect of wildlife trade, wet markets, and intensive farming practices.

There are many opportunities to partner with governments and industry in developing resilient infrastructure in the face of these threats. Just some of the industries with enormous growth potential in the face of global challenges are climate risk modeling, adaptive architecture, water reuse, and technical tools for insurance.

Decarbonization describes the reduction of carbon dioxide and other deleterious gas emissions to slow down climate change. The central task in this effort is the replacement of fossil fuels (oil, natural gas, and coal) with renewable energy (solar, wind, and hydro). A significant contribution can be made by increases in energy efficiency and conservation.

This noble effort sometimes flies in the face of local economic development, where massive interests in mining, drilling, or other resource exploration generate thousands of jobs and millions of dollars. Nevertheless, most governments are on board, and industrial sectors would be foolish to disregard the trend. It's a great time to see decarbonization as an opportunity, not a threat. Government incentives and opportunities for innovation and growth await the willing participant in the effort.

It is arguable that China is leading the industrialized world in this respect. Climate expert Tim Buckley reports that China is likely to hit its 2030 decarbonization targets six years early: "In 2024, it will break its coal addiction and start installing only renewables capacity" (Buckley, 2024, subheading).

AI plays a major role in addressing large environmental issues, including monitoring and reporting carbon emissions. Machine learning enables the prediction of extreme weather events, leading to better disaster responses. AI is of fundamental importance in managing renewable energy projects, as it is used to optimize energy distribution. AI-driven systems for detection of pollution levels, deforestation, and other negative trends provide data and decision-making capabilities for environmental management. Resource management can be significantly enhanced. Wildlife populations, habitats, free-ranging herds, pests, and predators can all be subjected to round-the-clock monitoring, with management using predictions and recommendations powered by AI.

Green energy is rapidly growing as a solution to the environmental and monetary effects of over-reliance on fossil fuels. Earlier, we gave several examples of large investments in renewable energy sources. Rural areas with very limited access to energy sources stand to benefit significantly from these developments.

Regenerative agriculture is expanding to reduce environmental impact. Sustainable land use is promoted by many governments as they struggle to cope with water scarcity, droughts, and deforestation. Water stress is an area of intense concern, driven by climate change and population growth. Emerging markets like Egypt, India, and South Africa are beset by severe shortages which impact agricultural productivity and industrial progress and can even fuel social or armed conflict.

Urbanization seems to be a corollary of development. It brings a host of environmental challenges, including air quality, waste, and water management. Plastic waste is possibly the most urgent issue, and unfortunately, emerging markets are among the largest producers and consumers of single-use plastics. Across these areas, initiatives to produce energy from waste, reduce emissions, and recycle waste are increasing in value and importance.

While environmental sustainability is frequently the most visible global demand, social dynamics are equally fragile and demanding of action to improve the future for emerging economies. AI-driven technological advancements also have profound social implications as they impact labor markets, financial inclusion, and governance structures.

Social

The Youth Bulge is one notable change in emerging market demographics. The swelling of the young population is a potential source of talent, labor, and market. Uzbekistan, for example, has 34 million citizens of which 60% are under age 30 (Jivraj, 2024). However, poor governance coupled with the energy and passion of a large young population can cause friction which seriously impairs social and economic development.

> Less than a quarter of the more than 350 million young Africans who will enter the labor force by 2035 will find formal wage employment. That demographic bulge could have scary implications for Africa and the world. Surging youth

populations can easily push fragile nations to the brink, driving food insecurity, migration, and violent extremism.

(Foote, 2018)

Aging populations, at the other extreme, can challenge social safety nets and deplete pension reserves. Advances in healthcare lead to longer life expectancies; if the birth rate declines as people focus more on education and career but less on family, an aging population begins to post severe challenges for the younger workforce that supports its elders.

Gig economies are growing rapidly. They can improve the lives and incomes of people who were previously completely unemployed, but at the same time expand the numbers of workers who are informally employed, without the protections and benefits afforded to regular employees. Gig economies are substantially driven by digital inclusion, but with automation and AI underpinning major improvements in efficiency, low-skilled workers have decreased job security.

Healthcare systems need to evolve alongside the populations that they serve. Healthcare is an area which we believe to be improving overall, despite rapid population growth and rising costs. AI is also playing an increasingly important role as it enables digital diagnosis, improved access, and cost control for providers. Beyond diagnosis, AI is increasingly used in predictive healthcare and in molecular analysis for drug development. AI can be used to predict disease outbreaks and suggest the likely outcomes of epidemics.

Financial inclusion continues to be a positive outcome from the fintech explosion, including mobile banking and other digital payment mechanisms. Emerging markets like Kenya have seen revolutionary changes wherein large populations of formerly unbanked people have leapfrogged traditional banking and accessed financial services for the first time on mobile devices. There is significant space for further development. For example, AI is being deployed in microfinance systems to develop credit scoring systems for unbanked populations where traditional credit data do not exist.

Aga Khan Rural Support Program, Northern Pakistan

The NGO-backed Aga Khan Rural Support Program (AKRSP) is a pioneering model case for participatory rural development. For over 40 years, it has operated in the mountains of northern Pakistan and has impacted more than 3,000 individual villages. Its work combines environmental stewardship, financial inclusion, and community governance. Consider the list of its achievements:

- Micro-hydropower plants provide clean energy to over 200,000 people.
- 5,249 village and women's organizations have disbursed over PKR 2 billion in loans, to increase women's access to small business financing.
- Climate-resistant agriculture and land management are widely promoted.
- Providing technical and digital training to thousands of young people, readying them for better jobs.

AKRSP's approach, which integrates multiple sustainability goals, is a leading example of developing local solutions to address global challenges (Aga Khan Development Network, n.d.).

Social mobility is a thorny area. While economic growth can move whole populations further from poverty, with its accompanying urbanization it can increase inequality and restrict rural residents from sharing in the new-found wealth. Many emerging markets have strong class structures which can deny upward mobility to the lower echelons.

The middle classes will continue to grow throughout emerging markets. As their incomes increase, consumer awareness grows and, with it, demand for sustainably produced goods and services. Money becomes available for energy-efficient appliances, organic food, and recyclable clothing. This trend is a notable feature of emerging markets, particularly among younger adults. Examples are easy to find – demand for solar panels in India (Jacobo, 2025), electric cars in Brazil (Els, 2024), reusable packaging in China (Research and Markets, 2024). Brazil is the fastest-growing EV market in the world, despite rising import tariffs (Albuquerque, 2025). In China, the sustainable packaging market in 2023 was worth $68.2 billion.

India is the outstanding example of middle-class growth and digital transformation; Brazil is the poster case for demographic shifting and increasingly a world leader in technology development. A permeative theme in studies of social mobility is the profound impact of educational improvements; AI's potential role in transforming learning access in underserved markets is one of its most promising features.

Social and political unrest are rising in emerging markets, driven by social media and increasing visibility of corruption and prejudice. The Center for Strategic and International Studies refers to our time as "The Age of Mass Protests," stating that there is an escalating global trend. In the decade from 2009 to 2019, the number of mass political protests increased by an average of 11.5% per year (Haig et al., 2020).

Philanthropy from emerging markets has increased over the last two decades. This is good news for education and social improvement. We saw earlier that impact investing is also gaining traction. There is an increasing role for businesses that are profitable but also have positive social impacts.

Governance

ESG-related financing is rapidly advancing. Disclosures are increasingly required by stock exchanges in emerging markets, for example in Brazil and India. Companies are increasingly adopting international codes as a precondition of securing foreign investment.

The connection between sustainability and investment is growing in strength and importance. Green finance – the issuing of bonds and loans specifically to support environmentally friendly initiatives – results in lower interest rates or better terms for borrowers who achieve sustainability goals. The World Bank, through its Green Bond Program, has raised billions of dollars for climate-change mitigation projects in emerging markets alone (World Bank Group, 2024).

ESG bonds are already in widespread use. Chile issues green bonds to fund renewable energy and sustainable infrastructure projects; Colombia issued the world's first biodiversity bonds late in 2024. Brazil, China, and India all have extensive issues of ESG bonds.

Corruption, bribery, and other financial offences will remain serious issues. Although there have been widely publicized crackdowns and exposures, our view is that the extent of financial malfeasance is still growing across emerging markets. We discussed earlier the worrying trend of emerging markets to make no progress, or fall backwards, in Transparency International's *Corruption Perceptions Index*. In 2024 Nasdaq reported that an estimated $3.1 *trillion* in illicit funds flowed through the global financial system. The United Nations reported that Southeast Asia has become "a hotbed" for cybercrime, with a one year haul of as much as $37 billion (United Nations Office on Drugs and Crime [UNODC], 2024). In better news, however, AI-driven forensic accounting tools are enjoying success in detecting money laundering and suspicious transactions.

In digital services adoption of *e-governance* is a spreading trend. Blockchain applications are growing in importance for fields such as land ownership and supply chain management. The same governments, such as India, which are leading the way in these areas are adopting AI for tax compliance and tax fraud prevention (BSWebTeam, 2023).

Cybersecurity, data protection, and **privacy** measures and laws are growing exponentially. We see vast opportunity for individuals and businesses in these areas, with no slow-down in sight for the growth trajectory.

Economic nationalism is a potentially negative trend. While this is highly topical in early 2025 due to the policies of the new American administration, there have been several more subtle developments throughout emerging markets over the last decade, as countries have sought to protect their economies from perceived threats. For example, after armed conflict between India and China in 2020, India tightened its restrictions on Chinese investments, inserting government approval into the process. A second example is Brazil's imposition of tariffs on Chinese electric vehicles, to encourage placement of manufacturing operations inside the country (Reuters, 2024).

Regulation of AI is a challenge for national governments, which lag the open market in response to AI's advances and threats. While most governments have taken some steps toward standard setting, they seem destined to remain permanently dated. Not surprisingly, given its enormous presence in the IT world, India is a first mover in regulation of AI, but its regime is very much a work in progress. The country has launched a national strategy to try to position itself as a leader in AI and established an "Ethics Committee" to develop a framework. It has moved more efficiently with respect to data storage and security but seems to be a long way from finishing a comprehensive regulatory framework. By the time it does, it will probably be outdated.

It is a positive sign that India is not all about proscription but has recognized the potential for leading by example. Governments the world over can provide leadership, moving promptly to improve their own processes using AI and employing them in a responsible manner. The organs of government responsible for fostering trade and internal development need to place particular focus on AI within their broader technological development initiatives.

Despite all the praiseworthy benefits brought by AI, with them come deep concerns about privacy and data security, bias, and labor displacement. Wherever regulatory oversight is weak, businesses must take the lead and proactively implement ethical AI practices to prevent the harms which can flow from irresponsible deployment.

Regulations and standards often struggle to keep pace in periods of rapid development. Industrial and commercial expansion bring with them a need for new legal regimes, strong institutions, and alignment with international standards. The pressure to evolve raises the specter of *regulatory capture*, where the regulators charged with keeping a watchful eye on their constituents fall under the control of those they are supposed to manage. The extreme manifestation of this is corruption of public officials by businesses wishing to avoid regulation. Today, businesses entering a new market are faced with several regulatory challenges, including digital, environmental, and financial. The key to coping with these demands is development of an effective legal and compliance team, supported by strong internal governance.

We see considerable evidence of increased demands for regulatory compliance in emerging markets. For instance, Mexico and Vietnam have made huge strides forward in their regulatory frameworks specifically with the purpose of becoming more attractive to foreign investors. Positive government intervention is a powerful force, especially when coupled with clear financial incentives.

Regulatory easing continues as several countries have enacted integrated packages of legislation aimed simultaneously at easing restrictions for inward investors. In 2020, Indonesia passed Law No. 11, commonly known as the *Omnibus Law*. It simplifies licensing processes and land acquisition, formalizes economic zones, simplifies environmental requirements, and provides financial incentives, all in one instrument (Indonesia, 2020).

Other fast-moving developments

Supply chain risk is an outcome of many vulnerabilities highlighted in our consideration of VUCA conditions; thus, it is exacerbated in emerging market operations.

AI tools increasingly support the analysis of data from multiple sources in material and product supply, logistics, production, and demand. AI models can synthesize these data, apply information from supplier finances, weather patterns, social media traffic, and other places, and predict supply chain disruptions with sufficient time to plan workarounds. Global shipping giant Maersk uses AI to optimize shipping routes, while Alibaba uses AI-sourced analysis of consumer behavior to fine-tune pricing strategies in new markets.

Political risk remains high and shows little sign of abating. The Russia-Ukraine War has resulted in significant sanctions activity, which has severely affected sourcing of many materials and the routes they take to manufacturers and markets. There are other countries where investors are very nervous due to political instability, including Türkiye. In addition, as the new American administration bares its teeth in the trade war arena, it seems we are destined for a period of increasing tariffs and economic nationalism.

Globalization is a clear trend throughout the world. As advances in technology, communication, and logistics increasingly connect almost the entire world, more people everywhere are connected to businesses, products, and services than ever before. The opportunity to supply ever more products and services to more people in emerging markets has created opportunities for strategically positioned countries like Türkiye and the United Arab Emirates to increase their roles as production and supply chain hubs. However, rising protectionism and the deployment of prohibitive tariffs, particularly between the United States and other major trade blocs, are a major threat to the atmosphere of open trade. At the time of writing, it remains to be seen whether trade access will revert to political stability and economic viability, which can no longer be taken for granted even among advanced economies.

Morocco

Morocco demonstrates the leveraging of geographic, political, and resource advantages to become a manufacturing hub. Ideally positioned on the north coast of Africa, close to Europe and connected to Africa, from 2014 to 2020, the government executed an Industrial Acceleration Plan and focused on transportation. These initiatives resulted in Tanger Med Port becoming the largest on the Mediterranean and the establishment of Africa's first high-speed rail system. The facilities attracted approximately 250 international suppliers to the automobile industry, including CITIC Dicastal, which invested $400 million in an aluminum cast parts factory to supply Peugeot. Although geographic position, stability, and facilities were enough to support this level of expansion, Morocco's advantage is capped by its cobalt reserves – an essential ingredient in EV batteries (Tanchum, 2022).

It is evident that the recent COVID-19 pandemic has driven reevaluation of global supply chain strategies, which deeply affects emerging markets. In the coming years, regional supply chains will assume greater importance as a result.

Increased competition from domestic and international players is common, especially in large promising markets. First-to-market advantage is priceless; brand loyalty is important to long-term success. Fierce competition can bring benefits to a population, as the mobile phone market in India attests. Competition among manufacturers, half of which are domestic, has brought down smartphone prices into the affordability range of a wider group of consumers, driving constant improvement, and enhanced the distribution network. Five major manufacturers hold 75% of market share (Statcounter GlobalStats, n.d.). It has also brought with it the foreseeable reams of government rules and regulations. Despite all this, there is still room for growth; the market grew 7% in the first half of 2024 alone (The Hindu Bureau, 2024).

Hello Tractor

The success of Hello Tractor[2] exemplifies how AI and digital transformation are delivering environmental stewardship and social impact in one emerging market.

Agriculture is the largest economic sector in Kenya (Stats_Kenya, 2024). It produces over 20% of GDP, employs over 40% of the workforce and over 70% of the rural population (Central Bank of Kenya, 2024). Yet it is fragile; poor weather in 2022 caused a contraction, followed by a boom in 2023. Initiatives which impact the productivity of smallholders and small farmers can have tremendous impact on millions of lives, not to mention the economy of the nation.

In 2012, Jehiel Oliver, a banker, founded a business which he intended to provide affordable access to agricultural machinery to small farmers who could not own such machinery outright (Foote, 2018). The first platform allowed tractor rentals and collaborated with dealerships to build a network of rental locations. Tractors are physical assets, and farming is physical work. Physical presence was essential to deliver the product and build a trusting client base.

Hello Tractor made an early and important investment in technology. Its mobile app enabled farmers to book rental tractors and allowed the business to monitor usage. An integration with GPS technology meant that the business always knew where the tractors were and planned to optimize their use. Data from the tractors were analyzed using AI, generating recommendations to return to farmers on areas such as planting and harvesting.

Hello Tractor is thriving, advancing a social cause, improving lives for farmers, and having an environmental impact. Its success created a need for expansion capital, which it secured from a combination of VCs and impact investment houses. It added further value to its customers by becoming a one-stop shop for farm financing (Agbetiloye, 2021), farm supplies, and continuing education. The business has made a valuable contribution to food security, rural development, and the livelihoods of its customers.

Today Hello Tractor has expanded across rural Africa and is a meaningful and major player in the application of technology, including AI, to the world's most basic industry.

Hello Tractor is a remarkable case which demonstrates the possibility of creating a profitable business model, combining technology, environmental consciousness, and social impact.

Conclusion: Embracing the future

In this chapter, we glanced into the proverbial crystal ball and shared our view of the developments and trends most affecting emerging markets in 2025. We looked at environmental, social, and governance aspects of these developments and shared our view that AI is the overarching technology that will change all of them for the better. AI is so much more than software – it's a generational change in the way we manage weather forecasting, banking, and regulatory compliance, to name just one example from each ESG component.

It does not overstate our case to say that the future of each emerging market is closely linked to its ability to harness ESG principles while leveraging AI to derive benefits in sustainable development, economic growth, and global relevance. Predictive analytics, automation, and analytical oversight will be the major sculptors of emerging markets for years to come.

In broader terms, we have seen that emerging markets exhibit a unique blend of opportunity, challenge, complexity, and risk. Planning for success requires adaptability, resilience, and innovation. The prospective player in emerging markets must prepare for rapid change and give close attention to strategy, all the while keeping focus on its environmental, social, and governance responsibilities. Emerging markets are key players in the future of the global economy, joining or leading the pack in sustainability and technology. Businesses that join this party proactively and remain agile will be best able to profit, thrive, and survive.

This brings us to our last paragraph. We hope that you have enjoyed the journey through these many interwoven topics and have a new, enhanced understanding of emerging markets. We hope that you have gained valuable insights and that your curiosity inspired to propel you toward further reading and research. As you continue your studies, please feel welcome to communicate your thoughts and ideas to us.

Notes

1 Migration is not always a bad thing in itself. The movement of people creates opportunities, especially for businesses that facilitate remittance flows, or promote diaspora engagement.

2 https://hellotractor.com

References

Aga Khan Development Network. (n.d.). Aga Khan Rural Support Programme. https://www.akdn.org/our-agencies/aga-khan-rural-support-programme

Agbetiloye, A. (2021, September 8). Hello Tractor is set to pilot a new PayG tractor-financing product with the $1 million prize award from Heifer International. https://venturesafrica.com/jehiel-oliver-founder-of-hello-tractor-intends-to-further-empower-smallholder-farmers-with-the-1million-prize-award-from-heifer-international/

Albuquerque, M. (2025, January 6). Brazil's EV sales hit record high in 2024. *Argus*. https://www.argusmedia.com/en/news-and-insights/latest-market-news/2644370-brazil-s-ev-sales-hit-record-high-in-2024

BSWebTeam. (2023, Dec 28). I-T dept leverages tech to scrutinize tax returns, recovers 36,000 cr. *Business Standard*. https://www.business-standard.com/india-news/i-t-dept-leverages-tech-to-scrutinise-tax-returns-recovers-rs-36-000-cr-123122800318_1.html

Buckley, T. (2024, August 12). China's early decarbonization holds lessons for the world. *fDi Intelligence*. https://www.fdiintelligence.com/content/opinion/opinion-chinas-early-decarbonisation-holds-lessons-for-world-84032

Centers for Disease Control and Prevention. (n.d.). *Zoonotic diseases spread between animals and people*. National Center for Emerging and Zoonotic Infectious Diseases. https://stacks.cdc.gov/view/cdc/89630

Central Bank of Kenya. (2024, January). *Agriculture Sector Survey January 2024*. Central Bank of Kenya.

Clement, V., Rigaud, K. K., de Sherbinin, A., Jones, B., Adamo, S., Schewe, J., Sadiq, N., & Shabahat, E. (2021). *Groundswell Part 2: Acting on Internal Climate Migration*. World Bank. https://doi.org/10.1596/36248

Els, F. (2024, September 3). Brazil's 2024 EV market is a tariff test case. https://www.adamasintel.com/brazils-2024-ev-market-is-a-tariff-test-case/

Food and Agriculture Organization. (2023). *The state of food security and nutrition in the world 2023: Urbanization, agrifood systems transformation and healthy diets across the rural–urban continuum*. FAO, IFAD, UNICEF, WFP, and WHO. https://doi.org/10.4060/cc3017en

Foote, W. (2018, August 14). Meet the social entrepreneur behind Africa's "Uber for the farm." Forbes. https://www.forbes.com/sites/willyfoote/2018/08/14/meet-the-social-entrepreneur-behind-africas-uber-for-the-farm/

Gerken, T. (2024, August 28). Klarna: AI lets us cut thousands of jobs – but pay more. https://www.bbc.com/news/articles/c80e1gp9m9zo

Haig, C. C., Schmidt, K., & Brannen, S. (2020, March 2). The age of mass protests: Understanding an escalating global trend. *Center for Strategic & International Studies*. https://www.csis.org/analysis/age-mass-protests-understanding-escalating-global-trend

Hajhamad, B. (2024, December 11). Quoted by InvestQatar. Qatar aims for growth through long-term transformation. *fDi Intelligence*. https://www.fdiintelligence.com/content/advertorial/qatar-aims-for-growth-through-longterm-transformation-84468

Indonesia. (2020). [Job Creation Law].

Jacobo, J.T. (2025, January 9). India installs record 24.5GW solar PV capacity in 2024. https://www.pv-tech.org/india-installs-record-24-5gw-solar-pv-capacity-in-2024/

Jivraj, H. (2024, September 2). Uzbekistan opening up, but yet to fulfil its FDI potential. https://www.fdiintelligence.com/content/News/uzbekistan-opening-up-but-yet-to-fulfil-its-fdi-potential-83947

Research and Markets. (2024, February). *Sustainable Packaging in China*.

Reuters. (2024, April 5). Brazil imports of Chinese electric vehicles surge ahead of new tariff. https://www.reuters.com/business/autos-transportation/brazil-imports-chinese-electric-vehicles-surge-ahead-new-tariff-2024-04-05

Statcounter GlobalStats. (n.d.). Mobile vendor market share India Dec 2023-Dec 2024. https://gs.statcounter.com/vendor-market-share/mobile/india

Stats_Kenya. (2024, July 14). *County contribution to agriculture, forestry and fishing*. DATA. https://statskenya.co.ke/at-stats-kenya/about/county-contribution-to-agriculture-forestry-and-fishing-data/41/

Tanchum, M. (2022, August). *Morocco's GreenMobility revolution: The geo-economic factors driving its rise as an electric vehicle manufacturing hub*. Middle East Institute.

The Hindu Bureau. (2024, August 13). Vivo, Xiaomi lead as Indian smartphone market grows 7% in first half of 2024: Report. *The Hindu*. https://www.thehindu.com/sci-tech/technology/gadgets/vivo-xiaomi-lead-as-indian-smartphone-market-grows-7-in-first-half-of-2024/article68520014.ece

UNODC. (2024, October). *Transnational organized crime and the convergence of cyber-enabled fraud, underground banking and technological innovation in Southeast Asia: A shifting threat landscape*. United Nations Office on Drugs and Crime.

World Bank Group. (2024, October 31). *IBRD funding program: Green bonds*. https://treasury.worldbank.org/en/about/unit/treasury/ibrd/ibrd-green-bonds

Appendix: Evaluation models

Introduction

Strategic analysis is an essential step along the road from theory to practice, from idea to implementation. A large amount of research, with a commensurate expenditure of time and money, will go into forming a proposition and gathering relevant data. To summarize all that scholarship and move toward decision-making, there are several models which may help to organize the process.

SWOT analysis

Every business student is familiar with SWOT analysis, exercised in classrooms and boardrooms around the world every day. The square or rectangle, divided into four quadrants, is tried, true, and dependable.

SWOT stands for strengths, weaknesses, opportunities, and threats. These are essentially two pairs of opposites. Often, however, a single feature of a market that credibly belongs is placed in different boxes depending on the precise nature of the business proposition. For example, a manufacturer might see an unreliable power grid as a threat, but a nuclear power supplier might see it as an opportunity. A manufacturer might see the exorbitant cost of power as a weakness in a model; an alternative power supplier might construe it as an opportunity.

A great merit of the SWOT model is that businesses can apply it from top to bottom of a proposition, from holistic evaluation of a continent, country, region, or discipline to consideration of one product for one market. Here is a broadly summarized SWOT analysis of the emerging markets sector worldwide.

Table A.1 Emerging markets SWOT analysis

Strengths	*Weaknesses*	*Opportunities*	*Threats*
Natural resources. Youthful populations. Low costs. Growth in disposable income. GDP growth.	Corruption. Educational standards. Social unrest. Political uncertainty. Deficient infrastructure.	Urbanization. Population growth. Demand for technology. Capital availability.	Climate change. Currency instability. Erratic economic growth. Regional aggression.

The purpose of the SWOT analysis is to present an at-a-glance summary of the pros and cons of a project or idea, so that the reader is rapidly informed of the most relevant arguments of the proposition. It is instantly recognizable, to the extent of being a requirement of many school projects and business proposals.

SWOT still works when applied to a single product in a specific market, as Table A.2 shows.

This SWOT analysis evaluates a theoretical proposition to establish a new campus of Hult International Business School in Brazil, providing only Portuguese-language instruction and targeting the populations of Brazil, Portugal, and other Lusophone nations and their diasporas (Davis, 2024).[1] Yet it will be seen that some of the entries are exactly the same ones that would have been inserted if the whole country was being assessed without a specific product.

Table A.2 Hult Brazil SWOT analysis

Strengths	*Weaknesses*	*Opportunities*	*Threats*
Hult's Global Brand. Fully developed curriculum. Strong international alumni network. Economic growth in Brazil. Massive digital lead.	Shortage of native speakers of Portuguese on faculty. Inflated cost of living in São Paulo. Inexperience dealing with corruption and governmental interference.	Growing demand for high-quality education. Providing hub for Brazil-wide and Lusophone expansion. Enhance global social contribution. Make cultural adaptations of existing programs. Build local partnership community. Build new alumni community.	Competitive reaction by established institutions. Regulatory interference. Economic volatility. Political instability. Currency instability. Organized and opportunistic local crime.

PESTEL analysis

PESTEL analysis focuses specifically on business risks and requires the establishment of a strategy to deal with each. It amplifies the right-hand side of the SWOT analysis, expanding on the exposures created by weakness, and the potential for damage from threats. PESTEL started life as ETPS (Aguilar, 1967), rebranded to PEST, but is now the subject of a debate between PESTEL and PESTLE. It is an imprecise exercise as some entries may fairly lie in more than one risk category, but that does not depreciate the value or importance of the assessment. The acronym reminds us to consider Political, Economic, Social, Technological, Environmental, and Legal Risks, alongside strategies to contain them. Again, we will employ the theoretical Hult Brazil assessment as a demonstration of PESTEL in action.

Table A.3 Hult Brazil PESTEL analysis

PESTEL Category	*Risk*	*Strategy*
Political	Bureaucracy	Employ competent local administrators who are seasoned experts in addressing in-country bureaucracy,
	Political instability	As Hult is in the private education sector, and political change has largely affected the public education sector, it is somewhat immune. Neither major party in Brazil has exhibited any real animus toward private education despite their political leanings. Monitor.
Economic	Economic volatility	Ensure scalability (up and down) of operations; set not-for-profit pricing at levels which generate a surplus in strong conditions and tolerable losses in worst-case situations.
	Currency fluctuations	Carefully model future income/expenses and arrange appropriate financial instruments (futures and options) to smooth out the variations.
Social	Reputational risks	Set exacting standards of conduct for all faculty, students, and staff and enforce them.
	Crime levels	Engage highly competent cyber security contractors or employees to advise on physical and online security. Protect assets with state-of-the-art security systems; promote policies which ensure the physical safety of staff, students, and visitors to campus.
	Cultural misunderstandings	Engage carefully, and listen to, local staff who have a good understanding of culture. Follow their advice in addressing a broad range of situations including crisis management.
	Faculty attrition	Ensure that superior quality faculty are compensated *at least* in line with top local levels and preferably at international levels.

(*Continued*)

Table A.3 (Continued)

PESTEL Category	*Risk*	*Strategy*
	Prohibitive costs	Keep tuition fees realistically low for this developing economy. Consider regional pricing to cope with the regional disparity in incomes, and special pricing for students from low-earnings regions. Grant scholarships to capable students from challenged economies especially from outside Brazil and Portugal.
	Student attrition	Create strong student support services and constantly remind students of their availability. Deploy hardship bursaries or fee forgiveness for students. Permit deferrals for students who have pressing needs for a break due to family, medical, military, or employment reasons, for example.
Technological	Quality Assurance Issues	Engage with outside auditors to ensure that quality in Portuguese programs is on a level with instruction and achievement at other Hult campuses. Publish results of all evaluations openly.
	Copycat activities by competing institutions	Keep standards high and tolerate emulation. There is a large enough market for all of us.
Environmental	No risks – many opportunities	Design physical facilities and course delivery on environmentally friendly principles. Demonstrate ESG leadership.
Legal	Regulatory changes, policy changes	Stay engaged with highly competent sector lawyers with strong government contacts, to secure early warning of proposed changes.
	Corruption and Dishonesty	Set a clear policy of no bribery or corruption, inbound or outbound. This will be challenging in Brazil, but over time, it will establish Hult as a leader in educational ethics.

PE diamond model

With more specific reference to acquisitions, a popular framework for evaluating an investment opportunity in the private equity world is often referred to as the "PE Diamond model," or "Private Equity Diamond model." Its attraction is that it provides a settled reference and framework for evaluation of propositions for purchase of investment of existing companies.

Its four elements (hence the "diamond" moniker) are Quality of Management, Market Opportunity, Business Fundamentals, and Deal Structuring. Unlike most evaluation models, this diamond has no clear originator or author; rather, it has evolved over time in various writings and applications by both academics and investors.[2]

POCD model

A close cousin of the PE Diamond is Professor William Sahlman's "POCD" model, which evaluates new ventures and start-ups (Sahlman, 1997). The four aspects are as follows:

People. Involves comprehensive evaluation of the individuals and teams supporting the venture. Do they have the skills, personal ambition, and experience to make this work?

Opportunity. Involves comprehensive evaluation of the market, competition, product design, and potential for growth.

Context. A broader examination of the entire environment in which the venture will operate. Internal drive and passion are essential to the venture; what external factors could make or break it?

Deal. A detailed look at the financial structure of the plan including timing and nature of investments, as well as the longer-term outlook. Even at this early stage, it is best practice to form a picture of the long-term cost or benefit to be derived from the venture and give some thought to an exit plan.

Notes

1 We wish to clarify that this is an academic exercise, not an official Hult document or plan.
2 It should not be confused with Porter's Diamond Model of National Advantage, which has some superficial similarities but is a vehicle for evaluation of a country's susceptibility to successful inward investment (Porter, 1990). The Porter Diamond Model is also, of course, of great relevance to evaluation of emerging markets.

References

Aguilar, F. J. (1967). *Scanning the business environment*. Macmillan.
Davis, R. (2024). *Escola Internacional de Negócios Hult*. Hult International Business School.
Porter, M. (1990). *The competitive advantage of nations*. Free Press, a division of Simon & Schuster.
Sahlman, W. A. (1997). How to write a great business plan. *Harvard Business Review*, 75(1), 98–108.

Index

Pages in *italics* refer to figures and pages followed by "n" refer to notes.

For Product Safety Concerns and Information please contact our EU
representative GPSR@taylorandfrancis.com
Taylor & Francis Verlag GmbH, Kaufingerstraße 24, 80331 München, Germany

www.ingramcontent.com/pod-product-compliance
Ingram Content Group UK Ltd.
Pitfield, Milton Keynes, MK11 3LW, UK
UKHW050230200926
475702UK00020B/2945
* 9 7 8 1 0 4 1 0 6 5 4 3 2 *